Media Education for a Digital Generation

Media education for digital citizenship is predicated upon the ability to access, analyze, evaluate, and produce media content and communication in a variety of forms. While many media literacy approaches overemphasize the end-goal of accessing digital media content through the acquisition of various technology, software, apps, and analytics, this book argues that the goals for comprehensive and critical digital literacy require grasping the means through which communication is created, deployed, used, and shared, regardless of which tools or platforms are used for meaning making and social interaction. Drawing upon the intersecting matrices of digital literacy and media literacy, the volume provides a framework for developing critical digital literacies by exploring the necessary skills and competencies for engaging students as citizens of the digital world.

Julie Frechette is Professor of Communication at Worcester State University, in Massachusetts, where she teaches courses on media studies, critical cultural studies, media education, and gender representations. Her book, *Developing Media Literacy in Cyberspace: Pedagogy and Critical Learning for the Twenty-First-Century Classroom* (2002), was among the first to explore the multiple literacies approach for the digital age. She is the coeditor and coauthor of the book *Media in Society* (2014), as well as numerous articles and book chapters on media literacy, critical cultural studies, and gender and media. She serves as a board member of the Action Coalition for Media Education.

Rob Williams teaches new/digital and social media, communications and journalism courses at the University of Vermont and Sacred Heart University. The cofounding president and current board chair of the Action Coalition for Media Education (ACME at www.smartmediaeducation.net), he is the author of numerous articles and book chapters about media education, lectures widely on topics and issues related to digital media literacy education, and consults with a number of organizations, including the College for America, PH International, and the U.S. State Department. His latest book is *Most Likely to Secede: What the Vermont Independence Movement Can Teach Us about Reclaiming Community and Creating a Human Scale Vision for the 21st Century* (2013).

Routledge Research in Cultural and Media Studies

For more titles in the series, please visit www.routledge.com.

Media Education for a Digital Generation

Edited by Julie Frechette
and Rob Williams

Routledge
Taylor & Francis Group

NEW YORK AND LONDON

First published 2016
by Routledge
711 Third Avenue, New York, NY 10017

and by Routledge
2 Park Square, Milton Park, Abingdon, Oxon OX14 4RN

First issued in paperback 2017

Routledge is an imprint of the Taylor & Francis Group, an informa business

© 2016 Taylor & Francis

The right of the editors to be identified as the authors of the editorial material, and of the authors for their individual chapters, has been asserted in accordance with sections 77 and 78 of the Copyright, Designs and Patents Act 1988.

Library of Congress Cataloging in Publication Data

   Media education for a digital generation / edited by Julie Frechette and Rob Williams.
      pages cm. — (Routledge research in cultural and media studies ; 74)
   Includes bibliographical references and index.
      1. Media literacy—Study and teaching. 2. Mass media—Technological innovations.
      3. Mass media in education. I. Frechette, Julie D., 1971- editor. II. Williams, Rob,
      1967 September 22- editor.
   P96.M4M38 2016
   302.23017—dc23   2015023537

ISBN 13: 978-0-8153-8641-4 (pbk)
ISBN 13: 978-1-138-92766-7 (hbk)

Typeset in Sabon
by codeMantra

To my family—Darryll, Hayden, and Connor—for always believing in me and for joining me in questioning reality.

To my family—Kate, Anneka, and Theron—for their extraordinary love, support, and shared adventures.

Contents

PART III
Local

PART IV
National

PART V
Global

Foreword

Douglas Rushkoff

Media literacy was always a tough sell.

After all, as most of us understood it, TV was supposed to be for entertainment—a respite from the drudgery of work or, worse, school. Just putting a word as severe as "literacy" next to "media" turns it from an escape into yet another chore. It brings to mind the educational programming of PBS, not the decadence of *I Love Lucy, Lucha Libre,* or even *Lost.* Media Literacy was for people who *read* TV, not for those who want to *watch* it. And if the subject somehow managed to deliver on its promise, it could render TV unwatchable forever more. The incomprehensible magic and storytelling replaced by the neutered crafts of technology and rhetoric, as well as the political economy fueling them. Instead of offering escape, the literalized media just extends the problems of the real world into that last refuge.

But that's precisely the point: media is not a refuge. Never has been. We didn't get mass media because Jack Benny and Milton Berle were sitting in their cabanas in Hollywood wondering how they could bring their music and comedy to the world. No, it was invented to serve the needs of the new giants of industry, who wanted to reach an entire nation of consumers with their brand mythologies. Without mass media, there would be no mass market.

Once we know things like that, however, we can't look at media content quite the same way. Magazines begin to feel less about the articles than the demographic niche they are delivering to their advertisers. Radio begins to sound like a string of commercials with a few bits of sports, weather, or news slipped in between to keep us listening. TV shows make sense only as environments fine-tuned to sell certain goods and lifestyles.

Being able to see through media's spell to the agendas driving it is a form of critical thinking. And it's not always fun—not for the audience, and certainly not for the programmer nor the sponsor paying him or her for our attention. Indeed, there's an argument to be made for rejecting this whole subject area as too disruptive, too disillusioning, too antagonistic to the marketplace for anyone's good. How are we supposed to grow the economy and sell more goods to more people in less time if everyone is busy deconstructing the media for its messaging techniques or, worse, the power structures behind it?

Every year in America, a new crop of students arrive at college, blissfully unaware of the forces shaping the media they watch and use. That's because the United States is the only developed Western nation without a mandated media literacy curriculum in elementary or secondary school. We just don't do that sort of thing. Maybe that's why we're the biggest consumer economy on earth. Or vice versa.

But kids grow up perfectly happy this way, and often right into adulthood. If it weren't for all of us well-meaning but cynical media educators, so many people would be spared the development of critical faculties and the attendant reluctance to believe, shop, aspire—at least in that naive way—ever again. In other words, why should it be so very important for people to know that the voting on *American Idol* is rigged, that automobile brands pay for placement on TV shows, or that dancers are hired for rock videos based less on their talent than the number of Instagram followers they can reach? If the middle class is happy this way, and they don't vote too much, where's the harm? If the system truly stops working for them, they'll take to the streets soon enough. Marxism and Madmen just don't mix, so why piss on what's left of the American dream?

It's a blinders-on argument espoused on talk radio to this day, and it does contain a grain of truth—at least as far as the GNP, military conscription, and mega-church enrollment are concerned. Like for the turncoat in *The Matrix* who decides to forget everything and return the illusion, the steak tastes real—and maybe that's good enough.

But no more. While ignorance may have been an option in the era of broadcast media, it can't work in a digital environment. The luxury of ignorance only works in a landscape where we are reading the media, not one in which we are *making* the media. In the read-only media universe of television, we are already in the position of consumers. Sure, we can read deeply, deconstruct the imagery, and alter the cognitive frame through which we receive our media. But we're still essentially consumers. That's why they call the stuff on television "programming": they're not programming a schedule or a TV set, they're programming *us*. We can pick which channel to watch, but we're still the ones being programmed. In such a media environment, critical distance is still just an upgraded style of *reception*.

In a digital environment, we are no longer just the audience but the programmers—or at least the content creators. No, many of us may not realize it quite yet. The tools of new media are as simple and user-friendly as a TV remote—in many cases, easier. Posting an update on Facebook is simpler and more commonplace than recording a season of *Game of Thrones* on the DVR.

Besides, instead of watching TV shows, young people today are spending more time shooting and posting their own programs to YouTube—and then watching those of their peers. Sure, they know what's on in primetime, but that's all just part of the same sea of video, and just as easily time-shifted. Likewise, they know what a professional site or sponsored Tweet looks like, but they're just pages on the same web and messages in the same stream that they post to themselves.

There's an unintentional media literacy that comes along with learning to do all this oneself. You can't look at a news report the same way once you've edited your own news story. Nor can you see a branded Facebook page the same way once you have solicited the very same Likes as it did from your friends for your own new profile picture. As content creators, most digital natives now read content as well as any 1980s semiotician. They know how Disney creates a pop star like Ariana Grande, and they really don't mind because they feel they are part of the same machine.

But that's not enough. For just as our reception of content was limited by our ignorance of its construction, our creation of content is now limited by our ignorance of the platforms on which we do it. Media literacy addressed our ability to read the media. Digital media literacy must address our ability to make it.

Digital technologies cannot simply be read. They do not impose themselves on us solely through their content. They express themselves in the ways that they dictate what we create on them, and whom those creations serve. Facebook is not a neutral social networking platform any more than FOX News is a neutral television network. But understanding a technology's biases is a dimensional leap beyond reading a piece of content.

The choice between YouTube and Vimeo, Facebook and Twitter, Wordpress and Squarespace, Google and Bing, Apple and Linux, are choices between different architectures, business models, abilities, and limitations. In some cases, the distinction may be as ethereal as branding; in others, as fundamental as the ownership of one's own creations, or the acquiescence to surveillance and predictive analysis. In still others, it can mean the difference between creating apps that enable and encourage peer-to-peer value exchange, and those that require transactions to go through a centralized, extractive authority.

The platforms we use are embedded with values that inform more than how we see the world; they inform how we create the world. As participants in a digital media environment, our interaction with and dependence on media extend far beyond what we are choosing to read and watch. Digital media literacy means seeing the values embedded in the highly mediated world of social interaction, business transaction, and even healthcare. Amazon and Uber are as much media in a digital age as *Xena* and *Knight Rider* were in a broadcast one. The behaviors they encourage, the platform monopolies they create, and the financial destruction they leave in their wakes are now the province of media literacy. If not us, then whom?

This is about so much more than entertainment. The structure of a television network may dictate what sorts of sitcoms we see, but the structure of a digital network can dictate who we're friends with, what our parents know about us, what we can earn money for, what the government knows about us, what mechanisms we use to vote, who informs us about the world, whether a robot or AI takes our job, or who controls the terms of the user agreement on our cochlear implant.

Our society seems hell-bent on creating an app for every desire, and a platform for every major challenge. And so our solutions come increasingly in the form of new media, which are then implemented with far too few questions about what values they bring along with them. As Frechette and Williams advocate, digital media literacy is the art and discipline of asking those questions. It is crucial that we follow their lead. Herein lie the first great probes into what it means to be literate in a digital age, and how educators can still take us there.

Douglas Rushkoff
Professor of Media Theory and Digital Economics, Queens College/
CUNY, New York February 2015

Preface

"It is not the consciousness of men that determine their being, but on the contrary, their *social being* that determines their consciousness" [emphasis ours]*(Karl Marx, 1859)*.

Marx's nineteenth-century projections remind us twenty-first-century "netizens" that it is not the technology of a generation that materializes its future, but the social and constructivist uses of human communication that determine its destiny. From Facebook and Twitter, to Instagram and Snapchat, we are inundated with new and emerging social media whose conceptual purpose is to provide us with the means to express ourselves and enhance our daily communication with others in varied networked environments. At the dawn of the twenty-first century, Marc Prensky presciently considered the ways in which K-12 students are the first generation born into a world where technology has redefined who they are and how they learn. He explains that they "have spent their entire lives surrounded by and using computers, videogames, digital music players, video cams, cell phones, and all the other toys and tools of the digital age" (para. 3, 2001). As a result of growing up in this new digital age, he aptly contends, "today's students are no longer the people our educational system was designed to teach" (para. 1, 2001). Given this important change, the challenge facing us all is to consider the ways in which the ubiquity of digital technology, and the ways that students interact with it, demand a new type of learning philosophy and methodology for our digital age.

Media Education for a Digital Generation lays the groundwork for establishing a curriculum that fosters critical autonomy for users of digital technology by outlining how critical digital literacy skills can be maximized through defined learning goals, strategies, and outcomes. By creating new criteria for evaluating online networks, social media, and mobile technology, our book provides new perspectives to help people judge the validity and worth of digital media content as they strive to become critically autonomous in a robust high-tech world.

If we are to best prepare young people for their roles as informed and active citizens in our globally connected world, then we must learn from recent scholarship in the area of emerging technologies as it affects a new generation of learners. *Media Education for a Digital Generation* fulfills this goal in both theoretical and pragmatic ways, offering empirical research, pedagogical tools, methods, and insights to critically analyze digital media while creatively and mindfully exploring ways they can be used to discover more essential truths about our relationships with others in profound and often transformational ways.

By exploring new innovations in hands-on, student-centered learning, readers will benefit from our exploration of key issues and pedagogical practices affiliated with multi-literacies—namely digital literacy, media literacy, and critical literacy—which inform and challenge our understandings of digital media and their impact. Using theoretical and conceptual constructs, case studies, pedagogical strategies, curricula, and examples devised around issues of digital literacy for today's generation of media users, our book is designed to help readers envision how new modalities of learning and social engagement can emerge for a new generation of students.

We've structured our book around five key lenses—self, social, local, national, and global—that provide five different but complementary windows into the world of Media Education for a Digital Generation. Part 1, the Self, features three chapters exploring the relationship between the constructed self and our digital age. Through the aperture of photography and photographic practice, Daniel Hunt considers the ways in which the constructed nature of "selfie"—the Oxford English Dictionary's 2013 word of the year—provides deeper understandings about our digital world and new pedagogical possibilities for visual literacy to merge with digital culture. Meanwhile, Chyng F. Sun, Rachael Liberman, Allison Butler, Sun Young Lee, and Rachel Webb look at Asian Americans as an often-stereotyped social group within U.S. culture, and how digital media literacy education helps us understand ways in which Asian Americans navigate "shifting identities" through the intentional deployment of social media. In his "Who's Tracking Me?" chapter, Thomas Corrigan fuses a study of surveillance with digital media education to help students develop deeper understandings of how they are being systematically surveilled by corporations interested in aggregating youth market user data, and how to respond proactively.

Part 2, the Social, explores digital media literacy education across a wide range of social norms and practices. Pediatrician Victor Strasburger, a longtime proponent of synthesizing public health research with media literacy education, considers how digital culture has generated new research opportunities for considering the relationship among youth, digital media use, and public health issues. As both parent and professor of marketing, Elaine Young offers a blueprint, born of both personal experience and research, for raising kids and families—the "Connected Generation." Girl Tech is the focus of our third chapter, in which Andrea Quijada, Jessica Collins, and Kandace Creel Falcon discuss how grassroots production teaches young women of color in the desert Southwest to be film directors. Finally, Morgan Jaffe considers how digital media platforms create "virtual and social affinity spaces" to advance the cause of social justice for LGBTQ communities, and how media literacy education helps provide deeper understandings of this phenomenon.

Local impacts of the digital age form the focus of Part 3. Allison Butler considers how legislation and regulation have both helped and hindered the deployment of media literacy education initiatives in U.S. public schools, while Ben Boyington explores the pedagogical consequences to date of 1:1 technology initiatives within secondary educational spaces in his chapter. Erica Scharrer and her research team—Christine Olson, Laras Sekarasih, and Ryan Cadrette—look at middle school cyber-bullying, and how digital media literacy education can encourage more critical thinking about this troublesome and pervasive phenomenon. Finally, in a provocative chapter entitled "The Text and the Image," Bill Yousman considers the generational divide—analog versus digital—between professors and their students around the teaching of texts in the classroom, and what might be done to improve educational experiences through thoughtful sustained application of digital media literacy educational approaches.

Focused on the National, Part 4 brings a range of critical voices to bear. In "Breaking the Corporate News Frame," Andy Lee Roth highlights the work of Project Censored, a national news watchdog organization that has challenged dominant U.S. corporate commercial mainstream news reporting for more than three decades with an innovative crowdsourced approach to "validated" independent news research and media production. Chenjerai Kumanhika and Paradise Gray share stories from the 1Hood Media Academy, where digital literacy and video production provide young students of color with creative and thought-provoking opportunities to participate in the exploding national conversation around race, police brutality, and social justice in the wake of the highly publicized Ferguson, Missouri, and Staten Island, New York, news stories. Next, Christopher Boulton looks at issues of digital copyright and its impact on authorship, creativity, and the cultural reproduction of ideas, while Satish Kolluri considers the importance of *The Daily Show* and *The Colbert Report* on our national news dialogue. Finally, Lori Bindig makes a case for more graduate programs nationally to train teachers and other educational practitioners in digital media literacy education.

The Global is the focus of Part 5. Paul Mihailidis makes a case for "the mobile citizen," looking at how digital media literacy education is reshaping the global public sphere. Bettina Fabos and her colleagues—Leisl Carr Childers and Sergey Golitsynskiy—detail how a new crowdsourced, cross-national digital photo archiving platform from Europe to the U.S. —FORTEPAN—provides a new, grassroots opportunity for nations around the world to capture lost history and collective cultural memory through the power of digital photo sharing. Nicki Lisa Cole's chapter provides insights into the environmental impacts of technology, using Apple's ubiquitous global mobile presence as a case study for exploring the natural consequences of living, working, and playing in the digital age. The final chapter by Julian McDougall offers new conceptual ways of creating digital media education praxis through 'mediapting' and curation.

Employing a cross-disciplinary approach, the twenty chapters in our book span outward to include practitioners interested in media literacy education, multiple literacies education, digital literacy, information literacy, computer literacy, trans-literacy, critical cultural studies, media studies, critical pedagogy, and political economy. Our emphasis is on providing dialogical inquiry and conversations between and among academics, educators, activists, parents, physicians, policy makers, students, and engaged citizens from across disciplines and fields. Our book is also essential for administrators, legislators, and the public at large interested in examining the trends of digital media and their impact, along with those seeking literature outlining a praxis of effective engagement in the digital age. In sum, our book is written for anyone interested and involved in effectively interrogating new digital technologies, as well as effectively integrating critical multi-literacies into the educational process.

Our hope is that *Media Education for a Digital Generation* offers multiple vantage points from which to creatively and meaningfully engage in digital media literacy education (DMLE) in the classroom, at home, and in everyday moments. Our chapter contributors provide innovative and thoughtful insights into DMLE today, as they ambitiously combine recent communication and educational scholarship about networked technology with theoretical visions and pragmatic possibilities for our twenty-first century digitally supported learning communities. The culmination is a critical pedagogy that values self and social empowerment over technical skills, and suggests new learning modes, approaches, and initiatives for teaching and learning across the digital spectrum.

REFERENCES

Marx, K. (1859; repr., 1979). Preface to *A contribution to the critique of political economy*. Moscow: Progress Publishers.

Prensky, M. (2001). Digital Natives, Digital Immigrants. *On The Horizon, 9*(5). Retrieved from http://www.marcprensky.com/writing/Prensky - Digital Natives, Digital Immigrants - Part1.pdf.

Acknowledgments

We would like to thank all those who contributed their ideas and feedback during the span of creating this book. We had a stellar team of contributors that we would like to thank for their scholarship and groundbreaking work in digital media literacy education. We feel a special connection to each and every one of them as we work in solidarity to expand media literacy initiatives locally, nationally and globally. We would also like to thank our dedicated team at Routledge who believed in the importance and timeliness of our project from the beginning, and who worked with us throughout the publication process. We would like to thank the members of the Action Coalition of Media Education who, over many years, have carried out our collective mission to advance media literacy at all levels of education and activism. In addition, we want to recognize the inspirational work of Project Censored, as this book was conceived at their motivating conference in San Francisco. We dedicate this book to our families for their sustained love and support as we ventured on this writing project. They have made media literacy personally transformative in our lives. Finally, a special thanks to all of our media education mentors, colleagues, students, friends, and supporters—for their vision, courage, and groundbreaking work in developing our field. May this book do justice to their pioneering efforts.

Introduction

Julie Frechette and Rob Williams

As part of a longstanding globalized movement, Digital Media Literacy Education (DMLE) is predicated upon the ability to access, analyze, evaluate, and produce media content and communication in a variety of forms. Rather than teach one-dimensional approaches for using media platforms, DMLE offers us a way to become media literate by providing tools through which to examine the political, cultural, historical, economic, and social ramifications of all media in a holistic way (Frechette, 2002). While many media literacy approaches overemphasize the end-goal of accessing digital media content through the acquisition of various technology, software, apps, and analytics, we argue that the goals for comprehensive and critical digital literacy require grasping and evaluating the means through which communication is created, deployed, used, and shared, regardless of which tools or platforms are used for meaning making and social interaction.

Undoubtedly, the speed and immediacy of technological advancements and mediated information are radically changing the nature of contemporary media and communication. As mobile technology, social media, and converging web content drive the new information economy, *Media Education for a Digital Generation* has become paramount. Parents and educators continue to extol the need for current and relevant curricular models equipped to encourage critical and effective engagement within our media landscapes at a time when digital media have become extensions of self, social, local, national, and global constructs at the core of human communication. As media educators committed to fostering critical thinking and informed engagement at all levels, we explore how a critical pedagogy of digital literacy leads us forward into the twenty-first century in order to provide purpose in our classrooms and learning communities for individuals and citizens interested in engaging in transformative communication.

Despite an unprecedented amount of new digital media content and technology that pervade our lives, few curricular models are poised to comprehensively address the question: "What does it mean to be digitally literate in our new media age?" We argue for a dialectical approach that carefully questions and examines the benefits of innovative, decentralized digital media, enabling self, social, and civic participation within a paradigm that values digital media for its transformative potential. Drawing upon the intersecting matrices of digital literacy and media literacy, we offer a framework for developing critical digital media literacies by exploring the necessary skills and competencies for engaging as citizens of our connected global world. Specifically, the chapters in this volume represent new insights and exciting opportunities from within the disciplines of Communication, Media Studies, and Cultural Studies, along with progressive media education action that effectively propels our pedagogical efforts forward to enable DMLE.

The Digital Revolution has provided remarkable new challenges and opportunities for the global media literacy education movement, which emerged during the Analog age. Twenty-five years ago, three national broadcast networks and PBS dominated the U.S. television airwaves; many national movie theaters sported single screens; Google, Facebook, Amazon, and Apple were in their infancy; mobile technology did not exist; and the Internet was just beginning to permeate daily life through desktop computing. Pedagogically speaking, media literacy educators worked with still images, short video clips captured and converted from analog VHS tapes to digital files via hypercard and other emerging presentation platforms, and organizations like the Center for Media Literacy, the New Mexico Media Literacy Project, and the Media Education Foundation produced films, CD-ROMS, and other multimedia packages that allowed for easy collection and sharing of rich multimedia for teachers and classrooms.

Fast forward to today. Screens of every size dominate every aspect of our lives, and it is the image, rather than the word, that commands our attention. Most all media—music, magazines, newspapers, books, television, radio, film, and games—have been digitized via the power of the binary code, and anyone with Internet access can personally participate in robust online conversations about almost any media text as soon as it "drops." Mobile technology creates convergence everywhere we turn, as once separate and discrete media experiences combine with one another through ubiquitous new small but powerful devices—mobile phones, tablets, phablets, wearable technology (think Google Glass and Timex watch screens). The Lords of the Cloud—Amazon, Apple, Facebook, Google, and other giant digital media corporations—partner with government agencies like the CIA and the National Security Agency to collect mounds of metadata and track our every e-move in real time, while providing undeniably exciting new digital platforms for people and organizations to connect in unprecedented ways. Today, the challenge for educators is not finding access to content—we swim in a sea of digital media—but developing powerful pedagogical approaches that foster new knowledge, skills, and meaningful engagement in our emerging digital world.

Just as new digital technologies have proliferated, DMLE must offer an inventive, developmental model of learning that considers the ways in which our sense of discovery and engagement are enhanced with access to new technologies, accompanied by smart media education. This approach requires both epistemological and empirical inquiry into the best practices for using new media to cultivate awareness, critical analysis, engagement, reflection, and production. For example, in what ways do young people create a sense of self-realization and esteem through the curation of content using photos, videos, text, audio, and other media (see Hunt, Chapter 1, this volume)? How can young people effectively interact with others developmentally and socioculturally as they learn to define their sense of communal connections locally, regionally, nationally, and globally? How can the use of digital tools and social media platforms foster substantive interaction, affinity spaces, activism, and global citizenship (see Jaffe, Chapter 7, this volume)? In what ways can the power of social media be leveraged to transcend the stereotypes and representational constructs that have epitomized mainstream media depictions (see Sun, Liberman, Butler, Lee, & Webb, Chapter 2; and Quijada, Collins, & Creel Falcon, Chapter 6, this volume)? These are the central questions that drive our inquiry.

Our framework for conceptualizing the impact of digital media is to view them as appendages of human communication and interaction that offer both constructive possibilities and limitations for the development of self and social constructs, along with communal linkages to local, national, and global spheres of interactivity that are increasingly and comprehensively defining a new generation of citizens. The idea of digital media as appendages hearkens back to Marshall McLuhan's famous analogy of the media as "extensions of man" that impact us through their design and structure. So if digital media serve as appendages/extensions of how we communicate, interact, create, and engage today in ways that are far more creative and decentralized than they were during the Age of Analog, should we not develop new visionary paradigms and pedagogies of media literacy education for the digital generation of learners we teach and interact with? At the 2014 International Media Literacy Education Summit in Prague, there was a lot of discussion about how to analyze the unique characteristics of digital media within paradigms of media education. We fall in the camp that believes that we need to precede our conversations and approaches to media literacy education by denoting the concept, structures, and applications of 'digital' media, or else the characteristics of digital ecosystems, and the ways they alter our sociocultural participation, go unremarked in the subsequent analysis of their role in our lives, for better, worse, or somewhere in between. Since digital media are personal, multidirectional, participatory, global, networkable, and more affordable than mainstream media, we make important inquiries into how these characteristics make digital media new and different from analog media. As such, the chapters in this collection consider the ways in which *digital* media literacy education must explore the impact of digital culture at home and at school, and in the various five key strata—self, social, local, national, and global—that define the new ecology of human interactivity today.

SELF

For starters, we contend that digital media have become appendages of *SELF* and identity as conceptualized and enacted within society. In spite of its clichéd use and limitations stemming from the digital divide, young people are often referred to as digital natives (Prensky, 2001) because they are born into a culture that is immersed in media and technology in which they are versed speakers "of the digital language of computers, video games and the Internet" (para. 5). Today, young people define their sense of self, identity, and place through social media that provide platforms for using visual media tools and technology to represent themselves.

Whereas children were once encouraged to develop a sense of self-actualization through 'show and tell' at school or by having their work exhibited in communal spaces, young people are now presented with new opportunities by using digital modes of self-expression and creativity from home and school for audiences that spread beyond their immediate domains. Using the rich affordances of digital technology, today's youth can access knowledge and information from innumerable media sources in ways hitherto unfathomable. With social media, they can chronicle their daily lives, experiences, and travels with 'selfies' and 'vines' of events in which they've participated, decide with whom to share this information, 'snap chat' to friends and strangers alike, and invite others to join in by tagging people and places in their posts. Using mobile devices, hash tags, and the power of online search engine optimization (SEO), young people can seek out others who share the same interests, hobbies, and passions they do, while imparting new perspectives, ideas, and behaviors that spread from niche groups to larger organizational structures. Through the amalgamation and mobilization of their collective voices, today's generation can also take part in conversational exchanges and collective action beyond their inner circles that impact people's lives personally and politically.

Although there is cause for celebration over theories espousing the "networked self" (Papacharissi, 2011), social "connectedness" (Christakis and Fowler, 2009), "the power of organizing without organizations" (Shirky, 2008), and living in "the age of engage" (Shiffman, 2008), there are bodies of literature that are equally concerned with overstating the case for digital media's progressiveness, ubiquity, and favorable impact on culture (boyd, 2014; Turkle, 2012; Steyer & Clinton, 2012; Ratner, 2014; Bauerlein, 2008; and Linn, 2009). The most influential structural critique of the digital revolution comes from Robert McChesney (2013), who argues in his book *Digital Disconnect: How Capitalism Is Turning the Internet Against Democracy* that the Internet's commercial colonization has led to the demise of credible journalism and made the Internet an antidemocratic medium.

Likewise, projections for technological learning gains are often unempirical and market-driven, thereby sustaining a corporate capitalist ideology and function (see Frechette, 2002, and Fuchs, 2014). When the funding mechanisms for urban schools and households are contrasted with those in suburban areas, the educational and social goals for children's digital media usage differ sharply. In a study that sought to find out where K-12 students develop their digital skill sets, it was discovered that children from Silicon Valley learned digital media skills outside of school because they had access to technology and instruction at home. However, in select media literacy programs in Chicago, children learned digital media literacy mostly in school and afterschool programs because those environments offered them access to production tools and instruction (Pinkard, 2014).

Although we need more demographic data to evaluate the accessibility and implementation of DMLE for all schools and homes, protectionist attitudes about digital media continue to vacillate between approval and dismissal along the high cultural/low cultural contingency. This is not unique to digital technologies, as these same sentiments were manifested during the film and broadcast eras when new media were entering both public and private social spheres. Ironically, those who wield cultural capital in the technology sector, in particular, believe that their children should be shielded from using digital gadgets at home and in schools in order to "protect" and "preserve" an essentialist purity of childhood learning. In a *New York Times* article entitled "Steve Jobs Was a Low-Tech Parent" (2014), journalist Nick Bilton reveals how, when he asked how his children liked the iPad, Jobs acknowledged that he had *not* exposed his kids to the very product he had launched in millions of families' lives. Jobs explained, "We limit how much technology our kids use at home" (Bilton, 2014). Bilton discovered that this practice represents a parenting pattern among other technology chief executives and social media CEOs who impose similar restrictions by limiting their children's screen time, forbidding Snapchat and other social media, implementing parental controls on every device, and encouraging book reading over digital content.

Parenting and educational differences like these are meaningful because they tell us that socioeconomic demographics affect pedagogical and curricular emphases. What's more, they indicate that access to technology at home and in schools, and policies toward them, are important determining variables that can lead to different skill sets and learning outcomes in students. For these reasons, DMLE requires more funding and research, cutting edge curricular initiatives, thoughtful and creative pedagogy, and strong technological infrastructures to overcome the digital divide.

In addition to cognitive and developmental concerns, there are also new studies that document the long-term physiological impact of using digital media. Brain researchers are uncovering both the collaborative educational possibilities and powerful addictive effects of twenty-first century media experiences, like first-person gaming (Gee, 2013). The physical impacts of a sedentary screen-driven life for our youth—increasing obesity, sleep deprivation, hearing loss, back pain, distraction, and depression—have been well documented (Strasburger, Chapter 4, this volume; Samakow & Leibovich, 2013). And what is the Internet doing to our brains? In the first full-length popular book to ever grapple with this question, *The Shallows* author Nicholas Carr highlights what he calls our "Juggler's Brain," a phenomenon we all experience when we are called upon to keep too many cognitive plates spinning simultaneously. The Internet, Carr concludes, is an "attention dividing" technology—we are no longer "SCUBA divers" immersing ourselves in a sea of words and ideas, but "Jet Skiers" distractedly skimming over the surface of our information world at high rates of speed (Carr, 2010).

Carr's book helps highlight many ambiguities regarding digital media. While on the one hand, technology affords enhanced mobility, on the other hand, it encourages stasis through physical and mental inactivity for those who remain tethered to their digital devices. Findings continue to document the impact of 'apptivity,'[1] which refers to gadget gaming activities through digital technology and tablet-based app games. The most prevalent concerns over 'apptivity,' gaming and social media are their impact on traditional communication, namely face-to-face and real time social engagements, even during daily routines like having family dinner conversations and chatting with people in the same room. As reported in the Kaiser Family Foundation's study *Generation M2: Media in the Lives of 8-to 18-Year-Olds*, the 24-hour access of media through digital technology means that children and teens, especially minority youth, are increasing the amount of time they spend with entertainment media (2010). The report documents that "8–18 year-olds devote an average of 7 hours and 38 minutes (7:38) to using entertainment media across a typical day (more than 53 hours a week). And because they spend so much of that time 'media multitasking' (using more than one medium at a time), they actually manage to pack a total of 10 hours and 45 minutes (10:45) worth of media content into those 7½ hours" (2010).

Behavioral changes such as these are troubling for parents, educators, and physicians alike. In fact, the American Academy of Pediatrics (2013) has developed a media kit for physicians and nurses to use as a means to inquire about their patients' screen time, as "excessive media use has been associated with obesity, lack of sleep, school problems, aggression and other behavior issues." Dr. Matthew Davis, director of the C. S. Mott Children's Hospital National Poll on Children's Health, explains "it's not so much the content of the entertainment that is the problem. Rather ... it's what the children and students are missing while they are glued to the screen," which includes other activities that promote cognitive and physical growth like reading and physical activity (cited in Huffman, 2014; see Yousman, Chapter 11, this volume).

Likewise, despite the ways that social media can embellish self-esteem, "Facebook envy" and FOMO (fear of missing out) have emerged as new pathologies, causing some to lose self-worth and purpose when comparing with other friends' social media profiles, highlights, and post "likes" (McCleod, 2014; Poswolsky, 2013). Thus, a balanced assessment of the benefits and drawbacks of digital connectivity is needed in order to fairly weigh the prosocial benefits of new digital media technologies against antisocial ones.

SOCIAL

Moving beyond self, digital media have redefined and altered our sense of *SOCIAL* place and interaction within the digital world. The impact of digital media on social networking and engagement cannot be overstated, as each year, young people continue to expand the time they spend in online spaces. According to the PEW Research Internet Project, "95% of teens are online, 81% of online teens ages 12–17 use some kind of social media, and three in four teens access the Internet on cell phones, tablets, and other mobile devices" (2013). As for owning personal media devices, "78% of online teens ages 12–17 own a cell phone, 8 out of 10 teens own a desktop or laptop computer, and 23% of teens have a tablet computer" (Pew Research, 2013).

In the gaming world, multiplayer games, like X Box Live, are now a defining component of social interactions among young people, particularly for boys and teenagers, as they experience virtual play in real time within autonomous heterogeneous environments. Pro-game researchers like linguist James Paul Gee argue that games can provide "well-designed problem-solving experiences" that "enable good learning" (Gee, 2013). Other observers are less sanguine, highlighting games' addictive, distractive, and antisocial tendencies. While literature on pop and fandom culture celebrate the creative aspects of digital modalities and engagements that come from media convergences (Jenkins, 2006; Bowman, 2010; Gee, 2013), others question their social effects, asking if the alleged benefits that accompany immersive gaming practice are truly worth the costs (Anderson, 1997; Anderson, Gentile, & Buckley, 2007).

Living in a tech-saturated world is complicated and ambiguous because it offers either / or binary possibilities for social engagement / disengagement, transparency / opacity, community / isolation, and shared civic values / dogmatism. As Young's research explains, parents are discovering the challenges of raising children whose ultra-connected lives often compete with their family values and routines (Chapter 5, this volume). Teachers and administrators are also finding it harder to deal with the behaviors that emerge when children socialize in unsupervised online environments. As Carrie James (2014) contends in her book, *Disconnected: Youth, New Media, and the Ethics Gap*, young people are faced with unique ethical dilemmas in online communities and digital contexts that require new philosophical and pedagogical approaches to engender fairness and civility. She describes a wide range of unethical behaviors, which can include anything from posting photos or videos of others in compromising situations, to adapting articles from Wikipedia for college papers, to using one's gaming experience to cheat new online multiplayers by selling them virtual accessories for a profit.

What's more, as the #GamerGate debacle has exposed, the privacy and anonymity of online social environments can be a hindrance to inclusivity if used to intimidate and bully, particularly in the male-dominated gaming world where sexism and misogyny run rampant in online multiplayer games and in subsequent real-world cultural interactions. Gendered intimidation, sexual violence, and even death threats are now more common in the encoding and cultural decoding of online social networks. As Natasha Lomas explains,

> The underlying agenda of GamerGate has always been an attempt to intimidate and drive women out of the games industry. While the threats of violence have been exceptionally crude, the tactics have been relatively sophisticated, with co-ordinated online attacks aimed at amplifying the impact and noise, and exerting commercial pressure on digital advertisers ... Bottom line: this is an online bullying issue, not a free speech issue (2014).

Similar antisocial behaviors are increasingly policed at school, as forty-nine states in the U.S. have anti-bullying laws that now require school administrators to deal with inappropriate emails, text threats and sexting, even if these negative behaviors occur outside school grounds and hours (see StopBullying.Gov). The research of Scharrer, Olson, Sekarasih, and Cadrette on cyberbullying explains this phenomenon at length (Chapter 10, this volume).

LOCAL

Digital media have also redefined our sense of, and connection to the LOCAL, including our classrooms and communities within the digital world. Looking locally, collective storytelling opportunities have never been more robust, and wikis, blogs, listserves, and hyperlocal community platforms proliferate. On the positive side, the Digital Age has made possible the creation and sharing of more flesh-and-blood community resources than ever before, as community organizations with limited resources scramble to leverage new digital opportunities. Local PEG-access community cable television stations, helmed by the national Alliance for Community Media (ACM), are now able to shoot and share local programming with both local and larger audiences via the power of the digital Web, and can digitally "bicycle" local programs to other networked PEG stations across any given state. In tiny Vermont, home to one of our coeditors, hyperlocal and privacy-focused digital platforms like iBrattleboro, Burlington-based Front Porch Forum, and the new Ello social media network are providing new digital opportunities for neighbors to connect and share information within their communities without neighbors having to rely on digital giants like Facebook as an organizing medium. Local schools, while struggling with the problems and opportunities presented by mobile'ly focused students trapped in more traditional low-tech classrooms, are also relying more and more on digital media platforms and initiatives to collect, measure, assess, and share data and information to track and ideally improve student performance. Teachers and students alike, meanwhile, are working and playing with new digital tools and platforms that dramatically increase the reach of research, storytelling, production, and presentation possibilities in our twenty-first-century schools.

The digital world has also created new challenges for classrooms and communities. Data mining and surveillance (Corrigan, Chapter 3, this volume); the ubiquitous, intrusive, distracting presence of mobile devices in classrooms; the constant pressure underfunded public schools feel to accept corporate commercial partnerships and sponsorships to pay for school equipment, buildings, and programs (Boyington, Chapter 9, this volume); the perceived and all-too-real digital homogenization of local and regionally unique cultures and communities—all of these are acute issues for local communities and classrooms in the twenty-first century. "You are not a gadget," warns futurist, programmer, and father of virtual reality Jaron Lanier, reminding us that technology both gives and takes away—and there are no easy answers to the vexing questions that all classrooms and communities face (2010).

NATIONAL

Moving into larger social arenas, digital media have redefined our sense of, and connection to, NATIONAL constructs within the digital world. Illinois Democratic Senator Barack Obama's successful if perhaps illusory 2008 presidential "Hope and Change" campaign proved a historic watershed moment for the United States, ushering in a full-blown digital/political communications revolution at the national level that took full advantage of both the new crowdsourcing and crowdfunding opportunities that have emerged through mobile and social media. The digital era has also encouraged grassroots organizing across the political spectrum: witness the national creation of the TEA party and #OccupyWallStreet communities in record time. And in 2003, when the Federal Communications Commission declared their intent to lift cross-ownership caps on U.S. media outlets, making it possible for a single corporation to own as many as eight radio stations, three television stations, and the monopoly newspaper and cable franchises in a single city, millions of outraged Americans from all political corners barraged FCC commissioners and congressional representatives with angry emails and telephone calls denouncing the impending decision. Media literacy education and reform groups, such as Free Press and the Action Coalition for Media Education (ACME), mobilized their national memberships to defeat an impending FCC decision that everyone, regardless of political affiliation, agreed was a bad one for democracy.

Digital and social media platforms also have facilitated ordinary citizens' remarkably easy access to national news about any topic: politics, music, sports, celebrities, extreme weather events, and the latest economic trends. Mere consumers no more, Americans of all stripes are embracing "prosumerism"—living the life of both media producer and consumer. Here again, an explosion of digital platforms and new approaches to copyright and information sharing—wikis, blogs, Creative Commons licensing, petition sites, and crowdfunding platforms—have allowed citizens from across the country to share, collaborate, argue, debate, discuss, support, work and play together (see Roth, Chapter 12; Boulton, Chapter 14, this volume). The result? "Here Comes Everybody!" exclaims NYU scholar Clay Shirky. With one million hours of collective leisure time (as of 2009), Americans live in an age of "Cognitive Surplus"—and our new digital universe, Shirky concludes, turns "consumers into collaborators" (Shirky, 2008; Shirky, 2010). Nicholas Carr, on the other hand, is less enthusiastic, arguing in his latest book that our digital technologies, with their focus on automation and the offloading of data from our brains to digital devices, imprison us in a "glass cage" of our own making (Carr, 2014).

GLOBAL

Moving from national to global, it is tempting to invoke the late Marshall McLuhan's famed "global village" as a metaphor to describe the sense that all of us on planet earth are "connected" via the power of the digital Internet. With seven billion plus people now occupying the globe, citizens have never before had an easier time reaching across the world to converse or collaborate with people and organizations in distant lands (see Fabos, Carr Childers, & Golitsynskiy, Chapter 18, this volume). A telling example: Wikipedia, perhaps the best single example of a globally created and shared information site, is now available (as of January 2015) in close to 300 languages. Powerful crowdfunding sites like micro-funding platform Kiva.org connect entrepreneurs (mostly women) in the developing world with first world citizens in the West interested in supporting small business start-ups. In Kenya, social media platform Ushahidi helps map incidents of election-related violence (Shirky, 2010). Using social media platforms and digital spaces, college students in the tiny state of Vermont gave birth to 350.org, a global grassroots movement in dozens of countries dedicated to climate change education and political action. In the Middle East, Facebook and Twitter provided important cyber-platforms for ordinary citizens to challenge long-standing government repression and organize, protest, and share ideas in virtual spaces, catalyzing a grassroots political movement across the region that transformed the status quo in Tunisia, Egypt, Yemen, Bahrain, Syria, Algeria and Libya beginning in 2011 (Ghonim, 2013). And in China, home to the Great (Fire)Wall, one of the world's most heavily policed and censored Internet networks, a single artist named Ai Wei Wei, armed only with a mobile phone and a robust Twitter network, so threatened the power of the Communist Party with his art and political activism that he was placed under house arrest, his Twitter feed all but shut down (Klayman, 2012).

Amidst all the digital hoopla, however, are some troubling global trends. Cyber-activists, reporters, and whistleblowers like Wikileaks' Julian Assange, Chelsea Manning, NSA whistle blower Edward Snowden, documentary filmmaker Laura Poitras, and investigative journalist Glenn Greenwald have exposed the dramatic depth and reach of U.S. digital surveillance and data mining across the globe—a form of Internet information imperialism (Assange, 2014). Longstanding, largely secret partnerships between U.S. intelligence agencies (namely, the CIA and the NSA) and giant global digital corporations like Google and Facebook are now being exposed by investigative journalists, such as former *Guardian* reporter Nafeez Ahmed (Greenwald, 2014; Ahmed, 2014). Repressive governments all over the world, meanwhile, are using digital tools to track, detain, arrest and imprison citizen activists. We must beware "the dark side of Internet freedom," cautions Evgeny Morozov in his 2012 book *The Internet Delusion*, pointing out that the very same platforms and digital spaces so celebrated by cyber activists are being coopted by governments unfriendly to increased citizen participation, democracy, and grassroots political challenges to the status quo. Finally, we must consider, as Annie Leonard reminds us in her sensational 21-minute viral Internet film and accompanying book *The Story Of Stuff*, the environmental consequences of our digital "materials economy" (Leonard, 2010). Namely, the extraction, production, distribution, consumption and disposal cycle that creates our digital technologies exacts a huge toll on Mother Nature. From the mining of coltan and other minerals for mobile phones to the enormous amounts of electricity needed to power an ever-growing global network of massive server centers, the digital age has created a voracious demand for energy and resources on a finite planet, and our one trillion dollar annual consumer economy in the U.S., driven by big business, does a fantastic job of keeping these "externalized" costs hidden from global public view (Cole, Chapter 19, this volume; Dawson, 2003).

While we argue that digital media have become appendages of self and social constructs through developmental behaviors and experiences, this is not to say that we believe in a technologically determined framework of DMLE that is solely propelled by aspirations for young people to acquire digital literacy skills to gain a "leg up" in the marketplace. Instead, we believe that DMLE requires us to analyze how human interaction and transformation are contingent upon the evolving ways that we conceptualize, develop, and use new tools and modes of communication—from the oral tradition to writing, print, broadcast, and digital culture. In his critical analysis of algorithmically determined modalities of networks and social media, Douglas Rushkoff reminds us in *Present Shock: When Everything Happens Now* that we need to move beyond extant approaches offered by the technology and commercial media complex that condition us to use technology for its own sake. He contemplates the impact of living in a digital age where trending events and social media usurp our critical competencies and deliberate proclivities:

> By dividing our attention between our digital extensions, we sacrifice our connection to the truer present in which we are living. The tension between the faux present of digital bombardment and the true now of a coherently living human generates the second kind of present shock, what we're calling *digiphrenia—digi* for "digital," and *phrenia* for "disordered condition of mental activity." This doesn't mean we should ignore this digitally mediated reality altogher ... [but] instead of succumbing to the schizophrenic cacophony of divided attention and temporal disconnection, we can program our machines to conform to the pace of *our* operations, be they our personal rhythms or cycles of our organizations and business sectors. Computers don't suffer present shock, people do. For we are the only ones living in time.
> (Rushkoff, 2013, p. 75)

Following Rushkoff's forewarning, the primary goal of DMLE should be to keep the focus off of the novelty of "present shock and awe," and on the social and relational outcomes of digital media through three modes of inquiry: 1) what we want to do with technology in the digital age; 2) how do we critically analyze and assess the changing dynamics and challenges of communication in digital culture; and 3) how can we effectively create, curate, engage, and transform ourselves through digital media. As such, rather than overextend the cybernetic techno-determinist and capitalistic prospects of digital media's ubiquity in our everyday lives which often (mis)represent the need for computer and information literacy, DMLE is well poised to provide both a humanistic focus and critical inquiry by offering students, parents, educators and community members the conceptual and practical means to analyze and evaluate constructs of identity, knowledge, values, and engagement from past to present as they continue to evolve in the digital age.

For some time now, cross-disciplinary research and scholarship have encouraged us to embrace and progressively experiment with the ways in which young people are already invested in their own self-determination through a variety of communication modes, media tools, programs, apps, and portals (Masterman, 1985; McLaren, 1986; hooks, 1988; Freire, 2000; McRobbie, 2000; Giroux, 2006; Goodman, 2003; Fabos, 2004). But as the latest iterations of digital culture permeate the boundaries between self / social, home / school, personal / political, and local / global, we need to encourage ourselves to assess the pedagogical effectiveness of whether or not, and how, we teach *and* learn from youths reciprocally in the digital age. The challenge is to provide learning communities that promote meaningful exchanges of knowledge, values, and diverse perspectives between and among all members in offline as well as online spaces (see McDougall, Chapter 20, this volume). More often than not, curricular and pedagogical walls continue to separate theory from production and analog from digital so that even contemporary modes of teaching and assessment reify the very generational divides that keep teachers and students, parents and children, activists and youths in different realms of reality.

Pedagogically, the insights and experiences of young people are essential to DMLE's success. Regardless of what temporal or spatial places they embody, young people should be encouraged to express themselves in responsible and meaningful ways through engaging curricula, workshops, and activities *as well as* media and technology so that they learn to see themselves as global citizens in both the physical and digital worlds (see Kumanhika & Gray; Chapter 13; Kolluri, Chapter 15; Mihailidis, Chapter 17, this volume). With so much emphasis on globalized learning, contemporary pedagogies and programs— from K-12 to higher education and graduate programs— need to embrace the potential of digital tools to accompany the developmental phases that lead from self-discovery to purpose, agency, and transformation (see Bindig, Chapter 16, this volume). DMLE provides the best hope for cultivating and materializing this developmental and educational paradigm from theory to praxis.

Other challenges for DMLE include the digital divide, budgetary constraints, traditional didactic pedagogies, and a culture of testing that stifles diverse and creative modes of teaching, learning, and assessment. Given these limitations—whether in part or in whole— most curricular approaches fall short of providing rich learning opportunities that embrace comprehensive approaches for DMLE, such as multi-literacies or trans-literacies. For instance, Frechette (2002) draws from Meyrowitz's media education theory to create a 4-step model of *multiple media literacy*: 1) media *content* literacy that allows us to decode and deconstruct meaning from various texts, narratives, and genres; 2) media *grammar* literacy that focuses on the distinct syntax and design elements of each medium; 3) *medium* literacy that examines the specific traits of each technology as it alters communication; and 4) *institutional analysis* of media to explore the financial and political constraints that affect message production, dissemination, reception, and impact.

Similarly, Frau-Meigs (2013) discusses the notion of "trans-literacy" as a means to "grasp the multi-media dimensions and trans-domain skills needed for information cultures to thrive" (p. 175). Her epistemological model involves the understanding of information through computation (code), communication (news), and information/library science (document and data). Combined, both of these types of multiple literacies are ideally suited for DMLE and will need further enrichment, advocacy and implementation.

In its projections for a digital curriculum, the Center for Digital Education (2014) endorses explorations in many areas: e-texts, open-source material, multimedia learning objects, apps, games, and online assessments. Touting the benefits of new digital technologies, they promote infrastructural tools such as Google Glass, robotics and programming, drones, 3-D printers, game-based learning and immersive learning, simulations, and augmented reality. Yet despite the promises these tools hold for fun and nimble learning, it's not yet clear how effectively they will be used by teachers and students alike to foster and improve learning across subjects, and how extensive their reach will be in all educational environments.

Ultimately, given the promises and challenges ahead for effectively integrating digital media into curricula and the lives of students of all ages, we believe our DMLE approach provides us with a strategic purpose, renewed dialogical inquiry, and collegial engagement that is thoughtfully proactive and visionary, rather than obsolete and reactionary in the digital age. With this approach, we hope to stimulate collaborative, action-oriented, and networked engagement for today's generation and future generations to come.

NOTE

1. Fisher Price has trademarked the term 'apptivity' for its Laugh & Learn Apptivity Case designed for iPad devices in order to "protect your iPad, iPad 2 or iPad 3 device from dribbles, drool, and sticky little fingers." The company touts that its product will help babies practice eye-hand coordination through on-screen activities, enhance fine motor skills though a textured handle and rattle beads, and offer parents baby-appropriate learning through free downloads of interactive apps (see http://www.fisher-price.com/en_US/brands/laughandlearn/products/Laugh-and-Learn-Apptivity-Case-for-iPad-devices-Blue).

REFERENCES

Ahmed, N. (2014, January 1). How the CIA made Google: Inside the secret network behind mass surveillance, endless war, and Skynet, Parts 1 and 2. Retrieved from https://www.patreon.com/nafeez.

American Academy of Pediatrics. (2013, October 28). Managing media: We need a plan. Retrieved from http://www.aap.org/en-us/about-the-aap/aap-press-room/Pages/Managing-Media-We-Need-a-Plan.aspx.

Anderson, C. A. (1997). Effects of violent movies and trait irritability on hostile feelings and aggressive thoughts. *Aggressive Behavior, 23*, 161–178.

Anderson, C. A., Gentile, D. A., & Buckley, K. E. (2007). *Violent video game effects on children and adolescents.* New York: Oxford University Press.

Assange, J. (2014). *When Google met Wikileaks.* New York: OR Books.

Bauerlein, M. (2008). *The dumbest generation: How the digital age stupefies young Americans and jeopardizes our future (or, don't trust anyone under 30).* New York, NY: Jeremy P. Tarcher/Penguin.

Bilton, N. (2014, September 10). Steve Jobs was a low-tech parent. *The New York Times.* Retrieved from http://www.nytimes.com/2014/09/11/fashion/steve-jobs-apple-was-a-low-tech-parent.html?_r=0.

Bowman, S. (2010). *The functions of role-playing games how participants create community, solve problems and explore identity.* Jefferson, N.C.: McFarland.

boyd, d. (2014). *It's complicated: The social lives of networked teens.* Hartford, CT: Yale University Press.

Carr, N. (2014). *The glass cage: Automation and us.* New York: W.W. Norton.

Carr, N. (2010). *The shallows: What the internet is doing to our brains.* New York: W.W. Norton.

Christakis, N., & Fowler, J. (2011). *Connected: The surprising power of our social networks and how they shape our lives: How your friends' friends' friends affect everything you feel, think, and do.* New York: Back Bay Books.

Dawson, M. (2003). *The consumer trap: Big business marketing in American life.* Illinois: University of Illinois Press.

Fabos, B. (2004). *Wrong turn on the information superhighway: Education and the commercialization of the Internet.* New York: Teachers College Press.

Frau-Meigs, D. (2013). Transliteracy: Sense-making mechanisms for establishing E-presence. In *Media and information literacy and intercultural dialogue: MILID yearbook 2013.* Göteborg, Sweden: Nordicom.

Frechette, J. (2002). *Developing media literacy in cyberspace pedagogy and critical learning for the twenty-first-century classroom.* Westport, Conn.: Praeger.

Freire, P. (2000). *Pedagogy of the oppressed.* New York: Continuum.

Fuchs, C. (2014). *Social media: A critical introduction.* London: Sage.

Gee, J.P. (2013) *Good video games and good learning: Collected essays on video games, learning and literacy* (2nd ed.). New York: Peter Land Publishing.

Ghonim, W. (2013). *Revolution 2.0: The power of the people is greater than the people in power—A memoir.* New York: Houghton Mifflin.

Giroux, H. (2006). *America on the edge: Henry Giroux on politics, culture, and education.* New York, N.Y.: Palgrave Macmillan.

Goodman, S. (2003). *Teaching youth media: A critical guide to literacy, video production & social change.* New York: Teachers College Press.

Greenwald, G. (2014). *No place to hide: Edward Snowden, the NSA, and the U.S. surveillance state.* New York: Metropolitan Books.

Grossman, L. (2006, December 25). You, yes, you, are TIME's person of the year. *Time.* Retrieved from http://content.time.com/time/magazine/article/0,9171,1570810,00.html.

hooks, b. (1988). *Talking back: Thinking feminist, thinking black.* Boston: South End Press.

Huffman, M. (2014, May 20). Survey: U.S. kids getting too much screen time. Retrieved from http://www.consumeraffairs.com/news/survey-us-kids-getting-too-much-screen-time-052014.html.

James, C. (2014). *Disconnected: Youth, new media, and the ethics gap.* MIT Press.

Jenkins, H. (2006). *Convergence culture: Where old and new media collide.* New York: New York University Press.

Kaiser Family Foundation. (2010, January 20). Daily media use among children and teens up dramatically from five years ago. Retrieved from http://kff.org/disparities-policy/press-release/daily-media-use-among-children-and-teens-up-dramatically-from-five-years-ago/.

Klayman, A. (2012). Ai Wei Wei—Never sorry. DVD.

Lanier, J. (2010). *You are not a gadget: A manifesto.* New York: Vintage Books.

Leonard, A. (2010). *The story of stuff: The impact of overconsumption on the planet, our communities, and our health—and how we can make it better.* New York: Free Press.

Linn, S. (2009). *The case for make believe: Saving play in a commercialized world.* New York: New Press.

Lomas, N. (2014, December 19). GamerGate Harassment Of Zoe Quinn stoops to new low. Retrieved from http://techcrunch.com/2014/12/19/gamergate-e-book/.

Masterman, L. (1985). *Teaching the media.* London: Comedia Pub. Group.

McChesney, R. (2013). *Digital disconnect: How capitalism is turning the Internet against democracy.* New York: New Press.

McLaren, P. (1986). *Schooling as a ritual performance: Towards a political economy of educational symbols and gestures.* London: Routledge & Kegan Paul.

McLeod, L. (2014, March 18). How to get over Facebook envy. Retrieved from http://www.huffingtonpost.com/lisa-earle-mcleod/social-media-envy_b_4598284.html.

McLuhan, M. (1964; reprint 1994). *Understanding media: The extensions of man.* Cambridge: MIT Press.

McRobbie, A. (2000). *Feminism and youth culture* (2nd ed.). New York: Routledge.

Meyrowitz, J. (1998, Winter). Multiple media literacies. *Journal of Communication,* 96–108.

Morozov, E. (2012). *The net delusion: The dark side of internet freedom.* New York: Public Affairs.

Norton, A. (2014, July 9). Kids still getting too much 'screen time': CDC— WebMD. Retrieved from http://www.webmd.com/children/news/20140709/kids-still-getting-too-much-screen-time-cdc.

Papacharissi, Z. (2011). *A networked self: Identity, community and culture on social network sites.* New York: Routledge.

Pew Research Internet Project. (2013, December 17). Internet user demographics. Retrieved from http://www.pewinternet.org/data-trend/teens/internet-user-demographics/.

Pinkard, N. (2014, December 3). Creating city-wide learning ecosystems to build 21st century digital savvy citizens. *Lee Gurel class of 1948 lecture.* Lecture conducted from Clark University, Worcester, Massachusetts.

Poswolsky, A. (2013, March 19). Three ways to avoid Facebook induced FOMO. Retrieved from http://www.huffingtonpost.com/adam-smiley-poswolsky/fear-of-missing-out_b_2499490.html.

Prensky, M. (2001). Digital natives, digital immigrants. *On the Horizon, 9*(5). Retrieved from http://www.marcprensky.com/writing/Prensky - Digital Natives, Digital Immigrants - Part1.pdf.

Ratner, B. (2014). *Parenting for the digital age: The truth behind media's effect on children, and what to do about it.* Sanger, CA. Familius.

Rushkoff, D. (2013). *Present shock: When everything happens now.* New York: Penguin Press.

Samakow, J. and L. Samakow (2013, October 17). Here's what a constantly plugged-in life is doing to kids' bodies. *Huffington Post.* http://www.huffingtonpost.com/2013/10/17/teens-on-screens_n_4101758.html.

Shiffman, D. (2008). *The age of engage: Reinventing marketing for today's connected, collaborative, and hyperinteractive culture.* Ladera Ranch, CA: Hunt Street Press.

Shirky, C. (2008). *Here comes everybody: The power of organizing without organizations.* New York: Penguin Press.

Shirky, C. (2010). *Cognitive surplus: How technology is turning consumers into collaborators.* New York: Penguin Press.

Steyer, J., & Clinton, C. (2012). *Talking back to Facebook: A common sense guide to raising kids in the digital age*. New York, NY: Scribner.

StopBullying.Gov. (n.d.). What educators can do to stop bullying. Retrieved from http://www.stopbullying.gov/what-you-can-do/educators/index.html.

Turkle, S. (2012). *Alone together: Why we expect more from technology and less from each other*. New York, NY: Basic Books.

Part I

Self

The first section of *Media Education for a Digital Generation* focuses on the construct of SELF as it is being reconceptualized and affected by digital media. In 1965, Marshall McLuhan presciently used the analogy of the media as "extensions of man" that affect us through their design and structure. Similarly, the chapters in this section consider how the design, structures, and functions of digital media affect the nature and delivery of our communication and social engagement in the Digital Age. Mobile devices, apps, and the portability of the Internet now serve as human appendages or extensions of 'the self,' as our sense of identity is increasingly defined by the technologies we use to represent ourselves as we interact in the digital world. In this section you will find explorations of the 'Selfie,' and arguments for adding visual literacy and photographic communication into the digital media literacy mix as a means to enhance self-representation. You'll also find an empirical study that questions whether or not marginalized individuals can leverage the power of social media platforms like Facebook to make inroads into more equitable self-representation. By design, we'll also consider the ways in which digital media literacy education teaches us to comprehend and make smart choices about our self-explorations online, especially given the ways in which we are increasingly tracked by the new surveillance economy that profits from following our every step. Collectively, these chapters offer pedagogical possibilities as a means of empowering us to make knowledgeable and creative choices in this new era.

1 The Selfie, Photographic Communication, and Digital Literacy

Daniel S. Hunt

Comedian Jena Kingsley created a "selfie free" zone in New York City's Central Park and recorded herself mock-ticketing people taking selfies within her designated boundaries. By creating the video she was trying to make the point that the act of taking selfies has gotten out of control. A few years ago, the word "selfie" held very little meaning to adults and was predominantly used only by socially networked teens. A lot has changed in a few years. In 2014, ABC aired a short-lived sitcom titled, "Selfie." The Chainsmokers song "#Selfie," a humorous account of club goers taking selfies, became a recent viral sensation. A selfie of Ellen DeGeneres and other A-list celebrities at the 86th Academy Award celebration made major headlines when it became the most retweeted microblog to date, surpassing President Obama's election night record. When the Oxford Dictionary deemed "selfie" the 2013 word of the year is when the media really took notice (Killingsworth, 2013) and the term entered mainstream vernacular.

The Oxford Dictionary defines selfie as "a photograph that one has taken of oneself, typically one taken with a smartphone or webcam and uploaded to a social media website" (Oxford Dictionaries, n.d.). Today, due to the popularity of social networking platforms, online representations of the self have become a necessity in both our professional and social lives. Selfies are one form of photographically representing the self to others online. Digital literacy curricula need to stay current and incorporate practical applications of how young people use social media in an image-based culture. Teaching students, especially teenagers, how to make ethical choices regarding photo composition can prepare students for more positive social interactions and give them a sense of professionalism in their digital presence. This type of training can foster a shared understanding of the consequences of posting and sharing images online. Digital literacy education should focus on issues such as privacy, the permanency of the social web, and practicing patience and caution when posting images online.

The importance of personal photography has gained attention recently due to the widespread adoption of photo-based sharing sites and social media (Duggan, 2013). In addition, the technical advances of digital cameras on mobile phones have allowed sending and sharing photographic images to become a fluid and common practice. Mobile phone adoption is significantly increasing among teenagers with text and image messaging the preferred method of communication by teens (e.g., Lenhart, Ling, Campbell, & Purcell, 2010). While "digital natives" are often considered to be visually literate, research testing this claim has found that individuals who have grown up using digital tools are not particularly proficient in interpreting or producing visual imagery (Brumberger, 2011). Photographic communication, defined as the exchange of messages primarily consisting of photographs, allows people to communicate through a rich medium and to tell image-based stories to their peer groups (Hunt, Lin, & Atkin, 2014b). These images can be markedly personal or a documentation of shared experiences. Whether people are frequent posters or those who occasionally update their profile, they will need to determine the type of image they will use to represent who they are to online audiences.

There are two objectives of this chapter. The first is to highlight the key areas that educators should focus on when teaching digital literacy skills related to photographic representation of the self. The second goal is to provide a lesson plan framework demonstrating how digital literacy skills for photographic communication can be taught through Kolb's Experiential Learning Model (Kolb, 1984). By adopting Kolb's model educators can balance teaching both theoretical and practical applications of photographic communication. By teaching important theoretical concepts students can better understand the consequences of their online behaviors, develop an ethical awareness for photo sharing, and foster a sense of accountability for their actions. The practical applications will increase students' visual literacy in regards to both image creation and analysis. This chapter will begin by outlining the relevant research on photographic communication. Subsequent sections will present a framework for curricula involving photographic composition and image analysis. Finally, the four stages of Kolb's model will be presented as they apply to photographic communication and digital literacy. In the following section, research on photo sharing will be discussed.

PHOTOGRAPHIC COMMUNICATION

In the last decade, scholars have studied people's motives for sending and sharing photographs. These motives can be grouped into five key areas: relationship maintenance, relationship formation, memory, self-expression, and self-presentation (Van House & Davis, 2005). The last two motives, related to the self, are of particular concern to digital literacy educators. Goffman (1959) explained that there are two types of expressions given off when making an impression, intentional and unintentional cues. When sharing photographs both types of cues contribute the symbolic representation of one's social self. Self-presentation refers to images of the self, such as the selfie or a portrait, but also includes images of personal belongings and objects with emotional meaning to the creator. Images of self-expression typically are more creative, abstract representations taken from the viewpoint of the creator. When individuals share images of the self, they form impressions online that contribute to their perceived self-image. Motivations to express and represent oneself online increase the frequency in which users send and shared images to their peers (Hunt, Lin, & Atkin, 2014a). The quantity and frequency of shared images can create problems, especially for younger content creators.

Digital literacy educators need to teach students about privacy and image content when photo sharing. The transitory nature of image sharing and the permanence of the social web are also of particular concern to educators. There have been instances where images posted on social networking sites have been stolen and used to create a false identity (Reznik, 2013). There is evidence that employers have elected to not hire individuals after reviewing applicants' social media profiles and finding inappropriate photos (Weber, 2014). As educators we can provide students with formative photo sharing experiences that will help them to foster a solid comprehension of their image sharing choices.

Certain images of the self should not be shared publicly. While this seems obvious, for young image producers creating photo-sharing boundaries can be problematic. Educators need to include course modules that explain how to set up privacy filters on social media platforms. More importantly, teaching students the power of exercising patience before capturing and sharing images is of critical importance. The instant gratification of using social platforms has been one reason for their growth and enjoyment but it does not come without consequences. When posting an image, often one does not stop and ask questions such as "who will see this image" and "how long will this image exist on the web." Murray (2008) commented that photo sharing "has become less about the special or rarified moments of domestic living, and more about an immediate, rather fleeting, display and collection of one's discovery and framing of the small and mundane" (p. 147). Murray's words also highlight the trivial nature of the image content shared online. The decision to post a photo is made in a fleeting moment and too often is not thought about until after the fact. Hand (2012) explains that "after the fact ethics" is more common in the world of ubiquitous photography. Digital literacy can serve as a preventive measure against such acts.

One of the most important and overlooked areas of digital photo sharing is the permanency of the social web. The shelf life of online content is much longer than what one expects. We have become so accustomed to constant contact and instant gratification that we lose sight of practicing self-control and patience. It is almost impossible to un-forget a powerful image. It is equally difficult to remove an unwanted image from the social web once it is in the hands of someone else. In today's mediated world, imagery is part of one's personal brand. Students need to find a balance between incessant, narcissistic posting and developing their personal brand online. Many of these issues can be controlled if students learn the principles of photographic composition and image analysis before sharing photos online.

PHOTOGRAPHIC COMPOSITION

Several online media outlets, such as *The Huffington Post* and *W Magazine*, provide tips on how to take a good selfie. Articles such as these represent the growing concern for photographic self-presentation. While some digital literacy educators might not want to teach students to "create" media, many would agree creating media helps students develop stronger digital literacy skills. Messaris (2012) noted visual literacy should move beyond developing an understanding of digital manipulation and should endorse the creative opportunities afforded by digital technology. Some of the basic rules of photographic composition include avoiding mergers, the rule of thirds, simplicity, lines, balance, and framing. By developing a sense of photographic composition, photo sharing will be a deliberate process and the photographer's aesthetic schema should provide caution to them before posting images online.

When teaching photography, one of the most important areas covered is the subject of the image. Often in the interest of time, the photographer will forget about secondary elements that are in the background of a photograph. By teaching compositional elements students will learn to consider the layers within their images of the self and will also be more cognizant of distracting background elements when using photographic representations of the self. These background elements, especially when documenting personal events, often reveal unwanted information to audiences. Examples of these instances can be seen the multitude of "selfie fails" images curated online.

The rule of thirds and framing will help students learn to compose aesthetically pleasing images. Avoiding mergers and using lines will help students develop the focal point of their image and become aware of distracting background elements. By considering how to frame images and create balance in photographs the final product will most likely be an image that represents the true intentions of the photographer. Images of self-expression and self-representation will be of a higher caliber and less likely to cause post-sharing regret. Image creation is only one part of this process. To increase one's digital literacy in the area of photographic communication, one must also learn to analyze images.

IMAGE ANALYSIS

While there are several analytical strategies for image deconstruction and analysis, visual semiotics is well suited for teaching students the consequences of photo posting behavior. Visual semiotics involves deciphering the layers of meaning within a photograph, specifically the denotative meaning and the connotative meaning (Barthes, 1977). The denotative meaning involves understanding the face value of the image while the connotative meaning involves a complex comprehension of the various image elements.

One might examine the aesthetics, pose, objects, syntax, and photogenia while examining the connotative layer of an image (Barthes, 1977).

At the connotative level, students will decipher the multiple interpretations of an image's meaning. They will learn how photographic technique and digital enhancement can change the meaning of a photograph. They will begin to understand how certain poses contain implicit meanings to viewers and learn how the presence or absence of certain objects also changes the meaning of the image. The syntax of the image might also be considered—the corresponding text or categorization of the image could reveal unintended messages to audiences. An awareness and understanding of these concepts is of critical importance in an image-based society.

By teaching visual semiotics, the learner will begin to understand how the various elements of a photograph work individually and collectively to create various meanings. Students of digital literacy will benefit from this awareness of implicit meaning when they view photos and when they create images. Both image creation and image analysis can be powerful tools that are most effective if taught through experiential learning.

EXPERIENTIAL LEARNING

Many teachers of new media have developed lesson plans that incorporate experiential learning. Kolb's Experiential Learning Model (Kolb, 1984) is a four-stage cycle of experiential learning. In the cycle, the stages are concrete experiences, reflective observation, abstract concepts, and active experimentation. Using this model, educators can teach photographic communication in a way that meets course objectives and provides a practical learning experience for students.

While learners can enter the cycle at any point in time, there are benefits to starting with *reflective observation*. In reflective observation, students might review the images posted by members of their network and use visual semiotics to analyze the images. Students will learn how the various layers of meaning impact their perceptions. Areas of focus during this stage might include how one's frame of reference and background influence their perceptions of the various layers of meaning within the photograph.

Next students should be taught concepts such as impression management, privacy, narcissistic behavior, ethics, and developing a personal brand. Through these activities students enter the stage of *abstract conceptualization*. This stage helps learners make connections between their observations and important digital literacy concepts. One useful exercise at this stage is to have students develop a photo-sharing code of ethics. The code can be tied to a larger discussion on moral philosophy or to a discussion of professional codes. Privacy can be discussed related to the technical settings of social networking sites and to help students develop boundaries between their private and social lives. Challenging students to become aware of narcissistic behaviors related to posting could also be covered in this stage of the model. Mendelson and Papacharissi's (2010) discussion of whether frequent photo posting is a step towards self-reflection and self-actualization or a form of self-absorption would make for an engaging discussion. During this stage, students should learn the difference between how they choose to present and express themselves online.

Following the cognitive stage of abstract conceptualization, students engage in *active experimentation*. In this stage of the cycle, students create and share images with their classmates on a simulated or closed social networking site. This will provide students with a practical application of photographic composition as it relates to sharing images of the self. Elements of photographic composition should be employed through assignments based on techniques such as the rule or thirds or simplicity. Students will be exposed to media aesthetics during these assignments that will help shape their photo-sharing behaviors.

Finally, students enter the *concrete experience* stage. Students will develop feelings towards their own photographic communication behaviors during the concrete experience stage. The affect associated with photo sharing should provide students with a more complex cognitive framework in future instances of image capture and image sharing. By the end of the lesson, students should develop a sense of ethical awareness related to photo sharing. After students complete each stage, the cycle can begin again. By following Kolb's Experiential Learning Model, educators can provide an engaging and active lesson plan with ties to theoretical and practical educational outcomes.

CONCLUSION

As photographic communication continues to increase in our society, educators need to teach composition and analytical skills. These skills can be taught through experiential learning inside and outside of the classroom. The goal is to slow down the process of photo sharing and to help communicators develop a sense of photographic ethics that focuses on goal-directed photo-sharing behavior. Providing these skills early on will prepare young people for adulthood in a world where their professional and personal lives are visually displayed in the public eye. Increased knowledge of visual concepts and technical skills will allow for more creativity (e.g., Messaris, 2012) in how people present and express themselves online. At the very least, after these digital literacy skills are introduced, the number of "selfie fails" should decrease over time.

REFERENCES

Barthes, R. (1977). *Image, music, text*. New York, NY: Hill & Wang.
Brumberger, E. (2011). Visual literacy and the digital native: An examination of the millennial learner. *Journal of Visual Literacy, 30* (1), 19–46.

Duggan, M. (2013). Photo and video sharing grow online. Pew Internet and American Life Project. Retrieved from http://pewinternet.org/~/media/Files/Reports/2013/PIP_Photos%20and%20videos%20online_102813.pdf.

Goffman, E. (1959). *The presentation of self in everyday life*. New York, NY: Anchor.

Hand, M. (2012). *Ubiquitous photography*. Cambridge, UK: Polity Press.

Hunt, D. S., Lin, C. A., & Atkin, D. J. (2014a). Communication social relationships via the use of photo-messaging. *Journal of Broadcasting & Electronic Media, 58* (2), 234–252.

Hunt, D. S., Lin, C. A., & Atkin, D. J. (2014b). Photo-messaging: Adopter attributes, technology factors and use motives. *Computers in Human Behavior, 40,* 171–179.

Killingsworth, S. (2013, November 19). And the word of the year is.... *The New Yorker*. Retrieved from http://www.newyorker.com/online/blogs/culture/2013/11/selfie-word-of-the-year.html.

Kolb, D.A. (1984). *Experiential learning: Experience as the source of learning and development*. Englewood Cliffs, NJ: Prentice Hall.

Lenhart, A., Ling, R., Campbell, S., & Purcell, K. (2010). Teens and mobile phones. Pew Internet & American Life Project. Retrieved from http://www.pewinternet.org/2010/04/20/teens-and-mobile-phones/.

Messaris, P. (2012). Visual literacy in the "digital" age. *The Review of Communication, 12* (2), 101–117.

Murray, S. (2008). Digital images, photo sharing, and our shifting notion of everyday aesthetics. *Journal of Visual Culture, 7* (2), 147–163.

Mendelson, A., & Papacharissi, Z. (2010). Look at us: Collective narcissism in college student facebook photo galleries. In Z. Papacharissi (Ed.), *The networked self: Identity, community and culture on social network sites*. London: Routledge.

Reznik, M. (2013). Identity theft on social networking sites: developing issues of Internet impersonation. *Touro Law Review, 29* (2), Article 12. Retrieved from http://digitalcommons.tourolaw.edu/lawreview/vol29/iss2/12.

Selfie. (n.d.). In *Oxford Dictionaries* online. Retrieved from http://www.oxforddictionaries.com/us/definition/american_english/selfie.

Weber, J. (2014, May 11). Should companies monitor their employees' social media? *The Wall Street Journal*. Retrieved from http://online.wsj.com/news/articles/SB10001424052702303825604579514471793116740.

2 Shifting Identities through Social Media

Asian American Stereotypes and the Exploration of Comprehensive Media Literacy

Chyng F. Sun, Rachael Liberman, Allison Butler, Sun Young Lee, and Rachel L. Webb

INTRODUCTION

Asian Americans represent nearly 5% of the U.S. population. They are America's fastest-growing racial group, and in the past decade their numbers have increased by 43% (U.S. Census Bureau, 2010). However, they are nearly invisible in the mainstream media (Aoki & Takeda, 2011). According to the *Fall Colors 2003–2004: Prime Time Diversity Report*, Asian Americans play just 3% of all characters in network shows and 1% of opening-credit characters, and when compared with other racial groups, they are the least likely to play primary roles. In a more recent study, Dana Mastro and Elizabeth Behm-Morawitz (2005) similarly found that Asian Americans comprised just 1.5% of the 1,488 characters tabulated during their content analysis of prime-time programming. Further, Karen Narasaki (2005) argues that network television has increasingly marginalized Asian American characters in recent years. In contrast, programs produced in Asian countries—recently available on U.S. cable, satellite television (Thussu, 2006), and the Internet, (especially YouTube)— have created more opportunities for Asian American media makers to produce programs (Balance, 2012). However, are these alternative and additional images reaching beyond the niche of Asian American youth to a more mainstream demographic?

While media stereotypes may not have a strong, direct, causal connection with racial attitudes and behaviors, they nonetheless have a significant impact on racial perceptions of the self and others over time (Derman-Sparks, 1989; Greenberg, Mastro, & Brand, 2002; Huntemann & Morgan, 2001). Audience research on Asian American media representations and their influence has been scarce, but available studies highlight the effects of white beauty standards on Asian Americans (Mok, 1998), on perceived attractiveness and dating desirability of Asian American men (Chan, 2001), and on white college students' notions of Asian Americans based on model minority stereotypes (Lee, 2008). This study was designed to understand college students' perceptions of Asian American media images—including the construction of these images, whether the Internet has any impact on them, and in what ways the subjects believe that media representations can be improved in the digital age.

In this study we compare two sets of data, one collected in 2002 and the other nearly a decade later, in 2011. Specifically, we were interested in recontextualizing the findings from 2002 to see if the affordances of digital media have led to increased representational production, channels, and distribution among a new generation of social media users. Each set of data consists of focus group interviews of male and female college students from three different racial backgrounds (Asian Americans, European Americans, and African Americans). The interviews were designed to address the following questions: (a) How do college students from different racial backgrounds perceive Asian Americans in the media? (b) Have the perceptions of Asian American media representations changed in the past decade as the cable and satellite TV, Internet, and social media have provided more diverse images of Asians and Asian Americans? (c) What did the subjects think were possible ways to improve media representations? This paper addresses these research questions and argues that while today there are more diverse images of Asians and Asian Americans available online, their impact on the general public is limited. The data also reveal that although Asian American respondents were able to locate and enjoy a limited amount of alternative representations, they were unaware of the logic of political economy, and the possibility of producing media themselves through new digital media tools.

Two avenues of study are employed to help contextualize the findings of this study. First, we present an overview of Asian American media stereotypes, their historical roots, and their racist functions. Second, we examine the development of new digital media and analyze both its possibilities and limitations in terms of helping the public access alternative media.

ASIAN AMERICAN MEDIA STEREOTYPES

In the United States, media are the key political instruments and driving forces of social life, serving as cultural pedagogues to educate individuals as to how to survive and succeed in a dominant culture (Kellner, 2003). Media also play a crucial hegemonic role in justifying the status quo and perpetuating the ideology of the natural and rightful superiority of political, social, and cultural elites over subordinated groups (Hall, 1996; Lull, 2011). One particularly effective strategy that reinforces the myths of the deviance and inferiority of oppressed groups is the use of media stereotypes.

Snead (1994) theorizes that the nature of stereotypes is to resist change and ultimately live forever within the culture and the public imagination. Ideological constructs—including stereotypes—almost always reflect, shape, and are shaped by their material conditions; therefore it is important to review the historical, political, and economic circumstances that led to the development and propagation of the major Asian American stereotypes.

With historical roots that go back to the 1840s, when Chinese men came to the United States as cheap labor for West Coast gold mines and later as railroad construction workers (Chen, 1996), Asian American male stereotypes include the evil Fu Man Chu plotting to take over the world (Chin & Chan, 1972; Hamamoto, 1994) and the effeminate detective Charlie Chan (Xing, 1998; Chin, Chan, Inada, & Wong, 1974, p. xvi), a stereotype that later morphed into the socially awkward computer programmer (Cao & Novas, 1996, p. xvi; Sun, Miezan, & Liberman, 2008). Later, in the 1970s, Bruce Lee ushered in the stereotype of the Kung Fu master (Chihara, 2000). Asian American women, for their part, have been hypersexualized on screen as, for example, Lotus Blossom and Dragon Lady (Tajima, 1989; Hamamoto, 1994), as well as prostitutes, bargirls, and geishas (Villapando, 1989). But if sexuality set Asian American male and female stereotypes apart, the "model minority" myth united them (Zia, 2000). It is important to note that stereotypes often evolve and merge with each other to create "hybrids," but overall, Asian Americans in the mainstream media have changed little in the past decade. This is a curious phenomenon for a decade in which digital and Internet technology has revolutionized how media are produced, distributed, and consumed. As scholars have theorized, however, the Internet has the potential to diversify ownership and representation, thus mitigating the dissemination of stereotypes, but digital technology alone cannot destroy these myths and symbols. In the following section, we focus on the political economy of new media.

New Media, New Limitations

In the mid-1990s, when the Internet garnered a great deal of popular attention, new media theorists projected that a new electronic terrain of democratic interaction and representation was emerging (Poster, 1995; Castells, 1996; Levy, 2001). They predicted that engaged citizens and alternative communities would gain increased control over symbolic representations (Miller, 2011, Rheingold, 1993). In particular, Mark Poster (1995) argued that new media represented a dynamic system that would usher in postmodern interests such as multiple realities, virtual communities, and personal narratives. Manuel Castells (1996) also echoed the belief that new media afforded an unprecedented degree of prosumption, and argued that, "For the first time in history, the human mind is a direct productive force, not just a decisive element in the production system" (p. 32). Indeed, highly relevant to this study, we found that young Asian American media makers have produced nonviolent, non-racist, and non-sexist and highly entertaining web series.

However, alongside these optimistic views of new media, political econo-mists and digital theorists argued that the Internet was beginning to resemble other capitalist mass media (Bagdikian, 2004; Curran et al., 2012; Miller, 2011; Papacharissi, 2002). As Vincent Miller (2011) states:

> However, as the Internet has become something used by the majority of the population in advanced economies, that population has brought with it all of the habits, inclinations and prejudices which are endemic to society as a whole. As a result, much of this early optimism that the Internet would radically change our culture in some sort of knowledge revolution has begun to fade in light of the realization that our culture has transformed the Internet more than vice versa (p. 1).

Lev Manovich (2001) makes a similar argument about cultural conventions that influence the human-computer interface, or what he calls "cultural inter-faces." He writes, "a new media designer or user approaches the computer through a number of cultural filters" (p.117). Both Miller and Manovich remind us that while new media has the technical capacity for interaction and virtual community development, it is also programmed and constructed within the same cultural codes, symbols, and ideologies that design other forms of media. As Zizi Papacharissi (2002) points out: "New technologies offer additional tools, but they cannot single-handedly transform a political and economic structure that has thrived for centuries" (p. 20).

Finally, it must also be recognized that new media is dominated by main-stream media conglomerates—just like the offline sphere—who control most of the production and consumption of information. Recent reports from the Pew Research Center for the People & the Press and The Nielsen Company show that the public is still seeking mainstream and dominant sources for its news and information. According to a September 2012 Pew Report, there has been little change since 2010 in the websites people go to most for news and information. Yahoo, mentioned by 26% of online news users, is the top destination, as it was two years ago, followed by Google or Google News, CNN, local news sources, and MSN (Pew Research Center for the People & the Press, 2012). In a report released by The Nielsen Company in January 2013, the top four U.S. web parent companies (home and work) were Google, Microsoft, Facebook, and Yahoo! (Nielsen, 2013). These trends echo the earlier arguments of Miller and Manovich, who reminded us that offline cultural activities and behavior have a direct con-nection to the practices surrounding new media. Legacy media is dominated by a handful of media conglomerates, so it is no surprise that the Internet would be managed in a similar fashion.

When comparatively examined, traditional and new mainstream media depictions have not altered in any significantly positive ways after the Internet revolution, underscoring how problematic Asian American repre-sentation continues to be. Although a plethora of websites have erupted, issues of access, awareness, and ritual act as barriers to the creation of a larger distribution network for these alternative sources of information. As a result, the same political economy issues that drive the circulation of stereotypes offline is also the case online. New media and the opportunity for increased audience participation has not changed the field in any structural or ideological way, which illustrates a gap between the use of new media technology and the knowledge of how to harness these tools to create alternative imagery.

Method

Heeding Douglas Kellner's (2003) advice to have a holistic view of media—by way of texts, audiences, and media systems—this study focuses on the respondents' perceptions on Asian American media images. The questions in the research instrument were designed primarily to elicit detailed information on students' perceptions of Asian American media representations, and ways in which they might act to improve media images. To examine those questions, we drew primarily on focus group interviews with male and female college students who identified as European Americans, African Americans, and Asian Americans, divided by both gender and race.[1] The fall 2011 study is an update of and comparison to a previous study conducted by one of the authors in 2002. We found the pattern revealed in the 2002 focus group results to be very interesting: although the subjects complained about the problematic representations of Asian Americans, they nonetheless affirmed that media corporations have the right to maximize their profits—even if the profit motive results in harmful products. The Internet and social media have seen tremendous growth in the decade between 2002 and 2011, and we have also witnessed the decline of mainstream network media. Our research question was to explore if the development of the Internet and the possibilities of alternative media would indeed change Asian American representations and affect people's perceptions of Asian Americans. Both studies used a similar methodology: we began with respondents who belong to the gender and race group in which we were interested, and we used snowball sampling from these multiple starting points. Both studies recruited students from large northeastern universities, but in the earlier study, most students attended a state school in a college town, while the later study exclusively recruited students from an urban, private university.

Participants

In the 2002 study, the data was collected with the purpose of answering questions on Asian American identity issues (Sun, 2002); thus, many more Asian Americans than members of other racial groups were recruited. This approach resulted in 7 Asian American male groups (N=18), 7 Asian American female groups (N=27), and a relatively smaller number of groups from other racial identities: 1 European American male group (N=3), 2 European American female groups (N=8), 2 black male groups (N=4), and 2 black female groups (N=7), for a total of 21 groups and 67 participants. The purpose of the 2011 study was to update and compare the respondents' perception of Asian American media representations, but not specifically Asian American identity issues as explored in the 2002 study. However, we still utilized the same number of focus groups (2 groups) across different genders and races, so there were two groups per category, each with these participants: 8 Asian American men, 7 Asian American women, 6 European American men, 7 European American women, 6 black men, and 6 black women, for a total of 12 groups and 40 participants. The focus group facilitators included one of the authors (Asian female), two female assistants (one European American and one African American), and a male assistant (European American). Each focus group session lasted between 60 and 90 minutes.

Results

Asian American Media Representations

The decade between the two studies saw digital technology revolutionize the way in which media are produced, distributed, and consumed. However, comparing the subjects' perceptions of Asian Americans in the media in these two studies yielded remarkably similar results: Asian Americans are mostly invisible. The most well known Asian American stars that all groups could name in 2002 were Lucy Liu, Jackie Chan, and Jet Lee; 10 years later, it was still the same three people. The respondents in the 2011 study also mentioned Sandra Oh (*Grey's Anatomy*) and Chow Yuan Fat, but less frequently than the respondents in the 2002 study. But other than these few actors, respondents tended to remember the characters but not the actors' names, for example: "the funny Asian guy in *The Hangover*" or "Harold and Kumar." Comparatively speaking, Asian Americans could name many more Asian American actors or roles than could any other group, which may be due to their hyper-awareness of the presence of their own kind on the screen. As July (Korean American, 2011)[2], said: "I get excited when I see Asian in a movie or TV show—just because they're Asian, I notice them."

The Asian American media characters that the respondents remembered in the two studies were almost identical in nature. The common stereotypes of Asian American men that the participants identified included: (a) karate masters, (b) nerdy and socially awkward male students or professionals in high-tech or financial fields, and (c) shop owners or food delivery men who have thick accents. In the 2011 study, Charles (Chinese American, 2011) and most other Asian American respondents said that most Asian American characters are minor, "sidekick" roles designed for "comic relief." These comments are consistent with the respondents' comments a decade earlier when Nelon (Korean American, 2002) called the Long Duk Dong character in *Sixteen Candles* a "quintessential Asian man" stereotype:

> He is basically a fresh off the boat kind of exchange student ... and is portrayed as a geek or a nerd. He portrayed that comic relief Asian who doesn't fit in, and tries to [fit] in American society, and is very, very awkward.

Lynn (Chinese American, 2002) suspected that these unattractive Asian American male portrayals were purposefully constructed to fit certain Hollywood modes of representation.

There was also agreement across groups in both studies that an additional aspect of Asian American men's media persona is that they always lack emotion. Though they may be "wise" sages, or skilled in Kung Fu, or intelligent in high technology, Asian American men are "never vulnerable," or "sensitive to love," as Rolan (Korean American, 2011) described it. Indeed, across all focus groups, respondents noticed that Asian American men in the media rarely "get the girls" or have any love interest—the opposite of Asian American women, who are usually hypersexualized and most often paired with European American men.

Moreover, the portrayals of Asian American women's submissiveness and sexiness are often combined to suggest a deviant and manipulative sexuality, as three respondents in the 2002 study observed in *Rush Hour 2* or the Asian Bond girls. That observations were reinforced by 2011 groups when they discussed the geisha characters in *Memoirs of a Geisha*, or Lucy Liu's roles as an undercover massage girl in *Charlie's Angels* (2000), a sexual, dominant, and manipulative character in *Kill Bill* (2003) and *Dirty Sexy Money* (2007).

The respondents also acknowledged that media representations might have real-life consequences. Shana, a European American woman (2002), admitted that when she sees an Asian American woman in real life, the idea of this person being "submissive" just automatically "pops into" her head. Claude, an African American man (2002), assumed that Asian women in real life were quiet, but also had a "fiery kind of temper" like Lucy Liu's character Ling Woo in the TV drama *Ally McBeal* he saw. Ten years later, respondents such as Ronelle (African American, 2011) often used Asian American media representations as the main source for their knowledge of Asian Americans in real life, or even measured the real Asian Americans by a yardstick taken from media images. For instance, Ronelle said that she never thought of Asian American men as sexy until she saw the movies of Bruce Lee, who was the "sexiest" Asian man she has ever seen. She said, "I started looking at Asian men and I could never find an ideal—Bruce Lee was the standard." When asked what she thought of Asian American women, she described them as "smart, intelligent, sexy, good at math, and family-oriented." Seeking evidence to prove the validity of her statement, she immediately said, "One of my favorite movies was the *Joy Luck Club*, it was all about family and they each turn to their mother and their family for that support and that approval."

This pattern of using media images to form perceptions of Asian Americans is prevalent in both African American and European American groups. Asian Americans expressed the most intense reaction to how media representations may have affected how others perceive them. In both studies, almost all Asian American men had had people ask them if they knew how to perform Kung Fu. Some even went on to take classes and learn martial arts to fulfill that expectation.

In addition, the Asian or Asian American characters the Asian American respondents saw as children sometimes evoked memories of pain and embarrassment, as the following examples illustrate:

> *Victoria (Chinese American, 2002)*: I was five or six, and *Mr. T* used to be my favorite show [sic]. He was a Black man, had a big chain, and I remember they always went in this big school bus. Once he talked to an Asian character and ... it was demeaning and disrespectful, and I was like "Jesus Christ, I can't believe Mr. T did that!"

Feeling angry and betrayed, Victoria did not watch *The A-Team* anymore.

Some respondents were aware of certain depictions of Asian Americans but did not comprehend the meaning of them until they were adults.

> *Ed (Korean American, 2002)*: I remember the Chan Clan ... about a really fat Asian American man who was a detective, no wife of course, and he had 12 children who were little munchkin children, who would run around with him and they solved mysteries. At the time it was made, I thought it was funny, this is really good. ... But as I grew older I found that less amusing because obviously that had a lot of political criticism of China at the time.
>
> *Robert (Chinese American, 2002)*: In elementary school, I remembered watching cartoons, like Tom and Jerry, a mouse and a cat show. When a paddle was smacked over a dog's head, the next moment, the dog is shaking and he would have a rice hat on, grew buckteeth, and there would be some Asian music on. ... Of course I knew they were portraying me. But when I saw it, I would start laughing because it was funny when I was a kid.

When they were young, both Ed and Robert found that the "Asian" type of representations were either harmless or even positive, but when they reached adulthood and gained an awareness of stereotypes, they realized what the images meant. Robert, in particular, connected these seemingly innocent images with the racism he experienced, and implied that media representations were functioning as what scholars such as Hamamoto (1994) call "controlled images."

> *Robert (Chinese American, 2002)*: I resented more and more as I grow older. Life is harder, and society puts a stamp on you and says "you are Asian and we are going to put you in place," then you view back and see that episode now ...

Since old cartoons and popular programs are constantly recycled and rerun on cable TV, the unflattering Asian American images would sometimes produce an "Aha!" realization for some respondents who, as children, did not "get it."

In the 2011 study, Asian American respondents did not mention the shows and the racist moments referred to above, perhaps because the shows the 2002 respondents grew up with were no longer aired. However, some respondents did mention the "injustice" they felt when a Hollywood studio hired European American actor Justin Chatwin to play the Japanese character Goku in *Dragon Ball: Evolution* (2009), after the Japanese cartoon series *Dragon Ball* had become immensely popular in the United States. Still, some Asian Americans in the 2011 study expressed much hope and confidence about Asian American media representations that were unseen in the previous study, as articulated by Adam: "If Asian Americans won't be allowed to cast leading roles in great movies like *Dragon Ball: Evolution*, we have other outlets such as YouTube, such as the Internet for us to carve out our own niche ... We'll innovate." His sentiment is echoed by Paul, who sees alternative images of Asian Americans that are already "here and now":

> There isn't really an impetus for more representations ... Asian Americans have a solid representation already ... there's no shortage of talent or means to publicize that talent at all. People want to go see Asian Americans in media, they can go anywhere and find them in the Internet.

Responses that projected favorable representations of Asian Americans in new digital media were pivotal for our study, and led us to pose the question, Is the enthusiasm of these young Asian Americans regarding what the new media can do justified or erroneous? To answer that question, we need to examine what media developments have offered potential or limitation.

Alternative Images

In the past decade, the proliferation of cable network channels, satellite television, YouTube, and other social media into the mainstream have given some Asian American college students access to alternative Asian and Asian American images, as expressed in their interviews in 2011. For example, Gloria (Chinese American) said: "If we want Asian idols, we have them because we will go to the Internet and look at Korean dramas and Asian pop stars ... you can like American shows but then always go back to your Asian dramas." These respondents were not only drawn to media produced in Asia so they could see people who "look like them" or where their parents came from; they are also fans of Asian American youth-produced amateur videos on YouTube by media creators such as Nigga Higga and Kev Jumba that have drawn millions of viewers worldwide. One of the most successful examples is Wong Fu Productions, where founders Philip Wang, Wesley Chan, and Ted Fu started making videos in 2003 as students at the University of California, San Diego. They currently work full time to create drama and comedy shows for the web and often collaborate with other independent producers. This new wave of Asian American filmmakers and entrepreneurs who use YouTube and other social media to distribute their own creations encourages and speaks to the importance of teaching production skills in the media literacy curriculum.

Asian American producers such as Wong Fu Productions indeed provide refreshing, diverse, and holistic representations of Asian Americans while showcasing the team members' talents in directing, writing, acting, dancing, and singing. But in the 2011 study, when answering the question "What Images of Asian Americans have you seen in the media?" only 4 of 15 Asian Americans (26.7%) and none of the European and African American subjects mentioned the existence of those new alternatives. This led us to question, How widespread are such alternative images created by Asian Americans? We contend that, since our identities are shaped by both social identity (how others perceive us) and self-identity (Wise, 2008), and if alternative images of Asian Americans cannot be distributed widely to mainstream audiences, then their ability to counter deeply entrenched stereotypes is limited. And if one sees media representations as a means for social change, disseminating these alternative images in the mainstream is mandatory (Jenkins, 1995).

HOW TO IMPROVE OUR MEDIA

In our two studies, all respondents across race and gender were dissatisfied with the U.S. mass media in general and television networks in particular; they all expressed the need for more frequent and diverse portrayals of Asian Americans and other minority groups. Some respondents distinguished media companies from other types of businesses, since the products they produce and sell are not necessary commodities (such as food products). As Alice (European American woman, 2002) put it: "Media form a lot of people's thoughts ... playing with your mind ... food [industry's] responsibility is just ... safety." When respondents pointed to TV, movies, newspapers, and magazines as the major source of the general public's information and entertainment, they often articulated that the media have a responsibility for what kind of images they bring to the public. The participants, however, were very cynical about how seriously media corporations take that responsibility, suggesting that their only incentive is to make money, even if they might simultaneously cause harm.

This conundrum became apparent when the respondents reported that although media corporations should bear responsibility for what they produce, they also have every right to maximize profits—even if the profit motive results in harmful products. Furthermore, the participants often assumed that media representations were the "direct reflections" of public interests. That is, if the media images were racist, it was because such images were popular, and therefore audiences wanted to see them. This rationale underscores the widely held belief that any media production is actually the result of a democratic selection process that reflects the public's tastes and preferences. This perspective, of course, stands in contrast to the fact that mainstream mass media images are constructed, have historical roots, and are produced by large media corporations that are near-monopolies whose primary motivation is profit. None of the respondents addressed alternative ways to create public media, even though this transformation has occurred in many countries throughout the world (Benson & Powers, 2011).

In the 2002 study, Asian Americans tended to argue that the lack of diverse images of Asian Americans stemmed from Asian Americans themselves. For example, some blamed Asian American actors as well for perpetuating media stereotypes; in particular, Sandra (Chinese American, 2002) thought that the problem reflects the quality of Asian American actors. Robert (Chinese American, 2002) blamed the actors directly for their willingness to accept negative roles and felt they should be confronted and held accountable. But he also sympathized with the actors who rely on such roles as their "bread and butter."

Robert did touch on the dilemma many Asian American actors have faced for decades. Well-known actors, such as B.D. Wong and Ming-Na Wen, explained the shame and embarrassment they felt when they saw demeaning caricatures in the media growing up. When they became actors and were asked to play stereotypical roles, the internal struggles were deep and "added another layer to the trauma of having to act as a caricature of themselves" (Zia, 2000, p. 115).

Pam (Korean American, 2002) argues that the problem does not lie with the actors, but with the scripts: the roles available to Asian Americans are too few. However, when asked about increasing the opportunities for Asian American representations, she answered:

> The only way that you can motivate those companies is just through money. If they realize that they can make more money by welcoming Asians, they will probably do something more, but otherwise. ...

Once again, all questions elicit the same conundrum for respondents across a decade: If Asian American representations cannot make money for media corporations, there is no hope for better representations. It becomes an unbreakable cycle. That is, the solution (i.e., Asian Americans can help the corporations to make money) actually affirms the root of the problem (i.e., the corporations would not want to risk their profits).

In contrast, in the 2011 studies, Asian Americans predominantly expressed apathy regarding improving media representations and instead focused on how and where to find media that please them. For example:

> Jennifer (Korean American): "I honestly don't care ... It would be nice to see more minorities and there's definitely an improvement from the 1970s, but I feel like .... it's going to take a long time until we're not minorities anymore."
>
> Gloria (Chinese American): "if we want Asian idols, we have them because we will go to the Internet and look at Korean dramas and Asian pop stars ... you can like American shows but then always go back to your Asian dramas."

What is striking about the two comments is not only the contradiction that, on the one hand, the subjects "don't care" about how the media represent them while, on the other, most Asian Americans acknowledge that media affect people's perceptions about them, but further, that they do not seem to differentiate between Asians (foreign) and Asian Americans (U.S. citizens), which is actually one of the most prevalent stereotypes that Asian Americans suffered—forever foreigners. The following two examples are even more revealing about the subjects' sense of being "foreign."

> Ann (Korean American): I don't really watch television ... I don't really care. I know that if I wanted to watch Korean things, I could just watch Korean dramas, but I think it's like in the same way that when you watch Korean dramas and white people come out ... [It would be strange.]
>
> Allen (Chinese American): I don't think I have a problem with it because in China you don't see white people on their televisions or in Russia, you don't see like American people on there. I don't think it's just America that we should point our blame at.

Both subjects, participating in two different groups, came up with the same rationale that Asian Americans in mainstream media are as out of place as white people appearing in Asian TV. In other words, U.S. mainstream media should be "white," and if Asian Americans were to appear, they would be out of place and strange. This finding led us to ask: Did those subjects really not care that there were insufficient media images representing them? Would they be satisfied with Asian images that do not reflect their experiences as Asian Americans? Were they offering rationales so they would not need to change the status quo? Regardless of the answers to these questions, one explanation for the dominant representational justification we observed is that, if people do not find change possible, they rationalize a lack of need for change as a way of resolving cognitive dissonance (Festinger, 1957).

Discussion

The findings of the two studies on Asian American media representations in 2002 and 2011 demonstrate the urgent need for a comprehensive media literacy curriculum to help students acquire the knowledge and skills to critically examine the production, content, and consumption of media images. During a time when young people are capable of being "producers" through new media technology and social networking, comprehensive digital media literacy—with its emphasis on political economy—brings awareness to the importance of creating one's own stories instead of perpetuating corporate ideology through uncritically reposting mainstream mediations on YouTube or on Facebook pages.

The two studies, although a decade apart, show almost identical patterns in the respondents' analysis of Asian Americans in the mainstream media, including a lack of knowledge of the role the U.S. media system plays in shaping media representations. Although the respondents were keen to point out the common types of Asian American media stereotypes, they were generally ignorant about the historical, political, and social constructions of those images. No respondent expressed an understanding that the current U.S. commercial broadcast system is highly unusual compared to other industrialized countries, which use a public service model—albeit one that also has been eroded by neoliberal capitalism (McChesney, 1999, 2004). No one mentioned that social responsibilities could be imposed through regulations on media corporations for the benefit of the citizenry, which was clearly stated at the inception of the early broadcast system in the United States (McChesney, 1999, 2004). No one articulated how the FCC's media policy has changed over the years to help create the media conglomeration that has had devastating effects on the quality of news and children's programming (McChesney, 2004; Levin & Kilbourne, 2008). All in all, no one imagined that media could be a potential "public space" for exchanging diverse ideas democratically instead of serving the sole function of maximizing profits. Overall, respondents believe that the media come to them "as-is"; they do not possess a critical-based understanding that all media texts are constructed and that these constructions serve a particular purpose.

In short, the respondents' comments demonstrate what Lewis and Jhally (1998) call a "conceptual limitation": if students cannot conceptualize alternatives, it is rooted not in a lack of imagination, but in a lack of education. Indeed, it is the belief that the current commercial media system is natural, neutral, ever-present, and incapable of change that feeds corporate hegemony, rendering the socially conscious and well-meaning respondents paralyzed by their "moral dilemma." Without ever having been taught that alternatives do in fact exist, few can think outside the box. Thus, young people without training in media literacy are understandably not aware that most mainstream texts are made with profit as the primary goal, which results in support for the industry through a blithe acceptance of the "way things are."

COMPREHENSIVE DIGITAL MEDIA LITERACY:
A CASE FOR POLITICAL ECONOMY

There have been heated debates on what content should be included in a media literacy curriculum (Hobbs, 1998; Buckingham,1998; Kubey, 1998; Jhally & Lewis, 1998). This study, we believe, exemplifies the importance of teaching a critical cultural studies-infused approach to media learning that includes a contextual, comprehensive approach that analyzes texts, audiences, and media systems (Kellner, 2003). This approach teaches young people to analyze historical contexts and influences, hierarchies among social relations, and hegemony; they are taught theories of social production and reproduction. This learning is inherently political and subjective in its efforts (Kellner, 2003; Kellner & Share, 2007; Share, 2009; Hammer, 2009; Jhally & Earp, 2006) as it investigates how a capitalist framework "structures institutions and practices according to the logic of commodification and capital accumulation" (Kellner, 2009, p. 9). Mainstream media in the United States are organized, produced, and distributed in the service of maximizing profits, which results in "structural limits" that impose guidance on "what can and cannot be said and shown, and what sort of audience effects the text may generate" (Kellner, 2003, p. 12). Regulations put in place to constrain media corporations from total control have rapidly eroded in the last three decades (McChesney 2004, 2005). This is another crucial point of concern that can be addressed by critical digital media literacy.

In a cultural environment where five global firms own most of the media, it is important to make this fact widely known in media literacy pedagogy and prioritize the study how media industries are organized (Bagdikian, 2004; Lewis & Jhally, 1998; Kellner & Share, 2007; Kellner, 2009). Hammer (2009) asserts that when students are able to think beyond the dominant ideology and corporate system, they have the potential to seek and produce alternatives. As seen in the students' responses, or lack thereof, to improve media representations, critical media literacy, combined with an analysis of political economy, is a crucial aspect to the proposed intervention strategy for the students examined. We argue that our respondents were fairly typical college students in terms of their knowledge about media: they were equipped with the ability to recognize stereotypes but unable to critically analyze their structural implications. Comprehensive digital media literacy is thus crucial for students to gain a contextual understanding of the media images, to examine the power and threat posed by the increasingly monopolistic media conglomerates, and to seek alternative media as models for consumption and production. Moreover, as we continue to use social media, we need to critically analyze online powerhouses of production and distribution while engaging in diverse and creative production through user-friendly tools and apps.

Although the new development of social media and digital technology that emerged in the 2011 study has enabled individuals to self-publish their own versions of alternative media, these same avenues, such as YouTube and Facebook, have strong ties with conglomerates and corporate establishments. However, while they are no longer "alternative," they nonetheless provide opportunities for independent producers to reach audiences they never would have, such as Wong Fu Productions (which has attracted millions of subscribers worldwide). This new online dimension to media demonstrates the pressing importance of a digital media literacy curriculum that demands production skills. Only then can students not only know how to "read" the underlying meanings of media images and the conditions of why and how they are produced, but also how to "write" new and alternative texts.

NOTES

1. This project is a comparative study between focus group interviews conducted in 2002 and 2011. The university at which the first set of interviews was conducted (2002) had a small population of Latino students; as a result of this, the methodology for this study focused on racial identities that could provide a higher degree of representative data. Of the sample of 538 people, there were White (40.9%, N=220), Black (21%, N=113) and Asian American groups (34.8%, N=187), and Latino and other racial groups (3.3%, N=17). Furthermore, since race issues in the US have been predominantly framed as a black and white issue even in the early 2000s, both white and black groups were selected to contrast with Asian American students. For the comparison study in 2011, we thus followed the same methodology in 2002.

2. Each respondent is identified with his or her ethnicity and year interviewed, and both qualifications are indicated in parentheses. For example, July is an Korean American and was interviewed in 2011, is indicated as July (Korean American, 2011). They are identified in a concise way in order to provide correspondence between their racial identification, the year they were interviewed, and their individual responses.

REFERENCES

Aoki, A., & Takeda, O. (2011). *Asian American politics*. Cambridge: Polity Press.

Bagdikian, B. (2004). *The new media monopoly*. Boston, MA: Beacon Press.

Balance, C. B. (2012). How it feels to be viral me: Affective labor and Asian American YouTube performance. *Women's Studies Quarterly 40*(1 & 2), 138–152.

Benson, R., & Powers, M. (2011) *Public media and political independence: Lessons for the future of journalism from around the world*. Free Press. Retrieved from http://www.freepress.net/sites/default/files/stn-legacy/public-media-and-political-independence.pdf.

Buckingham, D. (1998). Media education in the UK: Moving beyond protectionism. *Journal of Communication, 48*(1), 33–43.

Cao, L., & Novas, H. (1996). *Everything you need to know about Asian-American history*. New York: Plume.

Castells, M. (1996). *The rise of the networked society*. Cambridge, MA: Blackwell.

Chan, J. (2001). *Chinese American masculinities: From Fu Manchu to Bruce Lee.* New York: Routledge.

Chen, C. H. (1996). Feminization of Asian (American) men in the U.S. mass media: An analysis of the Ballad of Little Jo. *Journal of Communication Inquiry, 20*(2), 57–71.

Chihara, M. (2000, February 25). Casting a cold eye on the rise of Asian starlets. *The Boston Phoenix, 26* (3).

Chin, F., & Chan, J. P. (1972). Racist love. In R. Kostelanetz (Ed.), *Seeing through shuck* (pp. 65–79). New York: Ballantine.

Chin, F., Chan, J., Inada, L., & Wong, S. (Eds.). (1974). *Aiiieeeee!: An anthology of Asian American writers.* New York: Mentor.

Curran, J. (2012). Reinterpreting the Internet. In J. Curran, N. Fenton, & D. Freedman (Eds.), *Misunderstanding the Internet* (pp. 3–33). London: Routledge.

Derman-Sparks, Louise (1989) *Anti-bias Curriculum: Tools for empowering young children.* Washington, D.C.: A.B.C. Task Force.

Fall colors 2003–2004: Prime time diversity report. (2004) Oakland, CA: Children Now.

Festinger, L. (1957). *A theory of cognitive dissonance.* Evanston, IL: Row Peterson.

Greenberg, B. S., Mastro, D., and Brand., J. E. (2002). Minorities and the mass media: television into the 21st century. In J. Bryant & D. Zillman (Eds.), *Media effects: Advances in theory and research* (2nd ed.) Mahwah, N.J.: Lawrence Erlbaum Associates.

Hall, S. (1980). Encoding/Decoding. In S. Hall et al. (Eds.), *Culture, media, language* (pp. 128–138). London: Hutchinson.

Hall, S. (1996). Gramsci's relevance for the study of race and ethnicity. In D. Morley & K. Chen (Eds.), *Stuart Hall: Critical dialogues in cultural studies.* New York: Routledge.

Hamamoto, D. (1994). *Monitored peril: Asian Americans and the politics of TV representation.* Minneapolis, MN: University of Minnesota Press.

Hammer, R. (2009). "This won't be on the final": Reflections on teaching critical media literacy. In R. Hammer & D. Kellner (Eds.), *Media/cultural studies: Critical approaches* (pp.164–193). New York: Peter Lang Publishing.

Hobbs, R. (1998). The seven great debates in the media literacy movement. *Journal of Communication, 48*(1), 16–32.

Huntemann, N., & Morgan, M. (2001). "Mass Media and Identity Development" in In D. G. Singer & J. L. Singer (Eds.), *Handbook of children & the media* (pp. 309–222). Thousand Oaks: Sage.

Jenkins, H. (1995). Out of the closet and into the universe. In J. Tulloch & H. Jenkins (Eds.), *Science fiction audiences.* London: Routledge.

Jhally, S., & Earp, J. (2006). Empowering literacy: Media education as a democratic imperative. In S. Jhally (Ed.), *The spectacle of accumulation: Essays in culture, media & politics* (pp. 239–270). New York: Peter Lang Publishing.

Kellner, D. (2003). Cultural studies, multiculturalism, and media culture. In G. Dines & J. M. Humez (Eds.), *Gender, race and class in media* (pp. 9–20). Thousand Oaks, CA: Sage.

Kellner, D. (2009). Toward a critical media/cultural studies. In R. Hammer & D. Kellner (Eds.), *Media/cultural studies: Critical approaches* (pp. 5–24). New York: Peter Lang Publishing.

Kellner, D., & Share, J. (2007). Critical media literacy, democracy, and the reconstruction of education. In D. Macedo & S. R. Steinberg (Eds.), *Media literacy: A reader* (pp. 3–23). New York: Peter Lang Publishing.

Kubey, R. (1998) Obstacles to the development of media education in the United States. *Journal of Communication*, 48(1), 58–69.

Lee, M. R. (2008). *The effects of Asian American studies on Asian American college students' psychological functioning*. University of Illinois at Urbana-Champaign, ProQuest, UMI Dissertations Publishing. 3337876. Retrieved from http://ezproxy.library.nyu.edu:2143/docview/304626040/abstract?accounti d=12768.

Levin, D. & Kilbourne, J. (2008). *So Sexy So Soon: The New sexualized childhood and what parents can do to protect their kids*. New York: Random House.

Levy, P. (2001). *Cyberculture*. Minneapolis: University of Minnesota Press.

Lewis, J., & Jhally, S. (1998). The struggle over media literacy. *Journal of Communication*, 48(1), 109–120.

Lull, J. (2011). Hegemony. In G. Dines & J. M. Humez (eds.), *Gender, race and class in media* (3rd ed.) (pp.33–36). Thousand Oaks, CA: Sage.

Manovich, L. (2001). *The Language of new media*. Cambridge, MA: MIT Press.

Mastro, D., & Behm-Morawitz, E. (2005). Latino representation on primetime television. *Journalism & Mass Communication Quarterly*, 82(1), 110–130.

McChesney, R. W. (2004). *The problem of the media: U.S. communication politics in the 21st century*. New York: Monthly Review Press.

McChesney, R. W. (2005). The emerging struggle for a free press. In R. W. McChesney, R. Newman, & B. Scott (Eds.), *The future of media: Resistance and reform in the 21st century* (pp. 9–20). New York: Seven Stories Press.

Miller, V. (2011). *Understanding digital culture*. Los Angeles: Sage.

Mok, T. A. (1998). Getting the message: Media images and stereotypes and their effect on Asian Americans. *Cultural diversity and mental health*, 4(3), 185–202.

Narasaki, K. K. (2005). *The 2005 Asian Pacific American report card on television diversity*. Washington, DC: Asian American Justice Center.

Nielsen (2013). Top 10 US web parent companies. *Top tens & trends*. Retrieved from http://www.nielsen.com/us/en/top10s.html.

Papacharissi, Z. (2002). The virtual sphere: The Internet as a public sphere. *New Media & Society*, 4(9), 9–27.

Pew Research Center for the People & the Press. (2012, September 27). Online and digital news. *Trends in news consumption: 1991–2012*. Retrieved from http://www.people-press.org/2012/09/27/section-2-online-and-digital-news-2/.

Poster, M. (1995). *The Second Media Age*. Cambridge, UK: Polity Press.

Rheingold, H. (1993). *The Virtual Community: Homesteading on the Electronic Frontier*. Reading, MA: Addison-Wesley.

Share, J. (2009). Young children and critical media literacy. In R. Hammer & D. Kellner (Eds.), *Media/cultural studies: Critical approaches* (pp. 126–151). New York: Peter Lang Publishing.

Snead, J. (1994). *White screens, black images: Hollywood from the dark side*. New York: Routledge.

Sun, C. (2002). Stories matter: Media influence on Asian American identities and inter-racial relationships. (Doctoral dissertation). *Electronic Doctoral Dissertations for UMass Amherst*. Paper AAI3068596.

Sun, C., Miezan, E., & Liberman, R. (2008). Model minority/honorable eunuch. In R. Hammer & D. Kellner (Eds.), *Media/cultural studies: Critical approaches*. New York: Peter Lang Publishing.

Tajima, R. E. (1989). Lotus blossoms don't bleed: images of Asian women. In Asian Women United of California (Ed.), *Making waves: An anthology of writings by and about Asian American women* (pp. 308–317). Boston: Beacon Press.

Thussu, D. K. (2006). *International communication: Continuity and change* (2nd ed.). London: Hodder Arnold Publication.

U.S. Census Bureau. (2010). *U.S. Census Bureau delivers final state 2010 census population totals for legislative redistricting.* Retrieved from https://www.census.gov/2010census/news/releases/operations/cb11-cn123.html.

Villapando, B. (1989). The business of selling mail-order brides. In Asian Women United of California (Ed.), Making waves: *An anthology of writings by and about Asian American women* (pp. 318–326). Boston: Beacon Press.

Wise, J. M. (2008). *Cultural globalization—A user's guide.* Malden, MA: Blackwell.

Xing, J. (1998). *Asian America through the lens: History, representations & identity.* Walnut Creek, California: Altamira.

Zia, H. (2000). *Asian American dreams: The emergence of an American people.* New York: Farrar, Straus and Giroux.

3 Who's Tracking Me?

Investigating and Publicly Documenting the Surveillance Economy Using Lightbeam and Wikipedia

Thomas F. Corrigan

INTRODUCTION: DE-CENTERING REPRESENTATION IN MEDIA LITERACY EDUCATION

Len Masterman's (1989) "Media awareness education: Eighteen basic principles" is a foundational text in media literacy education—one that laid the groundwork for subsequent interventions (Jolls & Wilson, 2014). In it, Masterman stressed the centrality of *representation* in media literacy education:

> The central unifying concept of Media Education is that of representation. The media mediate. They do not reflect but re-present the world. The media, that is, are symbolic sign systems that must be decoded. Without this principle no media education is possible. From it, all else flows (para. 2).

Following Masterman's lead, media literacy pedagogy has focused predominantly on media's textual representations: how and why media texts are made; how media technologies shape/constrain texts; how texts are constructed and construct reality; how we understand texts; how texts shape our social and political life; and whose interests texts serve. In each case, it is textual representation that is 'centered.' Take, for instance, the "key concept" of media literacy education most pertinent to the present chapter—that "media have commercial implications" (Aufderheide, 1993, p. 10; Pungente, 1999). Aufderheide (2000) explains that, "If you are going to be media literate, it's crucially important to know the economic basis of media production, and how that affects content, techniques, and distribution" (p. 306). In other words, it is important to understand media economics because they affect the range and nature of media texts we encounter on a daily basis.

This attention to textual representation is absolutely crucial for making sense of media and their political, economic, and sociocultural implications. Take advertising, for instance. In the twentieth century, newspapers, magazines, radio, television, and other advertiser-supported mass media operated in an 'attention economy.' These media attracted our attention, and then they sold corporate advertisers the opportunity to expose us to branded messages. Media literacy educators rightly stress that this economic arrangement fundamentally shaped the texts that ad-supported media produced for public consumption. Producers created media content, such as sports and celebrity fare, that was most likely to attract the types of people advertisers wanted to reach (18- to 49-year-old urban and suburban males, for instance). They also avoided certain topics and storylines that might alienate large audience segments or undermine advertisers' commercial interests (Bagdikian, 2004). Finally, advertisements themselves taught us as much about race, class, gender, and consumerism as they did about the goods and services available in the marketplace (Leiss, Kline, & Jhally, 1997).

Important as these insights are, textual representations are not the only ways media influence society. Media also have a direct, *material* impact on the distribution of wealth and power in society. Take ad-supported media's impact on the broader capitalist political economy, for instance. In the twentieth century, national advertising's costs raised barriers to entry in oligopolistic markets and allowed those oligopolists to compete over market share rather than prices (Meehan, 2005). In other words, national advertising contributed materially (not just ideologically) to the static handful of similarly priced providers in soda, airline, gasoline, and various other industries. And as revenues in ad-supported media grew, media firms themselves provided profitable opportunities for reinvesting overaccumulated capital from other oligopolistic industries. Sure, the media investments of General Electric, Texaco, Coca-Cola, and others helped shape public discourse in pro-industry ways, but the ultimate goals of these investments were market power and profit, not public interest. To the extent that these processes contribute to monopoly, inequality, and undermine democratic processes (McChesney, 2013), educators' attention to the material impact of commercial media on wealth and power asymmetries is just as pressing as their ideological implications (via textual representations). Such political-economic considerations only crystalize, though, when we 'de-center' our focus on media representations and shift at least some of our attention (and pedagogy) to the economic bases of these industries and their material connections to the broader capitalist political economy.

Such material analysis is fundamental if students are to develop a holistic understanding of digital media and their implications for contemporary social, political, and economic life. The attention economy described above still undergirds twenty-first century digital media industries, as evinced in a wide array of free, ad-supported sites and services; however, the attention economy now operates alongside and in conjunction with an emerging 'surveillance economy.' Digital sites and services give us tools to create, share, and consume, but under one stipulation: that we let media and marketers surveil nearly everything we do and say online, compiling valuable marketing data about our individual identities and consumer preferences. It is a process known as 'behavioral tracking' or 'behavioral targeting,' and it presents a whole host of social implications both ideological and material.

This chapter begins by describing these furtive commercial surveillance processes, particularly the role of so-called 'third-party trackers.' It then describes a class assignment for familiarizing students with the surveillance economy's existence, workings, and social implications. This assignment follows an "inquiry-based approach" common in media literacy education, wherein students learn to ask and answer key questions about media (Rogow, 2011). Rather than focus on media texts, though, questions about surveillance are 'centered': Who is tracking me online? What behaviors are they tracking, and how? Why are they doing this? And what are the social implications (textual or otherwise)? More specifically, students use a Firefox "add-on" named Lightbeam to visualize the surveillance economy and to identify some of the third-party trackers that actively surveil their individual digital media use. Students then investigate one of those third-party trackers' business practices, publish what they find in an original Wikipedia entry, and reflect on the experience. In doing so, students illuminate the surveillance economy in a personal way—one that is tied to their own digital media use. They also shed light on third-party trackers for the public. Finally, this chapter offers some suggestions for moving students beyond critiques of behavioral tracking as 'creepy' to consider the surveillance economy's ideological and material implications.

BACKGROUND: BEHAVIORAL TRACKING AND THIRD-PARTY TRACKERS

As Joseph Turow (2012) has thoroughly documented, nearly everything we do and say online and with digital technologies produces a digital paper trail. Media and marketers closely surveil these data to build profiles of our identities and preferences. These profiles determine what ads, media content, and services we experience during future visits, on other websites, and even in offline consumption contexts (e.g., direct mail; supermarket check-out coupons; location-based mobile marketing). Audience profiling is nothing new; corporations have long allocated their marketing dollars to media outlets that reach their target markets (Bagdikian, 2004). The difference is that our digital paper trails are so rich and detailed that marketers can slice and dice us, demographically speaking, with greater precision than ever—even on an individual-by-individual basis. Moreover, our digital paper trails provide marketers with behavioral data: "measurable physical acts such as clicks, swipes, mouseovers, and even voice commands" presumed to offer valuable insight into consumer preferences (Turow, 2012, para. 10). In marketing parlance, the monitoring and packaging of consumers' behavioral data is referred to as 'behavioral tracking,' and the analysis and monetization of those data for target marketing is called 'behavioral targeting' or 'predictive analytics.' When Netflix recommends movies for you 'because you watched Ace Ventura' (again), when Facebook pitches you ads based on your demographic information, 'likes', or location, or when drug store check-out coupons reflect your recent Web browsing (and vice-versa), you are seeing behavioral tracking and targeting at work.

The websites and apps that we use are not the only (or primary) parties surveilling our digital lives, though. The *New York Times*' Natasha Singer (2012) explains that "there may be dozens of third-party entities on an individual Web page, compiling and storing information about what a user reads, searches for, clicks on, or buys" (para.12). These third-party trackers operate under unfamiliar monikers such as Scorecard Research, Gravity, and New Relic. Few consumers have heard of these companies because we, as users, are *not* their customers. Rather, multinational Web firms and marketers, such as Facebook, Amazon, Nike, and Apple, *are* their customers. These multinationals turn to third-party trackers to better understand and capitalize on our identities and preferences. In short, the media business is no longer just about capturing our attention and selling it to advertisers; it is also about surveilling and studying our individual digital media use so that corporations—media and otherwise—can better know our identities and consumer preferences, and, thus, more efficiently and effectively market their goods and service. Governments, too, have gotten in on the tracking game, furtively collecting citizens' digital paper trails in bulk to look for potential terror connections and intentions (and raising civil liberties concerns in the process). As explained later, behavioral tracking *does* shape media representations, including the digital advertising and media content we each see (Turow, 2012); however, the implications go beyond matters of representation and ideology. The structure of contemporary capitalist enterprise and shifting relationships between citizens and governments are also crucial material, political-economic implications of digital media's surveillance economy.

The public is gradually awaking to these processes. Edward Snowden's revelations about NSA surveillance and Facebook's controversial social experiments have, among other news stories, lifted the veil on both government and corporate surveillance (Albergotti, 2014; "United States of Secrets," 2014). Students have told me that they have noticed ads specifically tailored to them based on their previous page views, searches, clicks, purchases, and chats; however, most students underestimate the scale and detail of behavioral tracking, misunderstand its basic processes (particularly the role of third-party trackers), and lack an appreciation for its social consequences (ideological or otherwise). Turow's (2012) more systematic studies of consumer knowledge yield similar insights: "although people know companies are using their data and do worry about it, their understanding of exactly how the data are being used is severely lacking" (para. 19). The following assignment seeks to address this lack of understanding.

ASSIGNMENT: TRACKING AND DOCUMENTING THE TRACKERS

In light of the public's limited understanding about the surveillance economy, I developed the following assignment to actively familiarize students with the surveillance economy's existence, workings, and social implications. This assignment was designed for an undergraduate Digital Media and Communication course; however, it would also be appropriate (in part or in whole) for high school students. This assignment follows an "inquiry-based approach" common in media literacy education (Rogow, 2011). Inquiry-based approaches are focused more on the learning process than 'covering the content.' Students learn to ask and answer key questions about media—a process that can be particularly powerful when exploring students' own media experiences (e.g., the actual sites they visit). Inquiry-based approaches also stress 'openness'; instructors aim to facilitate inquiry rather than guide students to a particular conclusion. The key difference in this assignment (compared to most inquiry-based media literacy approaches) is that surveillance is 'centered,' rather than media's textual representation.

In Part I, students familiarize themselves with behavioral tracking through a reading and a video. The assignment pairs well with an excerpt from Turow's 2012 book *The Daily You* published on *The Atlantic*'s website. The excerpt is titled, "A guide to the digital advertising industry that's watching your every click" (Turow, 2012). In it, Turow describes behavioral tracking, identifies some of the leading third-party tracking firms, and situates these processes and parties relative to "old media" marketing. He also argues that behavioral tracking can result in "social discrimination." In other words, the asymmetries in our marketing profiles can lead to different advertisements, media content, and life opportunities that may advantage some and disadvantage others. These social implications are considered in greater depth later. To supplement Turow's analysis, students also watch a TED Talk by Firefox CEO Gary Kovacs titled "Tracking our online trackers" (Kovacs, 2012). Kovacs is particularly concerned with behavioral tracking's 'creepiness'—a critique that, as I later argue, can actually distract from some of commercial surveillance's important social implications. However, Kovacs' video does illustrate for students how they can employ Firefox's Collusion browser add-on (now named Lightbeam) to find out which third-party trackers are surveilling them online. This add-on is the same one students use in Part II to visualize the behavioral tracking process.

With this background, Part II demonstrates to students both the scale of behavioral tracking and that third-party trackers are, in fact, gathering data about their personal digital media use. This component works best if students each have access to a computer, whether at home or in a lab. Students first download Firefox's Lightbeam add-on and open the program in a browser tab. They then open a separate tab and visit a few of their favorite websites—ESPN.com, TMZ, Facebook, and the like. When students return to the Lightbeam tab, they find a real-time visualization of the sites they just visited, as well as the third-party trackers that gathered data about them during those visits. The third-party trackers far outnumber the visited sites, sometimes by a 20-to-1 ratio. Students then visit more of their favorite websites, intermittently returning to the Lightbeam visualization to find it rapidly expanding. This use of Lightbeam makes behavioral tracking real and personal for students. These are no longer hypothetical Web experiences; these are individual students' actual visits to sites they frequent and trust being monitored by an extraordinary number of third parties without their knowledge. It is not uncommon to hear students audibly gasp when they see the visualization and watch it expand.

Although Lightbeam is effective for visualizing behavioral tracking and identifying third-party trackers, the add-on provides limited information about each specific tracking firm. Accordingly, in Part III, students pick one of the third-party trackers from their visualization, and they engage in a structural analysis of that firm. Consistent with inquiry-based learning's focus on question-asking, students learn to ask and answer a handful of basic structural questions about that tracking firm: What product or service does the company provide? Who are their clients? And how does my data factor into their business model? Students start by visiting the company's website and looking for clues, particularly those available on the 'About' page. A company's website can provide a wealth of useful information; however, students must be reminded that they are *not* the intended audience of this information—Web publishers and marketers *are*. Thus, students need to look at these websites from a publisher or marketer's perspective: What service is the tracker offering *those firms*? Further, since these web pages are themselves marketing materials, they can include a great deal of 'corporate speak': 'Reading between the lines' is crucial. For an independent perspective on these third-party trackers, students conduct Google and LexisNexis searches for reporting about their tracking firm in newspapers, trade publications, and on blogs. Some companies are quite difficult to find independent coverage of, but such information *is* out there, particularly if students look beyond the first page of search results. Students take notes about what they find, and they are constantly encouraged to inquire about the company's business model: What do they do? Who buys their services? And how does my data factor in?

Having gathered information about their third-party tracking company, Part IV asks students to publish an original Wikipedia entry about that firm. In nearly every case, the tracking companies identified using Lightbeam do not have Wikipedia entries describing them, so students are able to create an original entry about their firm from the ground up. Contrary to popular belief, Wikipedia will not just publish *any* entry. Students need to adhere to Wikipedia's basic editorial guidelines if they are to be published. These guidelines include: (1) explaining why the company is notable, (2) using reliable published sources, (3) writing from a neutral point of view, and (4) using their own words. Wikipedia's editorial guidelines complement this assignment's inquiry-based approach in that students need to ask tough, evaluative questions about both their tracking firm and their investigation: What does a reader absolutely need to know about my company? How can I put 'corporate speak' in my own words? Have I culled enough information from reliable published sources? The primary purpose of composing the Wikipedia entry, then, is not to develop editorial skills or an appreciation for the constructed nature of Wikipedia entries (as is common in representation-centered media literacy approaches). Rather, the purpose is to get students to synthesize and evaluate what they have learned about their tracking firm. Any deeper understanding of Wikipedia, itself, is a side benefit.

Finally, given the importance of critical reflection in inquiry-based approaches, Part V asks students to consider what they learned during their investigation. There are, of course, any number of reflection prompts to respond to; however, I like to ask students: (1) what they found most surprising in learning about third-party trackers, and (2) what they hoped people would learn from their Wikipedia entry. Responses vary widely, from the astonished to the unsurprised, and from the highly critical to the supportively celebratory. Some delve into the specific practices of tracking firms, while others express surprise that behavioral tracking is happening at all or on the scale that it does. The latter response might seem underwhelming or obvious; however, they illustrate just how veiled this basic structure of digital media actually is. Ultimately, students' responses prove useful for subsequent in-class debriefing and discussion. Specific examples of companies, services, and relationships provide fodder for considering the social implications of behavioral tracking.

REFLECTION: TEACHING THE SURVEILLANCE ECONOMY'S SOCIAL IMPLICATIONS

When students reflect on this assignment, one word comes up again and again: 'creepy.' Many are uncomfortable with the idea that commercial firms furtively monitor their page views, searches, clicks, purchases, and chats. This is a perfectly reasonable reaction; however, a strong, holistic digital media education framework requires a sharper critique of the surveillance economy—one that connects the specificity of individual surveillance to broader social issues. Rather than dwell on behavioral tracking's 'creepiness,' a more productive pedagogical response is to shift the focus from behavioral tracking to the personalized marketing it facilitates and the ideological and material implications that follow.

Again, Turow's (2012) work is insightful. Turow highlights the three-fold potential for "social discrimination" arising from personalized, data-driven marketing. First, targeted ads function as "status symbols," providing information about one's position in the social pecking order. When online marketers tailor a payday loan ad to one Web user and retirement services to another, they signal to consumers how they should think about their life opportunities and relative worth compared to their peers. One effective way to illustrate this disparity is to have students take out their mobile phones, pull up their Facebook page (or another ad-supported website they frequent), and then trade phones with their neighbor. While directed not to alter or further explore their peer's profile, students scroll through their neighbor's Facebook page and focus on the types of ads presented there. As students look at the ads, they reflect on how their peer's ads differ in meaningful ways from those on their own Facebook page. With those differences identified, students then consider how personalized advertising might shape one's view of one's self.

A second form of social discrimination concerns the data-driven personalization of media content. Media are our chief sources of information and ideas for navigating the world around us, and personalization of media content means that each of us may operate on very different facts and assumptions than others. People have long gravitated to media that fit their worldviews; however, behavioral targeting means digital media can be tailored to specific individuals in ways that are less apparent to users. From Eli Pariser's (2011) TED Talk, "Beware online 'filter bubbles,'" students learn how the Web algorithms employed by Netflix, Facebook, and others give us content we are presumed to enjoy. In this, information and ideas that challenge our assumptions about the world are filtered out. To illustrate this, Pariser recommends a simple experiment—one that works well in class. Have two students self-identify as 'very conservative' and 'very liberal,' then have them conduct Google searches for polarizing political topics (e.g., 'Obamacare' or 'immigration'). Their divergent search results illustrate the extent to which data-driven algorithms filter some information and ideas in and others out.

These first two forms of social discrimination are ideological: personalized marketing affects the digital advertisements and media texts we see and, thus, our informational and cultural environment. However, Turow's third form of social discrimination shifts attention from behavioral tracking's ideological implications to material ones. Increasingly, our marketing profiles will guide the deployment of personalized retail offers and pricing schemes based on an individual's presumed ability and willingness to pay, as well as our relative desirability as consumers (a particular concern in taste-based industries, such as fashion and food and beverage). In a 2012 *Wall Street Journal* article titled "Websites Vary Prices, Deals Based on Users' Information" students learn that websites routinely adjust prices based on individual consumers' marketing profiles (Valentino-Devries, Singer-Vine, & Soltani, 2012). On Staples.com, for instance, users from more affluent ZIP codes received lower prices than those from less affluent areas (where, presumably, there is less competition). Emerging mobile marketing services, such as Apple's iBeacon, mean that personalized offers can even reach our smartphones as we approach a given product in the supermarket. In these respects, digital media are not only important in the information and ideas they communicate, but also in the revenue potential they confer on corporations. In other words, digital media's impact, here, is material; the data they produce are instruments for increasing consumer transactions and revenue. To the extent that these processes affect broader wealth and power asymmetries, they are of basic social importance. Any ideological impact on advertising texts or media content is a by-product of the pursuit of market power and profits.

When confronted with differentiated offers and prices, such as at Staples. com, students often characterize these processes as 'smart marketing' (which they are); however, some examples can raise their ire. One is a *Fast Company* article titled "Colleges are using big data to predict which students will do well—before they accept them" (Ungerleider, 2013). The article details how some universities use predictive analytics to determine which students are likely to succeed or struggle. They then make admissions decisions and allocate resources to at-risk students. The data upon which these predictions are based include "the amount of hours [the student] is enrolled during each semester, whether they're working part-time or full-time or not at all, the amount of assistance from family and a host of other factors" (para. 3). Work/school balance and family assistance clearly stand to mark some segments of the socioeconomic spectrum as more risky applicants than others, creating the very real potential for discriminatory college acceptance processes. Some students recoil at the idea that marketing data could shape one's privileges in ways that are divorced from individual merit. Others still see it as 'smart marketing.'

The distribution of scarce resources, such as capital or education, is always a political matter; however, commercial surveillance also affects governance in more direct ways. In 2013, NSA contractor Edward Snowden revealed the agency's secret program for collecting users' phone and Internet data, including that of U.S. citizens. Launched under the auspices of the War on Terror, 'The Program' has been framed primarily as a matter of *government* surveillance of citizens. This program could not have operated at the scale or level of detail that it did, though, without data from and advances in *commercial* behavioral tracking (Schneier, 2013). Indeed, the Frontline documentary "United States of Secrets" (2014) stresses to students that the NSA program's growth coincided with a "golden age of surveillance." Increases in digital media use, commercial behavioral tracking, and computing power each made it easier for governments to gather and analyze information about our digital media use. Indeed, when *The Washington Post*'s Barton Gellman preemptively ran a story about The Program by the intelligence community to avoid any genuine national security threats, the element of the story intelligence officials most wanted him to conceal from the public was the names of the participating Internet corporations ("Reporter had to decide," 2013).

There are, of course, various directions that productive class discussions of government surveillance can take. A chilling effect on political speech is one crucial ideological concern. So, too, is the potential for racial profiling and discrimination. However, these social implications flow not from digital media's textual representations, but from material processes—the gathering, packaging, analysis, and monetization of commercial behavioral data. The present assignment provides a starting point for 'connecting the dots' between commercial surveillance, on the one hand, and these seemingly disparate processes of social discrimination and government surveillance, on the other. A holistic understanding of the surveillance economy's implications requires pedagogical openness to both ideological and material analysis.

CONCLUSION

Media literacy education has traditionally focused on matters of textual representation. Given media's ideological importance, this emphasis is completely understandable; however, ideological analysis alone is ultimately insufficient for a holistic understanding of media's social implications. Commercial media have material consequences. They shape the distribution of *both* ideas *and* resources.

The emergence of digital media's surveillance economy underscores the importance of teaching both ideological and material frameworks. As Turow (2012) explains, commercial behavioral tracking impacts the advertisements and media content to which we are each exposed. In this, surveillance has ideological implications for how we each make sense of the world and our place in it. However, behavioral tracking also influences society through material processes that are only tangentially related to textual representations. Behavioral tracking facilitates the personalization of retailers' offers and prices. In doing so, it raises concerns about asymmetries in the distribution of individual offers and life opportunities, as well as the general distribution of wealth and power in society. Further, those behavioral tracking data operate as the basis for not just commercial surveillance of consumers, but government surveillance of citizens. In short, digital surveillance does not just influence commerce and governance through media texts. It also influences these spheres through the provision of behavioral data about citizens and consumers.

The assignment detailed in this chapter offers one starting point for a holistic approach to digital media literacy education. Rather than start with media texts, this assignment 'centers' the commercial surveillance process. Through an inquiry-based approach, students shed light on the surveillance economy, they investigate one of the third-party tracking firms that are studying their behavior, and they share what they learn with the public in the form of a Wikipedia entry. Skills and understanding are developed through asking and answering key questions: Who is tracking me online? What behaviors are they tracking, and how? Why are they doing this? And what are the social implications (textual or otherwise)?

Advocates of inquiry-based learning emphasize the approach's openness. Rather than simply telling students the information they need to know, inquiry-based learning develops students' independent, critical thinking skills, including the capacity to ask and answer important questions. This is an admirable way to develop critical and ethical media producers, consumers, and citizens; however, to the extent that media literacy education maintains an important-but-narrow focus on asking questions about textual representation, we actually close other important avenues for inquiry. A more radical form of openness would encourage students to not only ask important questions about media and ideology, but also to inquire about media's material influence on economics, politics, and social life. The emergence of digital media's surveillance economy demands that we teach students to ask and answer these sorts of questions.

REFERENCES

Albergotti, R. (2014, June 30). Furor erupts over Facebook's experiment on users: Almost 700,000 unwitting subjects had their feeds altered to gauge effect on emotion. *The Wall Street Journal*. Retrieved from http://online.wsj.com/articles/furor-erupts-over-facebook-experiment-on-users-1404085840.

Aufderheide, P. (ed.) (1993). *Media literacy: A report of the national leadership conference on media literacy*. Aspen, CO: Aspen Institute.

Aufderheide, P. (2000). *The daily planet: A critic on the capitalist culture beat*. Minneapolis & London: University of Minnesota Press.

Bagdikian, B. H. (2004). *The new media monopoly*. Boston: Beacon Press.

Jolls, T., & Wilson, C. (2014). The core concepts: Fundamental to media literacy yesterday, today and tomorrow. *Journal of Media Literacy Education, 6*(2), 68–78.

Kovacs, G. (2012, February). Tracking our online trackers. *TED*. Retrieved from http://www.ted.com/talks/gary_kovacs_tracking_the_trackers?language=en.

Leiss, W., Kline, S., & Jhally, S. (1997). *Social communication in advertising: Persons, products and images of well-being* (2nd ed.). London & New York: Routledge.

Masterman, L. (1989). Media awareness education: Eighteen basic principles. *Center for Media Literacy*. Retrieved from http://www.medialit.org/reading-room/media-awareness-education-eighteen-basic-principles.

McChesney, R. W. (2013). *Digital disconnect: How capitalism is turning the Internet against democracy*. New York: New Press.

Meehan, E. R. (2005). *Why TV is not our fault: Television programming, viewers, and who's really in control*. Lanham, MD: Rowman & Littlefield.

Pariser, E. (2011). Beware online 'filter bubbles.' *TED*. http://www.ted.com/talks/eli_pariser_beware_online_filter_bubbles?language=en.

Pungente, J. (1999). Canada's key concepts of media literacy. *Center for Media Literacy*. Retrieved from http://www.medialit.org/reading-room/canadas-key-concepts-media-literacy.

"Reporter had to decide if Snowden leaks were 'The real thing'" (2013, September 11). *Fresh Air*. Retrieved from http://www.npr.org/2013/09/11/221359323/reporter-had-to-decide-if-snowden-leaks-were-the-real-thing.

Rogow, F. (2011). Ask, don't tell: Pedagogy for media literacy education in the next decade. *Journal of Media Literacy Education 3*(1), 16–22.

Schneier, B. (2013, July 31). The public-private surveillance partnership. *BloombergView*. Retrieved from http://www.bloombergview.com/articles/2013-07-31/the-public-private-surveillance-partnership.

Singer, N. (2012, October 13). Do not track? Advertisers say 'don't tread on us.' *The New York Times*. Retrieved from http://www.nytimes.com/2012/10/14/technology/do-not-track-movement-is-drawing-advertisers-fire.html?_r=0.

Turow, J. (2012, February 7). A guide to the digital advertising industry that's watching your every click. *The Atlantic*. Retrieved from http://www.theatlantic.com/technology/archive/2012/02/a-guide-to-the-digital-advertising-industry-thats-watching-your-every-click/252667/.

Ungerleider, N. (2013, October 21). Colleges are using big data to predict which students will do well—Before they accept them. *Fast Company*. Retrieved from http://www.fastcoexist.com/3019859/futurist-forum/colleges-are-using-big-data-to-predict-which-students-will-do-well-before-the.

"United States of Secrets" (2014, May 13). *Frontline*. Retrieved from: http://www.pbs.org/wgbh/pages/frontline/united-states-of-secrets/.

Valentino-Devries, J., Singer-Vine, J., & Soltani, A. (2012, December 24). Websites vary prices, deals based on users' information. *The Wall Street Journal*. Retrieved from: http://www.wsj.com/article_email/SB10001424127887323777204578189391813881534.

Part II

Social

Part 2 of *Media Education for a Digital Generation*—the SOCIAL, explores the vast potential and possibilities for media literacy education to reenvision itself by drawing from a range of fields and practices that harness the power of digital media for social empowerment and activism. In this section, we consider the ways in which communication is influenced by the social exchange of ideas and information in networked environments that are uniquely structured to increase flow and activism among peers. We ask questions about the most effective means of using the tools of the Digital Age to enact positive sociocultural interactions and outcomes at home and at school, through research and advocacy. What are the best ways to encourage positive social interactions online and offline? How can the power of social media be leveraged to distribute abundant information and diverse perspectives among the widest networks of people to encourage them to self-organize? How can people use the sociocultural influence of digital technologies, platforms, and applications to challenge traditional forms of media and other formal structures? These questions pave the way to this section's inquiry. Here, we read arguments for synthesizing public health research with digital media literacy education in order to make a significant impact on the health and development of children and adolescents, particularly in areas related to aggression and violence, substance use, and obesity. In conjunction with public health media literacy campaigns led by pediatricians and schools, we also consider the role of parents in mediating children's digital lives at home, and how to find the right strategies to foster a balanced life that encourages all family members to make smart and ethical media choices. With online video hosting sites like YouTube, Vine, and Vimeo proliferating, we also explore community based digital media making through access to video cameras, smart phones, and video editing software. While the digital tools of production and their use continue to grow, this section addresses the pedagogical means for community based programs to tackle the lack of diversity, unequal access, and (mis) representation found within mainstream media. In tandem with this theme, we conclude by analyzing how digital media platforms create virtual and social affinity spaces to advance the cause of social justice for members of underrepresented groups, and how digital media literacy education can advance the goals of inclusive peer-to-peer and local-to-global dialogue and understanding.

4 The New Technology Revolution

Collaborative Efforts between Pediatricians, Schools, and Millennials for Media Education

Victor C. Strasburger

INTRODUCTION

Nearly all pediatricians, most media researchers, some parents, and a few schools now acknowledge that modern media can be tremendously important in teaching children and adolescents about health issues. When children and teens spend an average of > 7 hours per day with a variety of different media (Rideout, 2010), it seems inevitable that they will learn important messages about aggressive behavior, sex, drugs, obesity, and other health problems. While there is ample research documenting health effects of traditional media (e.g., TV and movies) (see Figure 4.1) (Common Sense Media, 2008; Strasburger, Jordan, & Donnerstein, 2012), there is far less research on the potential impact of "new" digital media and technologies (e.g., Web 2.0, social networking sites, mobile phones) on health issues (Strasburger, 2014). This prompts two questions: which media—traditional or new/digital—will be more effective in preventing unhealthy health behaviors and encouraging positive public health attitudes? And how can pediatricians, schools, and parent maximize the prosocial potential of media while minimizing the potential harmful effects?

Although traditional media (e.g., TV and movies) have been linked to a variety of potential health problems (Strasburger, Jordan, & Donnerstein, 2012), they have also been used to try to produce widespread public health changes. Today, new digital media are increasingly being tried as a means of reaching a broad audience of teenagers in ways that traditional media cannot (Lenhart, 2014; Yager & O'Keefe, 2012). The twenty-first century new media landscape is evolving quickly, so it is extremely difficult to assess what impact new media are currently having. For example, MySpace has been completely replaced by Facebook, which is now in danger of being supplanted by Instagram and Snapchat among youth users. From a research viewpoint, such rapid shifts make studying new media difficult—which media do we choose to study, and how quickly can we conduct research? On the other hand, older "traditional" media (e.g., TV and movies) have been present for decades and have a rich research literature associated with them. Therefore, the discussion below will discuss common public health issues from each perspective, focusing on both traditional media and new/digital media.

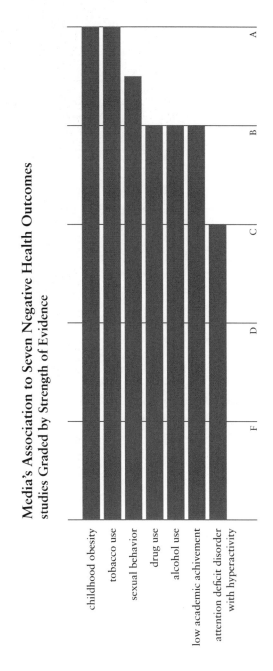

Media's Association to Seven Negative Health Outcomes studies Graded by Strength of Evidence

Strength of Evidence by Grade

Figure 4.1 From Common Sense Media (2008), reprinted with permission.

Regardless of whether children are consuming traditional or new media, there are three "bottom lines" here: (1) To be educated 100 years ago meant that someone could read and write. To be educated in 2015 means that someone can read, write, download, text, and perhaps even tweet. (2) At the moment, traditional media should be considered predominant in their behavioral impact, not only because abundant research says so but because TV and movies tell stories. And as George Gerbner was quick to point out many years ago, those in society who tell stories are the most powerful influencers (Gerbner & Morgan, 2002). (3) Researchers are far from understanding the impact of newer media on important public health behaviors like aggression, sex, smoking, and drinking. Newer media could potentially turn out to be even more potent than older media, but far more research will be needed to determine behavioral influences, and conducting research will be difficult because newer media are a "moving target."

MEDIA VIOLENCE

Since U.S. Senate hearings in 1954, media violence has been known to be an important factor in aggressive and even violent behavior. Although popular media and the general public still seem to remain skeptical, more than one thousand studies have made the connection between heavy media consumption and acts of violence (Council on Communications and Media, 2009; Media Violence Commission, 2012; Strasburger & Wilson, 2014). The problem in making connections between the two seems to be that people misunderstand the very rich communications literature, have a difficult time believing that entertaining programming could have such negative consequences, and expect a 100% cause-and-effect connection between viewing media violence and, for instance, the rate of homicide in the U.S. (Strasburger, Donnerstein, & Bushman, 2014). In addition, media are clearly not the leading cause of *any* violence-related public health problem; estimates are that they may contribute to 10% of violence in society (Strasburger, Wilson, & Jordan, 2014).

Traditional media: Although there are hundreds of studies linking the viewing of media violence to real-life aggression, there are very few studies on media-based violence prevention programs or mass public education programs. Thirty years ago, researchers had 169 second and fourth graders from Oak Park, Illinois, write essays about the unrealistic nature of media violence and its impact on young viewers. In three hour-long sessions over 6–8 weeks, they taught the students about the differences between characters in violent shows and real-life people, displayed the production techniques used to make TV characters violent, and showed how real people used different strategies to solve problems. Interestingly, the intervention had *no* effect on peer-assessed aggression or viewing levels of violence. However, when the researchers modified their intervention to include having the students make a film depicting children who were harmed by media violence and then write papers about violent media, those children displayed more negative attitudes about TV violence and less aggressive behavior four months later when compared with a control group (Huesmann, Eron, Klein, Brice, and Fisher, 1983). So the primary message is that simplistic teaching about media violence may do no good, but carefully planned and targeted interventions can be effective (McCannon, 2014).

In another interesting experiment, Court TV funded a study of 513 teenagers from three different middle schools in California who were randomly assigned to receive or not receive the "Choices and Consequences" curriculum that involved videotaped court cases of real teens who had engaged in risky behaviors resulting in someone's death (Wilson et al., 1999). The three-week curriculum involved watching videos of actual court cases in which teens had engaged in risk behaviors resulting in someone's death. The students discussed the cases, engaged in role-playing exercises, and completed homework assignments based on the cases. Compared with the control group, the intervention group had significantly reduced verbal and physical aggression and increased empathy (Wilson et al., 1999).

Most recently, California researchers assessed 1580 students in 20 different schools after implementing *Beyond Blame*, a violence prevention media literacy curriculum. Compared with controls, students reported increased knowledge of media literacy concepts and increased sensitivity to media violence exposure. By contrast, students in the control group reported more media consumption and greater likelihood of pushing or shoving another student or threatening to hit or hurt someone (Fingar & Jolls, 2014).

Overall, a recent meta-analysis of 51 media literacy interventions found nearly all had positive effects on media knowledge, criticism, perceived realism, attitudes and beliefs, and behavior (Jeong, Cho, & Hwang, 2012). The effects were moderate in size (mean effect size = 0.37), but nine studies showed that media literacy programs can be effective in how children respond to screen violence in terms of all of the aspects mentioned above. Finally, in 2014, a national campaign to encourage parents to ask about the presence of guns in households where children may be playing was begun using Juliana Margulies from "The Good Wife" as a spokesperson (Figure 4.2). The American Academy of Pediatrics strongly supports this aspect of firearm safety (Council on Injury, Violence and Poison Prevention Executive Committee, 2012). However, as with most public health campaigns, no data were collected about the efficacy of the campaign.

New / digital media: New / digital media have been implicated in two areas—cyberbullying and first-person shooter video games. Estimates of teens who have been cyberbullied range widely, from 7% to 72% (although 20–40% seems more accurate); and there is considerable concern that the effects of cyberbullying may be more severe than in-person bullying (Donnerstein, 2014; Selkie & Kota, 2014). First-person shooter

Figure 4.2 A public service ad about asking parents if there is a gun in the home.

video games have been implicated in nearly every recent mass shooting, from Norway to Aurora and Newtown. Yet the U.S. Supreme Court found no substantial evidence that such games lead to mass murder (Brown, Governor of California, et al. v. Entertainment Merchants Association et al., 2011). Nor could they: mass murders—even single homicides—are extremely rare, and millions of children and teenagers play video games daily. The connection is impossible to make from a research standpoint, but that doesn't mean that first-person shooter games don't contribute in a significant way (Strasburger, Bushman, & Donnerstein, 2014). One possibility is that a teen or young adult who has two or more risk factors (social isolation, history of childhood abuse or being bullied, mental illness, obsession with first-person shooter video games) might be more likely to do mass harm. A case control study would be useful to delineate how strong these risk factors actually are. Clearly, more research is needed to examine the relationship between new digital media and potential aggressive behavior among youth.

SEX

There is now no question that sexual content in the media can influence adolescent sexual beliefs, attitudes, *and* behavior (Strasburger, 2012a; Wright & Donnerstein, 2014). Currently, twenty studies that use longitudinal data have found a significant relationship between the viewing of sexual content at an early age and earlier onset of sexual intercourse (Strasburger, 2012a). One recent study has found that traditional media content may actually be more important than Internet content (Ybarra, Strasburger, & Mitchell, 2014). But both traditional and new media seem to represent the most "fertile" area for public health efforts via the media.

Traditional media. Several TV shows have engaged in public health efforts, including "Felicity" (date rape), "Friends" (condoms), "ER" (human papillomavirus, emergency contraception) (Figure 4.3a), and "Gray's Anatomy" (HIV-positive pregnancies) (Figure 4.3b) (Strasburger, Wilson, & Jordan, 2014). This is sometimes called "edutainment"—the practice of embedding socially responsible messages into mainstream programming. The effectiveness of these efforts has been evaluated (Folb, 2000; Collins, Elliott, Berry, Kanouse, & Hunter, 2003; Brodie et al., 2001; Rideout, 2008; Romer et al., 2009). A two-part episode on *Felicity* resulted in more than 1,000 calls to a rape crisis hotline immediately after the show aired (Folb, 2000). A 2002 episode of *Friends* concerned condoms, and 27% of a national sample of teens saw the program, nearly half with an adult; and 10% talked about condom efficiency as a result (Collins, Elliott, Berry, Kanouse, & Hunter, 2003). Collaborative efforts between the Kaiser Family Foundation and the producers of the hit shows *ER* and *Grey's Anatomy* resulted in viewers' increased knowledge about the use of emergency contraception, human papillomavirus, and the fact that the perinatal transmission of the HIV virus can usually be successfully prevented (see Figure 4.3) (Brodie et al., 2001; Rideout, 2008; Romer et al., 2009). Thus, the media can successfully educate the public about important public health issues in an entertaining and non-threatening way that does not interfere with any writer's or producer's First Amendment rights.

Other mass media have been employed as well: in North Carolina, billboards were created with the message, "Talk to your kids about sex. Everyone else is." A study of 1,132 parents of adolescents living in the 32 counties covered by the campaign found that exposure to the billboards or a radio or TV public-service announcement (PSA) significantly increased the likelihood of a parent-teen conversation taking place during the following month (Evans, Davis, Umanzor, Patel, & Khan, 2011). And media literacy has been shown to be effective here, too. A Washington state program found that a five-lesson plan targeting 532 middle school students resulted in their being less likely to overestimate sexual activity among their peers and be more aware of sex and sexual imagery in media (Pinkleton, Austin, Cohen, Chen, & Fitzgerald, 2008; Pinkleton, Austin, Chen, & Cohen, 2012).

New / digital media: The Internet could prove to be the best, most efficient sex educator for adolescents (Strasburger & Brown, 2014). Unlike

Impact of TV Show *ER* on Viewer's Health Knowledge and Behavior

Among regular viewers of the TV show *ER*, the percent who say they have...

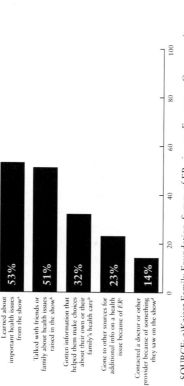

- Learned about important health issues from the show[a] — 53%
- Talked with friends or family about health issues raised in the show[b] — 51%
- Gotten information that helped them make choices about their own or their family's health care[b] — 32%
- Gone to other sources for additional info on a health issue because of *ER*[c] — 23%
- Contacted a doctor or other provider because of something they saw on the show[d] — 14%

SOURCE: a)Kaiser Family Foundation, Survey of ER viewers: Emergency Contraception Pre-show, April 1997; b) Kaiser Family Foundation, Survey of ER Viewers: Emergency Contraception Post-show, April 1997; c) Kaiser Family Foundation, Survey of ER Viewers: Wave 1, September 1997; d) Kaiser Family Foundation, Survey of ER Viewers: Emergency Contraception Post-show, April 1997, Wave 1, September 1997, and Wave 4, May 1998, N=300–500 per survey.

Health Knowledge Gain and Retention from Television

Percent of viewers aware that there is a more than 90% chance a baby will be born without having contracted HIV when an HIV-positive woman receives proper treatment during pregnancy

- 15% — Before *Grey's* episode
- 61% — One week after *Grey's* episode
- 45% — Six week after *Grey's* episode

SOURCE: Kaiser Family Foundation, *Television as a Health Educator: A Case Study of Grey's Anatomy,* September 2008.

Figure 4.3 Two Kaiser Family Foundation studies documenting the effectiveness of TV shows on public health information. Reprinted with permission.

traditional one-semester sex education classes in school, it has the advantage of being available 24/7 throughout a teenager's adolescence and does not need approval from a conservative school board. Many new websites have been developed that provide accurate and responsible sex information to teens (e.g., Bedsider.org and StayTeen.org from The National Campaign to Prevent Teen and Unplanned Pregnancy, Go Ask Alice! and Scarleteen). A new app is entitled "My Sex Doctor" and offers comprehensive sex education in easy-to-understand language (Costello, 2013).

Clinics and state health departments are increasingly using texting to remind patients of appointments and even answer sex-related questions (Jones, Eathington, Baldwin, & Sipsma, 2014; Reed et al., 2014). MTV has pioneered an iPhone app that uses GPS to search for the nearest place that sells condoms (Sniderman, 2011). And health department officials in North Carolina used social networking sites to locate 80% of at-risk individuals during an outbreak of syphilis (Clark-Flory, 2012).

Future research needs to elucidate how much sex information young people actually obtain from new/digital media versus traditional media, how useful new media are in actually changing risky behaviors like sexting and "hooking up," how accurate sex information is on the Web, and whether new media can successfully supplant traditional, school-based sex education programs (Strasburger & Brown, 2014).

DRUGS

Media use has long been associated with an increased risk of substance abuse, particularly smoking and drinking, largely due to the influence of advertising (Smith & Foxcroft, 2009; Morgenstern, Sargent, Isensee, & Hanewinkel, 2013). More recently, viewing scenes of smoking and drinking in mainstream Hollywood movies have been implicated as a major factor in the onset of adolescent substance use (Dalton et al., 2009; Hanewinkel et al., 2014; Hanewinkel & Sargent, 2009).

Traditional media: Public health campaigns have been extremely popular for trying to prevent drug use and abuse. However, their effectiveness remains debatable. The best known efforts have been done by the Partnership for a Drug-Free America (PDFA), the White House Office of National Drug Control Policy (ONDCP), and the Truth campaign (Figure 4.4). Only the Truth campaign has taken on tobacco, however, and there has never been a national campaign to prevent underage or binge drinking (Strasburger, Wilson, & Jordan, 2014). A study of PDFA ads found that more than 80% of nearly 1,000 public school students ages 11 to 19 could recall such ads, and half of the students reported that the ads convinced them to decrease or stop using drugs (Reis, Duggan, Adger, & DeAngelis, 1992). However, a more recent study has questioned the effectiveness of such ads and actually found some evidence for a boomerang effect (Hornik, Jacobsohn, Orwin, Piesse, & Kalton, 2008).

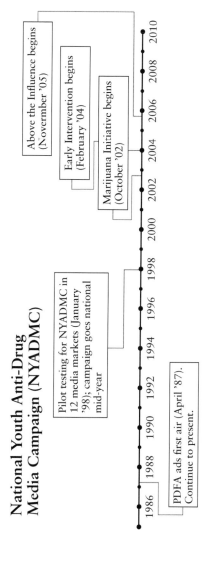

National Youth Anti-Drug
Media Campaign (NYADMC)

Pilot testing for NYADMC in 12 media markets (January '98); campaign goes national mid-year

Above the Influence begins (November '05)

Early Intervention begins (February '04)

Marijuana Initiative begins (October '02)

PDFA ads first air (April '87). Continue to present.

Partnership for a Drug-Free
America (PDFA) Media Campaign

Figure 4.4 National anti-drug campaigns.

As with media violence and sex, media education efforts have been largely successful in dealing with the subject of substance use and abuse among adolescents. Drug Abuse Resistance Education (DARE)—currently used in 70% of school systems around the U.S.—has been shown to be ineffective (Botvin & Griffin, 2005; Pan & Bai, 2009). Instead, a number of more psychologically attuned programs have demonstrated efficacy (Austin & Hust, 2005; Bickham & Slaby, 2012; Kupersmidt, Scull, & Austin, 2010; Pinkleton & Austin, 2013; Primack, Fine, Yang, Wickett, & Zickmund, 2009; Primack & Hobbs, 2009; Weichold, Brambosch, & Silbereisen, 2012). But these programs use media effectively and go far beyond the scare tactics of DARE.

New / digital media: Of all of the health aspects of old and new media, substance use may be the least likely to be influenced by new media compared with traditional media. Concern has focused primarily on the images of kids getting drunk, passing out, or using drugs on social networking sites and how to counteract those images. One correlational study found that compared with teens who spend no time on social networking sites, those who do were five times likelier to use tobacco, three times likelier to use alcohol, and twice as likely to use marijuana (NCASA, 2011). This may reflect the "super-peer" aspect of media (Huang et al., 2014; Strasburger, Jordan, & Donnerstein, 2014). Another, six-month longitudinal study of 1,563 10th grade students in five Southern California high schools found that exposure to friends' online pictures of partying or drinking was significantly associated with both smoking and alcohol use (Huang et al., 2014). Alcohol manufacturers are increasingly using Internet and social media websites to advertise their products (Winpenny, Marteau, & Nolte, 2014). Only one study thus far has tried to reduce adolescents' displays of risky behaviors on social networking websites (Moreno et al., 2009).

Much more longitudinal research is needed to verify the impact of social profiles on young adolescents' drinking and smoking behavior. In addition, knowing whether social networking sites can be harnessed to counteract depictions of risky behaviors in social networking profiles would be tremendously useful. Spending on Internet advertising is likely to continue, but there are virtually no data on the reach or the impact of such advertising on young people.

OBESITY

Obesity is not just a major public health issue in the United States, where one-third of children and teens are now obese or overweight (Cunningham, Kramer, & Venkat Narayan, 2014; Skinner & Skelton, 2014). It has become a worldwide problem, with rates increasing dramatically in nearly every country (Guthold, Cowan, Autenrieth, Kahn, & Riley, 2010; Ng et al., 2014). As rates of teen pregnancy continue to decrease internationally, and rates of substance use remain stable, obesity has now become the most urgent public health problem in the world.

Traditional media: Media research is clear that traditional media play an important role in the etiology of obesity (Council on Communications & Media, 2011; Hingle & Kunkel, 2012; Jordan, Kramer-Golinkoff & Strasburger, 2008). What is not so clear is the mechanism (Strasburger, Jordan, & Donnerstein, 2012): Is it the displacement effect of seven hours of media per day that minimizes physical activity (Guthold, Cowan, Autenrieth, Kahn, & Riley, 2010)? Is it the impact of the 5,000 ads on TV mostly for junk food or fast food that children see annually (Dembek, Harris, & Schwartz, 2012)? Is it the fact that more calories are consumed snacking while watching TV (Blass et al., 2006)? Or is it the impact of TV-viewing on sleep (Zimmerman, 2008)? The answer is that it is probably all of the above in combination, yet which factor predominates may vary from individual to individual.

New / digital media: New media may be contributing to childhood and adolescent obesity as well (Figure 4.5). Advergames—online games that are really surreptitious ads—are common: a study of the top five brands of food and beverages found that 63% had advergames and half used cartoon characters (Weber, Story, & Harnack, 2006). Advergames are online video games with a subtle or overt commercial message. For example, Candystand.com features dozens of candy-related games including Gummi Grab (involving Gummi Bears) and Match Maker (involving Life Savers). Children playing these games are exposed to multiple images of very attractive candy, which could easily help to build brand loyalty. There are currently nearly 150 websites that use advergames to market foods with low nutritional value to young children (Weatherspoon et al., 2013). Between July 2009 and June 2010, there were 3.4 billion food advertisements displayed on kids' websites and two-thirds were for breakfast cereals or fast food (Ustjanauskas, Harris, & Schwartz, 2013). In 2009, food companies spent nearly $2 billion on online, mobile, and viral marketing to children and teens (Federal Trade Commission, 2012). Research shows that it is highly unlikely that self-regulation by the food industry will lead to any significant improvement in this situation (Dembek, Harris, & Schwartz, 2012; Kunkel, Castonguay, & Filer, 2014).

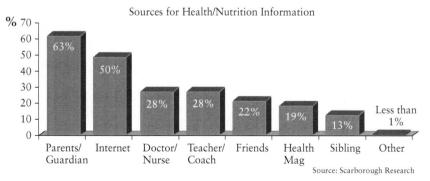

Figure 4.5 The Internet ranks 2nd only to parents as a source of nutritional information for children and adolescents.

As a means to counter the impact of online ads and advergames, public health campaigns have been tried and may or may not be effective (Jordan, Piotrowski, Bleakley, & Mallya, 2012). The Center for Disease Control created a campaign called VERB that used social marketing to "apply commercial marketing strategies to influence the voluntary behavior of target audiences to improve personal and social welfare" (VERB, 2010). The campaign spent $59 million on slick ads that portrayed exercise as being "cool" and resulted in a 30% increase in exercise among the preteens who saw it; but the federally-funded campaign was cut by the Bush administration in 2006 (Neergaard, 2006). Other campaigns in Atlanta and New York (see Figure 4.6) have been more controversial while also yielding fewer empirical results. It may be that rather than using "scare tactics," simply educating the public about the risk of overweight and obesity leading to diabetes will be most successful (Jordan, Piotrowski, Bleakley, & Mallya, 2012). When it comes to digital media campaigns, social media interventions have also been tried, but thus far have not demonstrated significant changes in either physical activity or weight (Williams, Hamm, Shulhan, Vandermeer, & Hartling, 2014).

Figure 4.6 Some observers have labeled this ad as "scare" tactics from a recent Atlanta anti-obesity campaign.

The exciting new development in this area is the use of prosocial, exercise-related video games to keep children fit. Popular video games like Dance Dance Revolution (NICE!) are increasingly being used to encourage exercise at home and treat or avoid obesity, and an increasing number of studies seems to be documenting at least some effectiveness (Bailey & McInnis, 2011; Ellis, 2007; Harrison, 2014; Lanningham-Foster, 2006; Trost, Sundal, Foster, Lent , & Vojta, 2014).

Solutions. Public health problems are typically multifactorial in origin. Therefore, solutions need to be multifactorial as well (e.g., media producers, the federal government, educators, administrators, parents, and activists). While it would be ideal for the entertainment industry to produce healthier, less violent, less sexually suggestive and graphic TV and movies, that is not likely to happen in the foreseeable future. With so much profit at stake, entertainment writers, producers, and directors are often quick to assert their First Amendment rights. The federal government could certainly do a lot more to initiate and/or fund public health campaigns and media research while simultaneously providing and enforcing regulatory measures to restrict alcohol advertising and ban food advertising aimed at young children. A possible 2017 National Institutes of Mental Health comprehensive report on media—similar to the 1982 report (Pearl, 1982)—would be most welcome but would need to be funded. Finally, media producers constantly try to shift the blame for any negative media effects onto parents, even though parents are incredibly busy and overburdened, and should not have to continuously police media content. Notwithstanding, parents *can* observe the American Academy of Pediatrics' media guidelines to (AAP, 2013):

- Avoid screen time for babies < 2 years old.
- Limit total entertainment screen time to < 2 hours/day.
- Co-view and discuss content with your child or teenager.
- Avoid allowing technology (e.g., TV, Internet connection, cell phone) in a child's or teen's bedroom.

WHAT ROLE SHOULD PEDIATRICIANS PLAY?

The American Academy of Pediatrics has had a long-standing interest in elucidating the effects—both positive and negative—of media on children and adolescents. In 2010, it issued a policy statement on Media Education in which it urged its 62,000 members to ask two media-related questions at every well-child and well-adolescent visit (Council on Communications and Media, 2010):

1 How much entertainment media is the child or adolescent watching per day?
2 Is there a TV set or Internet access in the child's or adolescent's bedroom?

In addition, it strongly supports teaching children and teens media literacy and has urged Congress to consider mandating and funding universal media education in U.S. schools.

WHAT ROLE SHOULD SCHOOLS PLAY?

Media education has been shown to be effective in "immunizing" children and teens against advertising, decreasing aggressive behavior, decreasing substance use, and increasing sexual knowledge (Council on Communications & Media, 2010; McCannon, 2014). Most Western countries—aside from the U.S.—either mandate media literacy education in schools or strongly encourage it (Beach & Baker, 2011). Unfortunately, without standardized curricula, U.S. public schools remain subjected to political pressures aimed at increasing performance standards. In this culture of standardized tests and high stakes assessments, comprehensive media and health education, such as effective drug prevention and/or sex education programs, remain marginalized (Bruckner et al., 2014; Strasburger, 2012b). The inevitable result is that the U.S. has the highest rates of teen pregnancy, obesity, and substance use in the world.

A century ago, to be literate meant that a person could read and write. In 2015, to be literate means a person can read, write, download, text, tweet, and be able to sift through the extraordinary amount of information available online while left to separate accurate information from the inaccurate. In the rush to adopt digital technology, many schools and administrators believe that if they simply make new online tools available to their students, then they will provide students with a leg-up in the competitive marketplace. Instead, what new technology has done is to shift the basic paradigm of learning from acquiring information—which can now be done almost instantaneously with the use of electronic devices—to assessing information through critical thinking skills. Rote memorization (other than, perhaps, multiplication tables) should be a thing of the past. Instead, students should be taught how to use new technology wisely and analyze the information so easily available to them.

Both traditional media and new digital media have great potential for increasing media literacy in children and adolescents. As previously mentioned, in a study of 51 media literacy interventions over the past three decades, researchers found that such programs were generally effective (Jeong, Cho, & Hwang, 2012). Knowledge, criticism, perceived realism, behavior beliefs, attitudes, and even behavior were affected. Although media literacy efforts have been criticized for being ineffective against risky behaviors (e.g., violence, smoking, underage drinking), this meta-analysis found that media literacy interventions actually may be effective in reducing potentially harmful media messages. The interventions studied were primarily using traditional media, but the authors commented, "Media literacy interventions [are] particularly important with the development of social media because the quality of information circulated through social media (e.g., Twitter) is not guaranteed, and thus, audiences' literacy has become more important than ever." In the future, a combination of traditional and newer media in media literacy programs could prove a powerful weapon in moderating harmful media effects and improving public health in crucial areas like violence, risky sexual behaviors, childhood and adolescent obesity, and underage drinking.

REFERENCES

Austin, E. W., & Hust, S. J. T. (2005). Targeting adolescents? The content and frequency of alcoholic and nonalcoholic beverage ads in magazine and video formats. November 1999–April 2000. *Journal of Health Communication, 10,* 769–785.

Bailey, B. W., & McInnis, K. (2011). Energy cost of exergaming. *Archives of Pediatrics and Adolescent Medicine, 165,* 597–602.

Beach, R., & Baker, F. (2011). Why core standards must embrace media literacy. *Education Week.* Available at: http://www.edweek.org/ew/articles/2011/06/22/36baker.h30.html.

Bickham, D. S., & Slaby, R. G. (2012). Effects of a media literacy program in the US on children's critical evaluation of unhealthy media messages about violence, smoking, and food. *Journal of Children and Media, 6,* 255–271.

Blass, E. M., Anderson, D. R., Kirkorian, H. L., et al. (2006). On the road to obesity: television viewing increases intake of high-density foods. *Physiology & Behavior, 88,* 597–604.

Botvin, G. J., & Griffin, K. W. (2005). Models of prevention: School-based programs. In J. H. Lowinson, P. Ruiz, R. B. Millman, & J. G. Langrod (Eds.), *Substance abuse: A comprehensive textbook,* 4th ed. (pp. 1211–1229). Philadelphia, PA: Lippincott Williams & Wilkins.

Brodie, M., Foehr, U., Rideout, V., Baer, N., Miller, C., Flournoy, R., & Altman, D. (2001). Communicating health information through the entertainment media. *Health Affairs, 20,* 1–8.

Brown, Governor of California, et al. v Entertainment Merchants Association, et al. No. 08–1448. (2010). Argued November 2, 2010. Decided June 27, 2011. http://www.supremecourt.gov/opinions/10pdf/08-1448.pdf.

Bruckner, T. A., Domina, T., Hwang, J. K., et al. (2014). State-level education standards for substance use prevention programs in schools: a systematic content analysis. *Journal of Adolescent Health, 54,* 467–473.

Clark-Flory, T. (2012, April 1). Facebook: The next tool in fighting STDs. *Salon.* Retrieved from http://www.salon.com/2012/04/01/facebook_the_next_tool_in_fighting_stds.

Collins, R. L., Elliott, M. N., Berry, S. H., Kanouse, E., & Hunter, S. B. (2003). Entertainment television as a healthy sex educator: The impact of condom-efficacy information in an episode of *Friends. Pediatrics, 112,* 1115–1121.

Common Sense Media (2008). *The impact of media on child and adolescent health.* San Francisco, CA: Common Sense Media.

Costello, K. (2013, October 8). My Sex Doctor: a new app for sex education. Available at: http://www.dailycampus.com/news/view.php/284003/My-Sex-Doctor-A-new-app-for-sex-education.

Council on Communications and Media. (2009). Media violence (policy statement). *Pediatrics, 124,* 1495–1503.

Council on Communications and Media. (2010). Media education (policy statement). *Pediatrics, 126,* 1012–1017.

Council on Communications and Media. (2011). Children, adolescents, obesity, and the media (policy statement). *Pediatrics, 128,* 201–208.

Council on Injury, Violence and Poison Prevention Executive Committee. (2012). Firearm-related injuries affecting the pediatric population (policy statement). *Pediatrics, 130,* e1416–e1423.

Cunningham, S. A., Kramer, M. R., & Venkat Narayan, K. M. (2014). Incidence of childhood obesity in the United States. *New England Journal of Medicine, 370,* 403–411.

Dalton, M. A., Beach, M. L., Adachi-Mejia, A. M., et al. (2009). Early exposure to movie smoking predicts established smoking by older teens and young adults. *Pediatrics, 123,* e551–e558.

Dembek, C., Harris, J. L., & Schwartz, M. B. (2012). *Trends in television food advertising to young people.* New Haven, CT: Yale Rudd Center.

Donnerstein, E. (2014). The Internet. In V. C. Strasburger, B. J. Wilson, & A. B. Jordan, *Children,adolescents, and the media* (3rd ed.) (pp. 401–434). Los Angeles: Sage.

Ellis J. (2007, February 21). New DVD game battles childhood obesity. Available at http://content.usatoday.com/topics/topic/Col%20Estorol.

Evans, W. D., Davis, K. C., Umanzor, C., Patel, K., & Khan, M. (2011). Evaluation of sexual communication message strategies. *Reproductive Health, 8,* 15.

Federal Trade Commission. (2012). A review of food marketing to children and adolescents. Washington, DC: FTC.

Fingar, K. R., & Jolls, T. (2014). Evaluation of a school-based violence prevention media literacy curriculum. *Injury Prevention, 20,* 183–190.

Folb, K. L. (2000). "Don't touch that dial!" TV as a—what!?—positive influence. *SIECUS Report, 28,* 16–18.

Gerbner, G., & Morgan, M. (2002). *Against the Mainstream: The Selected Works of George Gerbner.* New York: Peter Lang Publishers.

Guthold, R., Cowan, M. J., Autenrieth, C. S., Kahn, L., & Riley, L. M. (2010). Physical activity and sedentary behavior among schoolchildren: A 34-country comparison. *Journal of Pediatrics, 157,* 43–49.

Hanewinkel, R., Sargent, J. D., Hunt, K., et al. (2014). Portrayal of alcohol consumption in movies and drinking initiation in low-risk adolescents. *Pediatrics, 133,* 1–10.

Hanewinkel, R., & Sargent, J.D. (2009). Longitudinal study of exposure to entertainment media and alcohol use among German adolescents. *Pediatrics, 123,* 989–995.

Harrison, L. (2014, June 4). Video games can improve fitness. Available at http://www.medscape.com/viewarticle/826170.

Hingle, M., & Kunkel, D. (2012). Childhood obesity and the media. *Pediatric Clinics of North America, 59,* 677–692.

Hornik, R., Jacobsohn, L., Orwin, R., Piesse, A. N., & Kalton, G. (2008). Effects of the National Youth Anti-Drug Media Campaign on youths. *American Journal of Public Health*, *98*, 2229–2236.

Huang, G. C., Unger, J. B., Soto, D., Fujimoto, K., Pentz, M. A., Jordan-Marsh, M., & Valente, T. W. (2014). Peer influences: The impact of online and offline friendship networks on adolescent smoking and alcohol use. *J Adolescent Health*, *54*, 508–514.

Huesmann, L. R., Eron, L. D., Klein, R., Brice, P., & Fischer, P. (1983). Mitigating the imitation of aggressive behaviors by changing children's attitudes about media violence. *Journal of Personality & Social Psychology*, *44*, 899–910.

Jeong, S., Cho, H., & Hwang, Y. (2012). Media literacy interventions: A meta-analytic review. *Journal of Communication*, *62*(3), 454–472.

Jones, K., Eathington, P., Baldwin, K., & Sipsma, H. (2014). The impact of health education transmitted via social media or text messaging on adolescent and young adult risky sexual behavior: A systematic review of the literature. *Sexually Transmitted Diseases*, *41*, 413–419.

Jordan, A., Kramer-Golinkoff , E., & Strasburger, V. (2008). Do the media cause obesity & eating disorders? *Adolescent Medicine: State of the Art Reviews*, *19*, 431–449.

Jordan, A., Piotrowski, J. T., Bleakley, A., & Mallya, G. (2012). Developing media interventions to reduce household sugar-sweetened beverage consumption. *Annals of the American Academy of Political and Social Science*, *640*, 118–135.

Kunkel, D., Castonguay, J., & Filer, C. (2014, May). Evaluating industry self-regulation of food marketing to children: A longitudinal study. Presented at the annual conference of the International Communication Association, Seattle, WA.

Kupersmidt, J. B., Scull, T. M., & Austin, E. W. (2010). Media literacy education for elementary school substance use prevention: Study of Media Detective. *Pediatrics*, *126*, 525–531.

Lanningham-Foster, L., Jensen, T.B., Foster, R.C., et al. (2006). Energy expenditure of sedentary screen time compared with active screen time for children. *Pediatrics*, *118*, e1831–e1835.

Lenhart, A. (2014). Teens & technology: Understanding the digital landscape. Pew Research Internet Project. Available at http://www.pewinternet.org/2014/02/25/teens-technology-understanding-the-digital-landscape/.

McCannon B. (2014). Media literacy/media education: Solution to big media? A review of the literature. In V. C. Strasburger, B. J. Wilson, & A. B. Jordan. *Children, adolescents, and the media* (3rd ed.) (pp. 507–558). Thousand Oaks (CA): Sage.

Media Violence Commission, International Society for Research on Aggression (ISRA). (2012). *Aggressive Behavior*, 38, 335–341.

Moreno, M. A., VanderStoep, A., Parks, M. R., Zimmerman, F. J., Kurth, A., & Christakis, D. A. (2009). Reducing at-risk adolescents' display of risk behavior on a social networking Web site. *Archives of Pediatrics and Adolescent Medicine*, *163*, 35–41.

Morgenstern, M., Sargent, J. D., Isensee, B., & Hanewinkel, R. (2013). From never to daily smoking in 30 months: The predictive value of tobacco and non-tobacco advertising exposure. *BMJ Open*, *3*, 6.

National Center on Addiction and Substance Abuse at Columbia University. (2011). *Adolescent substance use: America's #1 public health problem.* New York, NY: Author.

Neergaard, L. (2006, September 14). Obese kids not getting right help. *Albuquerque Journal*, p. A6.

Ng, M., Fleming T., Robinson, M., et al. (2014). Global, regional, and national prevalence of overweight and obesity in children and adults during 1980–2013: a systematic analysis for the Global Burdens of Disease Study 2013. *Lancet*. Published online May 29. Available at: http://www.thelancet.com/journals/lancet/article/PIIS0140-6736(14)60460-8/abstract.

Pan, W., & Bai, H. (2009). A multivariate approach to a meta-analytic review of the effectiveness of the D.A.R.E. program. *International Journal of Environmental Research and Public Health*, 6, 267–277.

Pearl, D., Bouthilet, L., & Lazar, J. (1982). *Television and behavior: Ten years of scientific progress and implications for the eighties*. Rockville, MD: National Institute of Mental Health.

Pinkleton, B. E., & Austin, E. W. (2014). Young people's attitudes and decision making concerning tobacco and tobacco-use prevention advertising. In: Esrock, S.L., Walker, K.L., & Hart, J. L. (eds.). *Talking Tobacco*. New York: Peter Lang, pp. 157–171.

Pinkleton, B. E., Austin, E. W., Cohen, M., Chen, Y.-C., & Fitzgerald, E. (2008). Effects of a peer-led media literacy curriculum on adolescents' knowledge and attitudes toward sexual behavior and media portrayals of sex. *Health Communication*, 23, 462–472.

Pinkleton, B. E., Austin, E. W., Chen, Y., & Cohen, M. (2012). The role of media literacy in shaping adolescents' understanding of and responses to sexual portrayals in mass media. *Journal of Health Communication*, 17, 460–476.

Primack, B. A., Fine, D., Yang, C. K., Wickett, D., & Zickmund, S. (2009). Adolescents' impressions of antismoking media literacy education: Qualitative results from a randomized controlled trial. *Health Education Research*, 24, 608–621.

Primack, B. A., & Hobbs, R. (2009). Association of various components of media literacy and adolescent smoking. *American Journal of Health Behavior*, 33, 192–201.

Reed, J. L., Huppert, J. S., Taylor, R. G., et al. (2014). Improving sexually transmitted infection results notification via mobile phone technology. *Journal of Adolescent Health*. Published online June 23. Available at: http://www.jahonline.org/article/S1054-139X(14)00221-3/abstract.

Reis, E. C., Duggan, A. K., Adger, H., & DeAngelis, C. (1992). The impact of anti-drug advertising on youth substance abuse [Abstract]. *American Journal of Diseases of Children*, 146, 519.

Rideout, V. *Television as a health educator: A case study of* Grey's Anatomy. Menlo Park, CA: Kaiser Family Foundation, 2008.

Rideout, V. J., Foehr, U. G., & Roberts, D. F. (2010). *Generation M²: Media in the lives of 8- to 18-year-olds*. Menlo Park, CA: Kaiser Family Foundation.

Romer, D., Sznitman, S., DiClemente, R., Salazar, L. F., Vanable, P. A., Carey, M. P., Juzang, I. (2009). Mass media as an HIV-prevention strategy: Using culturally sensitive messages to reduce HIV-associated sexual behavior of at-risk African American youth. *American Journal of Public Health*, 99, 2150–2159.

Selkie, E., & Kota, R. (2014). Cyberbullying and online harassment in adolescents. *Adolescent Medicine: State of the Art Reviews*, 25, 564–573.

Skinner, A. C., & Skelton, J. A. (2014). Prevalence and trends in obesity and severe obesity among children in the United States, 1999–2012. *JAMA Pediatrics*, *168*, 561–566.

Smith, L. A., & Foxcroft, D. R. (2009). The effect of alcohol advertising, marketing and portrayal on drinking behaviour in young people: Systematic review of prospective cohort studies. *BMC PublicHealth*, *9*, 51.

Sniderman, Z. (2011, August 11). MTV app locates places to get condoms. *Mashable Social Media*. Retrieved from http://mashable.com/2011/08/09/mtv-condom-app/.

Strasburger, V. C. (2012a). Adolescents, sex, & the media. *Adolescent Medicine: State of the Art Reviews*, *23*, 15–33.

Strasburger, V. C. (2012b). School daze: Why are teachers and schools missing the boat on media? *Pediatric Clinics of North America*, *59*, 705–716.

Strasburger, V. C. (2014). Media matter—But "old" media may matter more than "new" media. *Adolescent Medicine: State of the Art Reviews*, *25*, 643–669.

Strasburger, V.C., & Brown, S. (2014). Sex ed in the 21st century. *Journal of the American Medical Association*, *312*, 125–126.

Strasburger, V. C., Donnerstein E., & Bushman, B. (2014). Why is it so hard to believe that media influence children and adolescents? *Pediatrics*, *133*, 571–573.

Strasburger, V. C., Jordan, A. B., & Donnerstein E. (2012). Children, adolescents, and the media: Health effects. *Pediatric Clinics of North America*, *59*, 533–588.

Strasburger, V. C., & Wilson, B. J. (2014). Television violence: 60 years of research. In D.A. Gentile (Ed.), *Media violence and children*. Westport, CT: Praeger, pp. 135–178.

Strasburger, V. C., Wilson, B. J., & Jordan, A. B. (2014). *Children, adolescents, and the media* (3rd ed.). Los Angeles, CA: Sage.

Trost, S. G., Sundal, D., Foster, G. D., Lent, M. R., & Vojta, D. (2014). Effects of a pediatric weight management program with and without active video games: a randomized trial. *JAMA Pediatrics*, *168*, 407–413.

Ustjanauskas, A. E., Harris, J. L., & Schwartz, M. B. (2013). Food and beverage advertising on children's web sites. *Pediatric Obesity*, published online July 2. doi: 10.1111/j.2047-6310.2013.00185.x.

Weber, K., Story, M., & Harnack, L. (2006). Internet food marketing strategies aimed at children and adolescents: A content analysis of food and beverage brand Web sites. *Journal of the American Dietetic Association*, *106*, 1463–1466.

Weichold, K., Brambosch, A., & Silbereisen, R. K. (2012). Do girls profit more? Gender-specific effectiveness of a life skills program against alcohol consumption in early adolescence. *Journal of Early Adolescence*, *32*, 200–225.

Weatherspoon, L. J., Quilliam, E. T., Paek, H-J., et al. (2013). Consistency of nutrition recommendations for foods marketed to children in the United States, 2009–2010. *Preventing Chronic Disease*, *10*, 130099.

Williams, G., Hamm, M.P., Shulhan, J., Vandermeer, B., & Hartling, L. (2014). Social media interventions for diet and exercise behaviours: A systematic review and meta-analysis of randomized controlled trials. *BMJ Open*, *4*, e003926.

Wilson, B. J., Linz, D., Federman, J., Smith, S., Paul, B., Nathanson, A., Donnerstein, E., & Lingsweiler, R. (1999). *The choices and consequences evaluation: A study of Court TV's anti-violence curriculum*. Santa Barbara, CA: Center for Communication and Social Policy, University of California.

Winpenny, E .M., Marteau, T. M., & Nolte, E. (2014). Exposure of children and adolescents to alcohol marketing on social media websites. *Alcohol and Alcoholism*, *49*, 154–159.

Wright, P. J., & Donnerstein, E. (2014). Sex online: Pornography, sexual solicitation, and sexting. *Adolescent Medicine: State of the Art Reviews*, *25*, 574–589.

Yager, A. M., & O'Keefe, C. (2012). Adolescent use of social networking to gain sexual health information. *The Journal of Nurse Practitioners*, *8*, 294–298.

Ybarra, M. L., Strasburger, V. C., & Mitchell, K. J. (2014). Sexual media exposure and sexual behavior and victimization in a national survey of adolescents. *Clinical Pediatrics*; *53*, 1239–1247.

Zimmerman, F. J. (2008). *Children's media use and sleep problems: Issues and unanswered questions*. Menlo Park, CA: Kaiser Family Foundation.

5 Parenting the Connected Generation

Raising Your Children in a Digital Age

Elaine Young

*Excerpts have been taken from Tuned-In Family: How to Cope, Communicate, and Connect in a Digital Age, *by Dr. Elaine Young, April 2014.*

INTRODUCTION

There are many challenges parents and families face when it comes to raising children in the digital age. As the result of living in an ever more connected world, it is often assumed that young children are naturally digitally savvy just because they were born into a world where technology is ubiquitous. Yet, the truth is that children need parents, adults, and teachers now, more than ever, to help them sort out the implications of these tools, learn how to balance "screen time," cope with technological innovation, and approach digital technologies with a healthy attitude.

We are now living in a digital age where we are becoming a "connected" generation. We are in a time when over 90% of U.S. children have an online presence created for them by the time they are 2 years old (Solis, 2012), and 7.5 million Facebook users are under the age of 13 (Martin, 2013). Moreover, the Pew Research Internet Project finds that, by 2025, "the Internet will become 'like electricity'—less visible, yet more deeply embedded in people's lives for good and ill" (Anderson & Raine, 2014). Regardless of age, we have to adapt to a society that is growing more connected, where digital technologies are not only transforming our daily lives; they are disrupting integral business models such as publishing and entertainment in ways we are just beginning to understand (Anderson & Raine, 2014).

Such vast changes in the digital age require parents, schools, and communities to help children learn how to function in a society that is not only different from the one of our own childhood, but different from what it was two years ago, two months ago, even two weeks ago. Digital media are ever changing, thereby challenging us to continually learn new apps and skills for effective communication. In unique ways, parents, children, schools, families, and communities are all affected by the impact of the digital media revolution (Young, 2014).

The first step toward understanding the impact of digital media on a family is to set the context for what it means to be raising children in a digital age. What follows is a set of brief guidelines, based on the advice provided in *Tuned-In Family* (Young, 2014), to help families with children of any age balance the benefits of technology innovation, without sacrificing individual family values and beliefs.

THE DIGITAL AGE AND WHAT IT MEANS FOR FAMILIES

Many adults compare their children's childhood to their own. They look back with nostalgia on their own childhoods as they worry and wonder about the complexities of a childhood so different from their own. This so-called "yearning for yesterday" (Davis, 1979) is a sociological phenomenon that emphasizes the power of nostalgia and its connection to the context of current fears and concerns. In today's digitally mediated society, it is no wonder that parents look to the past to frame the vision of what they want their children to experience. When today's communication technology enables real time communication and feedback and digital tools like iPads and mobile phones, as well as social apps, and toys that are connected to the Internet, it is clearly evident that today's children are not experiencing the same childhoods that their parents experienced.

In surveys of over 50 parents and informal interviews with parents, teens, and young adults conducted summer and fall 2012 for the writing of *Tuned-In Family*, parents revealed the challenges they are having as they try to find an appropriate balance of technology access for their children. They want to allow access to technology with the knowledge that, in today's society, to not have access could be a detriment as a child travels through school and into his or her own professional life. At the same time, parents also want their children to know what it is like to be "technology free", to spend a day disconnected, away from screens, immersing themselves in outdoor play, or social situations that are not mediated by technology. As mediated technology continues to evolve and becomes even more woven into individuals' daily lives, it is becoming harder for many families to pull their children away from their digital connections, or to find what they feel to be the right balance between mediated and non-mediated time. Experts agree. As Amy Jo Martin, a noted professional in social media, writes, "The way your kids use social today will shape their future. It's time for everyone to get educated on how—and how not—to live online" (Martin, 2013). At the same time, the Pew Internet and American Life Project highlights how teens have changed their Internet use "from stationary connections tied to shared desktops in the home to always-on connections that move with them throughout the day" (Madden et al., 2013). In their recent 2013 study on Children's Media Use in America, Common Sense Media finds that young children's mobile use has gone up dramatically since 2011, with time on mobile devices tripling. They also found that while kids' time with traditional screen media is down, TV still dominates many children's media time (Zero to Eight, 2013).

At the same time, schools are faced with an increasingly challenging situation to balance budgets, train teachers, and manage how technology continues to impact children in and out of the classroom. The nonprofit Educational Consortium EduCause (www.educause.edu), which publishes the Horizon Report on an annual basis, highlights a set of technology and digital trends for education levels K-12. Among the many challenges facing our educational system, and therefore our families, are the fact that:

- Educational paradigms now include online, hybrid and collaborative learning models.
- Social media is changing how people interact, present their ideas and information and communicate.
- As technology costs lower, and schools update their technology and access policies, more students are bringing their own mobile devices to school (Johnson et al., 2013).

Educational trends for 2014 and beyond include the increase of Bring Your Own Devices (BYOD) and cloud computing as well as adding games and gamification to learning approaches, and an increasing reliance by administrators on "learning analytics"(Johnson et al., 2014). These vast changes in the classroom, along with the overall concern of the impact of "screen time" on childhood development, (Rosin, 2013) serve to further highlight the tension family's face when negotiating digital technology use for their children. While each family's experience is unique, these trends highlight the challenge of parenting and educating in a digital age.

WHAT CAN A FAMILY DO?

Coping with the evolving nature of technology tools, and the growing social media network of content that can be placed online about families and children may not be easy, but there are things that every family can do. To better understand this landscape, current usage trends and individual experiences, provide insight. Some call it a "digital footprint" (Madden, et al. 2007) which in actuality is more passive than focusing more on "digital identity" (Young, 2014). A footprint is what is left behind by any action a user takes online, while an identity is more intentional and is something that individuals create and project about themselves online. "We have the ability to represent multiple identities across both offline and online environments" (Emanuel & Stanton Fraser, 2014). From large social networks such as Facebook and YouTube, to microblogging tools such as Twitter, to individual message sharing applications such as SnapChat, there are an increasing number of ways in which to create and share content in an online environment. As individuals create and share content, they become increasingly "findable" or, as PewResearch Internet Project Digital

Footprints report explains, "knowable" (Madden et al., 2007). As Martin (2013) explains, what a third grader posts today on Facebook and Instagram could impact him or her later when applying for college or jobs: "Everything they've posted online for the past decade is searchable, and social media only amplifies what already exists, both strengths and weaknesses."

In order for families to best address these mediated communication challenges, I recommend building a genuine learning community within the family. Rather than address technology issues with fear, anger, and frustration, it is important to capitalize on the knowledge base of the whole family, including the children, and to agree to learn and teach one another. While much has been written about "digital natives" vs. "digital immigrants" (Prensky, 2001), the fact remains that regardless of when they were born, or what experiences they have, today's families are all becoming part of Generation C (Solis, 2012). Generation C refers not to a specific demographic, but rather a group of individuals who have similar behaviors. As Solis (2012) explains Generation C, "is how people embrace technology, from social networks to smartphones to intelligent appliances, that contributes to the digital lifestyle." As such, when analyzed within a familial context, every member of the family has to learn how to cope and manage the best ways to deal with the integration of digital technologies into their lives.

In order to help address the challenges that come with digital media, families can enact a comprehensive media integration plan using the following steps:

1 Develop a family "Technology Philosophy"
2 Take a "Technology Inventory"
3 Agree to a "Content Sharing Plan"
4 Create an "Access Plan"
5 Set family "Ground Rules"

DEVELOPING A TECHNOLOGY PHILOSOPHY

A technology philosophy is a framework for families to use to help them navigate the challenges and opportunities that come from engaging in a digitally connected society. I developed this framework based on results of over 50 parent and young adult surveys and informal interviews conducted in 2012 for *Tuned-in Family*. The responses helped build the framework and guiding principles for families as they integrated digital technologies into their lives. The recommendations that I provide serve as the starting place for digital usage by grounding them in a family's unique values, beliefs, and culture. While further study should be conducted about the effectiveness of such approaches, this framework was developed specifically to provide families with a guided approach to come together to discuss what they each believe and value about digital technologies. Articulating a technology philosophy has the potential to help each family member acknowledge their overall attitude toward technology in the home and set a baseline that allows the framing of positive and productive conversations within the family unit. At the same time, it provides the needed flexibility to allow for adjustment and changes as technology continues to evolve.

An important place to begin a technology philosophy is for each individual in the family to assess their comfort level with technology and how they use technology on a daily basis. One tool that can help with this assessment is the Social Technographics ladder, developed by Forrester Research to help classify how individuals utilize digital communication tools (Bernoff, 2010). Within each echelon, analyst Josh Bernoff breaks down social media activities into seven different areas:

- Creators: people who publish blogs, upload videos and/or music, and post articles and stories.
- Conversationalists: people who posts status updates and share content via social network sites such as Facebook or Twitter.
- Critics: individuals who like to post reviews and ratings, comment on blogs, and contribute to online forums.
- Collectors: people who gather information from different news websites.
- Joiners: individuals who join social networking sites, mostly to read content, not post or engage a lot.
- Spectators: people who consume information but don't create online content.
- Inactives: individuals who do not use digital communication tools.

Based on these various echelons of online engagement, each family member should be encouraged to answer specific questions about themselves and to have a conversation as a family (Young, 2014).

- Where does each family member fall on the "Technographics Ladder"? How does that impact your attitude about online communication tools?
- Are you a family that is open to technological change? If parents are comfortable with changes, but tweens in the household aren't, how will you address this?
- Are you more conservative in your approach to allowing new technologies in the home? What happens if your child has a strong technological aptitude? How will you foster this while still being true to your family values?
- Are you education-centric and want just educational applications in your home? If so, how will you compromise with the gamer in the family?
- Are you concerned about privacy and security? How will you all agree on content that you will share, or not share? How will the impact family passwords or virus protection software, to name only two examples?

Here are some examples of technology philosophies listed in *Tuned-In Family* (Young, 2014) that provide an idea of how this can work.

As a family, we believe that technology:

- Is an important part of our daily lives. It makes things more convenient, is a big part of our entertainment, and helps us to stay connected. As a family we respect that each of us has a different comfort level with technology and, because we respect each other, we agree to ask permission before posting content about the family on open social networks. We will respect the importance of health and wellness and set guidelines that will help us all use technology wisely. We will share our knowledge with each other because technology always changes.
- While ubiquitous, technology should be managed carefully. We believe that all things should be balanced and come in moderation, and that technology is a tool that can help us get things done, but it should not be the focus of our lives. Screen time in all things will be limited, boundaries will emphasize the importance of face-to-face family time, and we will evaluate new technologies carefully.
- Helps us stay connected, have fun, and makes our lives easier and even more engaging. We will explore new technologies together as a family and evaluate each one as a unique learning opportunity. We'll set rules along the way, as we discover how each tool adds value to the individuals within the family or the whole family.

Once a family has developed their Technology Philosophy, it can provide a clear guide for future decisions for all family members. While designed to be a starting point, it is recommended that, as the family unit changes and as technology changes, the technology philosophy needs to be revisited and adjusted as necessary. The strength of any family technology usage plan comes from this philosophy, which is designed to be the foundation for negotiating all behavioral practices, from ground rules to solving disputes about technology use.

THE TECHNOLOGY INVENTORY

Digital technology and social networking sites have been around for a very long time. As early as 1997, the pioneering website SixDegrees.com emerged as a harbinger of social media sites to come, even though it was quickly surpassed by other startups after four years. From MySpace, to Friendster, to more popular and current social networks such as Facebook and Twitter, online social sharing sites have proliferated (boyd & Ellison, 2007). In fact, at any given time, an individual can be connected to ten or more online sites, with that many profiles. According to recent data from PewResearch, 74% of online adults are using social networking sites (Social Networking Fact Sheet, 2013). In *Tuned-In Family*, I recommend that the adults and teens in the family take some time to conduct what I have called a "Technology Inventory." This provides an opportunity for individuals to take stock of the different online tools they use every day, to consider carefully the purpose of each tool, and which tools are the most appropriate for sharing information and content about the family. The following worksheet is intended to help families conduct their Technology Inventory (Young, 2014).

Table 5.1

Our Family Social Media and Technology Inventory			
Website/Tool	Purpose	Person category	Notes
Facebook	*Information sharing, connecting with family and friends, entertainment, fun*	*family friends, current and former students, professional connections*	*use for both personal and professinal Careful to segment status updates prior to posting.*

The goal for filling out the form is designed to get each family member to become very aware of all the social and online tools they are using. Once completed the intent is that the adults in the family will have a much clearer picture of the value of each online tool they are using and how it can support, or at times cause conflict within, the family. The knowledge gained by completing this exercise allows individuals to better respond to interface changes and the changes that come when companies are sold or bought and when privacy and security settings change (Young, 2014).

THE CONTENT SHARING PLAN

The purpose of segmenting content is modeled on what marketers do when considering how to distribute their messages to consumers. Essentially, marketing professionals consider who their target market is based on who is most likely to find value in their products or services. Then they come up with a messaging strategy that includes how they will reach their target market. For example, they might decide that because their target market is more receptive to emails about specials, they will focus on creating interesting and engaging emails. Likewise, as a family considers the process of what content they want to share online and with whom, they should begin to think more like a marketer in order to design the most effective and desired approach. As a result of this approach, they will be better able to segment messages and content by the target audience and digital tools (Young, 2014).

The first step in this process is to carefully consider the private-to-public continuum of the content that will be shared. Simply put, private content is information that an individual would not want others to know about, while public content is content that an individual is comfortable sharing beyond a family or friend circle. Families need to ask a set of guiding questions in order to help develop a content sharing plan as follows:

- What content will we not share online?
- Who will we share our content with?
- Where will we share our content?

Table 5.2

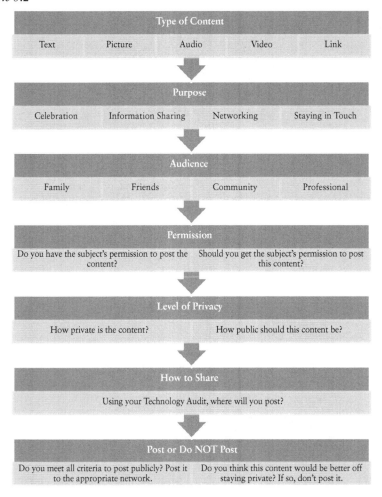

Type of Content				
Text	Picture	Audio	Video	Link

Purpose			
Celebration	Information Sharing	Networking	Staying in Touch

Audience			
Family	Friends	Community	Professional

Permission	
Do you have the subject's permission to post the content?	Should you get the subject's permission to post this content?

Level of Privacy	
How private is the content?	How public should this content be?

How to Share
Using your Technology Audit, where will you post?

Post or Do NOT Post	
Do you meet all criteria to post publicly? Post it to the appropriate network.	Do you think this content would be better off staying private? If so, don't post it.

When a family addresses the questions, they can develop a list of individuals they would like to connect with and share content with that includes close family members, extended family, work, and community. Once that step is complete, it is much easier to assess which online tools and platforms make the best sense for sharing of that content. For example if a family wants to create an online photo album that is private for the family, they might use a mobile application and website like Notabli.com. However, if the family wanted to create an online photo album that anyone can see, they might select a photo sharing tool like Flickr.

CREATE AN ACCESS PLAN

Keeping up with technology evolution is hard enough for an individual, but with the added responsibility of children, it becomes even more complex. Assessing the appropriateness of a tool for each family member, especially children, takes a lot of work along with drawing on outside resources and word of mouth. In order to address this challenge, I have developed the acronym PAVER as a simple way to assess the appropriateness of digital communication technology. Think of it as "paving the way to technology success" (Young, 2014).

- Purpose: First determine the purpose of the tool. Most social networking websites and mobile applications will explain what the intended purpose of the site is. Knowing the tools' purpose can help a family to first decide if the purpose of the site fits in with their overall technology philosophy.
- Age Appropriateness: Families with children must continuously examine the age appropriateness of media. This is no different with online tools. The important areas to emphasize, especially when it comes to games and social networks, include a child's maturity level to handle the environment and user interface, as well as their ability to manage the responsibility of the tool as a whole.
- Value: Each individual uses different technology tools for different reasons, but essentially, it comes down to the intrinsic value of that tool. For many, social networks are about connecting with like-minded individuals and sharing experiences. The value is the connection. For others, the value is in education and learning. In other contexts, the value of an online gaming environment such as Minecraft.com can be both educational and entertainment.
- EULA: Every online social network, game, mobile application, and software program has an End User License Agreement (EULA). This is where the company that makes the product lays out the legal implications for use of their product/service and explains limitations as well as what they do with content. It is imperative that individuals read the EULA of a site to be sure they agree are willing to conform to requirements. For example, the EULA for Facebook clearly points out that Facebook is for individuals 13 years old and older. It also clearly states

that individuals cannot have more than one account. Given current data on the amount of young people who have a Facebook account who are younger than 13, it is clear that parents and their children are not paying attention to the EULA for Facebook (Martin, 2013).

- Reviews/Resources: Finally, for most families, outside resources and reviews can provide much needed context. Individuals should take some time to read reviews, view videos, and utilize resources to learn more about specific tools. YouTube provides excellent tutorials and reviews on many different online games for families that want to better assess the helpfulness of an online environment like Mine Craft. CommonSenseMedia.org provides online reviews for age-appropriate software, games, videos, and movies.

Providing a framework like "PAVER" allows a family to quickly and easily determine if their child is ready to access and use a new technology tool.

SETTING THE GROUND RULES

Rules of digital media usage are an important component to teaching best practices, respect, and appreciation for what the tools can accomplish. They are also useful for dealing with the issues that can come with these tools. From health issues caused by too much screen time to user immaturity and misunderstandings of what content is private or not, families can run into many different issues when it comes to mediated communication. Setting strong ground rules within the family provides one way to appreciate the tools and respect the boundaries the family has set. As with all of the recommended processes for coping with digital technologies and mediated communication, these ground rules need to be revisited and discussed often.

While each family will need to determine the ground rules that work best for them, herein are a list of recommendations based on grounded experience, as well as survey data from families, to help create their own rules (Young, 2014):

- The "real friends" rule: When engaging in any online social context, the rule for children until they are older teenagers should be the "real friends" rule. Whether it is video games (computer or console), social networks, music services, or even texting, making sure everyone in the family understands the difference between real friends and virtual friends is important. The sooner young children understand this online / offline social distinction, the better off they will be as they grow older.
- Read the EULA rule: While the "legalese" can often seem overwhelming, and it is easier to just click the box and move on, there are many interesting things buried in the EULA, such as who owns the content that is posted, age restrictions, privacy information, and how sites use data collection to manage marketing and advertising efforts. All of this information is very important in a society that is moving more and more toward 24/7, always-on access.

- What's the value rule/Tell me why rule: This rule becomes more critical as children get older. Start them young and have them explain why a new tool would be valuable for them or why they need it. This rule is one that I have employed with my daughter a great deal. The justification "because my friends are doing it" is not a good reason. This is also a good way to ask children if they've read the EULA (reinforcing rule #2 above).
- Ask my permission rule. As we take sharing for granted we often forget that each of us has a different threshold for privacy and sharing. Making this a family rule means that all family members must ask permission before posting images or information about one another in social contexts. This is another important rule that will become more obviously important as children get older. Giving them a sense of control over what is posted and where it is posted sets a great foundation for good conversations. It's how my daughter and I have been operating for quite a few years now. I respect her privacy and her wishes on what I post on my social networks about her, especially with pictures. She does the same for me.
- Screen time rule. Rather than set time limits with the assumption that all screen time is "play time," emphasize the importance of walking away from screens for health reasons. Extended time in front of a screen, whether it is for homework, watching movies, or playing video games, is not healthy for the eyes, mind, or body. Taking breaks, moving around, and changing "visual inputs" are the foundations for this rule.

Each family should come up with rules that fit their needs. These should be utilized as a starting point, and, as with all rules, families will need to talk through the consequences for breaking the rules. One critically important component of this recommendations is that everyone in the family (including parents) needs to adhere to the rules and take the consequences for breaking them. Consequences can range from having to remove content from social media to permanent loss of access to a social network.

CONCLUSION

Raising a family in a digital age is not easy. Twenty-first-century parenting is especially challenging because most adults were not tethered to so many technological devices when they grew up, and did not have to learn to moderate or effectively engage with so many forms of digital media. Given the reality that technology will continue to evolve at a rapid pace, parents and educators should work together to take a proactive approach by fostering a learning community at school and at home. In so doing, families can successfully navigate the challenges that come with living in a continuously connected society. Creating and implementing a thoughtful technology philosophy will not only provide all media users with the means to make smart choices about the content they consume, produce, and share, but will also enable them to implement a personalized digital audit to better understand their usage habits. Likewise, the creation and implementation of a content sharing plan will provide each family member with well-defined criteria about what content should be shared or remain private. By clearly articulating a digital media access plan, all members of a classroom or household will better understand what they need to do before they can use a new technology tool, thereby enabling conversations around digital media to be more structured and easier to manage at home and at school. Finally, setting clear ground rules about media usage with enforced consequences will help build an overall culture of respect for the power of the tools that members of any learning community—whether at school or at home—can utilize as they engage in the digital world. While there are many challenges that come from a continuously connected society, there are also many benefits. By taking the time to set the proper foundation early on, students, teachers, and parents will be better able to fully embrace the benefits of media, find the right balance for consuming and participating in digital culture, and stay humanly connected in a digital age.

REFERENCES

Anderson, J., & Raine, L. (2014, March 11). *Digital life in 2025*. Pew Internet & American Life Project.

Bernoff, J. (2010, January 19). Social Technographics: Conversationalists get onto the ladder. Retrieved from http://forrester.typepad.com/groundswell/2010/01/conversationalists-get-onto-the-ladder.html.

boyd, d., & Ellison, N. (2007). Social network sites: Definition, history, and scholarship. *Journal of Computer-Mediated Communication*, 210–230.

Davis, F. (1979). *Yearning for yesterday: A sociology of nostalgia*. New York: Free Press.

Emanuel, L., & Stanton Fraser, D. (2104). Exploring physical and digital identity with a teenage cohort. *IDC '14 Proceedings of the 2014 Conference on Interaction Design and Children*, 67–76.

Johnson, L., Adams Becker, S., Estrada, V., & Freeman, A. (2014). *NMC Horizon Report: 2014 K-12 Edition*. Austin, Texas: The New Media Consortium.

Johnson, L., Adams Becker, S., Cummins, M., Estrada V., Freeman, A., & Ludgate, H. (2013). *NMC Horizon Report: 2013 K-12 Edition*. Austin, Texas: The New Media Consortium.

Madden, M., Fox, S., Smith, A., & Vitak, J. (2007, December 15). *Digital footprints*. Retrieved from http://www.pewinternet.org/2007/12/16/digital-footprints/.

Madden, M., Duggan, M., Cortesi, S., & Gasser, U. (2013, March 12). *Teens and technology 2013*. Retrieved from http://www.pewinternet.org/Reports/2013/Teens-and-Tech.aspx.

Martin, A. (2013, May 24). The Truth About Kids and Social Media. *Fast Company*.

Prensky, M. (2001). Digital natives, digital immigrants part 1. *On the Horizon, 9* (5), 1–6.

Rosin, H. (2013, March 20). The touch-screen generation. *The Atlantic*.

Social Networking Fact Sheet. (2013, December 27). Retrieved from http://www.pewinternet.org/fact-sheets/social-networking-fact-sheet/.

Solis, B. (2012, April 9). *Meet generation C: The connected customer*. Briansolis.com.

Young, E. (2014). Introduction: Why you need this book. In *Tuned-In Family: How to Cope, Communicate and Connect in a Digital World*. Burlington, VT: Champlain Publishing Initiative.

Zero to Eight: Children's Media Use in America 2013. (2013, October 28). Retrieved from https://www.commonsensemedia.org/research/zero-to-eight-childrens-media-use-in-america-2013.

6 Rectifying Social Inequalities through Actionable Pathways

How Girl Tech Teaches Young Women of Color to be Film Directors

Andrea Quijada, Jessica Collins, and Kandace Creel Falcon

Making the video was the most challenging and the most fun thing I have ever done. Sharing it with everyone, having something out there that I created makes me feel that I am actually doing something good in life and trying to accomplish my goals.[1]

—Girl Tech 2010 participant, age 16

Media Literacy Project (MLP) believes that media should build bridges between communities, spark transformational dialogue, and reflect the world both as it is, and how we want it to become. We understand the power of media to connect and inspire individuals to grow, challenge, and shape their communities. Based in Albuquerque, New Mexico, we have been providing media literacy education since 1993. We have created curricula, provided trainings, and presented workshops for schools and organizations across the United States and internationally in Mexico, Tunisia, Uganda, and the United Kingdom. During these past twenty-one years we have watched the media landscape shift dramatically due to both the rise of the Internet (and online video hosting sites such as YouTube, Vine, and Vimeo in particular) and the increased access by many communities to media making tools such as video cameras, smart phones, and video editing software. Social media sites such as Facebook and Twitter also serve to increase distribution avenues and create wide fan bases for some individual digital media makers. These shifts have substantially amplified public access to media creation and distribution resulting in cultural expectations and assumptions that everyone has access to this digital technology, knows how to use it, and should use it. However, many of the same issues of lack of diversity, unequal access, and (mis)representation that we experienced in radio, television, and cable before this digital technology appeared, are disappointingly reproduced in digital media despite the promise of equality these tools once made.

Some of the reasons for these disparities are rooted in policy decisions like some that have essentially created a digital divide whereby low-income and rural communities remain disconnected from Internet and mobile access.

Others are rooted in the culture itself that denies women and people of color access to large-scale media-making. For example, the number of women who directed Hollywood films that were released by a major studio between 2009 and 2013 was 4.7 percent (Silverstein, 2014), and 12.2 percent were directed by people of color (Ralph J. Bunche Center for African American Studies at UCLA, 2014). In television, women directors make up 14 percent of directors, with 2 percent being women of color (Directors Guild of America, 2013). The situation is slightly better in newspapers. At the nation's 10 most widely circulated newspapers, men garner 63 percent and women 37 percent of bylines (Women's Media Center, 2014). Over and over again, audiences are provided stories told primarily by white men—whether film, television, or print. In examination of who owns the media, it becomes apparent that media representation corresponds to media ownership. Women comprise over 51 percent of the U.S. population but hold less than 7 percent of all TV and radio station licenses, and people of color make up over 36 percent of the U.S. population but hold just over 7 percent of radio licenses and 3 percent of TV licenses (Free Press, 2012). It is difficult to measure online content creation and distribution and we do know that Black and Latino communities use the Internet 10 percent less than White communities (Zickuhr & Smith, 2012). Additionally, multiple factors exist that impede usage of the Internet including cost, infrastructure, and speed. Regardless of its current limitations, the potential for this new digital media culture to be shaped as a tool for social change is what inspires Media Literacy Project to do what we do every day.

This chapter demonstrates that simply having digital media technology in and of itself is not enough to create systemic social change (such as increasing women of color in filmmaking). Through the example of Media Literacy Project's Girl Tech program, we will reveal that in addition to the digital media technology there must be a framework and analysis that is offered to the creators and consumers of these digital media; policies in place to support access, affordability, and distribution of the technology; and a clear pathway to learn and utilize the digital tools in a safe and supportive environment. We contend that these three areas are embedded in MLP's theory of change, which directly informs how Girl Tech operates. In addition, the integration of Girl Tech participant feedback alongside media literacy educator reflection will offer qualitative analysis of why digital media technology does not serve young women of color in and of itself. We argue that the movies made in Girl Tech serve as tools, and not as the end products. This realization is crucial to create long-term, systemic change in our communities and in our media culture.

In order to effectively counter the mainstream media messages of racial, gender, and class stereotypes, MLP carefully roots all of our programs and campaigns in our theory of change, which stems from our definition of media literacy. We define media literacy as the ability to analyze, access, and create media. Therefore, our theory of change begins with teaching community members how to analyze corporate media by deconstructing it. We teach people how to deconstruct media by posing a series of questions with each media example. Questions such as, "Who paid for this piece of media? Who is the target audience? What techniques of persuasion are being used? What do we see and hear? Who is denied power or agency? Who is granted power or agency? What does this piece of media tell us about the product, policy, or idea that is being discussed? What stories are left untold?" (Media Literacy Project, 2014). These questions guide the conversation to issues of power, privilege, and profit. From there, we are able to deconstruct the corporate media system itself.

The second component in our theory of change is predicated upon digital media literacy to provide tools and technology to further analyze media, as well as to access and create media. We offer curricula for schools and organizations to analyze media, and provide digital tools like video and audio cameras for community members to create media. We ensure our communities have access to media tools by advocating for fair and just media policies such as reduced prison phone rates, net neutrality, and affordable and accessible Internet infrastructure.

Thirdly, we create, or support existing, pathways for individuals to take action. The action could be deconstructing a media example (analyze), submitting comments to the FCC in support of affordable phone rates (access), or directing a video project (create). Our fourth component is to offer encouragement and support to individuals on those pathways. Support comes in varying degrees—from a simple email alert to take action on a media justice or media policy issue, to offering a year-long media production program. While on any of these paths, the individuals become critical media consumers and engaged media justice advocates. For Media Literacy Project, it is this outcome that we strive for in each of our curricula, campaigns, and programs.

Girl Tech is MLP's flagship program that teaches young women of color to be film directors. The mission of Girl Tech is to develop the leadership and media-making skills of young women of color in New Mexico in order to advance reproductive justice and media justice in our communities. Launched in 2010, the year-long program teaches women to deconstruct media, to apply their critical analysis to the stories told in mainstream media, and to tell their own stories in their own words. Girl Tech is rooted in values including: We understand that access to communication tools and the complete well-being of women and girls are fundamental human rights and interrelated; We understand that media production is a skill that can allow individuals and communities to communicate, build power, and make change; and We value the leadership of young women of color and provide a safe space to learn and grow together.

GIRL TECH

> *I realize that I can use something that happened to me, like a story, in order to teach something or state a point I'm trying to make.*
> —Girl Tech 2012 participant, age 15 (MLP Girl Tech Evaluation, 2012)

Girl Tech effectively utilizes our theory of change because participants (1) hone their ability to analyze media and learn about the media system, (2) learn about media policies that provide or obstruct access, (3) are provided digital media making tools and are taught how to use them, and (4) create their own media. They learn all of the steps in the filmmaking process and are provided support in their production of a short film as part of the program. In encouraging young women of color to tell their own stories, their videos provide counternarratives to ubiquitous mainstream media that usually tells stories *of* communities of color, certainly not *by* them, and rarely *for* them. The young women of color who participate often enter the program with previous knowledge of race, class, and gender misrepresentation based in their lived experience. Girl Tech provides a place for them to delve into deeper dialogue about their lives, offers a framework and shared vocabulary to talk about their experiences, and validates their truths. The participant's quote (above) tells us that this process was instrumental in getting her to see a story—*her story*—as having legitimate value. In a culture where very little mainstream media is made by women of color, she has not had the opportunity, or privilege, of seeing stories like hers. It is clear that these conversations in Girl Tech are critical for the young women of color to have, for themselves, for each other, and for their creative process. These conversations are where the filmmakers come into their power, and it from that place of identity that their ideas for video projects emerge. Ultimately, the process of video making becomes where participants connect to, embrace, and share, their voice.

For other participants, learning to deconstruct media facilitated their video making abilities. One participant was working for New Mexico Teen Pregnancy Coalition when she participated in Girl Tech in 2010. She was 21 years old. She shared with MLP what influenced her video, *Teen Pregnancy: Stories from New Mexico*. She explains, "I remember during one of the Girl Tech trainings we had looked at various images that day, but I remember this one image that really stuck with me. It was a before and after image of a beautiful model on a magazine cover. To me she was flawless in the 'before' image, but I guess they had to pick out her 'flaws' in order to make her 'flawless.' They had to take out her wrinkles, make her abnormally thin, and just 'perfect.' I remember seeing just the fantasy of that image and how false it was, and it really stuck with me. So what I decided to do was make a video about real stories … I had never done anything with media. I had never edited a video and I had done very few interviews. That image helped keep me focused and keep sight of what I wanted to do which was tell the story of what being a teen parent is really like. It was a real video I wanted to make, a video different from what the mainstream media tells us which is often false and fantasized" (Media Literacy Project, 2012). Her experience with learning how to deconstruct media directly influenced her decisions in the creation of her own video. She did not want to repeat the patterns she had witnessed in the media literacy sessions where she had learned about

Photoshopped models. In those same sessions she also saw examples from "reality" television programs such as *16 and Pregnant,* and was taught the truth that reality television is staged. Learning to analyze media enabled her to tell stories about teen pregnancy not seen in mainstream media. As a result, she was able to stay focused and on message in her video making process.

Another 2010 Girl Tech alum echoes this experience when she shares, "Through my participation in the Girl Tech program, I was able to learn that media is important to understand because it helps us communicate with communities across the country. It is also important because it sends messages about who we are. I believe that people should study media literacy so we can make sure that our own information is communicated accurately" (Media Literacy Project, 2010). Her sister and co-director of their film, *Knowing is Protections: Thoughts on Sex Education,* says, "Through the Girl Tech program I have learned that media is a very powerful communication source that can influence our communities in many different ways. This is why media literacy is so important. After all, media targets and describes all of us and I believe we should be able to express ourselves with our own media" (Media Literacy Project, 2010). Here, these participants relay that the process of learning to deconstruct media informed how they wanted to construct media about and for their communities. Their experiences affirm that our theory of change is effective—not just as a theory, but more importantly, as praxis.

Girl Tech not only creates the space for young women of color to share stories that matter to them, but through MLP's leadership the program also helps young women of color develop lifelong skills and opportunities due to the technical knowledge they gain. For instance, a 2011 Girl Tech graduate who was 16 years old when she participated in the program is but one example of how Girl Tech develops lifelong passions for media literacy. Her involvement in Girl Tech had a profound impact on her life, and it continues to influence her today. Three different film festivals have screened her video, *Room to Improve: Albuquerque Schools' Sex Education.* Her volunteer work with Generation Justice, an Albuquerque youth radio organization, and her participation in Girl Tech inspired her to study journalism more intensely. In fact, she submitted her Girl Tech video with her college applications and talked about deconstructing media in her college interviews. During her senior year of high school, she received a full-ride scholarship to study journalism at Ithaca College. Her intent was to start a Latino radio show in Ithaca, continue her reproductive justice work, and fight for a just media system. Since creating her video in Girl Tech she went on to direct other video projects, including a video about a distance-learning program in Ethiopia.

In 2014, she wrote to MLP and said, "I just wanted to check in with you guys because a little less than a year ago I gave you some updates on my life as a Girl Tech alum and I have some new updates that have a lot to do with Media Literacy Project. First of all, I was really frustrated with the way

Journalism was taught at my school and thought it was annoying how a lot of personal narratives were stripped for the purpose of 'objectivity'. It caused me to change majors to Documentary Studies, which is a mixture between Journalism and Cinema Production, and it is allowing me to be way more open with the stories I tell and my activism. This summer, I wanted to expand on my research and production expertise, so I took an internship in Oakland with Making Contact which is a national radio project that does 30-minute in-depth pieces on important issues ... I am working on a media project, which I hope to someday turn into a documentary, on the Prison Abolition movement where I go to school in Ithaca, New York. I always want to thank MLP for being a real catalyst and support when I was just beginning multi-media story telling" (personal communication, May 27, 2014).

This participant's connection to Girl Tech and to Media Literacy Project is a direct result of a carefully constructed program that prioritizes the lived realities of young women of color, provides a space for reflection, and offers a clear pathway for participants to take action in the form of video making. Not only does Girl Tech provide support to them along the way, we wrap up the program year with a screening party. Prior to the screening party, each participant is prepped to speak about her film and is provided the chance to take questions from the audience at the event. This piece of the program furthers the leadership development of the participants and builds their media-making confidence. It encourages them to continue creating media to help meet the needs of their families and communities. Staff members and volunteers then remain connected to the participants after they leave the program.

MLP is now in the process of creating another pathway of connection through our newly formed Youth 4 Media Justice organizing program, whereby Girl Tech alums can continue their advocacy work once they finish Girl Tech. Advocacy work takes the shape of campaigns to increase media access, more filmmaking to elevate other community issues that the filmmaker wants to address, or even the continuation of deconstructing media as a daily practice. One participant who was age 15 at the time she participated in Girl Tech, shares how she still uses what she learned in Girl Tech today.

> I still analyze ads. It comes to the point where it is automatic. The video making experience has helped me so much. One of my best friends is making a video and I can help her. She wrote a script recently ... and I can point out little things that she isn't catching onto. I'm teaching her how to be a better filmmaker.
>
> (MLP Girl Tech Evaluation, 2012)

As a program, Girl Tech has shifted each year to address lessons learned by staff, volunteers, and participants. Funding sources have also impacted the shape of the program during its course. Funded first by New Mexico Community Foundation's Women Building Community Fund (WBC) and then by Catalyst Groundswell Fund, MLP has been able to strengthen the program each year. In our first two years, Girl Tech was funded by WBC. This fund supported a cohort of organizations in New Mexico that were collectively working within a reproductive justice frame. As a member of the cohort, MLP first conducted outreach to those organizations when recruiting participants. In this two-year time period, the Girl Tech videos were designed to also function as outreach and recruitment tools for the participating organizations. It required that the participants and the organizations decided together what the topics of the videos would be. Out of the seven organizations we partnered with those first two years, five were WBC cohort members. In our third year, we partnered with one organization from the cohort that had multiple participants (all but one of the four youth participants were from that organization).

In our fourth year, based on feedback and the realities that not all organizations had the capacity to use the videos the way we had envisioned, we reshaped the process so that the videos were focused on issues decided solely by the participants. Whether or not the participants were connected to other organizations, MLP was the only organization that reviewed and approved their video projects from beginning to end. MLP's role was one of guidance and support to ensure a successful execution of the vision laid out by the participants for their videos. In our fifth year, we chose to have the entire group make one collective video so that the participants could learn each film production role in more detail. This process allowed them the chance to individually be the director, writer, camera operator, sound technician, gaffer, lighting assistant, script supervisor, and editor.

Our ability to respond and adapt to the shifting media landscape, funding resources, and community priorities is what keeps Girl Tech relevant to the participants. In our five program years, 2010–2014, Girl Tech has involved 23 participants, one lead staff person, seven support staff, and 15 volunteers. A total of eight videos have been created. MLP takes our role in shaping digital media culture seriously and we do so through the creation of innovative curricula, programs, and campaigns. In particular, we created Girl Tech to counter the messages of mainstream corporate media that often deny the voices and experiences of women, communities of color, and low-income communities. Each of the participants have met that goal with the themes of the videos they have directed including: local organizing to support young parenting, the important role of traditional healing in community health, street harassment and prevention, positive body image, and the need for comprehensive sex education in high schools.

Our theory of change requires that we identify actionable pathways for the interests of those in our programs and support them on those pathways after they have left our programs. After the screening party, we place all videos online so that the filmmakers and general community can watch and use them. MLP knows that making the videos available online is not enough. Not all people have access to the Internet, or have the speeds necessary to watch streaming video. One way that we support participants is by submitting the Girl Tech films to film festivals across the country. Our program director takes time each year to match Girl Tech films to film festivals or conferences, submits the applications, and informs participants. To date, ten festivals and conferences have screened at least one Girl Tech video.[2] Our theory of change demands that these stories get heard, and therefore we have to actively seek audiences to increase our reach and build support, as well as work for equal access to affordable Internet for all of us. Simply put, the technology to make the films does not guarantee access to the technology to view the films.

Digital media technology offer powerful tools that have increased the ability for young women of color to create and distribute media. At the same time, policy battles over the Internet, such as the fight for net neutrality and the struggle to ensure that access is affordable, pose threats to its democratizing potential. The barriers faced by young women of color filmmakers are not easily erased by placing media making tools in their hands. They must have understanding of how to deconstruct and critically analyze media before creating more of it. There must be a place where their lived realities can be shared and discussed, particularly because they do not get to see themselves regularly represented in media as full, whole selves. For young women of color this piece is critical, and the participants in Girl Tech have clearly benefited from this approach. There must also be room to learn, fail, and succeed at learning how to use the digital media technology, along with technical and emotional support during and after the process. All of these components must be supported by a larger commitment to ensuring that federal and state policies support local needs for critical cultural analysis, production, and engagement. Media Literacy Project created Girl Tech as one small-scale, but significant, solution in helping young women of color explore pathways made possible by mentoring, new technology, and a sound curriculum. For MLP, we know our communities will not achieve media justice until and unless we invest in work that is rooted in anti-oppression and elevates the voices of young women of color. It is critical for all media advocates and media makers to foster spaces like Girl Tech for young women of color to fully participate and thrive in the world of digital media.

NOTES

1. Media Literacy Project. Girl Tech evaluations 2010. Qualitative evaluations in the form of in-person exit interviews are conducted with each of the three to eight participants at the end of each program year. The evaluations occur one week to one month of the program's end, contingent on the schedule of each participant.
2. Collectively, one or more Girl Tech films have been screened at the 2013 San Diego Latino Film Festival, 2013 and 2014 International Experiments in Cinema festivals (Albuquerque), 2013 Women & Creativity (Albuquerque), 2013 Allied Media Conference (Detroit), 2013 National Conference for Media Reform (Denver),

2013 University of New Mexico Indigenous Film Festival (Albuquerque), 2013 Bay Area Youth Media Network Festival (San Francisco), Loosening Our Minds Film Fest 2014 (Pennsylvania), and Youth Media Gallery at the National Alliance for Media Arts and Culture Conference 2014 (Philadelphia).

REFERENCES

Directors Guild of America. (2013). *DGA report finds director diversity in episodic television remains static.* Retrieved from http://www.dga.org/News/PressReleases/2013/100213-DGA-Report-Finds-Director-Diversity-in-Episodic-Television-Remains-Static.aspx.

Free Press. (2012). *Diversity in Media Ownership.* Retrieved from http://www.freepress.net/diversity-media-ownership.

Media Literacy Project. (2010). *Girl Tech Collective 2010.* Retrieved from http://medialiteracyproject.org/programs/girl-tech-collective/2010.

Media Literacy Project. (2012). *Girl Tech Report 2010–2011.* Retrieved from http://medialiteracyproject.org/sites/default/files/Girl%20Tech%20Report%202010-2011.pdf.

Media Literacy Project. (2014). *Intro to Media Literacy.* Retrieved from http://medialiteracyproject.org/intro-media-literacy.

Ralph J. Bunche Center for African American Studies at UCLA. (2014). *2014 Hollywood diversity report: Making sense of the disconnect.* Retrieved from http://www.bunchecenter.ucla.edu/wp-content/uploads/2014/02/2014-Hollywood-Diversity-Report-2-12-14.pdf.

Silverstein, M. (2014). *Infographic: Women directors in the studio system.* Retrieved from http://blogs.indiewire.com/womenandhollywood/infographic-women-directors-in-the-studio-system.

Women's Media Center. (2014). *The status of women in the U.S. media 2014.* Retrieved from http://www.womensmediacenter.com/pages/2014-statistics.

Zickuhr, K. & Smith, A. (2012). *Digital differences: Pew research internet project.* Retrieved from http://www.pewinternet.org/2012/04/13/digital-differences/.

7 Social Justice and LGBTQ Communities in the Digital Age

Creating Virtual and Social Affinity Spaces through Media Literacy

Morgan Jaffe

INTRODUCTION

Social justice is the idea or belief that all citizens, no matter their race, ethnicity, religion, ability, sexual orientation, or gender, should be allowed identical rights, protections, opportunities, obligations, and social benefits (Baker, 1991). While laws and protections have been put into place to protect individuals regarding housing, health, and education, as a nation we are still working on social justice issues with various groups within the United States, from Muslim and Native populations to the deaf community and those in low socioeconomic statuses.

Though social justice topics can incorporate many different types of people and communities, this chapter focuses on sexual orientation, gender identity, and other issues that effect the LGBTQ population. In this chapter I use LGBTQ (Lesbian, Gay, Bisexual, Transgender, and Queer and/or Questioning) as an umbrella term for all individuals who are impacted by their own and others' reactions to the lesbian, gay, bisexual, transgender, and queer or questioning community and issues.

When it comes to the LGBTQ community, members still lack equal rights and access pertaining to marriage, housing, education, and job opportunities. Many different types of people can be affected by LGBTQ issues, even if they do not self-identify as LGBTQ. This includes LGBTQ allies (i.e., family or friends) as well as those who are gender variant and do not adhere to strict gender presentation norms. Others may perceive allies or gender variant individuals to be a part of the LGBTQ community, and therefore bully, harass, or treat them as a member of the minority group (Muraco & Russell, 2011).

This chapter also focuses on LGBTQ social justice in online and offline spaces, and why and how to incorporate these topics into your classrooms. The solution to the modern day educational fear of "how can we ensure that students of today will be the digitally literate citizens of tomorrow?" starts with classrooms and students that are working towards critical thinking for real world situations and skills. By discussing how students can be social justice activists in online and offline spaces, educators can combine digital literacy with social justice, tying in the core issues with the technology of today for an ever changing tomorrow. This way, students can have the opportunity to educate and inform others who may not have the access or knowledge to become a part of LGBTQ and ally spaces.

Talking about LGBTQ issues within one's curricula might be difficult because of content restrictions, as well as the fear of becoming another educator fired as a result of being LGBTQ or being perceived as being LGBTQ and/or pro-LGBTQ (Edelson, 2014). Yet these concerns underscore the need to have the conversation. Efforts to create a more inclusive, diversity-friendly curriculum is especially important in the digital age, as students navigate their identities more fluidly and openly than in the past. The hope is that by merging online and offline spaces, inroads can be made between personal and communal spaces, home and school, to foster understanding and strengthen ties with allies to help put policies into place to protect the LGBTQ community. Accordingly, this chapter is not only a lesson about LGBTQ social justice in the digital age; it is about helping young people define the core values of social justice through an empowerment approach that embraces the tools of social transformation within the digital age.

LGBTQ STUDENTS BEING HARASSED

Schools are, unfortunately, unsafe environments for many LGBTQ youth. Elementary, middle, and high school can be hard enough for students with busy schedules, sports practices, plays, lunch, and fitting in socially (not to mention homework). But for many LGBTQ students, their everyday school reality also means being verbally (or physically) harassed and bullied. LGBTQ students who experienced frequent harassment and assault reported missing more days of school, lower GPAs, lower educational aspirations than students who were victimized less often, lower levels of school belonging, and poorer psychological well-being (Muraco & Russell, 2011). Though upsetting, these statements are not at all surprising. In a 2014 study conducted by Kosciw et al. in partnership with GLSEN, 55.5% of LGBTQ students felt unsafe because of their sexual orientation, and 37.8% felt unsafe because of their gender expression. If students feel unsafe, it may impede their desire to go to school, inasmuch as attending classes might be a difficult experience.

In addition to feeling unsafe, LGBTQ students hear negative remarks about gender and sexuality on a daily basis. According to Kosciw et al. (2014), 71.4% of students heard "gay" used in a negative way (e.g., "that's so gay") frequently or often at school, and 90.8% reported that they felt distressed because of this language; additionally 56.4% heard negative remarks about gender expression (not acting "masculine enough" or "feminine enough") frequently. What's even more distressing is that 51.4% of students reported hearing homophobic remarks from their teachers of other school staff, and 55.5% of students reported hearing negative remarks about gender expression from teachers or other school staff (Kosciw et al., 2014).

Beyond being verbally targeted, LGBTQ students and allies are also being physically targeted. According to Kosciw et al. (2014) during the 2012–2013 school year, 74.1% of LGBTQ students were verbally harassed (e.g., called names or threatened), 36.2% of LGBTQ students were physically harassed (e.g., pushed or shoved), and 16.5% of LGBTQ students were physically assaulted (e.g., punched, kicked, or injured with a weapon) because of their sexual orientation. Additionally, 55.2% of LGBTQ students were verbally harassed (e.g., called names or threatened), 22.7% of LGBTQ students were physically harassed (e.g., pushed or shoved), and 11.4% of LGBTQ students were physically assaulted (e.g., punched, kicked, or injured with a weapon) because of their gender expression (Kosciw et al., 2014).

While intimidation, provocation, and assault are experienced by LGBTQ students in schools, online spaces enabled by the Internet create another avenue for members of LGBTQ community to be bullied, harassed, or otherwise feel unsafe. With the advancement of the Internet and other digital technologies, forms of intimidation and harassment imposed upon LGBTQ students often manifest themselves online, from Facebook and Twitter to email and chat messaging. In their 2013 study, Palmer et al. found that 42% of LGBTQ youth have been bullied or harassed online, and 8% of LGBTQ youth have been bullied or harassed online at least once a week during the survey period of August 2010 through January 2011. One in four LGBTQ youth (26%) were bullied online specifically because of their orientation or gender expression during the survey period, and LGBTQ youth are nearly three times as likely as non-LGBTQ youth to have been bullied or harassed online (42% vs. 15%) (Palmer et al., 2013). Additionally, one in three (32%) LGBTQ youth have been sexually harassed online during the survey period, and LGBTQ youth are four times more likely than non-LGBTQ youth to have been sexually harassed online (32% vs. 8%) (Palmer et al., 2013).

Given these startling findings, students are doubly burdened with having to deal with bullying and harassment in and out of school, online and offline. Palmer et al. (2013) further document that 70% of LGBTQ youth have been bullied at least once in the past year via at least one mode, including 68% who said they had been bullied or harassed in person, online, or via text message; and for each medium surveyed, LGBTQ youth reported higher rates of bullying and harassment than non-LGBTQ youth.

AFFINITY SPACES

Whether they are out or closeted, it is not surprising that many LGBTQ students seek to find affinity spaces online as both a refuge from school and a means for participatory engagement. According to Gee (2004), affinity spaces are places (online, offline, or a mixture of the two) "where people can affiliate with others based primarily on shared activities, interests, and goals" (67). Even if these individuals never meet in real life, those within affinity spaces still see themselves as sharing interests within a community. For LGBTQ individuals, this could mean interacting with other members of the LGBTQ community, even if it does not involve sexual orientation, gender identity, race, ethnicity, class, or culture.

In many ways, the Internet can be "an agent of change" (Quinn & Reeves, 2009, 140), and many LGBTQ individuals spend much of their time online for a variety of different reasons. They include using the Internet to find more social supports online, getting answers to health and sex related questions, becoming more connected with others from the LGBTQ community (and further construct those communities), and feeling more out / open with themselves as well as others (such as opportunities for virtual coming out or establishing more of their identity). As Cooper and Dzara (2010) explain in their analysis of LGBTQ identity and activism on Facebook, "The Internet presents quite an opportunity for those who desire to 'come out online'" (p. 106). Regardless of what LGBTQ individuals do online, online spaces help to conquer isolation and create a place without rejection of sexual diversity (Pullen, 2010). Perhaps this is why LGBTQ youth spend an average of 5 hours per day online, or approximately 45 minutes more than non-LGBTQ youth (Palmer et al., 2013).

Most LGBTQ users are searching online for specific content, and this is a wonderful way to educate yourself (or others), find resources or answers to specific questions, and find online communities. In LGBTQ affinity spaces, users are actively seeking LGBTQ spaces (as websites or forums), choosing who or what groups and organizations to follow (websites and social media like Facebook, Twitter, or Tumblr), or are actively searching for or clicking on hashtags (in social media platforms that use them).

Despite numerous websites, online forums, and social media platforms that cater to the LGBTQ community and its allies, affinity spaces and online social justice can still be problematic. For instance, as many social media critics have argued, online spaces often reproduce social strata by creating inner circles of acceptance among like-minded participants (Zuckerman, 2013). That is, while digital spaces may provide users with a sense of safety and inclusion that they may not be able to feel in the physical world, these online affinity spaces can isolate these communities; they connect like-minded individuals who already agree that there needs to be more social justice for a particular cause (and in this case the LGBTQ community) rather than advocate their cause among groups who exclude them.

SOCIAL JUSTICE IN THE DIGITAL AGE

In America, the LGBTQ community has become more visible and accepted socially and culturally. But such gains are limited and have only recently been realized after a long and complicated history. Decades of inequality still exists in states where marriage for same sex couples remains illegal, and individuals in certain states can be fired from their workplace based on sexual orientation and/or gender identity. Hence, while strides for LGBTQ social justice have been made, there is still more work to be done.

In the digital age, social justice looks extremely different than it did during the Stonewall Riots or the 1979 National March on Washington for Lesbian and Gay Rights when people occupied a physical space and mobilized in public places, squaring off with those who tried to deny their rights. Today, the LGBTQ movement has shifted to online spaces due to social media, affinity spaces, and the surge of media outlets by both large corporations and smaller, independent outlets. Although activism can happen in both online and offline spaces, many argue that it may be harder to make a real world impact unless these users become more active in their non-virtual communities. This difficulty has been coined as "slacktivism" by Dwight Ozard and Fred Clark in 1995 (Christensen, 2011). "Slacktivism" is characterized by online political participation that has limited offline impact (Christensen, 2011). Whether signing a document on Change.org, liking a Facebook group, or hashtagging a tweet, online participation can be seen as simply enhancing the "feel-good factor" for participants (Christensen, 2011; Shulman, 2009; Hindman, 2009; Morozov, 2009). These factors all contribute to a disdain for online activism as less effective, and as a way to be involved without having any sort of real commitment.

Additionally, research argues that online activities replace traditional offline participation, thereby leading to lower levels of participation (Christensen, 2011). Sally Kohn (2008) agrees, stating insightfully that "real changes in society...won't politely go away with a few clicks of the mouse." As Kohn (2008) discusses, Internet activism is an individual activity: "It's great for a sense of interconnectedness, but the Internet does not bind individuals in shared struggle the same as the face-to-face activism of the 1960s and '70s did. It allows us to channel our individual power for good, but it stops there." Given these concerns, how might we rethink social activism and social justice in online and face-to-face spaces, from individual affinity sites to schools and public commons? How can we explore integrated spaces and environments that foster equality across all intersecting matrices of difference?

SOCIAL JUSTICE THROUGH AN LGBTQ LENS
IN THE CLASSROOM

In many states affected by the devastating consequences of cyberbullying, legislative mandates have held school administrators accountable for enacting anti-bullying awareness programs and for rectifying online bullying between students, even if it occurred outside of school (Sacco et al., 2012). In line with such measures, the time has come to combine offline and online activism through a pensive educational approach that advocates for social justice awareness and intervention. By teaching students about social justice, educators can help create opportunities for students to make a difference online and offline in both meaningful and systematic ways. In one offline example of LGBTQ social justice, a Massachusetts teen contacted Apple after finding that their programmed Apple dictionary listed a derogatory use as part of their definition of "gay" (Annear, 2013). In this case, the student took a stand so that the company would not propagate this definition. The value for such direct action is transformative, as students learn to critically analyze and evaluate knowledge dissemination online (in this case through Apple's online dictionary) and enact change to further social justice in physical spaces. Similar to how students are encouraged to contribute their knowledge sharing by using digital tools like wikis, blogs, and videos, students also need to use new digital tools for social change and advocacy if they are to see themselves as digitally savvy citizens of the world.

In order for social justice initiatives to take a stronghold among the next generation of citizens, pedagogical and curricular approaches must encourage students to participate in online and offline spaces, in and out of school. By using schools as spaces for students to discuss online and offline bullying, teachers can create a culture where students learn to listen, discuss, and process others' beliefs and viewpoints. This goes directly against the affinity spaces model, where individuals interact with others who already agree with their social values; this is why there is such a dire need to teach social justice for both online and offline spaces in the classroom. Additionally, students lives do not exist solely in physical spaces throughout the school day, so why should their curriculum? Teaching social justice through an LGBTQ lens also creates a wonderful opportunity to educate people, create allies, and change school culture to help make schools safer and feel more inclusive for LGBTQ youth.

Furthermore, "Students in schools with an inclusive curriculum were more likely to report that their classmates were somewhat or very accepting of LGBTQ people than other students (75.2% vs. 39.6%)" (Kosciw et al., 2014, xx). Having an inclusive LGBTQ curriculum could lead to having fewer homophobic remarks, epithets, or comments about someone's gender expression in and out of school, and on and offline. By changing even this one (seemingly) small part of school culture, the hope is that students would feel more safe at school and more inclined to attend. By including an LGBTQ curriculum in the classroom, LGBTQ students may feel more involved and accepted within school communities.

In terms of preparing for areas of resistance, changing the school culture to be more accepting of LGBTQ students and individuals is no easy task. Therefore, it is important to have an action plan to prevent and reduce student resistance and respond to resistance (Goodman, 2011, 67). For reducing student resistance, Goodman recommends building relationship and trust; affirming, validating, and conveying respect for individuals; and heightening student investment. For responding to resistance, Goodman recommends assessing the reasons for resistance, containing the behavior, and remembering to go with the flow. If needed, educators can also provide a break for students to do an individual activity or arrange a private meeting.

THE CURRICULUM

Without question, the ability for a school to effectively participate in online spaces will be easier to implement and more accessible to schools with more resources, particularly computers. Additionally, access may also be an issue, particularly if schools block social media sites and/or use Internet firewalls, filters, and/or have other computer and Internet restrictions and censorship.

In order to incorporate digital literacies into the classroom, it is extremely important that teachers begin by discussing sharing in online spaces with students. It seems that K-12 students, as well as college students, have been deemed the digital generation, and they are all treated as "digital natives" (Prensky, 2001, 2005). The term digital native becomes problematic, as the name implies that technology comes naturally to youth born into the digital native generation. Various researchers argue that digital natives need a more formal education, and that although they have been exposed to technology from a young age, they will not naturally and instinctively know how to think critically about mediated messages (James et al., 2010; Park, 2012; Selwyn, 2009). Consequently, educators should make sure that their students understand both how to share their work in online spaces (in terms of technology, social media use, and hashtags) as well as understand digital issues like privacy, copyright, and the pros and cons of posting in online spaces.

Once teachers have discussed with their students how to post in online spaces, as well as think critically about the messages they will create, it is then time to set up a social justice inclusive culture in the classroom. Adapted from Hasazi and Shepherd (2009, p. 93), educators can begin by having students:

1 Develop a shared vision and culture
2 Understand LGBTQ terminology, policies, and practices
3 Ensure that the structure and organization of the school and surrounding community reflects a commitment to LGBTQ policy and safety

1. Developing a Shared Vision and Culture

In order to develop a shared vision and culture, educators may benefit from giving their students a democratic approach to decision making and change. After all, students may resist if they feel uninvolved with the process, and "social justice curriculum does not mean dogma, it does not mean cramming the teacher's opinions into the students" (Ayers, 2009, p. 657). A community of learners (Rogoff, 1994) approach would work well in this type of classroom.

Additionally, because students will be discussing tough and personal LGBTQ topics in both online and offline spaces, the first step in laying a foundation should be putting ground rules into effect at the beginning of the school year or semester. All students, regardless of their sexual orientation or gender identity, whether they have liberal or conservative ideas and ideals, need to be comfortable and welcomed to voice their opinion. But that still entails having a set of expectations, and what Bradley and Nash (2009) refer to as "moral conversation":

> … good teachers and good students are primarily interested in *affirming and enriching* each others' perspectives and viewpoints rather than finding ways to *critique and ridicule* them. We try to do this by following what we call the "Golden Rule" of moral conversation: respond to others in the class the way you would like them to respond to you.
>
> (Bradley & Nash, 2009, p. 162)

In this way, students can learn to use affirmative communication skills and approaches to create a safe and open environment for thoughtful conversations.

Before starting a class discussion, it would be beneficial to allow students to write down their thoughts and feelings on sexual orientation and gender identity. As adapted from Bradley and Nash's social class work (2009, p. 163) and Lockhart and Shaw (n.d.), some prompts could include a session teaching about sexual orientation and an additional session on gender identity.

Questions about Sexual Orientation

1 Please complete this statement: Sexual orientation is_____.
2 Do you know anyone at your school whose sexual orientation is different from yours?
3 How do you know?
4 Are you comfortable with that person or those people? Why or why not?
5 Do you think that person or those people are comfortable with you? Why or why not?
6 Has your sexual orientation ever placed you at an advantage, or disadvantage, of any kind? If so, how?
7 Please complete this statement: When I think about sexual orientation, one stereotype I think about is_____.
8 What are some questions you have around the topic of sexual orientation?

Questions about Gender Identity

1 Please complete this statement: Gender identity is_____.
2 Do you know anyone at your school whose gender identity is different from yours?

3 How do you know?

4 Are you comfortable with that person or those people? Why or why not?

5 Do you think that person or those people are comfortable with you? Why or why not?

6 Has your gender identity ever placed you at an advantage, or disadvantage, of any kind? If so, how?

7 Please complete this statement: When I think about gender identity, one stereotype I think about is_____.

8 What are some questions you have around the topic of sexual orientation and gender?

By using these prompts, educators can both check their student's understanding of the topic, as well as direct class discussion around student questions and educating them about privilege and stereotypes.

When students answer these questions, teachers can include technology or not depending on their classroom resources and access, time, and comfort level. Educators with access to technology can provide students with options for answering these questions, such as starting a blog and writing their answers as a post, with added video, pictures, gifs, audio, or other media, as well as hashtags (depending on the platform they use). Students can also use YouTube, Vimeo, their smartphones, Flipgrid, Popcorn Maker, or other platforms to make a video of their answers. For educators unable to use any technology, students can also keep a journal or a diary of some kind, having the option to add clippings, pictures, or text from newspapers, magazines, or personal photographs, drawings or sketches, or use other available media.

Bradley and Nash (2009) also discuss doing a "me-search" with students. They define a me-search as "the intentional action of exploring oneself; of going beyond the surface self and digging deeper in an effort to extract new knowledge of one's self and one's place in the world" (2009, p. 152). After reading auto-ethnographies (perhaps narratives from the entire spectrum, from LGBTQ community members and allies to those unwelcoming of LGBTQ community members and allies), students can have the opportunity to write their own personal narrative. This activity is not about being LGBTQ or not, but rather allowing students to record their observations, tell their own story, and share their experiences and outlook. It might be that students were raised in an area where they didn't interact with the LGBTQ community or students were raised in an area where they did interact with the LGBTQ community. Students can explore if they were raised in an area where being in the LGBTQ community was seen as a negative or positive. No matter their experiences, it's important for students to analyze their experiences within a social, historical, and cultural context. The assignment goal should be for students to go beyond summary and autobiography to incorporate ethnographic analysis of the cultural contexts and practices, relationships, and dynamics of power that provide the broader context of their LGBTQ experiences. Readings, research, and discussion from class should be used to frame the analysis of their personal experience with the LGBTQ community.

When students create their me-search, teachers can also decide whether or not to include technology depending on their classroom's resources and access, time, and comfort level.

2. Understanding LGBTQ Terminology, Policies, and Practices

It is important for students to have a shared knowledge and understanding of LGBTQ terminology, policies, and practices. Websites like GLSEN, GLBTQ.com, or PFLAG can provide educators with resources to create a lexicon. Students may not understand the differences between sex and gender, let alone what transgender, intersex, or queer mean. Using this as a starting point, it may be interesting to teach students about federal and state laws or mandates. After students gain an understanding of LGBTQ terminology, policies, and practices, it would be useful for them to reflect on more questions such as (adapted from Lockhart & Shaw, n.d.):

1 What are some factors that might encourage or discourage a person (student, teacher, staff) about being "out" as LGBTQ in this class or your school?
2 What are, or what do you think would be, the consequences of a person (student, teacher, staff) being "out" as LGBTQ in this class or your school?

Bradley and Nash (2009) also discuss doing a "we-search" with students as a class. They define a we-search as a group discussion. As they explain, " … it is not only important to be able to be able to discover and express our own individual stories, but it is equally as important to be able to listen and engage with others around their stories" (Bradley & Nash, 2009, p. 152). Before doing this, it is important for teachers to (as discussed before) have set expectations that they create with their class.

When students respond in their we-search, they can either work individually to respond to their classmates, pair and share, or discuss as an entire classroom group, creating opportunities for collaboration. Regardless of technology, students can either work individually or multiple students may group together to respond to others' me-search. Ideally, whether students decide to respond individually, with a partner or group in whole class or small group sessions, there should at least be one classroom discussion with everyone present.

3. Ensuring that the Structure and Organization of the School and Surrounding Community Reflects a Commitment to LGBTQ Policy and Safety

Once students have taken the time to think about LGBTQ themes and issues as well as discuss with each other, teachers may want to talk about LGBTQ social justice issues within their own school or community, linking their learning and knowledge base to their everyday lives. When doing this, it may be beneficial and more engaging for students if they are in charge of the brainstorm, with the educator acting as a facilitator. This requires putting students in charge of taking notes in a space that everyone can see (whether it's a chalkboard, a large note pad in the front of the class, or a SmartBoard). If students are having a difficult time brainstorming, some possible topics include:

1 What do the anti-discrimination policies look like in our school? In other districts? In other states?
2 What are your state's policies on gay marriage? In other states?
3 What are your state's policies on workplace discrimination? In other states?
4 What does health coverage look like for LGBTQ individuals in our state? In other states?
5 What does the sex education curriculum look like in our school? In other districts? In other states?

Though some of these conversations may be uncomfortable for some students, faculty, and school administrators, they are important for enabling students to think about, analyze, and discuss with each other. After their brainstorming session, teachers may want to discuss with students what steps they can take—big or small, online or offline, in and out of school—to help make a difference and bring attention to these issues. Keeping in mind issues surrounding privacy, copyright, and pros and cons of sharing information online, educators should facilitate a brainstorming session that is action-oriented. Possible options include:

1 Boycotting a store or organization
2 A petition, either online of offline
3 Organizing or attending marches and/or protests and/or other demonstrations
4 Organizing a social event, educational event, or vigil
5 Writing an article or a blog post for the student newspaper or local newspaper
6 Creating a video or PSA for a school or community event and/or posting it online
7 Contacting your local and/or state representative through mail, email, or a telephone call
8 Interviewing LGBTQ individuals and/or organization, community leaders, politicians, or local celebrities through Skype and/or Google-Hangouts and later sharing those interviews in traditional print or digital media and/or through social media
9 Attending and speaking out at public forums and other meetings

10 Hosting a podcast combining different research, interviews, or other work
11 Volunteering and helping a local nonprofit or other organization

Naturally, students should be encouraged to share their work online and/ or use a hashtag to provide metadata on social media. Once students decide what local or global issue they wish to focus on, it may be beneficial to discuss the following questions:

1 Does having more voices from more places strengthen or weaken your position?
2 Should your movement focus on local or global communities?
3 If it is a local community, can it only take place in offline spaces? Why?
4 If it is a global community, can it only take place in online spaces? Why?
5 This is what we want to do offline. How would we do it online?
6 This is what we want to do online. How would we do it offline?

CONCLUSION

Social justice within the digital age requires participatory engagement in both online and offline spaces. As described in this chapter, the creation of safe spaces for the LGBTQ community in schools and online can be promoted by integrating digital media literacy skills with social justice awareness, understanding, and activism. Drawing from new digital media tools that encourage self-reflection through multimodal auto-ethnographies and social media, students can create and share narratives from their own unique vantage points relating to the LGBTQ community, either as direct members or allies to those unwelcoming of LGBTQ community members and allies. Regardless of the student perspective or experience, the goal is to foster reflections, understanding, and conversations aimed at situating LGBTQ concerns and issues within a social, historical, and cultural context. By incorporating ethnographic analysis of the cultural contexts and practices, relationships, and dynamics of power that provide the broader context of LGBTQ experiences, students can have the opportunity to educate and inform others who may not have the access or knowledge to become a part of LGBTQ and ally spaces. By using diversity lessons aimed at the LGBTQ community, the hope is that educators will combine their analysis of issues like bullying, cyberbullying, and harassment with discussions of digital topics like privacy, copyright, and the pros and cons of posting in online spaces. In so doing, teachers can synthesize digital literacy skills and social justice issues to create safer spaces for the LGBTQ community both in and out of school, online and offline, while raising awareness for other social justice movements as well.

REFERENCES

Annear, S. (2013, Nov. 12). Teen asks Apple to remove offensive definition of the word 'gay' from dictionary app. *Boston Magazine*. Retrieved from http://www. bostonmagazine.com/news/blog/2013/11/12/apple-dictionary-app-sudbury-teen-gay-defintion/.

Ayers, R. (2009). Classrooms, pedagogy, and practicing justice. In Ayers, W., Quinn, T. M., & Stovall, D. (Eds.), *Handbook of social justice in education* (657–660). New York: Routledge.

Baker, R. L. (1991). *The social work dictionary* (2nd ed.). Washington: D.C.: National Association of Social Workers.

Bradley D. L., & Nash, R. J. (2009). Helping college students explore the hidden injuries of social class. In R.G. Johnson, III (Ed.), *A twenty-first century approach to teaching social justice: Educating for both advocacy and action* (pp. 151–166). New York: Peter Lang Publishing.

Christensen, H. S. (2011). Political activities on the Internet: Slacktivism or political participation by other means? *First Monday, 16*, 2. http://dx.doi.org/10.5210/fm.v16i2.3336.

Cooper, M., & Dzara, K. (2010). The Facebook revolution: LGBTQ identity and activism. In C. Pullen & M. Cooper (Eds.), LGBTQ *identity and online new media* (pp. 100–112). New York: Taylor & Francis.

Edelson, J. (2014, June 26). Most Americans think it's illegal to fire someone for being gay. They're wrong. *Business Week*. Retrieved from http://www. businessweek.com/articles/2014-06-23/discrimination-at-work-is-it-legal-to-fire-someone-for-being-gay.

Gee, J. P. (2004). *Situated language and learning: A critique of traditional schooling.* New York: Routledge Press.

Goodman, D. J. (2011). *Promoting diversity and social justice: Educating people from privileged groups.* New York: Routledge.

Hasazi, S., & Shepherd, K. (2009). Leading beyond labels. In R. G. Johnson, III (Ed.), *A twenty-first century approach to teaching social justice: Educating for both advocacy and action* (pp. 91–106). New York: Peter Lang Publishing.

Hindman, M. (2009). *The myth of digital democracy*. Princeton: Princeton University Press.

Kohn, S. (2008). Real change happens off-line. *Christian Science Monitor*. Retrieved from http://www.csmonitor.com/Commentary/Opinion/2008/0630/p09s01-coop. html.

Kosciw, J. G., Greytak, E. A., Palmer, N. A., & Boesen, M. J. (2014). *The 2013 National School Climate Survey: The experiences of lesbian, gay, bisexual and transgender youth in our nation's schools.* New York: GLSEN.

Lockhart, J., & Shaw, S. M. (n.d.). *Writing for change: Raising awareness of difference, power, and discrimination.* Oregon State University. http://oregonstate.edu/dept/dpd/sites/default/files/1.04_talking_about_being_out.pdf.

Morozov, E. (2009). The brave new world of slacktivism. *Foreign Policy*. Retrieved from http://neteffect.foreignpolicy.com/posts/2009/05/19/the_brave_new_world_of_slacktivism.

Muraco, J. A., & Russell, S. T. (2011). How school bullying impacts lesbian, gay, bisexual, and transgender (LGBT) young adults. (Frances McClelland Institute for Children, Youth, and Families *Research Link, 4*(1). Tucson, AZ: The University of Arizona.

Palmer, N. A., Kosciw, J. G., Greytak, E. A, Ybarra, M. L., Korchmaros, J., & Mitchell, K. J.(2013). *Out online: The experience of lesbian, gay, bisexual, and transgender youth on the Internet.* New York: GLSEN.

Park, S. (2012). Dimensions of digital media literacy and the relationship with social exclusion. *Media International Australia,* 142, 87–100.

Prensky, M. (2001). Digital natives, digital immigrants. *On the Horizon,* 9(5), 1–6.

Prensky, M. (2005). *Listening to the natives. Educational Leadership,* 63(4), 8–13.

Pullen, C. (2010). The murder of Lawrence King and LGBTQ online stimulation of narrative correspondence. In C. Pullen & M. Cooper (Eds.), *LGBTQ identity and online new media (pp. 17–36).* New York: Taylor & Francis.

Quinn, A., & Reeves, B. (2009). The use of the Internet to promote social justice with LGBTQ individuals. In R. G. Johnson, III (Ed.), *A twenty-first century approach to teaching social justice: Educating for both advocacy and action* (pp. 139–148). New York: Peter Lang Publishing.

Rogoff, B. (1994). Developing understanding of the idea of communities of learners. *Mind, culture, and activity,* 1(4), 209–229.

Sacco, D. T., Silbaugh, K., Corredor, F., Casey, J., & Doherty, D. (2012). An overview of state anti-bullying legislation and other related laws. *The Kinder and Braver World Project Research Series.* https://cyber.law.harvard.edu/research/youthandmedia/kinderbraverworld.

Selwyn, N. (2009). The digital native—Myth and reality. *Aslib Proceedings,* 61(4), 364–379.

Shulman, S. W. (2009). The case against mass e-mails: Perverse incentives and low quality public participation in US federal rulemaking. *Policy & Internet,* 1(1), 23–53.

Zuckerman, E. (2013). *Digital cosmopolitans: Why we think the Internet connects us, why it doesn't, and how to rewire it.* New York, NY: W.W. Norton & Company.

Part III

Local

Part 3—LOCAL, explores how our connections to others increasingly involve the formative interactions we have with members of our local spheres through digital and social media. Using digital devices, our evolutionary predilection for human interactivity carries on through social and distributive online networks as we seek to develop our sense of shared meaning and understanding from individuals and social structures that shape and influence our worlds at the local level. In this section, we begin by assessing the state of media literacy education today in order to reflect on the ways in which local spheres of influence for youth have been altered by the speed and mobility of digital media. With young people having portable online access with them wherever they go, the boundaries of learning have shifted beyond familial and educational realms to include local peer networks of influence. While much has been made about how broader social connections are impacting children and youth, we'll learn about recent legislation and regulations that have both helped and hindered the deployment of media literacy education initiatives in U.S. public schools, and how policy efforts for media literacy are often reactionary and aimed at solving particular social and behavioral issues. Likewise, we'll explore the merits and drawbacks associated with 1:1 technology initiatives that seek to put a laptop or other Internet-enabled device in the hands of every public school student in the United States. We'll read why it's not enough to simply hand each student a Chromebook or an iPad, and will discover how meaningful digital media curricula, pedagogy, and connectivity outside the schools could provide a solid footing for digital media literacy education programs to overcome the limitations of the digital divide. To those ends, we'll discover how a partnership between a team of university researchers and a local middle school can empower young media users as members of virtual communities to engage in safe and respectful online behaviors as a means to curbing cyberbullying. Lastly, we explore how, with the right pedagogical strategies and approaches, digital media literacy education can bridge the generational divides between educators and students that manifest themselves in the classroom. We'll read arguments for the ways in which image-based orientations that prioritize speed, appearance, and emotion are at odds with what text-based educators hope to accomplish in the classroom through depth, critical analysis, and reason, and how imagery can encourage rather than disable critical thinking. As a whole, the chapters in this section consider the varied ways that comprehensive digital media literacy education provides one of the strongest means to provide students with the resources to think critically about their use of new technologies, while encouraging them to consider the relationship between their behaviors online and elsewhere within their local spheres of interaction.

8   Policy, Participation, and Practice

Assessing Media Literacy in the Digital Age

Allison Butler

INTRODUCTION

The first years of the twenty-first century are undeniably marked by rapid growth in digital technology; the quantity, perceived access, and perceived ease of digital media use is part of our everyday lives, in and out of classrooms. A cursory glance reveals that media use is everywhere, at all times, with little to no need for an "off" switch or "off" time. Despite the growth and apparent ubiquity of digital technology, many twentieth-century—and earlier— concerns remain active: What might these technologies *do to* our children and adolescents? What do young people *do with* their media? How do these technologies influence learning, brain, body, and social development? Are mainstream media—especially easily accessible and easily manipulated social media—responsible for increased violence, bullying, and antisocial behavior by youth? How are scholars, educators, and parents to make sense of, and make use of, digital media?

For 20+ years, media literacy in the United States has remained piecemeal. Interested teachers, community workers, and youth advocates are often isolated from each other's work. Despite being the largest producer and exporter of media in the world, the United States lags behind other English-speaking countries, especially the United Kingdom, Australia, and Canada, in media literacy education. This chapter explores the early questions and definition of media literacy in the United States, its growth—and often stagnation—to better understand where we are today and what changes can be made to move American media literacy forward. Specifically, it shares the work being done in Massachusetts to frame legislation, research, practice, and training.

THE EARLY QUESTIONS

In 1992, the questions of media's impact on youth were codified when a group of U.S. scholars met to discuss and grapple with questions of media literacy. The National Leadership Conference on Media Literacy grew from the observation that media literacy practitioners were not fulfilling their objectives because "funders and policy makers were confused by lack of clarity and understanding as to what the various organizations did, how they related, and what the overall goals are" (Firestone, 1993, *v*). The Aspen Group met to clarify the goals and vision of media literacy. In so doing, they developed a basic definition that, in various forms, has been the guiding model for the United States since 1992: "A media literate person ... can decode, evaluate, analyze and produce both print and electronic media. The fundamental objective of media literacy is critical autonomy in relationship to all media" (Aufderheide, 1993, p. 1). The conference noted that while media educators might approach their teaching in various ways, all media educators share the following beliefs: "media are constructed, and construct reality; media have commercial implications; media have ideological and political implications; form and content are related in each medium, each of which has a unique aesthetic, codes and conventions; receivers negotiate meaning in media" (Aufderheide, p. 2). The Conference noted the irony that the United States—the largest producer and exporter of media—remained woefully behind other post-industrialized nations in educating its youth.

Since 1992, there has been much work, but not much of a cohesive shift, within the U.S. media education landscape. There are many more initiatives; what took three paragraphs to detail in the Aspen Institute Report would now take many pages. However, there remains the same prevailing sense of isolation and disconnect: Teachers, academics, community workers, and youth interested in media literacy education often must figure it out alone, independent of the larger institution of which they are a part. For the most part, the United States teeters between a protectionist stance (Potter, 2010) that sees the media as inherently problematic and a celebratory position (Hobbs, 2011) that prioritizes young people's interests but does little to critique the larger system within which those interests are found. While much of American media literacy is ensnared in how to define it, what it means, and where it belongs, there is a new question added to the mix: How to incorporate digital media into the practice.

QUESTIONS FOR THE DIGITAL AGE

Moving further into the twenty-first century, there is still debate over the definition of media literacy, whether it works, and whether its implementation in various sites has been successful (Domaille & Buckingham, 2001; Hobbs, 2011; Potter, 2010). The literature of the early twenty-first century on young people and digital media reveals three prevailing themes: Quantity of time spent, especially with multiple media; how fast technology appears to be changing; and the mobility of media, which may (or may not) be indicative of a larger shift in society. Woven within these themes is the idea that education should play *some* role as problem solver, but it remains unclear *what* role.

The oft-cited Kaiser Family Foundation's 2010 report *Generation M²: Media in the lives of 8- to 18-year olds* (Rideout, Foehr, & Roberts, 2010) discusses how much time young people spend with multiple forms of media, often simultaneously. *Generation M²* reports, "media are among the most powerful forces in young people's lives today. Eight- to eighteen-year-olds spend more time with media than in any other activity besides (maybe) sleeping" (p. 1). Young people with regular media and technology access pack 10 hours and 45 minutes of media-related activities into 7 ½ hours per day (Rideout et al., 2010). Multiple-media use is reiterated in other studies (Bleakely, Vaala, Jordan, & Romer, 2014; Takeuchi & Levine, 2014) and becomes an overriding concern throughout much of the literature on youth and media in the twenty-first century (Arthur, 2005; Collier 2014; Flanagin & Metzger, 2010). Youth of all ages are growing up in homes with many diverse media, including traditional and new media (Bleakley et al., 2014) and by the 8th grade, the majority of youth with access are online regularly (Flanagin & Metzger, 2010).

A second theme is how *fast* change seems to occur, as well as the unique nature of these changes. Montgomery (2007) observes "never before has a generation been so defined in the public mind by its relationship to technology" (p. 2). Young people with access grow up with the Internet and a variety of wireless mobile devices that may define their prevailing communication. Takeuchi and Levine (2014) observe the rapid rate "at which these tools are invading family life and transforming daily routines" which are adopted by youth users within a matter of months (p. 28). With rapid and unfamiliar change comes the concern of what harm these technologies may incur (Collier, 2014), what impact may result from expression that were once private now lived and shared in a very public way (Potter, 2012) and what impact media multitasking may have on brain development (Takeuchi & Levine, 2014).

The third theme addresses the mobility of digital media and the potential societal shifts. According to Livingstone (2014) everyday practices "are being rewritten through the use of online digital technologies, especially mobile and social media" (p. 129; see also Takeuchi & Levine, 2014). Young people with access can bring their interests with them wherever they go, shifting the boundaries of in-and out-of-school learning (Takeuchi & Levine, 2014) and, conceivably, any other location. Indeed 'location' may be largely irrelevant, assuming there is a reliable Internet connection. Some of what is being rewritten includes how and what young people learn from their peers, who are ostensibly more accessible with portable media (Brown, El-Toukhy, & Ortiz, 2014). Further, digital, portable media allows the corporate structure, especially in advertising and marketing, to appear transparent even when it has a tighter hold over information (Montgomery, 2007; Potter, 2012).

While these technologies, their use, and their influence may indeed shift society in remarkable and dramatic ways, one needs to approach these changes with caution. Citing the trajectory of concerns over violence on TV progressing to violence in video games and song lyrics, Montgomery (2007) observes, "This explosion of 'new media' is occurring at a time when society has not yet resolved many of the issues related to 'old media'" (p. 7). A cautious approach asks us to explore for whom these changes are most apparent. There are inevitable intersections between race, class, and gender. The Annenberg Study (2014) gathers data from *parents* on their *children*'s use, yet a prevailing concern is that parents often do not know what, exactly, their children are doing on digital, mobile technologies (Takeuchi & Levine, 2014). Young people who use mobile, digital media independently from their parents may be self-exposed to more sexual images and messages, including pornography and sex advice (Brown et al., 2014; Livingstone, 2014; Montgomery, 2007). In middle-class families, arguably with more disposable income and therefore more access to a variety of technologies, mothers monitor and engage children's media use more closely than fathers (Arthur, 2005). Access to and possession of technology seems ubiquitous for middle- to upper-class youth while youth of color and working-class and impoverished youth remain isolated, thereby extending marginalization across technology and generation (Arthur, 2005; Dutta, Bodie, & Basu, 2008).

While we may be fascinated with new media, we cannot forget their broader social impact. Livingstone (2014) cautions against a fascination with technology, writing that it is the "anxieties, even moral panics, that dominate the agenda" when exploring children and media use (p. 130). What is tricky and difficult to untangle is that technology and use of technology moves rapidly and across large swaths of society while the support systems of education and policy move much more slowly, if at all, what Montgomery (2007) refers to as "tectonic shifts" that transform the media landscape (p. 2).

WHAT IS BEING DONE: LEGISLATION AND POLICY CHANGES

Generally speaking, current policy and legislation efforts for media literacy are compartmentalized into discrete, acute problem-solving efforts and are often trendy and reactionary. Examples from New Jersey, Massachusetts, and California illustrate ways current efforts at policy development put media literacy work into inflexible topic- and action-specific boxes.

In May 2013, the New Jersey General Assembly passed legislation that called for the inclusion of social media essentials for grades 6–8. The material was designed to be included in the technology education curriculum as part of the Core Curriculum Content Standards in Technology in the 2013–2014 school year. The bill's sponsor, Assemblyman Fuentes, states, "In an increasingly digital world, there are a growing number of opportunities for us to broaden our horizons. There are also opportunities for our young people to fall prey to the pitfalls of the many social media platforms at their fingertips" (New Jersey State Legislature, 2013). Fuentes developed the legislation in a space between reaction and prevention, promoting it as a way to "make sure that students know how to unlock social media's potential, instead of being held back late in life by a mistake" (New Jersey State Legislature, 2013). The legislation is limited to grades 6–8 and focuses on social media, not the broader media landscape of which young people are a part. What happens when social media morphs into something more advanced—as it inevitably will—or gets replaced by another advancement in media and technology (as it inevitably will)? This policy initiative, while it draws attention to a component of media literacy, emphasizes a techno-logical trend and has little foundational support—there is no explanation of *how* social media essentials will be brought to the classroom.

In 2010, Massachusetts passed anti-cyberbullying legislation,[1] which required schools to create and implement bullying prevention plans. The law was introduced in emergency session in the wake of two suicides by youth who had been harassed in-person and online (Bazelon, 2010). At the time, this was considered the most comprehensive and inclusive anti-bullying tactic, however, by 2013, the law was deemed largely ineffective because it had no comprehensive support, no funding for training, and no research on bullying incidents (Adams & Black, 2013). A noble effort, the anti-cyberbullying law was a reactionary measure that did not address the larger social context that asks where young people learn it is acceptable to be cruel to each other. In part because of its newness, and its flexibility with anonymity, it is easy to blame social media for bullying, but it cannot be held solely responsible.

In August of 2013, California introduced legislation to prepare students in the San Fernando Valley (and nationwide) for careers in computer tech-nology. The Computer Science in STEM Act will add computer science classes to the STEM curriculum, intended to develop students' computing skills. The sponsor of the bill, Tony Cardenas, states, "We have a duty to educate our children, so that each of them has the opportunity to find a well-paying job that will allow them create prosperity (*sic*), raise a family, and contribute to our economy. The tech industry is quickly expanding and adding middle class jobs to the US economy" (California State Legislature, 2013). This measure emphasizes skill-based learning, which runs the risk of succumbing to technological trends and then being left literally in the dust. This may be the twenty-first century equivalent of the late-twentieth century push to have more computers in classrooms, which succeeded in getting computers into classrooms—with little to no plan on how to use them or for what purpose (Tyner, 1998).

Many states are starting to explore legislating media literacy with vary-ing degrees of attention. Examples from New Mexico, Massachusetts, New Jersey, and New York illustrate varying degrees of attention to policy that includes media literacy in the public school curriculum. A close look shows the language of the bills to be tentative and susceptible to being buried. New Mexico was the first state to legislate media literacy inclusion in some capacity. Introduced in 2009, the 2011 rewrites state that, beginning in the 2014–2015 school year, media literacy "shall be offered as an elective" in grades 6–12. "Shall be offered" is vague and the brief phrases are buried within all the other requirements students are to complete in order to successfully graduate from school. It is vital to pause and explore the timeline of the bill: It was introduced in 2009, revised in 2011, and anticipated to go into effect in the 2014–2015 school year, a nearly five-year process.

Between 2011 and 2013, the Massachusetts state legislature was presented with *S213/H472: An act concerning media literacy*. As written, the bill was cumbersome and stipulated that the Department of Elementary and Secondary Education would "authorize and assist in the implementation of programs on teaching media literacy" (malegislature.gov).[2] Because Massachusetts will not mandate curriculum and continues to receive criticism because of the lack of follow-through on the cyberbullying law, the language used indicates the bill will not pass. After being presented at hearing in October of 2013, the bill was absorbed into bill *S2027: An act to involve youth in civic engagement*.[3] Unfortunately, this act buries and compartmentalizes media literacy within civics, thereby leaving out other core subjects where media literacy may be infused. New Jersey's Bill *S1761: An act concerning the teaching of media literacy*[4] uses similar language as Massachusetts and "encourages" boards of education to offer instruction in media literacy. The language in the New York bill is nearly verbatim to Massachusetts, differing only by not referencing the Department of Elementary and Secondary Education and clarifying professional development programs rather than points (assembly.state.ny.us). These examples, as they are written, show that media literacy cannot be taken seriously as a preventive, proactive measure when its implementation is merely "encouraged" or, worse, relegated to a group that will not mandate curricular change.

STRENGTHENING MEDIA EDUCATION IN THE DIGITAL REALM

Much of digital media, especially social media, is focused on young people and their role as producers: They create and redistribute the content of so much of social media, including but not limited to, what appears on Facebook, Twitter, Vine, Vimeo, Instagram, Pinterest, and YikYak. One current challenge of media literacy education is how to teach students to draw upon their strengths as users of new digital media, while also establishing a critical distance from their own lived media environments. Digital and social media know no boundaries these days and comprehensive media literacy must work to expand its own boundaries to move learning forward in a progressive, productive way. Greater attention needs to be paid to the inclusion of media literacy in undergraduate education, in teacher training programs, and ultimately, in the formal inclusion of comprehensive media literacy across the curriculum in primary and secondary schools. In order for media literacy to move forward, change must be predicated upon a collective grassroots effort that includes the legislative support of citizens and policy makers for mandated media literacy development and training for teachers and teachers-in-training.

Drawing upon my own research and practice, and capitalizing on the massive shifts brought about through digital, mobile technology, the time has come to enact media literacy inclusion for students learning within the digital age. In Massachusetts, Mass Media Literacy (MML) supports legislation and K-12 curriculum that infuses media literacy across all courses. We argue for comprehensive media literacy education, which includes addressing both the content/representation of media as well as the structural and institutional components and is grounded in a social justice framework (Mass Media Literacy, n.d.). Instead of compartmentalizing learning to specific topics, comprehensive media literacy argues that individual struggles are part of a larger tapestry and should be approached from a position of continuous inquiry, with respect to the larger context of which they are a part. Instead of seeking satisfaction in answers, the process of continuous inquiry invites participants to keep asking questions, both about what we know and how we know it. In this exploration, comprehensive media literacy focuses on intersectionality, exploring how questions of identity production and political economy overlap. That is, we not only address race, gender, sexuality, socioeconomic class, or ability, but rather how these (and many other identities) overlap and influence each other, and how the process of ownership, production, and distribution contribute to the sense making of media messages. This can be particularly challenging for youth who are immersed in their media world without reflecting on the external influences of media production and distribution in the digital age. In addition, it can be difficult for teachers to engage students in a mediated environment where they may have less digital media knowledge and experience than young people.

MML endeavors to create a space that supports teacher training and student learning in the foundations of media literacy within the classroom setting. Generationally and heuristically, students may have more direct and regular experience with digital media, but they deserve formal training in critical analysis, deconstruction, and production. MML develops curriculum for teachers who are invited to modify lessons to fit their teaching plans, thereby allowing for the integration of media literacy within pre-existing lesson plans that are part of classroom learning, rather than separated from traditional lessons. In addition to an integrative approach, MML provides a model of professional development whereby, through teacher training and classroom application, teachers serve as an integral part of the formation of curriculum; they are not handed one-off activities nor are they asked to squeeze in a lesson on which they have no training. Participating teachers are trained in the foundational work of media literacy, are provided with curriculum pieces, and are invited to contribute to and modify these pieces in order to best fit the topic and direction of their courses. In this way, we aim for the teachers (and, ultimately, their students) to be autonomous learners. The process is inherently dialogic. One of our goals is to make this learning more accessible to teachers across the state.

To that end, MML supports the development of legislation that emphasizes teacher training in media literacy. Asking schools to provide media literacy without providing teacher training almost ensures that media literacy will not be brought to the classroom sustainably. Teachers are trained in their subjects and deserve to have media literacy as part of that training. In addition, more research must be built on *how* media literacy works. Through pre- and post-surveys and evaluations, MML works to build research to measure what students know and what they learn.

Much of the history of media literacy has, even with the most anti-hierarchical intentions, been top-down, with adults and youth playing familiar roles as teacher and student. For instance, while students are often encouraged to direct the progression of analysis and deconstruction, they are rarely in charge of pedagogy, course planning, or curriculum development. Classrooms may be rearranged so students are active participants in their learning, but if digital and social media are teaching us anything, it is that these technologies target youth as the preferred demographic and, in turn, young people appear particularly adept at using new and emerging technologies as extensions of their communicative selves. The shift in technological know-how leads us to question how educators, families, and advocates invested in comprehensive media literacy can acknowledge the need for formal training while also respecting that young people have greater access to and engagement with contemporary media. The hope is that, by addressing these questions, adults will learn how to best educate today's youth to critically engage as informed citizens in the digital age, while youth are empowered to educate adults from their digitally savvy strengths and vantage points.

One possible innovation to include digital media learning into media literacy is upending of the classroom hierarchy and putting young people in charge of teaching about their unique skill sets and the communicative approaches they use in the digital worlds they are a part of. So much of their formal educational learning has already been decided for them— could digital and social media be a place where young people make their own decisions? What do young people want to talk about? What are their concerns? How do they make sense of social and digital media? What are young people's concerns in the digital realm? What do adults need to know about social networking that young people have mastered? What do young people want adults to know (or not know) about their media use?

Upending the hierarchy can be a classroom tool to help propel comprehensive media literacy forward and address young people's concerns from their own space. Admittedly, this deviates from the traditional classroom (and, it must be noted, plays no productive role in high-stakes test preparation or common core adherence) and may be intimidating to students who are resistant to—but familiar with—"normal" classroom arrangements. However, if we want student to grapple with major questions of identity production, political economy and participatory culture, and we want them to be more involved in the educational process, then self-directed learning initiatives and reflections about the tools and conditions of the digital age may be an effective way to achieve these ends.

CONCLUSION: NEXT STEPS

At a time when it is safe to assume that digital technology in some form is here to stay, and that young people with access will both adopt and adapt to it quickly, it is valuable to explore how we can make teaching and learning more productive and proactive for young people, teachers, families, and communities. While many schools and community organizations may be working to implement media literacy, empirical data on its effectiveness remain elusive. The small collection of research on media literacy efficacy finds that media literacy interventions seem most successful at: addressing harmful effects of mass media (Joeng, Cho, & Hwang, 2012); increasing children's understandings that violence is glorified and that advertisements make unhealthy foods and activities look healthy (Bikham & Slaby, 2012); and increasing knowledge of core concepts and critical analysis skills (Fingar & Jolls, 2013). As such, meaningful conclusions about media literacy's effectiveness in the digital age have been stymied by the lack of data collection and complex longitudinal studies (Wartella & Lauricella, 2014).

In order to best address the needs of today's students, comprehensive media literacy requires tackling more than violence prevention or advertising analysis; it must provide a holistic approach that draws from the whole child within his/her community and respects that much of what young people learn may not be quantifiable, especially if it involves shifting attitudes, behaviors, and content choices. Burniske (2008) offers the reminder that "introducing the 'boxes and wires' of telecomputing into schools is not merely a political or educational issue. It is a moral, philosophical, and cultural issue as well" (p. 9). Accordingly, the primary goal of comprehensive media literacy should be to advocate for its curricular integration as a means to prepare today's generation for moral, philosophical, and cultural excursions in the digital era. We believe this can be best achieved through legislation that supports teacher training, inclusive curriculum development that inspires teachers in the process, strong goals that empower community members with a common, shared outcome, and active and regular inclusion of young people in their own learning.

NOTES

1. Text of the anti-cyber bullying law:
   "Cyber-bullying", bullying through the use of technology or any electronic communication, which shall include, but shall not be limited to, any transfer of signs, signals, writing, images, sounds, data or intelligence of any nature transmitted in whole or in part by a wire, radio, electromagnetic, photo electronic or photo optical system, including, but not limited to, electronic mail, internet communications, instant messages or facsimile communications. Cyber-bullying shall also include (i) the creation of a web page or blog in which the creator assumes the identity of another person or (ii) the knowing impersonation of another person as the author of posted content or messages, if the creation or impersonation creates any of the conditions enumerated in clauses (i) to (v), inclusive, of the definition of bullying. Cyber-bullying shall also include the distribution by electronic means of a communication to more than one person or the posting of material on an electronic medium that may be accessed by one or more persons, if the distribution or posting creates any of the conditions enumerated in clauses (i) to (v), inclusive, of the definition of bullying.

2. Text of Massachusetts Bill S213/H472: An act for media literacy:
   To equip students with the knowledge and skills for accessing, analyzing, evaluating, creating and participating in the twenty-first century media culture, and to ensure students develop the independent thinking and critical analysis skills needed to navigate the messages of a media-saturated world, the department of elementary and secondary education shall authorize and assist in the implementation of programs on teaching media literacy. The components of media literacy covered in the program shall include: Accessing and evaluating information from a variety of internet and other media sources; Analyzing how media messages, including advertising, are constructed and for what purposes; Evaluating media's explicit and implicit messages, how messages can be interpreted, how values and points of view are included and excluded, and how media can influence ideas and behaviors; Creating media and messages using a variety of media tools, including the use of words, images, sound and other multi-media tools; Participating in a global media culture.
   The department shall develop standards and objectives for media literacy for grades kindergarten to 12, inclusive, within the existing curriculum. The department shall make available to school districts a list of resources to aid in the selection of materials and resources that contain substantive provisions on media literacy, and will ensure that approved media literacy training opportunities are made available for professional development points within the teacher recertification program.

3. Text of Bill S2027: An act to involve youth in civic engagement:
   The committee on Education to whom was referred the petitions (accompanied by bill, Senate, No. 203) of Harriette L. Chandler, Jason M. Lewis, Bruce E. Tarr, Eileen M. Donoghue and other members of the General Court for legislation to involve youth in civic engagement; (accompanied by bill, Senate, No. 213) of Katherine M. Clark, David M. Rogers, William N. Brownsberger, Tricia Farley-Bouvier and other members of the General Court for legislation concerning media literacy in schools; (accompanied by bill, Senate, No. 254) of Richard T. Moore, Michael F. Rush, Michael R. Knapik, James B. Eldridge

and other members of the General Court for legislation to involve youth in civic engagement.; (accompanied by bill, House, No. 330) of F. Jay Barrows and others for legislation to direct the Department of Education to include a course in civics as a high school graduation requirement; (accompanied by bill, House, No. 422) of Paul R. Heroux and others for legislation to develop an elective high school course on labor law and workers' rights; (accompanied by bill, House, No. 465) of Elizabeth A. Poirier and others relative to the awarding of diplomas for civics education by the Board of Education; (accompanied by bill, House, No. 472) of David M. Rogers, Katherine Clark and others for legislation concerning media literacy in schools; (accompanied by bill, House, No. 513) of Martin J. Walsh and others relative to requiring the teaching of civics in all public elementary and high schools in the Commonwealth; and (accompanied by bill, House, No. 535) of Jonathan D. Zlotnik and others establishing a personal finance, civic responsibility and general legal high school social studies curriculum,- reports the accompanying bill (Senate, No. 2027).

4. Text of New Jersey Bill S1761: An act concerning the teaching of media literacy:
   The department of education shall encourage each board of education to offer instruction in media literacy, including the means to demystify violent images, and shall study the feasibility of incorporating the instruction into the curriculum framework that is developed to implement the Common Core Standards in English Language Arts.

REFERENCES

Adams, D., & Black, S. (July 21, 2013). Massachusetts anti-bullying law seen as unfunded, ineffective. *The Republican*. Retrieved from masslive.com.

Arthur, L. (2005). Popular culture: Views of parents and educators. In J. Marsh (Ed.), *Popular culture, new media and digital literacy in early childhood* (pp. 165–182). London: Routledge/Falmer.

Aufderheide, P. (1993). *Media literacy: A report of the National Leadership Conference on Media Literacy*. Queenstown, MD.

Bazelon, E. (April 23, 2010). Bullies beware: Massachusetts just passed the country's best anti-bullying law. *Slate*. Retrieved from slate.com.

Bikham, D., & Slaby, R. G. (February 2012). Effects of a media literacy program in the US on children's critical evaluation of unhealthy media messages about violence, smoking, and food. *Journal of Children and Media, 6*(2), 255–271.

Bleakley, A., Vaala, S., Jordan, A. B., & Romer, D. (2014). The Annenberg Media Environment Survey: Media access and use in U.S. home with children and adolescents. In A. B. Jordan & D. Romer (Eds.), *Media and the well-being of children and adolescents* (pp. 1–19). New York: Oxford University Press.

Brown, J. D., El-Toukhy, S., & Ortiz, R. (2014). Growing up sexually in a digital world: The risks and benefits of youths' sexual media use. In A. B. Jordan & D. Romer (Eds.), *Media and the well-being of children and adolescents* (pp. 90–108). New York: Oxford University Press.

Burniske, R. (2008). *Literacy in the digital age* (2nd ed.). Thousand Oaks, CA: Corwin Press.

California State Legislature (August 6, 2013). Cardenas introduces legislation to encourage computer education. Retrieved from caredenas.house.gov.

Collier, A. (2014). Perspectives on parenting in a digital age. In A. B. Jordan & D. Romer (Eds.), *Media and the well-being of children and adolescents* (pp. 247–265). New York: Oxford University Press.

Domaille, K., & Buckingham, D. (2001). *Youth media education survey.* Retrieved from portal.unesco.org.

Dutta, M. J., Bodie, G. D., & Basu, A. (2008). Health disparity and the racial divide among the nation's youth: Internet as a site for change? In A. Everett (Ed.), *Learning race and ethnicity: Youth and digital media* (pp. 175–197). Cambridge, MA: MIT Press.

Fingar, K., & Jolls, T. (August 6, 2013). Evaluation of a school-based violence prevention media literacy curriculum. *Injury Prevention,* 1–8.

Firestone, C. M. (1993). Foreword. *Media literacy: A report of the National Leadership Conference on Media Literacy.* Queenstown, MD.

Flanagin, A. J., & Metzger, M. J. (2010). *Kids and credibility: An empirical examination of youth, digital media use, and information credibility.* Cambridge, MA: MIT Press.

Hobbs, R. (2011). The state of media literacy: A response to Potter. *Journal of Broadcasting and Electronic Media, 55*(3), 419–430.

Livingstone, S. (2014). Risk and harm on the Internet. In A. B. Jordan & D. Romer (Eds.), *Media and the well-being of children and adolescents* (pp. 129–146). New York: Oxford University Press.

Mass Media Literacy (2014). Retrieved from massmedialiteracy.org

Montgomery, K. (2007). *Generation digital: Politics, commerce and childhood in the age of the Internet.* Cambridge, MA: MIT Press.

New Jersey State Legislature. (May 20, 2013). Assembly passes Fuentes' 'Social media education act.' *New Jersey Legislation.* Retrieved from njleg5.com.

Potter, J. (2012). *Digital media and learner identity: The new curatorship.* New York: Palgrave MacMillan.

Potter, W. J. (2010). The state of media literacy. *Journal of Broadcasting and Electronic Media, 54*(4), 675–696.

Rideout, V. J., Foehr, U. G., & Roberts, D. F. (2010). *Generation M2: Media in the lives of 8- to 18-year-olds.* Menlo Park, CA: Kaiser Family Foundation.

Takeuchi, L. M., & Levine, M. H. (2014). Learning in a digital age: Toward a new ecology of human development. In A. B. Jordan & D. Romer (Eds.), *Media and the well-being of children and adolescents* (pp. 20–43). New York: Oxford University Press.

Tyner, K. (1998). *Literacy in a Digital World: Teaching and Learning in the Age of Information.* New Jersey: Lawrence Erlbaum Associates.

Wartella, E., & Lauricella, A. R. (2014). Early learning, academic achievement, and children's digital media use. In A. B. Jordan & D. Romer (Eds.), *Media and the well-being of children and adolescents* (pp. 173–186). New York: Oxford University Press.

Cited Bills

An act concerning media literacy (2013), Massachusetts Bill #S213/H472. Retrieved from malegislature.gov.

An act concerning the teaching of media literacy (2014). New Jersey Bill #S1761. Retrieved from njleg.state.nj.us.

An act to involve youth in civic engagement (2014). Massachusetts Bill #S2027. Retrieved from malegislature.gov.

An act relative to bullying in schools (2010). Massachusetts Bill H3909 Retrieved from malegislature.gov.

Media literacy as elective in public schools (2011). New Mexico Bill #233. Retrieved from nmlegis.gov.

Public school media literacy classes (2009). New Mexico Bill #342. Retrieved from nmlegis.gov.

Requires the development of standards and objectives for media literacy for grades K-12 (2013). New York Bill # AO8347. Retrieved from assembly.state.ny.us.

9   Digital Divides, Devices, and Destinations for 1:1 Technology Initiatives for U.S. Secondary Education

Ben Boyington

INTRODUCTION

The phrase "digital divide" refers to the gap between those with access to high-speed (broadband) Internet access and those who have no access or only low-speed access. The digital divide within the United States is significant in size and impact, creating digital segregations based on economic disparities, unequal access to information, and lack of voice. In March 2010, the federal government stepped forward to address this problem, creating the National Broadband Plan under the aegis of the American Recovery and Reinvestment Act. The plan emphasized the need for "greater broadband connectivity in anchor institutions, and improved broadband adoption and utilization, especially among disadvantaged and vulnerable populations" (*Congressional Digest*, 2013). With this action, the federal government clearly took the position that education generally and public schools specifically have integral roles to play in addressing the digital divide.

The schools-based approach to closing the digital divide is manifest in the so-called "1:1 initiative," in which every student in a school has his or her own Internet-enabled "screen" for academic use. Though this has not been without controversy, the intent is clear and laudable: to address digital and educational inequities by providing devices for use at school and at home. To help those who lack access at home, the federal government, through its E-Rate program and FCC initiatives, is encouraging telecommunications companies to provide low-cost Internet access (as low as $9.95 per month) to families who qualify for free or reduced-cost school lunches (Snider & Yu, 2011). But schools are left on their own to develop 1:1 programs, and not all stakeholders (educators, students, parents, taxpayers) have the same vision, or the same receptivity to a district's vision, regarding connectivity, digital literacies, and the role of screens in the classroom.

STORIES OF IMPLEMENTATION

The 1:1 movement dates back to at least 2000, when Delores Bolton, principal at Carmen Arace Middle School in Bloomfield, Connecticut (population

20,000), was facing low test scores and numerous disciplinary issues. As part of a plan to address these problems, Bolton persuaded the school board to purchase a laptop for every teacher and for each of the school's nearly 300 students. That same year in Maine, then-Governor Angus King proposed the nation's first statewide 1:1 initiative, under which each of the state's 17,000 7th graders would receive his or her own Apple laptop (Martens, 2000). In the intervening years, the movement has grown across the country.

Austin, Tex. In 2010, Westlake High School, an urban school serving about 2,600 students in grades 9 to 12, piloted a 1:1 initiative, providing iPads to all 11th and 12th graders as well as to those students' teachers (Foote, Jan/Feb 2012). The summer before implementation, teachers received professional development, while a limited number of students engaged in a trial rollout. Using iPad tools and apps, teachers provided assignments that required students to use new technology interfaces. The pilot included student submission of work via their tablets, assessment of work using digital tools, and an evaluative process that included both individual self-assessment and peer review. From the beginning, participants were concerned about the difference between simply automating processes and using screens in transformative ways (differentiation, creativity, communication, increased equity of access for special-needs students). As a result, Westlake engaged in serious examination of pedagogy and of the overall school experience. In a 2012 survey of 854 students, 88% reported that using iPads "enhanced their learning experience," 90% reported an increase in motivation, and 89% reported an increased "desire to dig deeper into a subject." A later report on the school's progress (Foote, Nov/Dec 2012) noted that teachers and students were involved in every stage, from planning to implementation, and observed fundamental changes in the following areas:

- individual reading and highlighting ebooks for classroom discussion
- student collaboration, merging new technology with older resources
- alternative assessments: filming skits and creating puppet shows and animations
- teachers accessing data collaboratively
- teachers co-planning and investigating software options

At Westlake, use of the 1:1 iPad technology "as an invisible aid" led to a culture of collaboration and learning together (Foote, Nov/Dec 2012).

Garrett, Ind. When Dennis Stockdale took over as superintendent of the rural Garrett-Keyser-Butler-Community School District in 2007, he had a vision: "The whole key is individualizing instruction and education for the student" (Davis, 2013). His path to reinvention was a 1:1 initiative, and by the 2012–2013 school year, "all three schools in this 1,800-student district [had] Wi-Fi, elementary school students [were using] iPads in class, older students [were taking] MacBook laptops home, [and a] totally wired high school [had] opened." This transition required much politicking, but

Stockdale's two greatest challenges were funding and equitable access. The solutions were integrally tied: "he redirected money that parents already were paying in state fees for printed textbooks" and the state department of education awarded a $300,000 classroom-innovation grant, enabling the purchase of 100 mobile WiFi "hot spots" that students can take home, establishment of WiFi in the community center, and the creation of a wireless area in the high school that is open until 10 p.m. on school days.

In the first year of the initiative, the school suffered an "implementation dip ... while educators worked out the kinks ... and continued training." The district earned a D rating from the state department of education, but that rose to an A the following year. This success is due in large part to belief in professional development and examination of pedagogy: for instance, in elementary mathematics, "students are grouped by learning level and outcomes, which can change daily or weekly," and more generally, "teachers are curating curricula and creating ... electronic-resource libraries to promote individualized learning."

Windsor, Vt. The Windsor Southeast Supervisory Union, a rural district of four schools and about 1,160 students, has been building its 1:1 initiative since the 2012–2013 school year. To help address connectivity outside the largest school, Windsor K-12, the town of Windsor has arranged for free WiFi access across much of downtown (T. Marsh, town manager, personal communication, Aug. 23, 2014). Implementation has been quick by education standards. Larry Dougher, Chief Information Officer, says the cost is not sustainable with grant funds, so it has to be built into the budget (personal communication, Aug. 23, 2014). This budget allocation works through reprioritizing and backing from the board, which, along with voters, has a history of deep support for technology. Chromebooks were a natural choice for this initiative because Windsor K-12 already uses Google Apps for Educators. Judging by changes from the faculty's move to 1:1 almost a decade ago, Dougher expects a culture of collaboration to grow among students across the supervisory union.

Teachers involved in the 1:1 before 2014–2015 were positive about the implementation of this initiative. Michelle Reidy, 7th and 8th grade English/language arts, said that this technology saves time with the writing-feedback cycle and noted that "being able to conference online seems to [lead] students to put forth greater effort" (personal communication, Aug. 20–21, 2014). In the pilot year, Destiny Lawyer, grades 5 and 6 reading and writing, noticed that students were more inclined to do their work than they had been before. Other benefits in her classroom include technology-based project choices for independent reading, greater depth in research, interventions such as a dictation read-and-write program, and differentiated or individualized instruction and assessment in the form of video clips to support in-class readings and online spelling and vocabulary tests. Colleen Deschamp, 5th and 6th grade science, experienced 1:1 in the second year of the program. She emphasized the benefits of self-direction: "[O]ur students have this head start … to learn how to browse appropriately, to find credible information, and to organize themselves" (personal communication, Aug. 20–22, 2014).

Parents of middle schoolers who have participated in the initiative observed the following benefits (personal communication, Aug. 20–22, 2014):

- increase in student engagement (preference for computer over textbooks)
- less resistance to writing assignments (distaste for handwriting; ease of editing)
- increased efficiency (students can work at school when staying late)
- more in-school learning activities (science in particular)
- additional option for communication between teachers and students
- more research-based assessments (making learning more interesting for students)

Parents were split, however, on funding. Their feedback echoes arguments found in the research: one parent opined that each student having his or her own device "is important [because] our students live in a world where computer proficiency and interface is a fact of life," while another suggested that "Having the school well-equipped for use during the day … and having a computer lab staffed before and after school may be a better use of resources." One parent echoed what we've seen in other districts: "If the devices aren't used for more collaboration between students, or between student and teacher, I don't really see an advantage." But in the end, parents expressed hope: "When teachers use the 1:1 well, … my sons thrive because it allows them to accelerate their learning."

The district should consider these observations as the initiative continues its expansion into the high school in 2014–2015 and beyond. Four months into the high school's adoption of 1:1, there is already much improvement in logistics: Before the 1:1, teachers had to share a limited number of Macbooks by signing out mobile laptop carts in advance. However, the biggest problem being reported by teachers is distractibility—students don't always know how to keep the focus on educational use. These concerns notwithstanding, teachers are interested in changes that the ubiquity and ease of access might bring to engagement and pedagogy. Although many WHS teachers were already using project-based learning with digital tools, Web-based lessons, and Google Docs, use and access of these digital tools should become easier. Overall, further professional development is essential, as is buy-in by all stakeholders, in order to adopt and assess instructional and learning goals and the methods teachers will use with these devices to create new classroom experiences. Meaningful transformation will require collaboration among teachers and administrators (including curriculum coordinators and instructional coaches).

Nationwide Trends. Across the country, administrators are asserting that 1:1 initiatives will lead to improvement in student performance, and with "99,000 K-12 schools spend[ing] $17 billion annually on instructional materials and technology" (Rotella, 2013), the technology industry is eager to capitalize on these assertions. In 2010, a study conducted by Project RED found that "schools with a 1:1 student-to-computer ratio outperform non-1:1 schools [academically]" (Salpeter, 2010). The study's authors offered three key best practices in the 1:1 programs of these schools:

- daily implementation in all classes (intervention or regular work)
- principal leadership
- pedagogical use of social media and games/simulations

The authors also emphasize collaboration among students and the importance of "proper implementation," asserting that districts "need to invest in the re-engineering of schools" (Findings, 2013). This prompts one to ask, what kind of reengineering? Physical reengineering (wiring and hardware), curricular reengineering (digital media literacy, information literacy, computer literacy), or metaphoric reengineering (pedagogy, school culture)?

In November 2013, panelists from *Tech & Learning*'s New York and Texas Tech Forums reported on implementation of technology in their districts and benefits they have observed:

- devices: Chromebook, iPad, Dell Latitude 10, Intel Ultrabook
- platforms: Google Apps for Education, Blackboard, Edmodo, eBackpack, Moodle
- software/apps: Garage Band, iMovie, Nearpod
- curricular and performance benefits: creation (higher-order thinking); technology-based intervention for special-needs students; inquiry-based learning; improvement in students' fact-based content; differentiation; collaboration
- systemic changes: team-building; personalizing education
- implementation procedures: teacher and student involvement in choice of devices; extended shared planning times and professional development/support; use of data to inform instruction (What hardware are you using and why?, 2013)

Clearly, there is great potential in 1:1 initiatives, including equitable access, blended learning, differentiation and individualization of learning, credit recovery options, online coursework, and collaboration among teachers and students. Robin Britt, director of Personalized Achievement, Curriculum and Environment at North Carolina's Guilford County Schools, believes that such implementation could transform not only classrooms, but the teaching profession itself. He emphasizes "a postindustrial workplace where temporary groupings of co-workers collaborate on tasks requiring intellectual, not physical capabilities" (cited in Rotella, 2013). Echoing the language of corporate reform, he goes on to say, "We need a schoolhouse that prepares students to do that kind of work" (Rotella, 2013). In Guilford County, over a dozen technology facilitators were hired, illustrating one of the central conundrums facing schools who wish to adopt 1:1 initiatives: budgeting. While new initiatives often lead to questions about purpose and methods, the biggest arguments arise when it comes to financing: How will communities fund this initiative? Will taxpayers fund the costs of digital access? Will schools have to adjust staffing in order to pay for such resources? If private sources or governmental funding support these projects, will impositions be made upon schools' curricular autonomy? Citizens and stakeholders often do not consider such infrastructural issues, but answers to such questions are necessary for effective digital media literacy to emerge in schools.

FUNDING

Education funding can be complicated, but for 1:1, there are three basic models (Dixon, 2007):

- State-Funded. Within the U.S., the state of Maine led the way in funding of 1:1 initiatives, going beyond hardware and software to address infrastructure and training. However, the sustainability of a model like Maine's is a challenge because state funding is always "vulnerable to political changes and new priorities."
- District-Funded. Schools in Henrico County, Va., enjoy "the benefit of sustainability while preserving local control" by increasing their technology budget through reprioritization. The board has made sure that laptop purchasing and support is part of the annual budget. However, district funding usually includes fiscal support from the state and federal levels, possibly bringing influence over local curricular considerations.
- Hybrid. "One-off grants or bonds from district, state, federal, corporate or philanthropic sources" can be found but "are [best] used to cover one-off start-up costs, such as infrastructure and professional development."

Ultimately, Dixon concludes, the cost of 1:1 "is much more than buying technology. [Successful districts] budget at least an additional 25–33 percent of the total costs for priorities such as professional development and support."

In short, the majority of districts rely to some extent on outside sources to provide technology funding. With most districts buying into the argument that educational technology is essential, schools often have to jockey for limited grant dollars, thereby increasing vulnerability to commercial enterprises seeking to profit from 1:1 technology initiatives. Moreover, the installation of hardware and software in schools often precedes curricular initiatives, professional development, and assessed learning outcomes, all of which are needed to provide a viable trajectory for effective digital media literacy.

Federal Government

In February 2014, President Obama announced that the ConnectEd initiative would provide "$2 billion in repurposed funding from the Federal Communications Commission's E-rate program ... to provide 99 percent of the nation's schools with high-speed broadband technology within five years" (Molnar, 2014). Older government programs, such as No Child Left Behind and its Race to the Top initiative, also provide funding. "With digital content becoming a primary source of instructional delivery ..., [f]ederal funds that used to be dedicated to equipment acquisition are now being integrated into [funds] to support teaching and learning" (House, 2012). However, funding access has become increasingly competitive: in a single year (2011 to 2012), the percentage of competitive funds rose by 8 percent, an increase of 4.9 billion dollars. Finally, there are strings attached to such grants: tying teacher evaluations to student performance has long been a requirement of Race to the Top grants, and "evaluation of ... principals, superintendents, and school boards" is new to this particular iteration.

Non-Governmental Sources

In that same speech, President Obama announced "a donation of $750 million in goods and services from seven companies for schools and students" (Molnar, 2014):

- Apple: iPads, MacBooks, content and professional development tools.
- AT&T: free Internet connectivity for educational devices over their wireless network for three years.
- Autodesk: expansion of its "Design the Future" program to every secondary school in the country.
- Microsoft: "deeply" discounting the price of Windows OS for all U.S. public schools, more than 12 million copies of Office free to qualifying institutions.
- O'Reilly Media: with Safari Books Online, free educational content and tools for every school in America.
- Sprint: free wireless service for up to 50,000 low-income high school students over the next four years.
- Verizon: cash and in-kind commitments to expand existing programs aimed at helping teachers use devices in STEM classes and to start new programs.

Noting these contributions, the president went on to challenge "every business leader across America to join us in this effort" (cited in Molnar, 2014).

Despite sustainability concerns, John Musso, executive director of the Association of School Business Officials International, supports this corporate involvement for financial reasons, though some ASBOI members have questions about guidelines. More pointedly, Alex Molnar (2014), director of the Commercialism in Education Research Unit at the University of Colorado–Boulder, who has studied the intersection of business interests and public education for 30 years, categorizes the contributions as "a self-interested effort to shape a marketplace in education, and to peddle their wares." Frederick M. Hess, director of education policy studies at the American Enterprise Institute, echoes this concern, questioning "whether a quid pro quo is implied in corporate donations of this magnitude" (cited in Molnar, 2014, p. 11). And Donald Cohen, executive director of In the Public Interest, a resource center on responsible contracting, asserts that "Education policy needs to be driven by public interest, not profit margins" (cited in Molnar, 2014, p. 11).

Given the magnitude of corporate funding options sanctioned by the federal government, public policy concerns over the autonomy of districts should be shared by every administrator, educator, parent, and citizen: Do schools, parents, and communities comprehend and support the influence that can come with grant funding from third parties? Besides corporations, where might funding come from?

Venture Philanthropy. Venture capitalism is the investment of monies in high-potential startup companies or companies undergoing major restructuring or redirection, and/or organizations that do not have access to public funding. With this model in mind, a new type of giving has been born: venture philanthropy. This is different from traditional philanthropy in a few significant ways (Gregorian, 2001):

- Venture philanthropists work intensely with a small number of nonprofit organizations.
- Venture philanthropists often play direct roles in daily operations, even joining boards of directors of recipient organizations.
- Venture philanthropists generally invest only in causes with outcomes that can be readily measured.

In describing the process of educational reform, Saltman (2010) writes that venture philanthropy "pushes privatisation and deregulation" and relies on central concepts of corporate reform "to describe [and drive] educational reforms and policies: choice, competition, efficiency, accountability, monopoly, turnaround, and failure" (p. 2). He also notes that "giving to public schooling [is] a 'social investment' that … must begin with a business plan and involve quantitative measurement of efficacy" (p. 2). Saltman asserts that these methods exert an insidious influence on the federal government, citing the Obama administration's championing of charter schools, reliance on standardized tests, and "data-driven policy making" (p. 66). Teachers' unions also express concerns: Karen Lewis, president of the Chicago Teachers Union, has said, "Venture philanthropy is a slow road to privatization" (Ahmed-Ullah, 2012).

While corporate education reform has deliberate financial and ideological agendas and outcomes, critics argue that the work of venture philanthropists is no less dangerous simply because it is more subtle. For instance, the Broad Foundation—one of the three most powerful venture philanthropists exerting influence on education—faces political and economic conflicts of interest, including integral ties to corporate reformers; a longstanding relationship with the Obama administration's secretary of education, Arne Duncan, the chancellor of New York City Schools, Joel Klein, and other reform "champions"; a "superintendents academy" predicated on the idea that education should be run like a business; and initiatives seeking to transform teachers' unions into company unions and thus open "the workforce to unfettered exploitation" (Derstine, 2013).

Public-Private Partnerships. Such partnerships have included three organizations devoted to the much-ballyhooed STEM problem in the country, the creation of learning labs in existing community spaces, and the Maker Education Initiative, which seeks to lead "young people to develop confidence [and] creativity [in] learning ... through making" (Guymon, 2014). But what does this look like? The Maker Initiative, for instance, is funded in part by Google, a proponent of the 1:1 initiative; so while one may see public-private partnerships as "contrary to ... the invasive privatization of a cultural institution [because they] are a community effort," concerns over fairness and equity abound, even in this seemingly benign hybrid model.

IMPLICATIONS

While issues of access tend to fuel the urgency to fund and create 1:1 programs, digital literacy initiatives and related competencies often remain marginalized. The movement toward putting a laptop or other Internet-enabled device in the hands of every public school student in the United States could be an effective means to resolving the access problem if meaningful digital media curricula, pedagogy, and connectivity outside the schools are addressed at the same time. But it's not enough to simply hand every student a Chromebook or an iPad. According to Joel Klein, former New York City chancellor of schools and currently the chief executive of Amplify—a division of Rupert Murdoch's News Corp. that is positioning itself as a major tablet and curriculum provider for middle schools across the country—"If you just stick a kid in front of a screen for eight hours and hope it works, it's not going to work" (Rotella, 2013). The success of the Amplify device—indeed, of any such device—lies with teachers' ability to exploit it. Research indicates that some district decision-makers understand this well: The most successful initiatives are investing in professional development for teachers, including blended learning, integration, differentiated and personalized instruction, and assessment tools. Without long-term commitment to such planning and without stakeholder buy-in, the 1:1 movement is just another fad. Indeed, there are those who argue that the movement is a waste of resources, especially given fundamental problems with student engagement, poverty, and societal lack of respect for the system and for teachers. In order to effectively integrate digital media literacy into today's classrooms, focused longitudinal studies are needed to analyze the 1:1 initiative's impact on learning.

Even if one believes the rosiest projections about 1:1 initiatives—and accepts the assertion of Amplify's Joel Klein that a tablet is the best tool for teachers and students to make progress, issues surrounding funding and risks must be weighed regardless of the 1:1 funding source. All grant organizations, including those that don't seem to have an obvious agenda, insist on accountability measures, and with such measures come questions about autonomy. Given the decentralization of education in the U.S., the onus falls upon each educational community to carefully examine the access they provide to those seeking to enhance digital portability, as well as the risks associated with accepting funding for hardware or software. Stakeholders must assess the political economy of 1:1 technology programs by looking into the motives and agendas that could potentially undermine the autonomy and viability of a public school system, even if gradually. Rather than rush to include technology without a clear purpose or designated pathways to digital literacy, decision-makers must engage in critical inquiry, researching the goals and mission of all granting organizations and opening up discussions with all stakeholders regarding grant criteria and possible influences. Creating a sustainable digital media education program across subjects requires investment by the community, so districts must persuade their citizens to support technological reform along with digital literacies over the long term. Due to the imbalanced "zip code" funding of American education, schools must work toward these goals one community at a time. This direction can best be achieved by fostering collaborative community relationships in the form of partnerships among taxpayers, local industry, and companies whose success relies on an informed and capable workforce. Collectively, these visionaries can leverage the power of all stakeholders to create and sustain a viable and comprehensive digital media education program for a new generation of learners.

REFERENCES

Ahmed-Ullah, N. S. (2012, June 19). New venture fund to focus on CPS education reform. *Chicago Tribune*. Retrieved from http://articles.chicagotribune.com/2012-06-19/news/ct-met-cps-new-venture-fund-20120619_1_chicago-public-education-fund-renaissance-schools-fund-education-reform.

Congressional Digest. (April 2013). *Access to telecommunications technology.* (Vol. 92, Issue 4). Washington, DC: Congressional Digest Corp.

Davis, M. (2013, February 6). Digital access. *Education Week, 32*(20), S24–S25.

Derstine, K. (2013, February 24). *Who is Eli Broad and why is he trying to destroy public education?* Retrieved from http://www.defendpubliceducation.net.

Dixon, B. (2007, March). Finding funds for student laptops. *District Administration, 43*(3), 72–75.

Findings. (2013). Section of research overview. *Project RED*. Retrieved from http:// www. projectred.org/about/research-overview/findings.html#one.

Foote, C. (2012, January/February). Learning together: The evolution of a 1:1 iPad program. *Internet@Schools 19*(1), 14–18.

Foote, C. (2012, November/December). The 1:1 experience: An idea worth watching. *Internet@Schools 19*(5), 26–27.

Gregorian, V. (2001, April 19). Putting venture philanthropy into perspective. *Chronicle of Philanthropy 13*(13), 43–44.

Guymon, D. (2014, June 17). Public-private partnerships: The real future of education. Retrieved from http://www.edutopia.org/blog/public-private-partnerships-future-of-education-dave-guymon.

House, J. (2012, August). 5 trends that follow the money. *T H E Journal 39*(6), 12–15.

Martens, E. (2000, May 1). A laptop for every kid. *Time 155*(18), 57.

Molnar, M. (2014, February 19). President's ConnectED effort garners major support from FCC, companies. *Education Week 33*(21), 10–11.

Rotella, C. (2013, September 12). No child left untableted. *Chicago Tribune*. Retrieved from http://www.nytimes.com/2013/09/15/magazine/no-child-left-untableted. html?_r=0&adxnnl=1&pagewanted=all&adxnnlx=1419192097-DTYMvcN+ b2AFsAUVjUzKYQ.

Salpeter, J. (2010, August). Study shows the benefits of 1:1. *Tech & Learning 31*(1), 16.

Saltman, K. J. (2010). *The gift of education: Public education and venture philanthropy*. New York: Palgrave Macmillan.

Snider, M., & Yu, R. (2011, November 9). Plan to help poor offers Net for $9.95. *USA Today* 3.

What hardware are you using and why? (2013, November). *Tech & Learning 34*(4), 40–41.

10 Encouraging Critical Thinking about Cyberbullying

Media Literacy Data from 6th Graders

Erica Scharrer, Christine J. Olson, Laras Sekarasih, and Ryan Cadrette

With television, video games, and the Internet occupying increasing amounts of children's and teens' time and attention, media literacy efforts designed to increase critical thinking about the role of media in society and in individuals' lives become more important than ever. One topic that registers as a particular area of concern for parents, teachers, and young people themselves is cyberbullying. Indeed, with tragic examples capturing headlines and prior studies showing bullying via social media to be relatively prevalent among youth (e.g., Roberto et al., 2014), there is no question the topic is socially significant. Yet, although many have called for the role of media literacy in policy initiatives on cyberbullying (Hobbs, 2010; Livingstone & Brake, 2010), it seems very little prior data exist that shed light on whether such efforts might shape views and practices of cyberbullying among young people (Worthen, 2007). Indeed, the introduction and impact of newer forms of media call for the extension and reimagining of literacy in a digital space (Meyrowitz, 1998). Cyberbullying is a prime example of a new form of a long-standing issue—bullying—that we argue requires newer modes and approaches to understand and to address.

CYBERBULLYING

Cyberbullying has introduced a number of new challenges to the existing problems that face-to-face bullying has caused. The current generation of adolescents are sharing and socializing online more than any other in history (Madden, Cortesi, Gasser, Lenhart, & Duggan, 2012). They have grown up using new social media such as Facebook, Twitter, and Instagram, incorporating these technologies into their developing social lives to an unprecedented extent. These platforms complicate the challenges of preventing bullying by allowing abusive and antagonistic behaviors to occur beyond the boundaries of the schoolyard. Online spaces not only allow social interaction to take place without immediate adult supervision, but also offer a degree of anonymity that can make it difficult to hold bullies accountable for their actions. Estimates of how frequently young people experience online bullying vary widely, with 22 peer reviewed studies published as of 2011 showing most rates of victimization ranging from 6 to 30%, while rates of bullying others online ranged from 3 to 44% (Patchin & Hinduja, 2012).

Concerns about cyberbullying and its potential implications have resonated beyond school communities: cyberbullying has also been spotlighted by policymakers, as evidenced by the growing number of attempts to legislate statewide anti-bullying policies (Hinduja & Patchin, 2014). While formal legislation has the power to provide the legal protection to the victims of bullying and their families, it is also important to empower young media users as members of virtual communities to engage in safe and respectful online behaviors. Media literacy education (MLE) is one of the possible strategies that provides this opportunity by giving students the resources to think critically about their use of new technologies, encouraging them to consider the relationship between their conduct online and elsewhere.

YOUNG PEOPLE AND INTERNET SAFETY

The availability of the Internet and new media opens various avenues for youth, ranging from educational experiences to self-expression, to friendship and intimacy. However, it also poses challenges and risks, such as Internet addiction, compromised privacy, risky interactions with strangers, exposure to violent and sexual content, and online harassment or cyberbullying (Leung & Lee, 2012; Livingstone & Brake, 2010). It is therefore important to "equip" young Internet users with media and information literacy. Youth need not only to understand technical knowledge but also be aware of the social construction and production of the information they receive and produce on the Internet. Additionally, they should also be capable of exercising critical assessment of information in order to navigate the virtual world (Dupuis, 1997; Frechette, 2006).

Despite the emergence of the use of ICTs and mobile communication among children and adolescents, literature that focuses on digital media literacy "intervention," including parental mediation, or, even more so, media literacy curricula, is still scant. However, some researchers have noted that facilitation that provides knowledge about the Internet for young media users might be beneficial for mitigating risky Internet use (Bhat, Chang, & Linscott, 2010; Leung & Lee, 2012; Lwin, Stanaland, & Miyazaki, 2008; Mesch, 2009). For example, Lwin and colleagues (2008) demonstrated that children aged 10 to 12 who received active mediation—in which parents discussed online activities with their children—were less likely to disclose personal information on the Internet, compared to children whose parents exercised no rules or only provided restrictions regarding their children's Internet use. Similarly, Mesch (2009) found that adolescents whose parents engaged them in discussions on online safety were more likely to be aware of virtual risks than those whose parents did not exercise such mediation. Leung and Lee (2011) reported that parental mediation, including providing recommendation of particular websites to their children and co-using the Internet, was negatively associated with exposure to pornographic and violent content. In sum, providing children with knowledge about online safety appears to empower them and reduce their vulnerability to risks in the virtual world.

OUR MEDIA LITERACY APPROACH

The current focus is the latest in a long-term University-community partnership in which annual versions of the same MLE program raising issues pertaining in some way to media violence have been offered multiple times (e.g., Scharrer, 2005, 2006, 2009; Scharrer & Wortman-Raring, 2012; Sekarasih, Olson, O'Malley, & Scharrer, 2014; Sekarasih, Walsh, & Scharrer, 2015). Indeed, most recently, Internet safety issues and face-to-face bullying as well as cyberbullying have informed our prior research and outreach efforts on the topic (Olson, Sekarasih, O'Malley, & Scharrer, 2014; Walsh, Sekarasih, & Scharrer, 2014). In the previous iterations of our MLE initiative, one of the lessons focused on different types of bullying—physical, verbal, social/relational, and cyberbullying—as part of aggressive behaviors, as well as their depictions in U.S. entertainment media (Walsh et al., 2014). Adopting the findings of the National Television Violence Study (Smith et al., 1998), students were introduced to the notion of high-risk depictions of bullying in media content (e.g., rewarded bullying, bullying done by the protagonist, bullying portrayed with humor). Analyzing students' homework responses that served as data source in the study, we found that students were able to recognize bullying in entertainment television programs that were oriented towards teens and preteens (e.g., *Glee*, *Victorious*). Some students even went further by offering a hypothetical scenario of how they would portray bullying responsibly on a television show, for example making the protagonist the victim of bullying instead of being the bully or depicting the role of bystanders in defending the victim.

In this current chapter, two primary questions are addressed (1) How does a group of young people view the issues of cyberbullying, especially (but not exclusively) in terms of the role of bystanders in the phenomenon? And (2) Does participation in our MLE program seem to shape those views? In posing these questions, the central issue of whether media literacy participation might promote critical thinking regarding topics pertaining to bullying in a digital environment is addressed.

The data for this chapter are drawn from student responses to a cyberbullying lesson within a broader MLE program. In March and April of 2014, the authors worked alongside a team of undergraduate students who were enrolled in an advanced Communication course with a Community Service Learning component to design and facilitate a program for 60 sixth grade students. All students attended the same school located in a predominantly White, middle-class rural New England community. During the 2013–2014 school year, 17.4% of students in the district were identified as low income, as compared to the state average of 38.3% (Massachusetts Department of ESE, 2013–14).

The MLE Program

Three classrooms of sixth grade students participated in four, 1-hour MLE lessons. The program's objective was to encourage students to think critically about their use and production of media. Multimedia presentations were used to introduce key concepts and to prompt student discussion regarding media violence, gender stereotypes, and cyberbullying. Additionally, between meetings, students were given homework assignments which prompted further reflection on each topic.

Each classroom participated in the same curriculum although the direction of discussion varied depending upon student responses. On the first day, students were introduced to the practice of asking critical questions about media and how to identify "high-risk" portrayals of media violence (as adapted from the National Television Violence Study; Smith et al., 1998). The second day's lesson concentrated on cyberbullying, the bystander effect, and responses to cyberbully behavior. Day three was specifically focused on gender stereotypes, beauty standards for men and women, and gendered advertising. The fourth and final day of the program was dedicated to a production activity in which the students designed a public service announcement (PSA) that addressed an issue related to media violence, cyberbullying, or gender stereotypes. These PSAs were then displayed in the elementary school to educate others.

Cyberbullying Lesson Materials

Materials collected during the cyberbullying lesson provided rich insight into student understanding of online bullying, their possible responses to such behavior, and their preferred methods for addressing the issue, and those data are the source of the current analysis. These materials included 60 responses to a closed-ended questionnaire administered prior to the lesson, 54 student "brainstorming journals" used to record students' thoughts during the lesson, and 3 "Online Constitutions" outlining guidelines for good online citizenship written and signed by all the students in each classroom. Textual analysis was used to highlight emergent themes, which were then refined using the constant comparison method.

The closed-ended questionnaire was completed as homework prior to the lesson to assess students' preexisting beliefs about cyberbullying. The questionnaire asked about their beliefs regarding bullying prevalence (e.g., Bullying happens more often online than it does in person) and about their likelihood to report bullying witnessed online. For these items students responded using a 5-point scale from "Strongly Agree" to "Strongly Disagree." The questionnaire also provided hypothetical scenarios regarding bullying among their peers (e.g., "Your best friend comments on a picture of a classmate calling him or her ugly. How likely are you to intervene and defend the classmate?"). For these scenarios students identified if they were likely to intervene using a

5-point Likert scale from "Very Likely" to "Not Likely At All." The final item asked, "If you were to report online bullying, how would you do it?" and directed students to select as many options as applicable from the list provided (e.g., Tell a parent, Tell a teacher, Tell a police officer, Comment online/Respond online, Talk to the bully in person, or Other).

Students used the brainstorming journals during the lesson to collect their thoughts on discussion questions. They were asked to write their reactions to the following hypothetical scenarios independently and then discuss their answers in small groups. Each small group was led by a facilitator from the university team. The first scenario placed their friend as the victim of bullying: "You go online and see a picture of your friend posted publicly on Facebook with the caption "Loser." What do you do?" The second scenario suggested their friend was the wrongdoer: "Amy, your friend, posts a mean tweet about your classmate Jessica's outfit. What do you do? Do you defend your friend, Amy, or your classmate Jessica?" In addition to their responses to bullying, students were also asked to brainstorm in their journals about what kind of rules or guidelines they would like to see enacted online to make it a safer and less hostile environment.

Students built upon the individual guidelines during a collaborative activity in which they worked together to draft an "Online Constitution" with guidelines for being a good online citizen. They began drafting their plans for a classwide "Online Constitution" in groups of four or five. Each group then pitched its list to the rest of the class until a master list was created with which the entire class agreed. Each of the three classes designed a unique classwide "Online Constitution" and then signed the document.

IN THE STUDENTS' WORDS: OUR FINDINGS

Students' Survey Responses

What to do if you see online bullying? The most common option that students selected, taken by 36 out of 58 students who responded to this question, was to engage in intervening action themselves by writing comments to respond to the online aggression. There was no gender difference among students in choosing to handle online bullying themselves as an option. Parents and teachers were also figures that students reported they would inform if they saw online bullying. Out of 59 students, 35 and 27 students reported teacher and parent, respectively, as adult figures to whom they would report online bullying. Twenty out of 27 girls included telling parent as an option if they saw online bullying, compared to 15 out of 31 boys ($\chi^2 = 3.98$, df = 1, $p < .05$) (See Table 10.1). No gender difference was found in whether students would tell a teacher about online bullying. "Talking to the bully in person" was fourth, following the aforementioned three options, and was chosen by 22 students. There was also no gender difference in whether students would consider talking in person to the bully.

Table 10.1 Gender differences in reporting online bullying to parent.

	Did Not Include Parent	Included Parent	Total	
Female	7	20	27	
Male	16	15	31	$\chi^2 = 3.98$ (df = 2, p < .05)
Total	33	35	58	

What to do if your friend is involved in bullying? In general, students reported that they would be "Very Likely" or "Likely" to defend victims of online bullying (See Table 10.2). However, further analyses revealed differences between the reported possible reaction for friends (presumably socially closer) and for classmates (presumably less close than a friend). They were more willing to write an online comment to defend their friend if they saw their friend's picture posted on a page with a mean caption (Mean = 1.66, SD = .92, n = 59), compared to if they saw a photograph of a classmate posted with the same mean caption (Mean = 2.24, SD = .1.12, n = 59)

Table 10.2 Students would be more likely to defend their friend than defend classmate.

Items	n	Mean	SD	T
You see a picture of one of YOUR CLASSMATES posted publicly on Facebook with the caption "loser". How likely are you to comment on the picture in that person's defense?	59	2.24	1.12	
				3.59 (df = 58, p < .01,)
You see a picture of YOUR FRIEND posted publically on Facebook with the caption "loser". How likely are you to comment on the picture in your friend's defense?	59	1.66	0.92	
Your best friend comments on a picture of a classmate calling him or her ugly. How likely are you to intervene and defend the classmate?	58	2.43	0.96	
				7.09 (df = 54, p < .001)
A classmate comments on a picture of your best friend calling him or her ugly. How likely are you to intervene and defend your best friend?	56	1.46	0.71	

*Students responded to each item using 5-point Likert scale (1 = Very Likely, 5 = Very Unlikely). Lower score indicates higher self-reported likelihood to defend the victim of online bullying.

(t = 3.59, df = 58, p < .01). Students also reported that they would be more likely to defend their best friend when the latter received an aggressive online comment from a classmate (Mean = 1.47, SD = .72, n = 55), rather than in the scenario where their best friend perpetrated bullying against a classmate (Mean = 2.42, SD = .94, n = 55) (t = 7.09, df = 54, p < .001). In other words, students' responses suggested the role of social distance in their likelihood to intervene in online bullying incident: they would be more willing to stand up if the victim were a friend than a classmate. On the contrary, however, students would be *less* willing to intervene if a friend was the one who committed online bullying than if the perpetrator were a classmate. These patterns appeared across gender. That is, boys and girls were both more willing to defend their friends than stand up for their classmates, and were less likely to intervene if the bully happened to be their friend.

STUDENT BRAINSTORMING JOURNALS

Scenario 1: A Friend as Victim

"The first thing I would do is comment." Consistent with the survey results, social proximity seems to be important in how students chose to address bullying in the data they provided in their brainstorming journals. In the first scenario, where the student's friend is a victim of bullying on Facebook, students favored direct intervention. Only two students said they would avoid the situation and not intervene. Students described this form of direct intervention as "standing up" or "sticking up" for the bullied.

Twenty-three students chose to confront the bully by commenting online at the site where the bullying occurred while an additional 14 wrote that they would "say" something to the bully, although they did not specify online. For instance, Tara wrote that she "would comment and say, "I can't believe[sic] you have the nerve to say that to my friend! I bet you wouldn't say that to her face so why would you say that to her now?! UNBEILIVIBLE [sic]!!!" Another student, Rachel, had a similar reaction to the scenario: "I would comment back "EXCUSE ME but what right do you have to be making fun of people. THIS IS MY FRIEND YOU'RE TALKING ABOUT HERE SIR. You cannot say that about her unless you could say that to her face." We can infer from these two examples that students may perceive online bullying as cowardly because it is not addressed "to the person's face." Even when students mentioned a variety of responses, the need to "comment" on the bullying publically was consistently foregrounded. Joe, for instance, explained the steps he would take as follows: "The first thing I would do was comment and say 'Well that's rude and not true. My friend is very cool.' And after that I would tell a parent and maybe call the person who posted." Carl also walked us through the steps in his response which began with a public comment: "1) I would say to that person (online) dude your [sic] just a jerk and then block the bully."

"**My first reaction is to put something positive.**" Eight students chose less confrontational approaches by way of indirect intervention, including reporting the bullying incident to either the website or a parent. Most students would consider engaging in multiple strategies (e.g., commenting on the picture to defend the victim *and* report the bullying incident), with only one student choosing to report the bullying without taking any other forms of action. The indirect interventions mentioned by students were more often focused on ways to build up or support the victim rather than point out the bad behavior of the bully, and some pointed to the importance of not escalating the conflict. Kenny, for example, wrote, "If I saw one of my friends post with the caption 'loser' my first reaction is to put something positive about that friend if that can't happen maybe just let the bully be and tell the victim that you like it in private to avoid further bullying." Similarly, Lisa wrote, "If I saw a picture of my friend with the caption 'loser' I would post a positive comment. Don't fight fire with fire." Again, however, these indirect interventions were not common and the students usually responded to the first scenario in a more direct manner.

Scenario 2: A Friend as Aggressor

"**I wouldn't stand up as much.**" In the scenario where their friend was the aggressor, students' preferred intervention strategies changed significantly. Some students mentioned directly that this complicated their desire to intervene. Jan, for example, did not seem willing to confront her friend: "If my friend was the bully I wouldn't stand up as much but I would just comment maybe you shouldn't post mean pictures or something and say delete the picture or apologize." Some students chose not to confront their friend on the bullying at all. Jackson, for instance, who wrote, "I would comment, 'leave him alone'" in the first scenario in which the friend was the victim, reported that he would "Do nothing" in the second hypothetical situation.

"**You should apologize.**" Unlike in the first scenario, where students would "comment" directly and "stand up" against the bully, in the second hypothetical case students said they were more likely to "talk" with the bully—their friend—and present opportunities for him or her to "apologize." Ashleigh, for instance, explained how confronting a friend was challenging and favored having a discussion: "I would most likely try to get them to stop, but it would be hard because there [sic] my friend. ... I would probably ask them why they did it and then what [would] you do if someone did that to you?" Most students were still willing to defend the bullied classmate but their approach favored more private discussions and efforts to understand the bully's motives. For instance, Tyler wrote, "I would go talk to my friend in person and tell him to stop bullying and say sorry and I would rethink our friendship." Julie had a similar approach, "I would talk to Amy personally and explain to her gently why it's wrong to say things like that and try to get her to apologize on the internet and take it back if that fails, I'll apologize to the classmate personally."

Constitution Activity

After group discussions on responses to bullying and the implications for victims, the group participated in a culminating activity that asked them to draft behavioral guidelines, called the "Online Constitution." The three classes were given the freedom to choose any guiding principles to add to their constitution, provided the majority of the class agreed. The students dictated their guidelines to the MLE facilitators who wrote them onto a final poster which the students then signed (See Figure 1).

Class 1
Online Constitution
"The Constitut- ia- gram"

- Be a source of help, not harm
- If mean, intervene
- No spamming
- Do not spread rumors about others
- Think before you "click"
- Make sure the things you post have a positive impact on others

Class 2
Online Constitution

- Be nice and don't be a bystander
- If you don't have something nice to say, don't say anything
- Stand with the bullied
- Police your friends
- Don't post something about someone else without their permission

Class 3
Online Constitution

- Don't fight fire with fire
- Treat others the way you want to be treated
- Stand up against bullies, even when you don't know them
- Think before you post
- Don't contribute to rumors

Figure 1

Although the three classes completed the activity separately, clear patterns emerged in their responses (see Table 10.3). Two categories of responses

Table 10.3 Themes emerging from Online Constitutions.

Strategy	Class 1	Class 2	Class 3
Actively Discourage Bullying	If mean, intervene	Stand up against bullies even when you don't know them	Stand with the bullied Police your friends
Avoid Escalation	Be a source of help, not harm	Don't fight fire with fire	
Avoid Instigation	Do not spread rumors about others	Don't contribute to rumors	If you don't have something nice to say, don't say anything
Consider consequences before you contribute online	Think before you click	Think before you post	Don't post something about someone else without their permission
Empathize to foster positivity	Make sure the things you post have a positive impact on others	Treat others the way you want to be treated	Be nice and don't be a bystander
Unrelated to Bullying	No spamming		

*The individual guidelines derived from the sixth graders that comprised the Constitutions have been reordered to highlight patterns in the responses.

emerged from these guidelines: (1) Proper intervention strategies when bullying has occurred and (2) Preemptive strategies to avoid bullying altogether.

Proper Intervention Strategies. All three classes highlighted the need to *actively discourage bullying*. Class 1 used the saying "If mean, intervene" to highlight the need to address bullying when it occurs. Additionally, two classes included practices to *avoid escalation*. Class 2, for example, used the familiar phrase "don't fight fire with fire" to define proper behavior when addressing bullying.

Proactive Strategies to Avoid Bullying. All three classes suggested ways to *avoid instigation* online. Rumors were of particular concern and students in Class 1 included the guideline "Do not spread rumors about others." All three classes also suggested that users monitor their own behavior by carefully *considering consequences before you contribute*. Class 3 specifically highlighted privacy concerns by adding "Don't post something about someone else without their permission." Finally, students in all three classes pointed to what we called *empathizing to foster positivity* as a preemptive strategy to curb bullying by considering the feelings of others. Class 2, for example, included the "golden rule" to "Treat others the way you want to be treated."

CONCLUSIONS

Despite the fact that cyberbullying, by definition, occurs through digital media (most often social media), and despite calls for media literacy education to be considered as a potentially fruitful path for understanding and perhaps even resisting cyberbullying (Hobbs, 2010; Livingstone & Brake, 2010), there are precious little data on how adolescents receive curricula that include cyberbullying as a topic within a larger media literacy framework, whether on the portrayals of cyberbullying in mass media or on how to cultivate responsible online behaviors among young media users (Walsh et al., 2014; Worthen, 2007). And yet, clearly, the stakes are high, with tragic examples of the consequences of cyberbullying on suicides capturing the headlines, and with recent rates showing many young people will encounter bullying online at some point in their adolescence (Roberto et al., 2014). Within the context of the pleasures and opportunities available to young people interacting socially in the contemporary digital environment as well as the risks (Leung & Lee, 2011; Livingstone & Brake, 2010; Madden et al., 2012), the potential for media literacy education to facilitate a critical engagement with digital technologies is profound. Indeed, given the findings from past research showing that parents can mediate their children's awareness of and exposure to online risks (Bhat et al., 2010; Leung & Lee, 2012; Lwin et al., 2008; Mesch, 2009), it seems that teachers and media literacy facilitators may be able to do to the same.

In this chapter we have detailed a media literacy education program in which sixth graders actively participated in a series of educational exercises and activities designed to spur and to voice their critical thinking about cyberbullying in general, and about the ways in which they can respond positively to bullying situations they may encounter online. Studying the input of a small sample of 11- and 12-year-olds from a relatively privileged setting both quantitatively and qualitatively, our data suggest they have internalized such axioms as "If you don't have anything nice to say, don't say anything at all" and "Don't fight fire with fire." The success of the Online Constitution construction activity and the relative homogeneity in the resulting constitutions themselves (despite their having been produced by each individual classroom) suggests they *have* thought critically about cyberbullying and are willing to make a pledge toward responsible and responsive online behavior, vowing to intervene rather than to be passive bystanders and pledging to promote positive dialogue in social media. The data also point convincingly to their desire to defend and therefore actively intervene when a friend is on the receiving end of an act of bullying. This reveals the strong attachments of friendships for our sample and their valiant desire to "stand up for" those they love.

Yet, our data also point to complexities, such as those that occur for the members of our sample when a friend is displaying cyberbullying behavior, in the statistical discrepancy between their reported plan to intervene when a friend is the victim compared to when a classmate is, and in some interesting patterns that differ by gender. The axioms they articulate appear to be a bit flexible, then, as the quantitative data reveal a higher likelihood of standing up for a friend who has been subject to a cyberbullying incident than for someone else they merely know from class and as the qualitative data show some may not intervene at all and many would intervene differently if a friend were the aggressor in a cyberbullying incident. What's also striking across all of the data is the self-reliance implied by this sample's responses. They appear much more likely to take matters into their own hands when encountering cyberbullying than to involve an adult, in general, and yet the girls in the sample were also more likely to turn to a parent during such encounters than were the boys. Given this self-reliance and the finding that parents and teachers are not always aware that cyberbullying has occurred (Byrne, Katz, Lee, Linz, & McIlraith, 2013), continued media literacy educational efforts such as these that give students the space to collectively consider and give voice to their experiences with negotiating bullying online are increasingly important.

Based on these results and others, we believe that the topic of cyberbullying calls for a unique approach to media literacy education—a specifically *digital* or digital media literacy education (DMLE) approach—that acknowledges and responds to the interactive nature of the media space, the relative anonymity that media users may feel within that space, and the sentiment among young users that, for the most part, this is *their* space, for them to use, to help form, and to actively regulate themselves. We hope to problematize the binary between a "top-down" approach that poses DMLE as a corrective response to the "moral panic" of cyberbullying and a "bottom up" approach in which young people's own meaning making regarding this new form of an old issue—recurring verbal, social, and physical aggression among youth stemming from power differentials—is at the center (Hoechsmann & Poyntz, 2012). In so doing, we hope to illustrate the contribution of a DMLE framework in foregrounding and helping to shape young people's own understandings of and interventions regarding cyberbullying.

REFERENCES

Bhat, C. S., Chang, S. H., & Linscott, J. A. (2010). Addressing cyberbullying as a media literacy issue. *New Horizon in Education, 58* (3), 34–43.

Byrne, S., Katz, S. L., Lee, T., Linz, D., & McIlraith, M. (2013). Peers, predators, and porn: Predicting parents' underestimation of children's risky online experiences. *Journal of Computer-Mediated Communication, 19,* 215–231.

Dupuis, E. A. (1997). The information literacy challenge: Addressing the changing needs of our students through our programs. *Internet Reference Services Quarterly, 2*(2–3), 97–111.

Frechette, J. (2006). Cyber-censorship or cyber-literacy? Envisioning cyber-learning through media education. In D. Buckingham & R. Willett (Eds.), *Digital generations: Children, young people, and new media* (pp. 149–171). Mahwah, NJ: Lawrence Erlbaum Associates, Inc.

Hinduja, S., & Patchin, J. W. (2014). *State cyberbullying laws: A brief review of state cyberbullying laws and policies.* Retrieved from http://www.cyberbullying. us/Bullying_and_Cyberbullying_Laws.pdf.

Hobbs, R. (2010). *Digital and media literacy: A plan of action.* Washington, DC: Aspen Institute.

Hoechsmann, M., & Poyntz, S.R. (2012). *Media literacies: A critical introduction.* Malden, MA: Wiley-Blackwell.

Leung, L., & Lee, P. S. N. (2012). The influences of information literacy, internet addiction and parenting styles on internet risks. *New Media and Society, 14* (1), 117–136.

Livingstone, S., & Brake, D. R. (2010). On the rapid rise of social networking sites: New findings and policy implications. *Children & Society, 24,* 75–83.

Lwin, M. O., Stanaland, A. J. S., & Miyazaki, A. D. (2008). On the rapid rise of social networking sites: New findings and policy implications. *Journal of Retailing, 84*(2), 205–217.

Madden, M., Cortesi, S., Gasser, U., Lenhart, A., & Duggan, M. (2012). *Parents, teens, and online privacy.* Pew Research Center's Internet & American Life Project. Retrieved from http://www.pewinternet.org/2012/11/20/parents-teens-and-online-privacy/.

Massachusetts Department of Elementary and Secondary Education (ESE). (2013–14). *2013–14 Selected Populations Report (District).* Retrieved from http://profiles.doe. mass.edu/state_report/selectedpopulations.aspx.

Mesch, G. (2009). Parental mediation, online activities, and cyberbullying. *CyberPsychology & Behavior, 12*(4), 387–393.

Meyrowitz, J. (1998) Multiple media literacies. *Journal of Communication, 48,* 96–109.

Olson, C., Sekarasih, L., O'Malley, D., & Scharrer, E. (2014, May). *"Sign up today for free!": 6th graders' perception of the Internet.* Paper to be presented at the annual meeting of the International Communication Association, Seattle, WA.

Patchin, J. W., & Hinduja, S. (2012). *Cyberbullying prevention and response: Expert perspectives.* New York: Routledge.

Roberto, A. J., Eden, J., Savage, M. W., Ramos-Salazar, L., & Deiss, D. M. (2014). Prevalence and predictors of cyberbullying by high school seniors. *Communication Quarterly, 62,* 97–114.

Scharrer, E. (2005). Sixth graders take on television: Media literacy and critical attitudes about television violence. *Communication Research Reports, 24,* 325–333.

Scharrer, E. (2006). "I noticed more violence": The effects of a media literacy program on knowledge and attitudes about media violence. *Journal of Mass Media Ethics, 21*(1), 70–87.

Scharrer, E. (2009). Measuring the effects of a media literacy program on conflict and violence. *Journal of Media Literacy Education, 1*(1). Retrieved from http:// digitalcommons.uri.edu/jmle/vol1/iss1/2/.

Scharrer, E., & Wortman-Raring, L. (2012). A media literacy curriculum on violence in the US: Studying young people's written responses for evidence of learning. *Journal of Children and Media, 6*(3), 351–366.

Sekarasih, L., Walsh, K., & Scharrer, E. (2015). "Media violence is made to attract and entertain": Responses to media literacy lessons on the effects of and institutional motives behind media violence. Journal of Media Literacy Education, 6(3), 1–13.

Sekarasih, L., Olson, C., O'Malley, D., & Scharrer, E. (2014, May). *Entertaining audiences, ensuring inclusivity, and considering media influence: Sixth-graders' understanding of media producers' responsibility.* Paper presented at the annual meeting of the International Communication Association, Seattle, WA.

Smith, S. L., Wilson, B. J., Kunkel, D., Linz, D., Potter, W. J., Colvin, C. M., et al. (1998). *National television violence study: Vol. 3.* Thousand Oaks, CA: Sage.

Walsh, K., Sekarasih, L., & Scharrer, E. (2014). Mean girls and tough boys: Children's meaning making and media literacy lessons on gender and bullying in the US. *Journal of Children & Media*, 8(3), 223–239.

Worthen, M. R. (2007). Education policy implications from the expert panel on electronic media and youth violence. *Journal of Adolescent Health, 41*, S61–S63.

11 The Text and the Image
Media Literacy, Pedagogy, and Generational Divides

Bill Yousman

"Seeing comes before words. The child looks and recognizes before it can speak."

(Berger, 1972, p. 7)

A TRUE STORY

I enter the classroom on a fall afternoon ready to introduce the topic of language acquisition to my Introduction to Communication students. I begin discussing language—how it works, how we acquire it. I notice a few students drifting away, so I say, "Okay, let's watch something." One of the drifters perks up and says "Oh good! I like to watch things."

I show a clip of linguist Noam Chomsky talking about the theory of generative grammar. My drifters slump back in their seats and glaze over. Most of the students remain silent for the next hour. I ponder what just happened as I walk back to my office.

This is what I think: I made a promise that I didn't fulfill. "Let's watch something" promised a visual experience. When the visual didn't meet expectations, there was a boomerang effect—students became even more disinterested in the ideas that I was presenting. "Let's watch something" hinted at something like a trailer for a Hollywood blockbuster: Explosions in the sky, giant interstellar robots, flying superheroes, fiery car crashes, beautiful people in tight clothes doing dangerous things.

My video didn't engage because it wasn't visual in the way that my students expect something to be visual. It was small v visual rather than VISUAL!!!!!!!

Honestly, it was simply text taken off the page and made auditory, with some bland visual accompaniment, but based in a verbal logic involving the sort of sequential, linear unfolding of meaning that most written texts follow.

I propose this anecdote reveals a profound cultural difference between how most educators approach knowledge and how many, if not most, of our students approach knowledge. And I believe that this difference originates outside, not inside the classroom.

TWO ORIENTATIONS

Media scholar Stuart Ewen eloquently describes the visual environment that marks the modern era:

> We are constantly addressed by alluring images; they speak to the universal language of the eye ... We are educated, from infancy, to *look*, we are not encouraged to see and interpret simultaneously. Our eyes imbibe images with little critical resistance (1988, p. 156).

Since the advent of photography, followed by film and television, and now digital mobile technologies, we have become more and more of an image-based culture. We are saturated with spectacular visual images and this has become commonplace, unquestioned by the youth born into this previously unimaginable visual environment.

This is not to say that humans have not always been visual beings, sight being our primary sense (Barnes, 2011; Berger, 1972; Lester, 2006). Face-to-face communication began nonverbally, and mediated communication could be found in the paintings that adorned cave walls in the prehistoric era. As far back as the Homeric period, philosophers privileged vision over other sensory experiences (Drucker, 2014; Jay, 1993). Later, Descartes claimed "sight is the noblest and most comprehensive of the senses" (2001, p. 65). Centuries after Descartes, Daniel Boorstin (1961) published a groundbreaking analysis of how imagery had taken over news and politics. Today, mobile and digital technologies allow us to access an ever-growing multitude of images from all over the world, wherever we are, whenever we are. As Sturken and Cartwright put it: "Every conceivable surface, from our car dashboards to our telephones, seems to hold potential as a site on which to put a visual screen" (2009, p. 1). From cave paintings to political ads to Instagram, humans have always told visual stories. Apkon notes, "The power of visual media has been with us from the beginning of our species, as we are physiologically constructed to consume and find meaning from images in a way that transcends other forms of communication" (2013, p. 13).

Text and images do share much in common (Hill, 2004; Müller, 2007; Seppanen, 2006). Printed words are visual images in their own right (Bernhardt, 2004; Lester, 2006) and Logan (1986) argues that the alphabet carries a visual bias by converting sound into appearance. Furthermore, most communication operates through a combination of these two modes (Barthes, 1972). YouTube videos usually include both words and pictures. Photographs on Tumblr or Instagram are often accompanied by text, and Facebook is a prime example of what Forceville (2005) calls the multimodality of communication.

But there are also real differences between the verbal and the visual. Messaris (2003) calls visual and textual communication two distinct modes, and Müller argues "visual communication and textual communication follow a different logic: while textual communication is based on argumentation, visual communication is based on association" (2007, p. 13). We can see this difference in contemporary advertising, which seduces not through step-by-step logical arguments for the value of products, but through encouraging positive associations in our minds (this beer will make me more masculine, this perfume will enhance my allure, this cereal will prove that I love my kids) or, most obvious in the case of political advertising, negative associations (Can't vote for her! She wants to raise my taxes!). And these differences play out in the classroom as the (primarily) text-based orientations of faculty meet the (primarily) image-based orientations of students.

There is also something both quantitatively and qualitatively different about the era of digital communication, something rooted in the twentieth century when images began to challenge text as the dominant mode of communication (Laspina, 1998; Mirzoeff, 1999; Mitchell, 1994). As Berger put it before the digital revolution, "In no other form of society in history has there been such a concentration of images, such a density of visual messages" (1972, p. 129). Imagine if the iPhone was a thing when Berger penned those words. Media scholar George Gerbner argued that this is the first time in history that images sponsored and created by massive global corporations have come to dominate to such an extent that they can no longer be thought of as separate or distinct from culture—they *are* the culture (Stossel, 1997). This is also the first time in history when all of these images, untold millions, can be carried in our pockets, accessed by the touch of a button.

Students grow up in an environment that is saturated with *particular* sorts of images, based in *particular* ways of defining the world, *particular* encouragements to think (or not think) in *particular* ways, ways that serve the interests of commercial entities. It's not that faculty don't also inhabit that world, but that we come from a different culture due to our immersion in texts throughout our academic training. The (non)thinking preferred by the commercial world of images is antithetical to the ways of knowing that most faculty were inculcated in throughout our academic careers. Colleagues and I regularly talk about the books and articles that made an impact on us, that affected the way we see the world. These are texts that are often rhetorically elegant, skillfully using language to build systematic arguments, or to tell compelling stories that unfold bit by bit.

Images, however, work holistically. As Ewen suggests:

> Basically, the word is something that unfolds over time. It's not that propaganda can't be created through words … but that the processing of written text is a deliberative process. People know that they're decoding letters. Images tend to speak very instantaneously … people involved in engineered persuasion view images as things that work very quickly and bypass reason (1998, p. 4).

Educators are in our comfort zones writing and reading. But most of my students don't have that same relationship to the written word. Many of my students can't easily recall books that they found significant. To test this hunch, I took an admittedly unscientific poll a few years ago. I asked students to list books, or any other texts, that affected their lives. I polled 84 students (45 women, 39 men, ages 18–25, two students in their 30s). 43% of them were not able to list anything: not a single book, not one essay, not even a story.

Part of this may be age—traditional students have not had as many years to encounter writing that affected them deeply. But I believe that this is also a reflection of differing orientations. Many of my students just do not relate to words the way I do. But they do have a strong connection to visual modes of representation.

Consider a 2007 report that "kids are actually watching more TV, not less, even with the multitude of other options, including iPods, videogames and online video" (Downey, 2007, no pagination). The media rising most rapidly in terms of daily use are image-based media—television, video, online gaming, and social media like Instagram, Snapchat, etc. A 2013 British study reported that while use of gaming applications and YouTube was rising, reading was on the decline and that nearly a third of British teenagers are now classified as complete non-readers (Dredge, 2013).[1]

CONFLICT IN THE CLASSROOM

So what are the consequences of this "visual turn" for pedagogy? I want to be clear that I am not making a moralistic argument framing verbal texts as inherently more edifying than images. I am not suggesting images must be purged from student's lives and we must flog them with the great books— Eat your Tolstoy or you won't get any Minecraft!

After all, as Sut Jhally argues:

> Images are the dominant language of the modern world. We are stuck with them. Further, we have to acknowledge the pleasure that such images provide. This is not simply trickery or manipulation—the pleasure is substantive (2003, p. 256).

Yet note the text-based orientation even from Jhally, who is arguing we need to work *within* an image-based culture: "we are stuck" with this. Not that this is something we love or embrace—but that we must come to terms with it, tolerate it, only because we have no choice. This is not the way students would see the issue. There is a cultural difference here.

So, how does this difference manifest itself? I propose three ways that image-based orientations are at odds with what text-based educators hope to accomplish in the classroom. These conflicts can be framed as speed vs. depth, appearances vs. analysis, and emotion vs. reason.

First, there is the issue of speed working against in-depth understanding. Cognitive scientists suggest the brain "begins to categorize and make sense of an image within 150 milliseconds of the first glimpse" (Apkon, 2013, pp. 75–76). Taylor (2014) connects speed to fragmentation—lack of connection between one idea and the next. He argues that the acceleration brought on by social and technological developments has led to our perceptive processes becoming increasingly scattered, sliced and diced, atomized. Jhally uses the world of television advertising as a paradigm example—thirty-second, or increasingly, shorter (Molla, 2014) clips that tumble one after another in rapid succession: "the generalization of this speed/fragmentation strategy to the entire domain of image culture may in fact mean that this is the form that thought increasingly is taking" (Jhally, 2003, p. 255).

Recent innovations in technology and marketing, the proliferation of social media and mobile devices, and ever-increasing media saturation have made his argument even more persuasive. Image-based culture discourages us from lingering too long on any one thing. Next time you go to a museum, try a little informal ethnography by observing how fast most people move—even through a location where the whole point is careful contemplation of the visual.

An image-based orientation is one that is predisposed to look quickly and then find something different to look at. Postman (1985) called this phenomenon "and now this": as in television news where there is a constant headlong rush to the next item and everything is distinct from what preceded it. No connections are made, just now this, now this, now this—creating what Postman called a "peek-a-boo world." Yet pedagogy often requires slowing down, lingering, even what students may consider belaboring a point.

When we move fast we tend to skim the surface, so a related issue involves the dichotomy between appearances and analysis. Ewen notes: "In advertising, packaging, product design, and corporate identity, the power of provocative surfaces speaks to the eye's mind, overshadowing matters of quality or substance" (1988, p. 22). Consider our relative willingness to accept the truth-value of images versus the truth-value of language (Barthes, 1972; Sturken & Cartwright, 2009). To a degree, this is a matter of cognitive processing. As marketing professor Richard Pollay says in the documentary *The Ad and the Ego*:

> We don't process images in the same way we process words. If I say something to you in order for you to sort of file that in your memory and to understand it, you match it up with what you already know and in your mind you may go, well that's true or maybe it's not true, or only if. You engage in a kind of counter-argument or cognitive processing. If I show you a picture, seeing is believing. A picture is an experience. It's not treated and processed in the same cognitive way. We still have this cultural predisposition to believe what we see. That the photo does not lie.
>
> (Boihem, 1997)

Images are not readily subject to critical thinking unless we set out specifically to analyze them—which most of the time outside of the classroom
we don't. Yet critical thinking and analysis are exactly what educators
want to encourage in students—moving beneath the surface, not accepting things at face value. An image-based culture encourages the opposite: Here it is, it must be true, don't think any further. The filmmaker
Errol Morris puts it like this: "vision is privileged in our society and our
sensorium. We trust it; we place our confidence in it. Photography allows
us to uncritically think. We *imagine* that photographs provide a magic
path to the truth" (2014, p. 92, emphasis in the original). Images thus
speak to us on the level of what comedian Stephen Colbert has called
"truthiness," an emotional sense that something is indeed true without
having to rely on antiquated notions like evidence or fact checking. One
early advertiser wrote: "There seems little doubt that the old fallacy that
the camera cannot lie greatly strengthens its appeal … It can emphasize
qualities of delicacy, elegance of line, mystery and glamour, and yet retain
the persistent atmosphere of reality. Cameraland is the land of dreams
come true" (Everard, 1934, pp. 2–3).

This leads to the third way that image-based orientations present a
challenge to pedagogy. Images engage us primarily on an emotional level.
Writing about photographs taken after the 1862 Battle of Antietam, Oliver
Wendell Holmes noted:

> It was so nearly like visiting the battlefield … that all the emotions
> excited by the actual sight … came back to us. [Photography] gives
> us … some conception of what a repulsive, brutal, sickening, hideous
> thing it is, this dashing together of two frantic mobs to which we give
> the name of armies (1864, pp. 267–268).

While emotion is powerfully persuasive, it's not the primary response we
are aiming for in the classroom. The insights of critical pedagogy (Friere,
2000; hooks, 1994) inform us that emotion does play a strong role in what
occurs between teachers and students, but when students with image-based
orientations come to class craving emotional stimulation, they are apt to be
sorely disappointed. I want my students to feel, but more importantly I want
them to *understand* and *evaluate* the substance of our discussions. I want
them to understand and evaluate *why* they feel what they feel—whether it
is about social inequality; or how media report on the Middle East; or even
just the necessity of doing good research before they deliver a presentation.

Images, however, work against asking why. Once we are emotionally
hooked into a belief it becomes very difficult to examine that belief critically
(Morris, 2014). Image-makers understand this very well and count on it to
bypass "inconvenient truths," to steal a phrase from Al Gore. This is why
SUV ads, for example, almost always depict wilderness settings, articulating
nature with a machine that is incredibly destructive to the natural environment

(Andersen, 2000). Or why political advertisements are so often deceptive while playing on emotions like resentment and fear (Apkon, 2013; Boorstin, 1961).

I want my students to examine ideas in terms of their logical construction, their reliance on evidence, the connection between evidence and claims. This is not how the image-based culture speaks to us—it operates on the gut level, not on the critical intellectual level. This cultural divide is one key reason why students often have difficulty making the shift from emotional to intellectual engagement.

While I have argued for the fast, superficial, and emotional ways that we encounter images, this is not to suggest that visual messages themselves are simple or easily understood. Sturken and Cartwright note: "All images contain layers of meaning that include their formal aspects, their cultural and socio-historical references, the ways they make reference to the images that precede and surround them, and the contexts in which they are displayed" (2009, p. 46). So, where then does this leave us?

MEDIA LITERACY EDUCATION AS A BRIDGE

> *"If the new language of images were used differently, it would, through its use confer a new kind of power."*
>
> *(Berger, 1972, p. 33)*

Media literacy education offers a bridge across the cultural divide between text-based faculty and image-based students. One central media literacy principle is that media play a key role in constructing our sense of reality (Aufderheide, 2000). The image industries (television, film, video gaming, social media, advertising, etc.) know that it is easier to capture our imaginations by visual rather than verbal modes of communication. If we agree that getting students' attention and exciting their imaginations are laudable pedagogical goals, then we can learn from commercial media. Not as an end place, not as an abandonment of the value of traditional literacy skills and critical thinking, but as a starting place to engaging students with image-based orientations (Hill, 2004).

The simplest way that many educators try to do this is by showing educational films. However, as my anecdote at the beginning of this chapter reveals, traditional classroom films are not really VISUAL in a way that captivates students. A series of middle-aged talking heads sitting in front of bookshelves does not truly speak to image-based orientations. If we are really interested in "meeting students where they live," we have to look beyond the traditional classroom film.

Dare I suggest that educators need to thoroughly understand the techniques of visual communication experts: those working in the fields of commercial media production? A second media literacy principle is that media have commercial implications (Aufderheide, 2000). The industrial aim behind most of the images students encounter is the generation of profit. In this pursuit of profit, Hollywood filmmakers, television producers, and advertisers know just how to engage people visually. When Apple introduces a new product, they don't promote long lists of technical specs. They fill the environment with intriguing images of cool people interacting with cooler devices. The problem with advertising and most other commercial media is that the visuals usually stifle critical thinking. It's all emotion and visceral reactions: We know that Big Mac is poisonous (and that it doesn't even really look like that), but when it flashes by juicy and plump on the screen we aren't supposed to contemplate McDonald's contributions to suppressed wages, environmental destruction, animal cruelty, and rampant diabetes and heart disease. Instead the appeal is to what some neuroscientists call the reptilian brain (MacLean, 1990), referring to our instinctual predispositions—the part of us that doesn't think but simply reacts (McClure et al., 2004). All we are supposed to feel is "yummy—give me one."

Remember Ewen's observation cited above: "people involved in engineered persuasion view images as things that work very quickly and bypass reason" (1998, p. 4). It's not just media critics that make this argument. One marketing guru actually uses the phrase "loyalty beyond reason" *uncritically* to refer to consumers' emotional attachments to brands (Roberts, 2005). Abandoning the human capacity to reason, to rational thought, is framed as a positive outcome. If we stop there, we are literally doomed to stupidity. I am arguing educators should *understand*, not *emulate* the techniques of commercial media. Captivating images can also be used as a starting rather than ending place—to make us want to know more, to make us curious, to spark the human propensity for exploration.

Thus, Jhally argues:

> The struggle to reconstruct the existence and meaning of the world of substance has to take place on the terrain of the image system. In some progressive cultural politics the very techniques associated with the image-system are part of the problem—that is, images themselves are seen as the problem ... I believe such a strategy surrenders the very terrain on which the most effective battles can be fought—the language of the contemporary world (2003, p. 256).

Notice, he suggests that text and images are actually more similar than we often imagine them to be. Images are language in the sense that they are communicative. My argument is not that we have to capitulate to the society of the spectacle, as DeBord (1995) labeled modern day culture, turning our classrooms into glitzy but empty visual circuses, but rather that meeting students where they live now means understanding their image-based orientation and using it as a starting place to encourage analysis, critical thinking, sustained rather than fragmented thought. In closing, let's consider some examples of how this can be done.

FROM THEORY TO PRACTICE

A third media literacy principle is that media messages have social and political implications (Aufderheide, 2000). Think about the possibilities of using iconic photographs, for example, to engage students in critical thinking about the relationships between culture, power, and resistance (Hariman & Lucaites, 2007; Hill, 2004). Imagine pairing images from 2014 protests in Ferguson, Missouri, with the famous 1989 photograph of the unknown Chinese man facing down tanks in Tiananmen Square as a way to get students to begin analyzing different (or not so different) manifestations of authoritarian political rule around the globe. Or consider a class on ethics, and the intense discussion that could be generated by examining photographic evidence of U.S. torture after 9/11 alongside calls from progressive media outlets for more widespread access to and distribution of these visual markers of history (see, for example, Meurer, 2014).

However, we also need to keep in mind that visual images cannot provide the effective pedagogy we strive for if they are asked to stand all on their own. As Morris notes, "Photographs reveal and they conceal" (2014, p. 118). Without discounting the potential power of images of violence, war, and atrocities, Sontag cautions us to be wary of the notion that just by viewing a picture we can really know "the pain of others":

> "We"—this "we" is everyone who has never experienced anything like what they went through—don't understand … We truly can't imagine what it was like. We can't imagine how dreadful, how terrifying war is; and how normal it becomes (2003, pp. 125–126).

Text, however, when coupled with imagery, can perhaps bring us a little closer to understanding. Apkon (2013) discusses the case of Neda Agha-Soltan, an Iranian woman whose death by a sniper's bullet during a 2009 protest was caught on film. Agha-Soltan became a symbol of dissent for the Iranian people because of the widespread distribution of this video. But Apkon points out the limitations of the image if it is completely decoupled from text:

> Yet understanding the larger meaning of the Neda Agha-Soltan death video is impossible without knowing the larger background on the state of affairs in Iran, and why people were out protesting that day … A broader conception is necessary, and text is an important element in supplying that context … Without it, you have only a meaningless act of violence. With the text and the accompanying context, the image becomes a powerful indictment of the sitting Iranian government and its callous treatment of its own citizens (2013, p. 29).

This is where media literacy "enters the picture." Images draw our attention and engage us emotionally, but for critical understanding we need textual context. After all, as Berger noted, images don't convey meaning in a vacuum: "The way we see things is affected by what we know or what we believe" (1972, p. 8). If we understand visual imagery as well as the media, advertising, and public relations industries do we can then provide the context that encourages the very sort of critical reflection the commercial industries strive to suppress.

I've had success fomenting critical reflection by using a visual quiz to get students talking about how the commercial media set the agenda for what we think is important (McCombs & Shaw, 1972). In the first half of the quiz, students view photographs of political leaders, activists, and places where there is social unrest, and I ask them to identify who or what is pictured. In the second half of the quiz they see celebrities and products, stills from Hollywood movies, etc. As you might expect, the scores on the two sections are radically different. This always leads us to useful discussion about the work of Project Censored, who track the most unreported news stories of the year and compare them to what they call "junk food news" (see, most recently, Roth, Huff, & Project Censored, 2014).

This exercise is related to another media literacy principle: media carry ideological and value messages (Aufderheide, 2000). Hill (2004) discusses how educators can use advertisements to get students to critically examine unspoken cultural values that are turned to commercial purposes. Many educators have seen students become outraged, and then motivated to social action, after viewing Jean Kilbourne's highly visual documentaries on the sexism at the heart of contemporary advertising (see, most recently, Kilbourne, 2010). This is a stunningly successful example of an argument that would not stick without both her verbal context and the advertising images that she archives. It is one thing to lecture students about advertising's constant degrading images of women. It is another thing entirely to show an actual ad for Bitch Skateboards, depicting a young man using a scantily clad woman as an ottoman, and then ask what this image is selling ... beyond skateboards. This is a sort of intellectual judo where Kilbourne turns the force of media images against themselves in order to have the opposite effect of what they intended—to get us to *start* thinking, not *stop*. The documentary series *Dreamworlds* (see, most recently, Jhally, 2007) embodies much the same strategy by using actual music videos to critique music industry misogyny.[2]

Mitchell argues for students also doing their own visual research and offers examples of potential assignments:

> 'Take photographs of where you feel safe and not so safe'; 'Produce a video documentary on an issue "in your life"'; 'Find and work with seven or eight pictures from your family photographs that you can construct into a narrative about gender and identity' (2011, p. 4).

Having students collect and/or create visual images enhances their understanding of another important media literacy principle: all media are constructions (Aufderheide, 2000). Or, as Barthes put it, the mediated image "is an object that has been worked on, chosen, composed, constructed, treated according to professional, aesthetic or ideological norms" (1972, p. 19). Educators might introduce the basics of a program like Photoshop, for example, and then have students reconstruct images of themselves, manipulate them, place them in different settings, with different people or objects, as a way to begin challenging the ubiquity and ethics of image manipulation in the digital age. This can be a useful antidote to our subconscious notion that photographs are unmediated, simple reflections of reality (Barthes, 1977; Drucker, 2014).

Educators across the curriculum are thinking about the importance of images in ways that would have been considered radical in previous decades when the bias against visual knowledge was still hegemonic (Drucker, 2014). We are starting to see resources that seek to bridge the divide between verbal and visual orientations. For example, a composition textbook called *Beyond Words: Reading and Writing in a Visual Age* (Ruszkiewicz, Anderson, & Friend, 2006) integrates a plethora of visual images with analytical essays while challenging students to think visually and critically at the same time. This verbal/visual text includes assignments like the following:

> Identify a text that you have experienced in at least two different media: book and film, stage play and film, film and TV version, TV and newspaper, magazine and newspaper ... As best as you can, explain and then analyze the differences you experienced between the works (2006, p. 25).
>
> [Next to an array of *Rolling Stone* magazine cover photos:] How does placing a year's worth of *Rolling Stone* covers side-by-side change your perspective on the cover photos? Use the portraits ... to prompt your thinking about gender and body issues as markers of identity. What might the covers suggest about the relative power of men and women in popular music? (2006, p. 143)

Of course there are numerous other possibilities for integrating images into the classroom, but these few examples offer some useful starting points, "ways of seeing" (Berger, 1972), how imagery can encourage rather than disable critical thinking. Image-based orientations do present challenges to pedagogical goals, but they can be met if we accept that this is a battle educators can join. Let's not leave control over the visual environment solely in the hands of advertisers and commercial media industries. Arguing for why the concept of literacy itself needs redefinition in the digital age, Apkon sums up both the challenge and opportunity that the image saturated environment presents: "The most persistent question now facing us is not how can we resist this revolution in thought, but how can we respond with the maximum amount of thoughtfulness, energy, and smarts? How will we present ourselves to the world? How literate will we be?" (2013, p. 36).

NOTES

1. I anticipate one of the objections to my argument might be to raise the specter of text messaging. After all, aren't young people thoroughly immersed in words through the astounding number of text messages that they read and compose every day? Due to both the brevity and instrumental nature of most text messages I believe they do not constitute sustained, logical, discursive arguments and narratives. I acknowledge, however that this is a complex issue that warrants further debate and analysis.
2. For a fascinating reflection on the logic behind the pedagogy of the *Dreamworlds* videos and why using the same visual style as MTV was crucial to its success, see Jhally, 1994.

REFERENCES

Andersen, R. (2000). Road to ruin: The cultural mythology of SUVs. In R. Andersen and L. Strate (Eds.), *Critical studies in media commercialism*, pp. 158–172. New York: Oxford University Press.

Apkon, S. (2013). *The age of the image: Redefining literacy in a world of screens.* New York: Farrar, Straus and Giroux.

Aufderheide, P. (2000). *The daily planet: A critic on the capitalist culture beat.* Minneapolis: University of Minnesota Press.

Barnes, S. B. (2011). *An introduction to visual communication: From cave art to second life.* New York: Peter Lang.

Barthes, R. (1972). *Mythologies.* New York: Hill and Wang.

Barthes, R. (1977). *Image-music-text.* New York: Hill and Wang.

Berger, J. (1972). *Ways of seeing.* London: Penguin Books.

Bernhardt, S. A. (2004). Seeing the text. In C. Handa (Ed.), *Visual rhetoric in a digital world*, pp. 94–106. Boston: Bedford St. Martin's.

Boihem, H. (1997). *The ad and the ego* [Video]. Los Angeles: Parallax Pictures.

Boorstin, D. (1961). *The image: A guide to pseudo-events in America.* New York: Random House.

DeBord, G. (1995). *The society of the spectacle.* New York: Zone Books.

Descartes, R. (2001). *Discourse on method, optics, geometry, and meteorology.* Indianapolis, IN: Hackett Publishing Group.

Downey, K. (February 8, 2007). TV viewing is up, despite online video. *Media Life Magazine.* No pagination. http://www.medialifemagazine.com/tv-viewing-is-up-despite-online-video/.

Dredge, S. (September 26, 2013). Children's reading shrinking due to apps, games, and YouTube. *The Guardian.* No pagination. http://www.theguardian.com/technology/appsblog/2013/sep/26/children-reading-less- apps-games.

Drucker, J. (2014). *Graphesis: Visual forms of knowledge production.* Cambridge, MA: Harvard University Press.

Everard, J. (1934). Advertising to women by photography. *Commercial art and industry* 17, 1–6.

Ewen, S. (1988). *All consuming images: The politics of style in contemporary culture.* New York: Basic Books.

Ewen, S. (January, 1998). PR! Interview with Stuart Ewen. *StayFree!* 14, 8–18.

Forceville, C. (2005). Cognitive linguistics and multimodal metaphor. In K. Sachshombach (Ed.), *Bildwissenschaft zwischen reflexion und anwendung* (pp. 264–284). Cologne, Germany: Herbert von Halem Verlag.

Friere, P. (2000). *Pedagogy of the oppressed*. New York: Bloomsbury Academic.

Hariman, R., & Lucaites, J.L. (2007). *No caption needed: Iconic photographs, public culture, and liberal democracy*. Chicago: University of Chicago Press.

Hill, C. A. (2004). Reading the visual in college writing classes. In C. Handa (Ed.), *Visual rhetoric in a digital world*, pp. 107–130. Boston: Bedford St. Martin's.

Holmes, O. W. (1864). *Soundings from the Altantic*. Boston: Ticknor and Fields.

hooks, b. (1994). *Teaching to transgress: Education as the practice of freedom*. New York: Routledge.

Jay, M. (1993). *Downcast eyes: The denigration of vision in twentieth-century French thought*. Berkeley, CA: University of California Press.

Jhally, S. (1994). Intersections of discourse: MTV, sexual politics and *Dreamworlds*. In J. Cruz and J. Lewis (Eds.), *Reconceptualizing audiences*. Boulder CO: Westview Press.

Jhally, S. (2003). Image-based culture: Advertising and popular culture. In G. Dines and J. M. Humez (Eds.), *Gender, race and class in media: A text-reader* (2nd ed.), pp. 249–257. Thousand Oaks, CA: Sage.

Jhally, S. (2007). *Dreamworlds 3: Desire, sex and power in music video* [Video]. Northhampton, MA: Media Education Foundation.

Kilbourne, J. (2010). *Killing us softly 4: Advertising's image of women* [Video]. Northampton, MA: Media Education Foundation.

Laspina, J. A. (1998). *The visual turn and the transformation of the textbook*. Mahwah, NJ: Lawrence Erlbaum.

Lester, P. M. (2006). *Visual communication: Images with messages* (4th ed.). Boston: Wadsworth.

Logan, R. K. (1986). *The alphabet effect*. New York: St. Martin's Press.

MacLean, P. D. (1990). *The triune brain in evolution: role in paleocerebral functions*. New York: Plenum Press.

McClure, S. M., Laibson, D. I., Loewenstein, G., & Cohen, J. D. (2004). Separate neural systems value immediate and delayed monetary returns. *Science, 306*, 503–507.

McCombs, M. E., & Shaw, D. L. (1972). The agenda-setting function of mass media. *Public Opinion Quarterly, 36*, 176–187.

Messaris, P. (2003). Visual communication: Theory and research. A review essay. *Journal of Communication, 53*(3), 551–556.

Meurer, M. (December 10, 2014). The missing photos from the Senate report on CIA torture. *Truthout*. No pagination. http://www.truth-out.org/news/item/27935-the-missing-photos-from-the-senate-report-on-cia-torture.

Mirzoeff, N. (1999). *An introduction to visual culture*. London: Routledge.

Mitchell, C. (2011). *Doing visual research*. Thousand Oaks, CA: Sage.

Mitchell, W. J. T. (1994). *Picture theory*. Chicago: University of Chicago Press.

Molla, R. (May 13, 2014). Commercials—like our attention spans—are getting shorter. *Wall Street Journal*. No pagination. http://blogs.wsj.com/numbers/commercials-like-our-attention-spans-are-getting-shorter-1364/.

Morris, E. (2014). *Believing is seeing (observations on the mysteries of photography)*. New York: Penguin Books.

Müller, M. G. (2007). What is visual communication? Past and future of an emerging field of communication research. *Studies in Communication Science, 7*(2), 7–34.

Postman, N. (1985). *Amusing ourselves to death: Public discourse in the age of show business*. New York: Penguin.

Roberts, K. (2005). *Lovemarks: The future beyond brands*. New York: power House Books.

Roth, A. L., Huff, M., & Project Censored. (2014). *Censored 2015: Inspiring we the People: The top censored stories and media analysis of 2013–2014*. New York: Seven Stories Press.

Ruszkiewicz, J., Anderson, D., & Friend, C. (2006). *Beyond words: Reading and writing in a visual age*. New York: Pearson.

Seppanen, J. (2006). *The power of the gaze: An introduction to visual literacy*. New York: Peter Lang.

Sontag, S. (2003). *Regarding the pain of others*. New York: Picador.

Stossel, S. (May 1, 1997). The man who counts the killings. *The Atlantic*, pp. 86–104.

Sturken, M., & Cartwright, L. (2009). *Practices of looking: An introduction to visual culture* (2nd ed.). New York: Oxford University Press.

Taylor, M. C. (2014). *Speed limits: Where time went and why we have so little left*. New Haven, CT: Yale University Press.

Part IV

National

In the fourth section of *Media Education for a Digital Generation,* we examine the ways that digital media have redefined our sense of, and connection to, NATIONAL frameworks, creating both new opportunities and challenges for what scholar Benedict Anderson famously called "imagined communities" of nation-states that have now entered the digital age. As people increasingly seek out and share a wide array of news sources beyond the mainstream, we begin by exploring the power of distributive online social networks to redefine national structures of power. In the past, the business model for print and broadcast news consisted of a process that homogenized narratives and frameworks into conventional tropes and hegemonic ideologies to appeal to a national audience for advertisers. Today, we explore new digital possibilities for crowdsourcing independent news stories that challenge hierarchical organizations and corporate commercial infotainment. As a pedagogical means to harness the collective energy of the groundswell, we'll learn about an innovative assignment that affords students the chance to use digital platforms to bring public attention to important but underreported social issues. By using Web 2.0 media to become part of the newly emerging Fifth Estate of bloggers, journalists, and non-dominant media outlets, and by creating alternative narrative frames, we discover how students can learn to participate outside of institutional channels. As part of the movement to maintain the porosity, transparency, and creativity of an open Internet, we'll hear arguments for enacting and maintaining fair use and cultural sovereignty as democratic cornerstones. Much has been written about the diffusion of information and ideas in the Digital Age, and how the success of social media is predicated upon dynamic, collective exchanges and cultural participation that include mashups, sampling, and remixing. Here, we consider the ways in which copyright impairs the process of information sharing and creative interplay by maintaining rigid hierarchical structures of control over the use and diffusion of cultural content found within social networks. In keeping with the theme of self-organization online and offline, we learn how community organizers use media production as a means of critical analysis, political activism, and entrepreneurship. By embracing a paradigm of production that involves "being the media" rather than remaining defined and controlled by them, we'll also discover how in the current technological environment, issues of social justice, representation, production, and surveillance are crucial digital literacy issues requiring careful attention. Next, we turn to a chapter exploring the opportunities and limitations presented by "fake" news programs produced by *The Daily Show* and the *Colbert Report*. As millennials turn to humorous and witty programs like these instead of more established news sources, we'll hear an argument for extending the scope and purpose of media literacy to include political literacy through satire as an effective means of fostering engagement and news judgment within the digital landscape. Resulting from the need for adequate training to address the changing structures and uses of digital media, this section concludes with a call for more graduate level media literacy programs across the United States. As the reach and impact of digital media continue to expand, educators, administrators, policy makers, and community activists alike seek a deeper understanding of digital media and their impact on individuals and culture. Inevitably, this will require comprehensive digital media literacy education, from K-12 through graduate programs of study suitable for the twenty-first century.

12 Breaking the Corporate News Frame through Validated Independent News Online

Andy Lee Roth and Project Censored[1]

"THE ART OF BREAKING OBNOXIOUS FRAMES"

A little more than two hundred years ago, English textile artisans protested against their employers' introduction of newly developing technologies, which threatened to put them out of work. From the owners' perspective, the new mechanized power looms and spinning frames promised to increase production and lower costs. From the textile workers' standpoint, the mechanization of labor would leave them more vulnerable to exploitation. Machines would make their skills unnecessary, permitting their bosses to replace them with cheaper, unskilled workers, including children. The textile workers were part of a broad swell of working-class discontent and protest in nineteenth-century England, as the Industrial Revolution radically transformed not only working conditions but also nearly every aspect of daily life.[2]

The Luddites responded in two ways. First, and most directly, under cover of night, they broke into shops that used power looms and spinning frames, and they destroyed those machines. Second, and less well remembered, the Luddites posted notices describing their grievances and often threatening future acts of sabotage. These public messages were sometimes addressed to the general public and, at other times, to specific shop owners and were usually signed on behalf of Ned Ludd or some variant. For example, a note posted on a village hosier's shop in late 1811 suggested that Ned Ludd and his "supporting Army" well understood "the Art of breaking obnoxious Frames." Another letter, from the same time period, issued from "Ned Ludd's Office, Sherwood Forest," informed its readers that the knitters were "empowered to break and destroy all frames and engines that fabricate articles in a fraudulent and deceitful manner."[3] Reviewing nineteenth-century Luddite resistance to industrialization, historian Peter Linebaugh (2014) has written that machine breaking was "a means of defending the commons," the natural and cultural resources held in common, rather than privately owned (Linebaugh, 2014, p. 79).

In many ways, today's millennials are remarkably different from the Luddite machine-breakers of nineteenth-century England. Millennials are "digital natives" who have grown up with (and, in many cases, helped to develop) the digital age communication technologies that define our networked society. They understand these technologies and use them to their benefit (Higdon, 2014). If revolutionary new technologies of media and communications define our twenty-first century, as industrialization defined the nineteenth century, then what "obnoxious frames" or "fraudulent and deceitful" articles threaten today's commons? And, how should we respond?

To address these questions, consider a different type of frame. In the late twentieth century, social scientists began using the concepts of "frame" and "framing" to analyze how we perceive, make sense of, and communicate about reality. In this usage, a frame refers not to a physical structure—such as those nineteenth century power looms—but, instead, to the *interpretive processes* that we use (often without any awareness of them) to make sense of the world.[4] From studies of everyday interaction to social movements and journalism, social scientists now use the concept of framing to understand a symbolic form of power. For example, Todd Gitlin applied the idea of framing to explain how journalists covered the Students for a Democratic Society (SDS) and other social movements in the late 1960s. Gitlin defined *media frames* as "persistent patterns of cognition, interpretation, and presentation, of selection, emphasis, and exclusion, by which symbol-handlers routinely organize discourse, whether verbal or visual" (Gitlin, 1980, p. 7). As such, media frames are "largely unspoken and unacknowledged," even though they serve to organize our collective understanding of the world. Gitlin argued that media frames emphasized aspects of SDS that ultimately destabilized it, resulting in the promotion of more moderate alternatives. Had SDS and other antiwar movements been better able to counter how news outlets framed them, they might have been more successful in their efforts.

As this chapter will describe, the Validated Independent News assignment affords students the chance to put their savvy understanding of these new digital platforms to good use, by bringing public attention to important but underreported social issues, by creating alternative narrative frames regarding those issues, and by using Web 2.0 to become part of the networked fourth estate (Benkler, 2013) themselves.

PROJECT CENSORED AND THE NETWORKED FOURTH ESTATE

Since 1976, Project Censored, a nonprofit news watch organization, has focused its efforts on informing students and the public about the importance of a robust free press for democracy. The Project's mission is dual: first, we critique the corporate-owned news media when they fail to provide the kind of reporting that members of the public need in order to be informed citizens and engaged community members. Second, we celebrate and draw attention to independent investigative journalists—and the organizations that support their good work—for covering newsworthy stories and perspectives that their corporate counterparts either ignore or treat in systematically slanted ways.

Project Censored can thus be understood as part of what Benkler (2013) describes as the newly emerging "networked fourth estate." More diverse and organizationally decentralized, the networked fourth estate challenges the previous dominance of an elite-controlled, centralized, top-down mass media. As Benkler argues, the networked fourth estate has "an agility, scope, and diversity of sources and pathways" that allow it to "collect and capture information on a global scale that would be impossible for any single traditional organization to replicate by itself" (Benkler, 2013, pp. 29–30).

In this chapter, we first argue that corporate news media often employ "obnoxious frames" that defraud and deceive the public, rather than inform and engage them. Against this backdrop, we then describe how Project Censored's campus affiliates program coordinates the efforts of hundreds of college and university professors and students across the country in an electronically networked, collective effort to "break" these corporate news frames. By identifying, evaluating, and summarizing what Project Censored calls Validated Independent News stories (VINs), students develop their critical thinking and digital media literacy skills in service of informing the public about significant news stories that the corporate media fail to cover adequately. The chapter's third and final section describes in detail how teachers might adapt the Project's Validated Independent News curriculum as an effective research assignment in a variety of different courses. This section also anticipates some of the challenges that students regularly face in successfully completing the assignment, and offers classroom-tested solutions on how to deal with them.

Critical thinking and media literacy are crucial to democracy. Even in a society with strong free speech protections, if powerful elites can significantly manipulate public opinion, then free speech may actually serve the interests of those in power more effectively than traditional censorship.[5] For this reason, the development of students' critical thinking capacities is crucial to democracy—especially for millennials who are bombarded with digital media that aim to colonize their attention through clicks and 'likes' (see Higdon, 2014). To formulate vital questions clearly and precisely; to gather and assess relevant information; to formulate well-reasoned conclusions and solutions that can be tested against relevant criteria and standards; to think open-mindedly across alternative systems of thought, while identifying underlying assumptions; and to communicate all of this effectively—these are elementary critical thinking skills that make free speech meaningful and robust democracy possible.[6] Researching Validated Independent News stories provides students with direct, hands-on opportunities to engage and hone these skills.

Furthermore, with the demise of traditional newspapers and the rise of the blogosphere, the need for trusted independent news perspectives is now more acute than ever. As Linebaugh (2014) acknowledges, the commons in need of defense includes language, and censorship of press and speech amounts to another kind of enclosure to be resisted (Linebaugh, 2014, p. 81). The research assignment we describe here not only sensitizes students to this concern, it also provides them with the opportunity to contribute to Project Censored's ongoing, collaborative effort to provide the public with trustworthy, validated news sources on important stories that the corporate media either ignore or distort.

CORPORATE MEDIA IN THE DIGITAL ERA OF "NEWS INFLATION"

In 2001, Project Censored founder Carl Jensen observed that Americans suffer from "news inflation"—"[T]here seems to be more [news] than ever before," Jensen wrote, "but it isn't worth as much as it used to be" (Jensen, 2001, p. 252). His observation took into account the rise of the 24-hour news cycle, which became conventional after the launch of CNN and other dedicated cable television news channels in the 1980s. But Jensen's critique of news inflation dates back to a time when just 46% of Americans reported using the Internet (today the figure is 87%), 53% owned cell phones (compared with 90% in 2014, including 58% who own smartphones), blogging was not yet widespread, and neither Skype nor Reddit existed.[7] As a result of these developments, news inflation is even greater today than when Jensen first made his observation.

A full discussion of this point's implications goes beyond this chapter's scope. Here we limit ourselves to two basic observations about news inflation that are directly relevant in the classroom. First, an overwhelming amount of information, combined with lack of skills for parsing what is valid and useful from what is distorted or trivial, threatens to leave us cynical or disengaged—not only about news but, more fundamentally, about the most important public issues that we as a society face.[8] With news inflation, we are more likely to suffer from what Susanne Moeller (1999) has described as "compassion fatigue"—a dulled public sensitivity toward societal crises like disease, famine, and war. The more media-saturated our society becomes, the more likely we are to suffer from the compassion fatigue-inducing consequences of news inflation, until some people reach the point where they disengage from news and politics entirely.

Engaging students in researching and validating independent news stories and then making their findings public through blogs, videos, and contributions to Project Censored's web site and annual book is a powerful antidote to cynicism. Our experiences are not unique, as Project Censored affiliate faculty from college and university campuses across the country attest.[9]

An ability to recognize institutional factors that reduce much of what passes as news to propaganda is a second crucial counter to the overwhelming impacts of news inflation.

Although news inflation has accelerated in the digital era, the framing assumptions that shape corporate news coverage in the new millennium have not significantly changed. Consequently, the propaganda model introduced by Herman and Chomsky in *Manufacturing Consent* (1988) remains useful as a basis for assessing twenty-first century corporate news coverage. Arguing that news is systematically structured to function as propaganda in service of elite interests, Herman and Chomsky (1988, pp. 1–35) identified *five filters* that "fix the premises of discourse and interpretation, and the definition of what is newsworthy in the first place" (p. 2):

1 *Ownership*: With consolidation, media are increasingly corporate owned, and information provided by corporate media typically serves corporate interests. News items that threaten media owners' financial interests face bias and, potentially, censorship.
2 *Advertising*: Corporate media are not commercially viable without advertising revenues. Media must generate audiences to produce profits. In this view, the audience is the product that content providers sell to advertisers. Herman and Chomsky argue that news takes whatever form is conducive to attracting large, affluent audiences.
3 *Sourcing:* News is primarily about what powerful elites do and say, because establishment journalists treat elites as the most newsworthy, reliable sources. Corporate news marginalizes or altogether excludes other views.
4 *Flak:* Herman and Chomsky use this term to describe negative responses to media content, including, for example, letters to the editor, phone calls, petitions, and lawsuits. Because flak can be expensive—think, for example, of lost advertising revenues and the costs of defending lawsuits—the prospect of generating flak can push news organizations to avoid certain types of stories or issues.[10]
5 *Fear*: News as propaganda highlights potential threats—whether real, exaggerated, or imagined—and frames issues in the dichotomized terms of Us/Them. Herman and Chomsky originally defined this fifth filter as "Anti-Communism," but taking into account more recent history, including the "War on Terror," they now identify this fifth filter in broader terms to address phenomena such as Islamophobia.[11]

In sum, the propaganda model suggests that these five filters structure news—at least in its corporate form—to keep audiences less than fully informed and potentially *mis*informed, thus weakening their ability as citizens and community members to engage in robust democratic self-government.[12]

   In the classroom, then, one beginning point is to ask students, what is censorship? And, why is it important to understand it? Here students might consider Project Censored's working definition of censorship as "anything that interferes with the free flow of information in a society that purports to have a free press."[13] Depending on the focus of the course, and the level of the students participating, an instructor might assign the "Propaganda Model" chapter from *Manufacturing Consent* as reading, or she might simply summarize the model and its five filters in class.

Once students begin working on assessing their own Validated Independent News stories, they can use the propaganda model and its filters as analytic tools for making sense of differences between corporate and independent coverage. Of course, it should not be treated as a foregone conclusion that every corporate news story suffers from filtering, or that independent media never reflect the filters' purging consequences (see, e.g., Phillips, 2007).

VALIDATED INDEPENDENT NEWS AND PROJECT CENSORED'S CAMPUS AFFILIATES PROGRAM

Students have played a crucial role in Project Censored's work since Carl Jensen founded it in 1976. Originally students and faculty at Sonoma State University undertook all of the news analysis and produced the Project's annual list of the Top 25 "Censored" news stories. In 2009–2010, Peter Phillips (the Project's second director) and Mickey Huff (its current director) pioneered Project Censored's campus affiliates program. They invited faculty and students from college and university campuses across the country to join in researching Validated Independent News stories and informing the public about them through the Project Censored web site and the Project's annual *Censored* book.[14]

Validated Independent News stories (VINs) are news stories reported in the independent media that have been ignored or only partially covered by corporate media. These VINs provide information and perspective that the public has a right and need to know, but to which it has limited access. Each year, college and university teachers and students participating in the Project's campus affiliates program review several hundred independently sourced news stories for their significance, accuracy, quality of sources, and competing corporate news coverage. We post news stories that pass this review process as Validated Independent News stories on our website.[15] And, in turn, these VINs join the pool of stories that are the candidates for that year's Top 25 list. To give some sense of the affiliate program's current scope, consider that the Top 25 story list in the most recent yearbook, *Censored 2015: Inspiring We the People*, represents the efforts of 219 students, 56 professors, and 13 community experts. This chapter describes the basics of the assignment that coordinates our efforts. Project Censored affiliated faculty have successfully implemented the Validated Independent News research assignment in courses that cover a range of disciplines and topics, and with students at different stages in their college education.[16]

In a book focused on media education in a digital age, it is worth noting that the Internet dramatically enhances this type of collaboration. With the combination of (1) such expanded participation, (2) tight deadlines tied both to the academic year and yearbook's production and publication, not to mention (3) a slim organizational budget, Project Censored contributors have neither the time nor the resources to gather in person to work; we cannot imagine hosting enormous 100-person phone conferences; and (much as we support them) the U.S. Postal Service can't deliver fast enough. Beyond the Internet-dependent researching of stories, communication among campus affiliates hinges crucially on the Internet. (We have a vested interest in promoting Net Neutrality—The Project, much like democracy in a digital age, may literally depend on it!)

HOW TO FIND, EVALUATE AND SUMMARIZE VALIDATED INDEPENDENT NEWS STORIES

Students who successfully complete the VIN research assignment will (1) develop their critical thinking skills (including interpretation, evaluation, and explanation) and media literacy, in service of (2) Project Censored's ongoing mission to highlight important but underreported news stories that the public has a right and a need to know. The assignment consists of three stages in which students—often working in teams of two or small groups—identify, evaluate, and summarize an independent news story. Here we describe this three-step process in some detail.

I. Find a Candidate Story

Students will search *independent* news sources to find candidate stories. In many courses, an important starting point is to help students understand the difference between *independent* and *corporate* news. The Project Censored website includes a listing of recommended independent news sources. Many school's libraries may provide access to ProQuest's Alt-Press Watch, which is also useful.

II. Evaluate the Candidate Story's Strength

The strongest candidate stories—those most likely to gain a spot among the top censored stories in a given year—are important, timely, fact-based, well documented, and underreported. Once students have found a candidate story, they should test its significance by considering these four questions:

1 Is it *important*? The more people that the story affects, the more important it is. Be careful to consider indirect impacts. For example, a story about electronic waste disposal in Africa might seem like it only involves the people exposed to the toxic waste. But the problem of electronic waste disposal includes Western consumers (mostly North Americans and Europeans) who discard as much as 40 million tons of electronic waste each year. So, that story involves a wider circle of people and is more important than it might first seem.[17]

2 Is it *timely*? News stories should have appeared within the last year. For example, *Censored 2015* covers the top stories from April 2013 to March 2014. Thus, stories submitted as candidates for *Censored 2016* should be no older than April 2014. Recent stories on older events will be considered if they report new, important information.

3 Is the story *fact-based* and *well documented*? The story's accuracy and credibility is crucial. Dramatic claims and seductive rhetoric do not matter if the journalist fails to provide *specific evidence* to support the story. How many different sources does the story use? How credible is each source? A story based on a number of reliable sources is harder to dispute than one based on a single good source or several biased sources. If a student's story cites other published work (for example, a scientific study, government document, or another news story), the student should track back and read the primary source(s). Does their story accurately depict the original?

4 Have the corporate media ignored or *underreported* the story? Students should evaluate their stories' coverage by using a news database (such as LexisNexis News, part of Lexis-Nexis Academic; ProQuest NewsStand; or Newspaper Source Plus) to search for corporate coverage of it.[18] Do not underestimate the importance of this crucial step in the process. When possible, in our classes, we schedule a session in a computer lab, sometimes with one of the school's reference librarians, to familiarize students with these databases and how to use them effectively. Decisions about what key terms to use in searches, for instance, are often new challenges for many students. It is worthwhile to take time to help students develop these skills. They matter, not only for the success of the assignment, but more importantly as "real-world" skills that may serve students well beyond their schoolwork.

Decisions about whether a candidate VIN has been adequately covered in the corporate press can be among the most challenging aspects of the assignment. The clearest "censored" stories are ones that corporate media have completely ignored. However, candidate stories that received some corporate coverage may still be considered "censored" if corporate coverage leaves the reader with an incomplete or distorted understanding of the story. Many students' initial reaction is to assume that, as soon as they find *any* corporate news coverage of their candidate story, that story is dead as far as the VIN process goes. This is not necessarily true, however. On finding corporate news coverage of their story, students have the rich opportunity to engage their critical thinking skills to compare and contrast the two stories' content and perspectives.

An example illustrates this crucial aspect of the VIN process. In spring 2013, Qui Phan, a student at the College of Marin, was researching a story published in the *Guardian* about journalists around the world imprisoned or killed because of their work. One day she came to class looking discouraged. Her story, she explained, seemed to be dead: The *New York Times* had subsequently covered it. I encouraged her to do a careful comparison of the two articles. Did the *Guardian* coverage include anything important that the *Times* did not? The next class session, Qui smiled as she explained that, although the *Times* coverage included the same figures (from the Committee to Protect Journalists) that the *Guardian* had reported, the *Guardian* story also presented crucial information about efforts to pass a resolution in United Nations that would provide additional protections for journalists. Here was a clear instance of the independent press providing a broader scope of information, not only identifying an important social issue, but also informing the public about one consequential effort to address it. On this basis, Qui continued to pursue the story, and Project Censored's panel of international judges eventually voted to make it story #16 in *Censored 2014* (Huff & Roth, 2013, pp. 56–57 & 75–77). Before making it to that stage, however, the exercise provided rich opportunities for student learning.

As students research their candidate stories, they should be alert for related stories that (1) contain information contrary to their original, (2) were published prior to their original story, or (3) contain more complete information than their initial story. Credit should be given to the first reporter(s) to cover a given story. Students may decide that a second story is superior to the one they were initially tracking, in which case they should continue their work using the second story. Or they may conclude that the second story supports the first and should be included along with it.

Students should be rewarded when they identify corporate news coverage that does effectively "kill" the story's status as a Censored story. From a strictly educational perspective, this is part of the critical thinking process, and should be acknowledged as such. Furthermore, from the point of view of Project Censored's work, we only want to critique the corporate media when they do indeed fail to fulfill their duty of fully informing the public—misleading claims about what the corporate media have failed to cover undermine the Project's reputation. Therefore, when students identify high quality corporate coverage of an independent news story they have been researching, this outcome should be seen in positive light: Not only have students usefully employed their skills as researchers and critical thinkers, they have also helped to uphold the Project's reputation for thorough, trustworthy news judgment.

III. Summarize the Candidate Story

All candidate stories submitted to Project Censored should use the following format.

<u>Title</u>   This captures the story's most important point in approximately five to ten words.

Summary

The first paragraph should provide a specific, concise and factual summary of the story's most important point. Students should use a *summary lead* to place this essential information up front. Encourage students to write a first sentence that introduces what happened, where, and when. This writing should be specific, use active verbs, and avoid passive constructions (for example, "Civilians were targeted") that tend to hide agency. The first paragraph should address the skeptical reader's questions, "So what? Why is this important?" If the main point of the story is controversial, which is often true for Project Censored stories, an attribution will add strength to the lead paragraph. For example,

> In January 2012, FairTest, the National Center for Fair and Open Testing, reported that a decade of No Child Left Behind (NCLB) policies has actually slowed the rate of education progress.

Purdue University's Online Writing Lab (OWL) provides useful guidelines on how to write a lead or opening paragraph, including several examples of summary leads.[19]

The following paragraph should go into more detail, elaborating on the story's main point and/or introducing secondary points. Good detail might include who stands to benefit from the action or policy in question, as well as who (if anyone) it harms.

A final paragraph should address *corporate media coverage* of the story. This is often as important as the story's summary lead. As already noted, it is essential that students do a thorough job of researching their story's coverage using a reliable news database. If there is no corporate media coverage of their story, students should state so directly and indicate a date as of which this was true. If their story has gotten some corporate news coverage, then they should identify what corporate news organizations covered the story, and when. In this case they should also describe how the independent news story that they are summarizing goes beyond the coverage provided by the corporate media. If students cannot identify any important differences between the independent and corporate coverage, then they need to reconsider whether their story is actually a "censored" story.

References   Following the summary, students should give a complete reference for the story using the *Chicago Manual of Style* format. For example:

Almerindo Ojeda, "Death in Guantánamo: Suicide or Dry Boarding?" *Truthout*, November 3, 2011, http://www.truth-out.org/death-guantanamo-suicide-or-dryboarding/13201˚82714.

If students' summaries draw on multiple stories, they should give a complete reference for each source.

<u>**Student Researcher(s):**</u>   List each student researcher's name and, in parentheses, school affiliation.

<u>**Faculty Evaluator(s):**</u>   List each faculty evaluator's name and, in parentheses, school affiliation.

CONCLUSION: TWENTY-FIRST CENTURY FRAME BREAKING AND THE NETWORKED COMMONS

The proliferation of media outlets in the digital age demands an informed public capable of distinguishing between valid news and propaganda. Teachers who bring Project Censored into their classrooms via the Validated Independent News assignment give their students direct, hands-on opportunities to develop their critical thinking skills and media literacy. In our experience, this assignment is especially effective because students who successfully complete it also contribute to a larger, cooperative effort to bring greater public attention to marginalized issues worthy of recognition, dialogue, and debate, whether in their communities or online, in what is an increasingly important virtual public commons. Time and again, as Project Censored's campus affiliates program grows each year, we hear stories from our faculty colleagues about how excited students are to work on an assignment that may result in contributing to some greater good. The prospect of sharing their work—via the Internet and potentially through the *Censored* yearbooks—motivates students to do their best on this assignment.

In a digital age, when the political economy of the corporate media is in crisis, and the framing of crucial social issues is more important than ever, engaging students in "breaking the frame" of the corporate news media is not only critical, pedagogically; it is also essential to defending the commons of information that we need to make our communities and the world a better place to live for all.

NOTES

1. The guidelines for the Validated Independent News exercise described here have been developed and refined over the years by a number of teachers affiliated with Project Censored. Among these, Peter Phillips, Mickey Huff, Susan Rahman, Susan Maret, Kenn Burrows, and the late Brian Murphy have made especially significant contributions. In addition to being constant sources of inspiration, Elizabeth Boyd and Mickey Huff offered helpful comments on earlier versions of this chapter.
2. The classic account of this history is Thompson (1964).
3. Both letters are quoted in Kirkpatrick Sale's (1995) highly recommended history (pp. 80, 99). As Peter Linebaugh documents, machine breaking was not limited to nineteenth-century England. U.S. slaveholders in the antebellum south

frequently reported broken plows, lost hoes, and ruined carts—evidence of resistance by insurrectionary slaves (Linebaugh, 2014, pp. 89ff.).

4. Sociologist Erving Goffman pioneered this perspective in *Frame Analysis* (1974).
5. See, for example, Marcuse (1969), available online at http://www.marcuse.org/herbert/pubs/60spubs/65repressivetolerance.htm, and Huff and Roth (2013, pp. 249–250).
6. On the import of critical thinking for democracy, see Cohen (2013).
7. Figures on Internet and cell phone use from Fox and Rainie (2014).
8. Roth and Huff (2013, pp. 27–28) discuss cynicism regarding news and disengagement from politics.
9. See, for example, Niman (2014) and the professor testimonials on the Project Censored web site: http://www.projectcensored.org/project-censoreds-commitment-to-independent-news-in-the-classroom/.
10. The networked fourth estate (Benkler, 2013) is subject to new forms of flak. For example, Fernández-Delgado and Balanza (2012) analyze "libel tourism," in which "wealthy and powerful claimants pursue (or threaten to pursue) actions in plaintiff-friendly jurisdictions regardless of where the parties are based" (p. 2717). In cases of libel tourism, plaintiffs take advantage of the Internet's global reach to argue that networked journalists who publish online are subject to libel laws anywhere that content might be read, including in nations like the United Kingdom, where libel laws strongly favor plaintiffs. Press freedom advocates recognize that libel tourism discourages critical media reporting.
11. On Islamophobia—a form of anti-Muslim racism that invokes the specter of a "Muslim threat" to justify aggressive U.S. foreign policy and imperialism—see Kumar (2012).
12. The contributors to Klaehn (2005) provide a critical review and assessment of the propaganda model. Parenti (2001) offers an alternative model of corporate news filtering.
13. This broader definition of censorship is necessary to understand the pervasive impact of corporate news media. At Project Censored we understand censorship as a specific form of propaganda—i.e., deceptive communication used to influence public opinion to benefit a special interest. In this view, modern censorship includes the "subtle yet constant and sophisticated manipulation" that results from systemic political, economic, legal, and professional pressures on news content (Huff & Roth, 2012, p. 30). The Project Censored documentary film is a valuable resource for introducing students to these issues. For information about *Project Censored the movie: Ending the reign of junk food news*, see http://www.projectcensoredthemovie.com/.
14. Phillips and Huff (2010) describe the campus affiliates program's early history.
15. See www.projectcensored.org/category/validated-independent-news/.
16. From first-years to graduating seniors, students of all levels have shown themselves able to complete the VIN research assignment successfully. The greatest variations that we see are in terms of how much time the professor needs to invest in helping students (1) to identify an article's key points and (2) to summarize these clearly in prose. Understandably, most upper-division students are better prepared than first-year students to handle these challenges, but in our experience the assignment may have its greatest positive impacts on first-year students. For many of them, this will be the first time they undertake a research assignment that could result in their work being deemed sufficiently important

and good to warrant publication. It would be difficult to overemphasize how motivating this is for many of the students with whom we work.

17. See, for instance, "What We Don't Know When We Throw Out Our Electronics," Project Censored, April 10, 2012, www.projectcensored.org/what-we-dont-know-when-we-throw-out-our-electronics/.

18. Experience shows that Google News is not always reliable. Although students may be most familiar with it, allow them to rely on it as a last resort, only if your school library lacks access to any of the previously mentioned databases.

19. See "How to Write a Lead," Purdue OWL, no date, http://owl.english.purdue.edu/owl/resource/735/05/.

REFERENCES

Benkler, Y. (2013). WikiLeaks and the Networked Fourth Estate. In B. Reveni, A. Hints, & P. McCurdy (Eds.), *Beyond WikiLeaks: Implications for the future of communications, journalism and society* (pp. 11–34). New York: Palgrave Macmillan.

Cohen, E. D. (2013). Digging deeper: Politico-corporate media manipulation, critical thinking, and democracy. In M. Huff and A. L. Roth (Eds.), *Censored 2014: Fearless speech in fateful times* (pp. 251–269). New York: Seven Stories Press.

Fernández-Delgado, F. C., & Balanza, M. T. V. (2012). Beyond WikiLeaks: The Icelandic Modern Media Initiative and the creation of free speech havens. *International Journal of* Communications, 6, 2706–2729.

Fox, S., & Rainie, L. (2014, February 27). The Web at 25 in the U.S. Retrieved from http://www.pewinternet.org/2014/02/27/the-web-at-25-in-the-u-s/.

Gitlin, T. (1980). *The whole world is watching: Mass media in the making & unmaking of the New Left.* Berkeley: University of California Press.

Goffman, E. (1974). *Frame analysis: An essay on the organization of experience.* New York: Harper & Row.

Herman, E., & Chomsky, N. (1988). *Manufacturing consent: The political economy of the mass media.* New York: Pantheon Books.

Higdon, N. (2014, February 14). The millennial media revolution: How the next generation is re-shaping the press. *Censored Notebook*, featured articles. Retrieved from http://www.projectcensored.org/the-millennial-media-revolution-how-the-next-generation-is-re-shaping-the-press/.

Huff, M., & Roth, A. L. (2013). *Censored 2014: Fearless speech in fateful times: The top censored stories and media analysis of 2012–13.* New York: Seven Stories Press.

Huff, M., & Roth, A. L. (2012). *Censored 2013: Dispatches from the media revolution.* New York: Seven Stories Press.

Jensen, C. (2001). Junk Food News, 1877–2000. In P. Phillips and Project Censored (Eds.), *Censored 2001* (pp. 251–264). New York: Seven Stories Press.

Klaehn, J. (2005). *Filtering the news: Essays on Herman and Chomsky's propaganda model.* Montreal: Black Rose Books.

Kumar, D. (2012). *Islamophobia and the politics of empire.* Chicago: Haymarket Books.

Linebaugh, P. (2014). *Stop, thief!: The commons, enclosures, and resistance.* Oakland, CA: PM Press.

Marcuse, H. (1969). Repressive Tolerance. In R. P. Wolfe, B. Moore, Jr., & H. Marcuse (Eds.), *A critique of pure tolerance* (pp. 95–137). Boston: Beacon Press.

Moeller, S. (1999). *Compassion fatigue: How the media sell disease, famine, war, and death*. New York: Routledge.

Niman, M. I. (2014). The SUNY-Buffalo State and Project Censored Partnership. In A. L. Roth and M. Huff (Eds.), *Censored 2015: Inspiring we the people* (pp. 193–198). New York: Seven Stories Press.

Parenti, M. (2001, May). *Monopoly media manipulation*. Retrieved from http://www.michaelparenti.org/MonopolyMedia.html.

Phillips, P. (2007). Left progressive media inside the propaganda model. In P. Phillips and A. Roth (Eds.), *Censored 2008: The top 25 censored stories of 2006–07* (pp. 233–251). New York: Seven Stories Press.

Phillips, P., & Huff, M. (2010). Colleges and Universities Validate Independent News and Challenge Censorship. In M. Huff & P. Phillips, (Eds.), *Censored 2011: The top censored stories of 2009–10* (pp. 355–369). New York: Seven Stories Press.

Roth, A. L., & Huff, M. (2013). Introduction. In *Censored 2014: Fearless Speech in Fateful Times* (pp. 25–34). New York: Seven Stories Press.

Sale, K. (1995). *Rebels against the future: The Luddites and their war on the Industrial Revolution: Lessons for the computer age*. Reading, Mass.: Addison-Wesley Pub.

Thompson, E. P. (1964). *The making of the English working class*. New York: Pantheon Books.

13 Teaching Digital Literacy and Social Justice at the 1Hood Media Academy

Critical Pedagogy and the Limits of Philanthropy

Chenjerai Kumanhika and Paradise Gray

The 1Hood media academy is a Pittsburgh-based educational program that aims at empowering African American males to "be the media" by using media production as political activism, entrepreneurship, and as a response to their own critical readings of media representation. I learned of the academy while researching their founders, Jasiri X and Paradise Gray, between 2011 and 2014. While problems of representation are typically discussed as *media* literacy issues, 1Hood's academy and similar interventions demonstrate that in the current technological environment, issues of social justice, representation, production, and surveillance should be also be understood as digital literacy issues. Although academy members don't use the specific terminology of "digital literacy" to describe what they do, the philosophy and cultivation of digital literacies are present throughout 1Hood's curriculum.

After establishing the stakes of digital literacy for African American males, and providing some background on the academy, this chapter will explore how 1Hood's approach to pedagogy involves critical digital media analysis, journalism, media-production, and social media management. I then examine how these elements come together in the context of a digital media focused activist project that academy students participated in during the fall of 2011. Ultimately, the chapter will describe the ways that 1Hood translates the concept of digital literacy in hopes of demonstrating that elements of their approach are innovative and necessary forms of democratic empowerment that should be widely available through publicly funded education.

THE STAKES OF DIGITAL LITERACY AND MEDIA REPRESENTATION FOR YOUNG AFRICAN AMERICAN MALES

In a society that is increasingly mediated by media and digital technologies, there are a variety of economic, social, psychological, and political stakes that surround issues of representation, production, and critical consumption of information. These stakes are particularly high for historically marginalized groups such as African American males. A range of research produced during the past decade describes a media environment in which it is easier to envision African American males as gangsters and criminals than to imagine them as fathers, sons, business owners, politicians, and other identity categories that foreground the diversity of their skills and interests and their human and civil rights. Related studies and recent protests have explored the material implications of these images which in the United States have particularly acute impacts on the lives of young African American males, families, and communities.

Typically, calls for curricula and regulation that promote the critical consumption of media texts are understood as issues of media literacy, but in order to design policy and education that is responsive to the problems and potentials of the expansive contemporary digital environment, scholars, educators, politicians, and activists should focus on the specific competencies embedded in definitions of digital literacy. Stephanie Couch, director of CA STEM network, defines digital literacy as "a life long process of capacity building where people are using technologies and networks to create, access, evaluate, and manage information that is required in a knowledge society or knowledge economy" (californiacio, 2010). This way of thinking about media engagement has particular relevance in the lives of African American males for several reasons. Technologies such as smartphones, mobile apps, the Internet, social media, and emerging technologies such as "smart wear" (Google Glass, screen wrist watches, etc.) have changed the contexts in which young people, police officers, and other citizens encounter and interact with information. The Center for Digital Democracy and The Berkeley Media Studies Group released a report identifying a number of marketing-focused concepts that describe important features of this digital environment (Center for Digital Democracy, n.d.), including user-generated content, personalization, immersive environments, opt-in default social networking, and ubiquitous connectivity. Citizens from a variety of social and ethnic backgrounds need specific literacies to assist them in accessing, evaluating, and managing information relevant to the systematic disparities and obstacles that they must overcome in such environments.

The importance of digital literacy must be understood in the broader context of media representation. In 2011, the Topos Partnership released a review of social science literature from a variety of disciplines and methods exploring media representations of African American males. The research covered in this review and other similar studies reveal a consistent pattern of overrepresentation of African American as criminals, entertainers, and athletes. Entman and Rojecki (2001) find that in popular media, Blacks are overrepresented as perpetrators of violent crime. Simultaneously, African American males tend to be underrepresented in roles such as computer users or technical experts in television commercials, instead tending to appear in roles that put less emphasis on physical performance (Kinnick,

White, & Washington, 2001). The tendency to present user-generated media platforms such as YouTube as alternative media spaces where dominant media patterns can be countered can sometimes create the impression that these sites are more progressive then they actually are. In their study of racial representation in YouTube videos, Guo and Harlowe (2014) found that over 64% of the most popular videos included a racial stereotype and 85% of those reinforced or supported a racial stereotype.

Related studies illustrate the societal impact of these media patterns, with particularly acute effects in African American communities. Patterns of media representation that contribute to the symbolic criminalization of African American men operate in the same cultural context where these men seek jobs, education, and entertainment.

These images and narratives also circulate in a context of law enforcement where local police departments are under pressure to rapidly and consistently raise funds through a variety of ethically questionable police practices. The lucrative but predatory ticketing practices of St. Louis, Missouri's police department, and New York City's "Stop and Frisk" are high profile examples of practices that are common in law enforcement throughout the United States. Such practices reveal that stereotypes can trump solid criminological research when deciding who to arrest. Furthermore, these stereotypes influence the interactions between officers and unarmed citizens. African Americans are disproportionately the victims of excessive force by police officers, and suspects killed in arrests are disproportionately Black (FBI Bureau of Justice Statistics, 2003–2009).

Retired Major Neil Franklin served for 34 years in the Maryland police department but now opposes the war on drugs. Commenting on the issues of officer bias, Franklin includes the media as an influence on perception of young Black males (Lopez, 2014).

> "[W]e all have this subconscious bias. Even me, as a black police officer, I felt the same," Franklin said. "When I would be in certain parts of the city and see young black males, it would run through my mind, 'What are they up to? Are they dealing?' That's because of what we've been bombarded with for so many years from so many different directions, including the media."

Franklin's insights point to the need for more a more representative range of stories in the mainstream media and by implication the need for what Baker (2006, p. 15) calls "source diversity" in media production and distribution. Ramasubramanian (2007) demonstrates that exposure to counter-stereotypical new stories can help reduce unconscious bias, but for groups that are marginalized due to class, race, gender, sexual orientation, ability, or other structuring forces, the costs of producing and distributing through mainstream media is highly prohibitive. The technologies of digital literacy offer much more accessible platforms for production and distribution of independent media, including, blogs, podcasts, music, and various kinds of video production. The 1Hood media academy emerged in 2010 as a response to these conditions.

Since 2011, the Heinz endowment has funded the 1Hood media academy, run by Jasiri X and Paradise Gray. In early 2011, the Heinz endowment—an influential funder of nonprofit cultural activities in the Pittsburgh region—founded the African American Men and Boys Initiative to improve a variety of life outcomes for African American young males. As part of this, the initiative funded two studies of the portrayal of African American young men and boys, both of which concluded that media outlets in Pittsburgh "reflect an incomplete and imbalanced view of African-American men and boys" (portrayal-and-perception: Two Audits of News Media Reporting on African American Men and Boys, 2011). In response to this, the endowment began looking for innovative approaches to improving media representation and increasing media literacy among this population. Fortunately, the incipient 1Hood media academy—run by Jasiri X and Paradise Gray—was selected for funding. 1Hood media academy was an outgrowth of the broader 1Hood coalition formed in Pittsburgh in 2006 (Ayad, 2007).

In many ways, the 1Hood Media Academy was an effort of Jasiri X and Paradise Gray to institutionalize their artist/activist work. In the course of their previous careers as hip-hop artists and activists, both men had developed experience with grassroots activism, cultural politics, cultural industries, and literacy with both analog and digital technologies of hip-hop production and promotion.

Paradise Gray gave the 1Hood coalition its name and has helped to turn the organization into a recognizable media production team. Since the 1970s, he has operated at various times as a hip-hop producer, activist, video director, writer, photographer, painter, social media connoisseur, scholar, and public speaker, frequently serving in multiple roles simultaneously. Starting in 1987, Paradise worked with Lumumba Carson to create the BlackWatch Movement, which spawned popular political hip-hop group "X-Clan," and several other hip-hop groups. Gray was a key member of the group's production team.[1] The X-Clan were nominated for an NAACP Image Award. Paradise also opened up a recording studio, an art gallery, and performance space, and participated in the launching of Pittsburgh's first hip-hop awards. He has remained in Pittsburgh since 1993, leaving only for a brief stint in California as a hip-hop consultant for mp3.com.[2]

The academy's cofounder Jasiri X is a prolific and internationally influential and political hip-hop artist. The techniques that X uses to navigate the relationship between critical consciousness, creative expression, media production, and self-promotion have also become central to the strategies of 1Hood and 1Hood Media. In September 2008, Smith and Gray started the online YouTube news series *This Week with Jasiri X*.[3] Eventually, Gray and Smith began to see the need to train a new generation of hip-hop activists. This required decoding and systematically teaching the media and digital literacy skills that they had learned through trial and error.

ELEMENTS OF 1HOOD'S HIP-HOP DIGITAL LITERACY CURRICULUM

Principles of digital literacy are present in four aspects of the 1Hood media academy's curriculum. First, class activities stimulate the production and ongoing critical media analysis of digital texts and contexts (such as YouTube channels, blogs, and hashtags). Lesson plans differ in structure, content, and mode of presentation on a daily basis, but they are consistently oriented toward identifying, denaturalizing, and challenging dominant themes in news and popular culture, as well as privileging marginalized voices. Second, the academy instructors promote innovative approaches to the concept of journalism involving several varieties of what I call "hip-hop journalism." Third, academy participants are taught approaches to Internet and social media–based engagement, marketing, and networking that are informed by underground hip-hop promotional strategies. Finally, 1Hood's production curriculum focuses on the computer-based production of music, videography, photography, and some graphic and web design. Digital skills such as hip-hop sampling are translated beyond music into a video production logic that requires politically informed and aesthetically savvy usages of found footage.

Critical media analysis runs through all of the other aspects of 1Hood's curriculum. As mentioned above, comprehensive definitions of digital literacy involve not simply producing texts and speech on digital platforms, or uploading content, but also being able to negotiate the specificities of digital contexts such as Twitter, Instagram, or email, and being able to tailor speech appropriately and *participate* in those contexts (californiacio, 2010). While the curriculum includes training in complex software such as ProTools, Sony Vegas, and the Adobe Suite, often youth in the academy do not need to be taught the basics of digital platforms such as those of social media. A recent Pew report on the technology use of African Americans finds that "73% of African American internet users—and 96% of those ages 18–29—use a social networking site of some kind." In fact, the study reports that while 16% of online whites use Twitter, 22% of online blacks are Twitter users (Smith, n.d.).

1Hood's critical approach to digital literacy therefore expands the definition of "understanding of digital contexts" to include the informed reading and interpretation of the broader sociopolitical, racial, and gendered environment that informs digital media content. Academy meetings often begin and end with recorded group discussions of community, news, and pop cultural events. The 1Hood YouTube channel features examples of these discussions on topics such as Trayvon Martin's death, the L.A. Clippers response to Donald Sterling's comments, and other contemporary sociopolitical issues.

In April 2014, 1Hood uploaded a video clip called "Young Black Men Discuss Donald Sterling, Call Clippers 'Slaves'" (2014). This video features

Jasiri X facilitating a discussion in which students critically analyze the events related to Sterling's comments and the response by the Clippers. Another video called "Being a Young Black in America: 1 Year After the Zimmerman Verdict" (2014), features the various youth in the academy expressing their views on the issue of extrajudicial killings of African American males. Commenting in the video, one youth says, "I realized that that could have been me walking home minding my own business."

Allowing youth to participate in producing this kind of content and then distributing it familiarizes them with seeing and celebrating their skills at media analysis and media production simultaneously. Additionally, academy instructors frequently explore the metrics of audience response and discussions of what leads to "virality" can help them think critically and strategically about what kinds of content gains views and what doesn't.

HIP-HOP JOURNALISM

The term "hip-hop" journalism[4] as it is being applied here might be defined as an approach to journalism in which the narrative styles, aesthetic elements, linguistic approaches, and political sensibilities align closely with the corresponding aspects of hip-hop culture. Writing on popular music and journalism, Mano (2007) concludes that in as much as "journalism" is a form of cultural expression, a way of inscribing the world that is informed by what takes place in society, popular music can be considered journalism. Mano also argues that "popular musicians, music performance, and lyrics at times compliment and even more effectively express what journalists fail to communicate." Students in the 1Hood media academy produce hip-hop songs, hip-hop videos, short documentaries, video blogs, and other media. Gray and Jasiri X consider all of these to be forms of Hip-hop journalism. Students in the first session of the academy helped produce installments in "Game Changers Project" about a Black male Pittsburgh based entrepreneur as well as short clips about survivors of police brutality such as Jordan Miles, or victims of extrajudicial killing such as Trayvon Martin, or Renisha McBride.

In developing and teaching 1Hood's curriculum, X and Gray draw heavily on strategies that have been successful in their own hip-hop journalist efforts. Their presence as active practitioners of activist digital literacy constitutes a tangible embodied curriculum. As templates for the future student production, instructors expose students to the 1Hood and Jasiri X YouTube channels containing over 100 videos that include music videos, news segments, documentaries, video blogs, and clips of protests and speaking engagements. The benefit of working with these archived examples in addition to other contemporary productions includes the insight that X and Gray can offer about the actual circumstances and techniques of production. In addition, their productions frequently reference specifics of black life in Pittsburgh and therefore relate to the lives of young African American male academy students. In some cases, academy students gain the opportunity to work as interns on projects that Jasiri X or 1Hood media are producing for their audiences or clients.

SOCIAL MEDIA

Smith and Gray also teach youth strategies of social media management that have been successful in their own activist and hip-hop careers. The focus here is teaching youth to navigate social media platforms as resources for gaining information, building and maintaining audiences, and the distribution of content. Gray points out that hip-hop artists and underground artists have always had to find alternative means of promoting their events and cultural products and spreading the relevant news to their communities. Furthermore, he argues that "hip-hop culture has always had social media, and the hip-hop flyer was one of the first social media innovations" (Personal Communication, June 14, 2012). 1Hood instructors promote their own artist activist brands, as well as 1Hood media's brand. 1Hood teaches youth to understand social media platforms such as Twitter, Facebook, and YouTube as virtual locations for the building of one's professional brand in addition to being vehicles for personal self-expression. An important element of this is lessons about how to curate social media accounts. The selective curating of content on these platforms by posting and sharing specific kinds of content, and the specific kinds of interaction with followers, subscribers, and friends is guided by political and entrepreneurial sensibilities rather than purely personal whims. More specifically, the concept and internalized logic of branding that 1Hood promotes both organizes and redeploys one's personal instincts about how to share. An important part of these lessons involves a relatively consistent pace of sharing news items on Twitter and Facebook, keeping their profile relevant to viewers. Additionally, by maintaining relationships with blogs and media outlets for which they can produce content, students can activate those relationships strategically when they have political or entertainment messages to distribute. Over time, both Amil Cook and Idasa Tariq—two younger 1Hood media academy instructors—have joined X and Gray in amassing significant followings through the uploading and sharing of cultural products.

Another essential aspect of the curriculum involves maintenance of 1Hood's own YouTube channel and Facebook page. 1Hood has a formal website and other accounts on websites such as Instagram, but YouTube and Facebook are also major online outlets. The 1Hood YouTube channel allows academy students to upload a variety of content documenting their activities and accomplishments of the academy as a whole, as well as spotlighting guest speakers and specific academy members. It serves as an online location where the youth in the academy can be featured as voices weighing in on various cultural phenomena. As of this writing, the 1Hood

YouTube channel features short pieces documenting the visits of artists, activists, and scholars such as Rapper David Banner, Producer 9th Wonder, Activist–Scholar Rosa Clemente, and police shooting victim Leon Ford. The channel also includes short clips of Academy youth weighing in on various social issues.

HIP-HOP ACTIVISM AS DIGITAL LITERACY CURRICULUM: PRODUCING "I AM TROY DAVIS"

An essential experiential component of the 1Hood Media Academy's curriculum is the student's involvement in Jasiri X and Paradise Gray's ongoing activist work. In 2011, students in the 1Hood media academy worked with Paradise Gray and Jasiri X to produce and distribute music videos for Jasiri X's song "I am Troy Davis" about the controversial execution of Georgia State Inmate Troy Davis. The video—produced before the execution had taken place—was intended to be a tool for citizens and activists to educate themselves about the case and to support global efforts to call off his scheduled execution. The academy's experience with the video illustrates its combination of hip-hop journalism, narrative, video production training, and social media distribution as elements of digital literacy.

TROY DAVIS CASE BACKGROUND

Davis was sentenced to death in August 1991 for the murder of police officer Mark McPhail in Savannah, Georgia. However, aspects of Davis's case raised significant doubts about his guilt for a wide range of observers. Questionable evidence included the fact that two witnesses implicated a different man as the shooter, most witnesses contradicted their testimony, and new analysis of physical evidence contradicted the state's case. Davis and his supporters built an influential movement in defense of his innocence over the next twenty years. The movement, which included celebrities, politicians, activist religious leaders such as Archbishop Desmond Tutu and Pope Benedict XVI, succeeded in staying the execution three times and producing a Supreme Court ordered evidentiary hearing. Ultimately, the conviction was upheld and on September 7, 2011 a new execution date was set for September 21, 2011. Students and instructors in the academy produced their video in between these dates.

The 1Hood Media academy's curriculum in this regard was experiential, involving students in every aspect of producing the music video. This began with discussions of the case's facts, discussions of what was missing from the dominant media narrative, and creative brainstorming about what kinds of production choices might most effectively challenge that narrative. The review of alternative online news sources, and the websites of news organizations to review mainstream coverage proved important components of this assessment of the most influential news frames up until that point in the case's development. A tight three-day production deadline was set. The short time frame was required to give academy participants the real-world experience of using digital production, distribution, and viral promotion strategies to offer timely artistic commentary on a current social justice issue.

The video centers on Jasiri X's performance of the song lyrics. Since there wasn't time for long-term and resource-consuming set development, the video was shot on location at the August Wilson Center. Several students tried their hand at recording pieces of Jasiri X's performances using the Canon 7D SLR cameras at various locations in and around the center in downtown Pittsburgh. Commenting on this, Jasiri X points out that "it showed those young men that participated in our media academy that they could do something at the August Wilson Center in Pittsburgh" (*Game Changers*, 2013).

In addition to these performance scenes, the students also received instruction in the creative use of news footage, which is captured digitally and used throughout the video. "Mashing up" the audio and visual aesthetics of journalism (headline banners, transcribed testimony graphics, interview footage) with the musical and visual aesthetics of hip-hop performance foregrounds the journalistic role of this hip-hop text. Choices about which news footage to include allows video producers to highlight elements of the case they deem important. The academy members captured CNN footage of a juror expressing regret over what she had not known during that trial, and footage of Davis's mother expressing confidence that the global movement to save her son's life could be successful.

The academy production team decided that, in addition to offering a celebration of Troy Davis's life and an exposure to the facts of the case, an important function of their production would be to find a way to creatively present what this case meant in their own lives. The problem was how to do this with limited resources in a tight time frame. Their solution ended up being low-tech but poignant. Copies of a black and white photograph of Troy Davis's face on an 8 ½ x 11 sheet of white paper were printed out and distributed to each of the several members of the production team. Each member was filmed holding the photograph in front of their heads and slowly lowering it to reveal their faces while reciting the phrase, "I am Troy Davis." This representational strategy had also been used by academy youth in an earlier academy production about Jordan Miles, but in the earlier video, youth walked silently while holding the pictures in the neighborhood where Miles was beaten. These scenes were included at the end of the video.

As demonstrated in 1Hood media's earlier series, "this week with Jasiri X," as well as in news comedy shows, such as *The Daily Show, The Colbert Report*, and John Oliver's *This Week Tonight*, the use of news footage also allows the producer to editorialize, add editorial commentary to mainstream news footage, and invite critical interpretations of events from marginalized or unheard stakeholders. Finally, the use of this footage allowed the youth to repurpose the production value of mainstream and local news journalism, saving time and money on expensive, potentially costly, and time-consuming graphic design techniques.

Ultimately, the academy members arranged news footage, live performances, and musical soundtrack into a text that loosely follows the narrative logic of the lyrics, offering lyrical performance, news clips, and various representations of the significant evidence raising doubt about Davis's guilt. From a digital literacy perspective, the process of producing and distributing the video accomplished more than simply relaying facts about the case. When considered within the aforementioned landscape of media coverage of African American males, and the posthumous criminalizing of African American shooting victims, the affective and factual appeal of the video did important "rehumanizing" work. During the weeks before the Davis execution, the video functioned as a set of important cultural political arguments to stay his execution so that there would be adequate time to revisit recanted witness testimony and other facts in the case. In the aftermath of Davis's execution, the video stands as a testament to Davis's success in making his life count by contributing to a movement against the death penalty and racially disproportionate incarceration on questionable grounds.

On September 15, 2011, the song was released as a free download on Bandcamp and the video was released online at YouTube. Academy members, instructors, and supporters shared the video with friends, families, communities, and broader networks—leading to a significant number of worldwide views. The YouTube video included information about the case links to petitions and links to campaigns by the NAACP, Colorofchange. org, and Amnesty International. As of this writing, the video boasts 92,522 views on YouTube. Speaking on the reach of the video, Jasiri X pointed out, "It showed them websites in Italy that it was on, Israel, China, Japan. So I'm showing them the different languages, and of course you can't understand, you had to translate it, but I'm showing them all of the different places around the world the people played that video" (*Game Changers*, 2013). One of the academy members, Gabriel Pierre Martin-Scrusc, spoke on how seeing the distribution of the video impacted him.

> I didn't know people in Greece really cared that much; I didn't know people in Japan really cared that much; I didn't know people really cared that much about Troy Davis; I didn't know people cared that much about what was happening in America. So like to see people responding the way they did kind of gives you hope that you can be heard.
>
> (*Game Changers*, 2013)

At a time when a prevailing mode of response to social injustice is semicoordinated, decentralized, spontaneous protest demonstrations with questionable sustainability, the 1Hood media academy aims to institutionalize its critical digital literacy curriculum, even as some of its members participate in these larger movements. Paradise Gray and other 1Hood instructors are working toward building the academy into an afterschool program that meets several times a week to being a full-fledged school, with its own curriculum specializing in media literacy and media arts. In this regard, the academy faces predictable challenges in terms of sustainability. These challenges include the procurement of long-term funding, adequate facilities, the maintenance of reliable and skilled instructors, and a consistent crop of participants in their target demographic of young African American males. Currently, the academy relies heavily on the consistent charisma, fund-raising skills, and embodied digital curriculum of Gray and Jasiri Smith and Sister Celeste Muhammad, Amil Cook, and Idasa Tariq.

NOTES

1. Other members of the team included Jason Hunter (The Grand Verbalizer Funkin-Lesson Brother J), Anthony Hardin (The Rhythm Provider Sugar Shaft), And Lumumba Carson (Professor X The Overseer).
2. Gray was offered this position based on his massive hip-hop collections, his influence in the entertainment industry, his influential online presence, and his fluency with both music and social media technologies such as MySpace. This experience gave Gray an unusual inside perspective on the challenges, potentials, legal components, and technological possibilities of music and social media.
3. Currently Smith is signed to Wandering Worx entertainment.
4. This should be understood as a distinct concept from journalism *about* hip-hop music, artists, or the hip-hop industry.

REFERENCES

Ayad, M. (2007, May 7). Shootings bring out determined Homewood residents for another anti violence rally. Retrieved from http://www.post-gazette.com/local/city/2007/05/07/Shootings-bring-out-determined-Homewood-residents-for-another-anti-violence-rally/stories/200705070151.

Baker, C. E. (2006). *Media concentration and democracy: Why ownership matters.* Cambridge University Press.

Being a Young Black Man in America: 1 Year After the Zimmerman Verdict. (2014). Retrieved from https://www.youtube.com/watch?v=gWgn51qNNSo&feature=youtube_gdata_player.

californiacio. (2010). *Digital Literacy Series–Part 4–Stephanie Couch* (Vol. 4). Retrieved from https://www.youtube.com/watch?v=KkBp6v0hU9M.

Center for Digital Democracy. (n.d.). Implications of digital food and beverage marketing to children and adolescents—an introduction. Retrieved from http://digitalads.org/how-youre-targeted/publications/implications-digital-food-and-beverage-marketing-children-and.

Entman, R. M., & Rojecki, A. (2001). *The black image in the white mind: Media and race in America*. Wiley Online Library.

Game changers: The One Hood media academy. (2013). Retrieved from http://www.youtube.com/watch?v=cP9j58O0IjY&feature=youtube_gdata_player.

Guo, L., & Harlow, S. (2014). User-generated racism: An analysis of stereotypes of African Americans Latinos, and Asians in YouTube videos. *Howard Journal of Communications, 25*(3), 281–302.

Kinnick, K. N., White, C., & Washington, K. (2001). Racial representation of computer users in prime-time advertising. *Race, Gender & Class*, 96–114.

Lopez, G. (2014, December 16). How subconscious racism complicates racial disparities in policing [News]. Retrieved from http://www.vox.com/2014/8/28/6051971/police-implicit-bias-michael-brown-ferguson-missouri.

Mano, W. (2007). Popular music as journalism in Zimbabwe. *Journalism Studies, 8*(1), 61–78.

portrayal-and-perception: Two audits of news media reporting on African American men and boys. (2011). Retrieved from http://www.opensocietyfoundations.org/sites/default/files/portrayal-and-perception-20111101.pdf.

Ramasubramanian, S. (2007). Media-based strategies to reduce racial stereotypes activated by news stories. *Journalism & Mass Communication Quarterly, 84*(2), 249–264.

Smith, A. (n.d.). *African Americans and technology use*. Retrieved from http://www.pewinternet.org/2014/01/06/African Americans-and-technology-use/.

Young black men discuss Donald Sterling, call Clippers "slaves." (2014). Retrieved from https://www.youtube.com/watch?v=BfKmUOgU-sk&feature=youtube_gdata_player.

14 Fight for Your Copyrights

Mashups, Fair Use, and the Future of Freedom

Christopher Boulton

In the summer of 2013, Elisa Kreisinger (AKA: Pop Culture Pirate) posted a mashup of Jay Z's "Picasso Baby" video with Taylor Swift's song "22" to YouTube, only to have it blocked seconds later. This came as a surprise, since Kreisinger had been successfully sampling, remixing, and posting subversive videos on YouTube since 2008. She would first record, select, and reedit dialogue from popular television series like Mad Men, Sex in the City, and The Real Housewives to reimagine their hetero-normative plot lines as feminist and queer-positive narratives. Then she would upload these mashups to the Internet so her media analysis—made more accessible and spreadable by its short-form video format and presence on YouTube—could, in turn, be embedded on feminist websites like Jezebel, promoted through social media curators like Buzzfeed, and even featured on more mainstream outlets like *New York Magazine*.

Importantly, Kreisinger did not ask permission to use the copyrighted content when creating or distributing her mashups, but instead claimed "fair use," a provision outlined in Section 107 of the United States Copyright Act of 1976 that allows scholars, journalists, and critics to quote from copyrighted material (remix someone else's material) in order to comment on it (U.S. Copyright Office, 2012). Furthermore, according to the Digital Millennium Copyright Act (DMCA), if a copyright owner asked YouTube to pull an unauthorized mashup, the creator could get it reinstated with a counter-notification explaining why the mashup qualifies as fair use (DMCA Info, 2010; Google Support, 2014). So, when Kreisinger's Jay Z/Taylor Swift mashup was blocked, she filed a counter-notification, but to no avail. After ten months of appeals, she hired a lawyer and finally found out why. Unbeknownst to Kreisinger, YouTube had made a private deal with Universal Music Group, giving them the power to take down any video involving their music, fairly used or not (Kreisinger, 2014).

I tell Pop Culture Pirate's cautionary tale for three reasons. First, her process exemplified many of the fundamental tenets of media literacy—asking critical questions of the media environment and using cultural interventions to spark conversations amongst peers by engaging with the media on their own terms. Second, she exercised her rights as a citizen by researching copyright law and—when these rights were infringed—fought to get them reinstated. Failing that, she exposed and objected to the private political-economic arrangement shaping what kinds of speech could be freely created and circulated online. This kind of engaged citizenship is crucial to the achievement of critical digital literacy; it combines knowledge of how media institutions are organized with a willingness to try to change them. And, finally, I open with Kreisinger's story as a way to introduce my own. I, too, have fought for my copyrights.

While a graduate student in Communication at the University of Massachusetts, Amherst (UMass), I sparred with my school and two publishing companies over copyright and permissions policies. The results were mixed, ranging from hard-fought victory to stalemate and withdrawal. My first round came back in 2006. Reviewing the submission guidelines for my Master's thesis, a textual analysis of print advertisements for designer children's clothing, I learned, to my shock and dismay, that rule number 88 of the Graduate School's Guidelines for Master's Theses and Doctoral Dissertations required me to secure permission from the copyright holders of any commercial images that I wished to include in my monograph. Otherwise I would have to excise the ads from the text and "include a note in the List of Figures that directs readers to the set of illustrations on file in your department" (p. 12). As you can imagine, this was a disheartening prospect. The 30 ads in my thesis were my data, the very basis of my analysis, and my argument would be incomplete without them. Rule 88 meant that any reader who wanted to see my data would be forced to travel all the way to the UMass campus, trudge up to the fourth floor of Machmer Hall, and then request that some unlucky administrative staff person go back into storage, thumb through a filing cabinet, and pull out my dusty manila folder of magazine ads. Unless I was looking for evidence to solve a homicide, I wouldn't go to such trouble, so how could I expect anyone else—especially since most of my potential readers would access my thesis online?

So, in my naive deference to a ridiculous policy, I dutifully spent months trying to track down someone, *anyone* who would give me an answer to my "Can I use your ad in my thesis?" request. *Cookie*, the magazine where the ads appeared, sent me to the clothing brands, who then sent me to the photographers, who then sent me to the child models who appeared in the ad, who then, surprise, were unreachable. At every step along the way, my requests for permissions baffled the supposed copyright holders. As a result, I was swept into a maze of endless referrals; no one knew what to do with me. In the end, I had gone down a multitude of rabbit holes with nary a "yes," or, for that matter, "no." With no permissions, rule 88 now had me in a terrible position since compliance would strip the data from my analysis. Clearly, the Graduate School's policy presented a serious hindrance to my intellectual freedom. Furthermore, the guidelines contained no mention of the fair use provision of copyright law. So, in the end, after making several unanswered petitions for policy reform, I simply asserted my fair use rights and ignored rule 88—including the ads and posting my thesis to a digital repository where it has, to date, been downloaded over seven thousand times (Boulton, 2007).

And if I thought my Graduate School was draconian in its copyright restrictions, I would soon discover that academic publishers could be downright nutty. In 2010, I received a contract for a book chapter submission from Routledge (also the publisher of this volume) holding me responsible "for obtaining written permission for the inclusion of any copyright material in the Contribution, whether text, illustrations or otherwise." I pushed back and the editors, more enlightened on the subject than the publisher, promised to pursue a "muscular interpretation of fair use" that would defend all of the contributors' right to quote from copyrighted material. But when I received another restrictive contract from Pearson Education just weeks later asserting that, "anywhere you use a direct quote we will need to secure and pay permissions fees," I would take on a much more stubborn adversary. Pearson's permissions policy was accompanied by the editor's nonchalant request that we (as authors in an anthology on race, class, and media, mind you) paraphrase and thereby avoid direct quoting of any and all "media texts—songs, films, ads, TV shows, newspapers, magazines, websites, etc. (for which others hold copyright)" because every quotation from these sources will "require permissions"—a process that the editor would like to avoid (Pearson Editor, personal communication, December 2, 2010). I responded immediately, drawing the editor's attention to the Code of Best Practices in Fair Use for Scholarly Research in Communication (International Communication Association, 2010), a document put forward by the International Communication Association (ICA), in collaboration with the Center for Media and Social Impact at American University, in order to help forge a consensus on the topic and help guide the field:

> Where it applies, fair use is a user's right. In fact, as the Supreme Court has pointed out (in its 2003 Eldred decision), fair use helps to keep copyright from violating the First Amendment. New creation inevitably incorporates existing material. As copyright protects more works for longer periods than ever before, creators face new challenges: licenses to incorporate copyrighted sources become more expensive and more difficult to obtain—and sometimes are simply unavailable. As a result, fair use is more important today than ever before (ibid.).

I also argued that, in helping Pearson to avoid permissions, the editor was passing the burden on to the author, who must now second-guess the "necessity" of every quote. In my own work, all quotes are necessary, yet none are absolutely crucial. This editor's approach, under the draconian (and I don't use that word lightly) Pearson permissions regime, would have made for a precarious writing process indeed. Thus, my resistance was equal parts practical and principal. First off, I simply couldn't imagine writing like that. I'd never had to work under such restrictions (not even with Taylor & Francis) and didn't want to start engaging in self-censorship just to get published. Second, providing that the use is proportional and transformative, quotation of copyrighted works does not require permissions and is one of the fundamental keystones of intellectual freedom in critical media studies (ibid.). For instance, inquiry should not be restricted by the good graces of our analytical objects, lest they be given free rein to block any author who dare cast them in a negative light. And while I well understood that authors should not reproduce entire poems, lyrics, or visual artworks, the Pearson permission-to-quote policy was so far-reaching as to be incomprehensible. Even if I wanted to comply, I wouldn't have known where to begin or, for that matter, stop. Many journal articles and books also constitute copyrighted material owned by for-profit publishing companies. Would I have needed to seek permission to quote a colleague? Would my colleagues have had to seek permission to quote me? Moreover, this sort of blanket policy didn't strike me as a very tenable regime. Perhaps I was being too literal in my interpretation of Pearson's policy, but my requests for clarification went unanswered. So, in the end, I refused to sign the author agreement and, ultimately, withdrew my chapter from the volume.

I recount this episode to illustrate how the copyright conservatism of corporate publishing houses, along with academics incentive to "publish or perish," can persuade a fellow media scholar to justify restricting the speech of her colleagues. This matters because fair use is not merely a defense; it is a right—and one that will be taken away by skittish publishers if not claimed and exercised by authors. Of course, turning down a publishing opportunity is not a viable option for most graduate students hoping to get jobs in the academy—where publications are the coin of the realm—but I was in a unique position. First, I already had a few articles under my belt, and so did not necessarily *need* this chapter, which, in turn, made it easier for me to play hardball. Second, I had already used the threat of withholding my work to successfully pressure an academic publisher to change their copyright policy. This happened in 2008 and the company was Taylor & Francis, who also owns Routledge. The Communication Review accepted my article submission for an upcoming special issue and instructed me to transfer my copyright to the publisher, Taylor & Francis. Reading the fine print, I discovered that this would prevent me from posting the article to my website or any digital repository for an embargo period of 18 months. This was problematic for several reasons. First, the purpose of the embargo is to create scarcity and protect a pay-wall, which journal publishers use to charge libraries database subscription fees that can run in the thousands of dollars. In other words, my friends, family, students, or even colleagues at less well-endowed universities would have to pay to see my work— work I had given to the journal for free. This struck me as unacceptable, so I decided that I would exercise the option, allowed by the company,[1] to retain my own copyright. My repeated requests were denied. So I decided to contact the other authors in the volume and organize a general strike. In sum, it took three months of negotiation and the collective resistance of multiple authors threatening to hold up the issue to get Taylor & Francis to reverse their policy and accept the SPARC addendum, a free legal instrument developed in partnership with Creative Commons that modifies the publisher's agreement and allows authors to retain key rights for posting and distributing their own work (SPARC, 2006). In our case, I even posted the signed addendum online to help establish a precedent.[2]

My experience with Taylor & Francis taught me a very important lesson: when it comes to copyright policy change, there is power in numbers. For instance, that same year, the MacArthur and Ford Foundations supported a collective effort among multiple organizations[3] to establish a Code of Best Practices in Fair Use for Media Literacy Education.[4] The development of the Code began with a series of meetings with over 150 media educators and advocates in ten cities all over the United States. The resulting consensus around commonly held understandings was then vetted by a committee of legal scholars and endorsed by leading media literacy organizations. Such a "bottom-up" approach not only exemplified a democratic and participatory process of deliberation but also helped forge a set of principles that are relevant, practical, and clear to the stakeholders who would implement them. Best of all, the Code is concise and quite readable, avoiding jargon in favor of concrete examples of classroom practices—the kind of document one could easily pull out to calm skittish colleagues and supervisors.

The Code's five principles apply across media forms (from newspapers to YouTube) and educational settings (from schools to nonprofits) and focus on "the unlicensed fair use of copyrighted materials for education." So, if you wish to copy a movie clip for class, you can disregard that scary FBI warning providing that you follow the "rule of proportionality." In other words—and this is a central theme of the Code—only use what you need to accomplish your curricular goals. Depending on the lesson, this could range from a short excerpt to the entire work. Such flexibility emphasizes how fair use can vary according to context and situation. Another central theme in the Code concerns whether the use transforms, repurposes, and/or adds value to the copyrighted material. If it does, then it's probably fair.[5]

For each of the five principles, the Code outlines a set of related instructional activities and then states both the rights and limitations of fair use. And while the first three focus on fair use from the perspective of educators—(1) teaching, (2) preparing curriculum, and (3) sharing resources—the last two consider the (4) production and (5) distribution of student work. This move illustrates how the concept of fair use can cover both the pedagogy of media critique and the process of media production. Thus, while the Code could inspire an instructor to show clips that demonstrate the commercial nature of powerful media institutions, it could also encourage students to sample and reedit those same clips to tell a different story ala Pop Culture Pirate's mashups.

For instance, way back in 1991, fair use pioneer Sut Jhally began selling a video entitled *Dream Worlds* that critiqued the sexist tropes of music videos and MTV threatened to sue him for copyright infringement. Jhally stood his ground, publicly shamed MTV for censorship, and the network caved. Today, Jhally's Media Education Foundation (MEF) continues to produce and sell films that quote copyrighted media material without permission under the provisions of fair use, which they explicitly reference in the opening credits. As Aufderheide and Jaszi (2011) note in their book *Reclaiming Fair Use*, Jhally has publicly welcomed a lawsuit from copyright holders, as he is confident that it would set important legal precedent, but has yet to have any takers. And, in a more recent example, Matthew Soar and his students at Concordia University used animation to transform and add value to an existing concert video of Girl Talk—an artist who himself claims fair use when remixing hundreds of samples from copyrighted songs.[6] To date, neither Soar nor Girl Talk has been sued for infringement.

The Code of Best Practices in Fair Use for Media Literacy Education insists that "the social bargain at the heart of copyright law" grants "limited property rights" as an incentive for generating culture but also adds the important caveat of fair use that can allow that same property to be reused by still other creators, without permission or payment, to generate new culture. Thus, fair use promotes a dynamic atmosphere where culture remains in a constant cycle of transformation—every remix inventing potential ingredients for the next. The current dearth of legal precedent means that educators have an opportunity to influence both current practice and emerging policy by openly and publicly asserting their right to transform copyrighted material. In anticipation of potential obstacles to this effort, the Code concludes by dispelling some of the common myths around fair use that characterize it as: (a) too complicated, (b) subject to iron-clad "rules of thumb;" (c) only for critical commentary; (d) only for noncommercial work; (e) a big hassle with lots of paperwork; (f) and just plain risky. "Nonsense!" cries the Code. Fair use is a right, not a defense, and its flexibility makes it adaptable to rapid technological change.

Here's the take-home message: if the use is transformative and proportional, then unlicensed copyrighted material is fair game for both teachers and students either inside or outside the classroom. In other words, this Code argues that the remixing of culture in educational settings is not only perfectly legal but can even be done for fun and/or profit. No one has been sued for this yet and as more teachers exercise and loudly proclaim their fair use rights, the already remote possibility of a lawsuit will simply fade away.

Encouraged by the success of the Code, I pursued a similar strategy within the academy to enact permissions reform, working with colleagues to develop a set of general guidelines and argue that transformative and proportional quotation of copyrighted material without permission was an inalienable right of free academic inquiry. From 2008 to 2010, we followed a three-step process. First, we convened a preconference to form the International Communication Association (ICA) Ad Hoc Committee on Fair Use and Academic Freedom (Pre-Conference Workshop, 2009). Second, we conducted a broad survey of the field, resulting in a report outlining how concerns over copyright have created a widespread chilling effect on scholarship, resulting in quotation avoidance and self-censorship (Ad Hoc, 2010). Finally, the Ad Hoc Committee consolidated the findings of the report and vetted them through a legal team before issuing a Code of Best Practices in Fair Use for Scholarly Research in Communication through the ICA and the Center for Media and Social Impact at American University. The National Communication Association (NCA) would eventually sign on as well (Best Practices, 2009). To be sure, such a document cannot, as evidenced by my unsuccessful negotiation with the Pearson editor chronicled above, reregulate the publishing industry into full compliance with the fair use provisions of copyright law. However, it can help contribute to a wider consensus—and even momentum—around best practices for fair use online. And the tide seems to be turning.

In February 2014, Liberation Music agreed to add fair use considerations to its copyright policies and pay compensation to Lawrence Lessig as an out of court settlement for blocking his YouTube video. Lessig's video included a mashup of Phoenix's song "Lisztomania" with scenes from *The Breakfast Club*. As Phoenix's label, Liberation Music ordered YouTube to take down the mashup and, when Lessig issued a counter-notification, threatened to sue. But Lessig, like Jhally before him, didn't blink; he was, after all, a cofounder of Creative Commons and arguably the world's most famous fair use lawyer, so he countersued and won: "Too often, copyright is used as an excuse to silence legitimate speech," said Lessig. "Hopefully this lawsuit and this settlement will send a message to copyright owners to adopt fair takedown practices—or face the consequences" (Electronic Frontier Foundation, 2014).

For scholars who study media, the Internet has broadened research horizons and expanded the reach of teaching and publication. But powerful gatekeepers remain. From academic journals seeking to control our intellectual property to music company lawyers blocking mashups on YouTube, we are bombarded with a myriad of confusing and dubious restrictions. In short, the implied threat of legal action creates a chilling effect that impacts us all. Some have pushed back, founding open access journals that don't require expensive subscriptions or impose embargoes on their authors and while also allowing for quotations and remixes of copyrighted material as protected under the "fair use" statute. But more needs to be done to encourage emerging scholars to stand up for their copyrights. With such a vulnerable population so desperate to publish pitted against a deeply entrenched and powerful publishing industry, change will require a united front. More senior, already tenured scholars can lead the way by insisting on the SPARC addendum and joining the editorial boards of open access journals. Similarly, if YouTube users want to protect their access to Pop Culture Pirate–style content, then they'll need to either get together and organize a viable resistance to the kinds of private deals that block legally protected forms of speech (like mashups) or seek out more fair-use friendly video-sharing platforms.

In sum, if we want to win the copyright fight, we will need more democratic participation, engaged citizenship, and critical digital literacy. The future of freedom, both online and beyond, depends on it.

NOTES

1. "Whilst Taylor & Francis strongly recommends to authors that they transfer copyright, it is not necessarily a condition of publication. An author can retain copyright in her or his paper, but we must receive a formal signed statement licensing us to publish the work exclusively, worldwide, and in all forms, in the journal" (http://www.tandf.co.uk/journals/copyright.asp). "We prefer authors to assign copyright to Taylor & Francis or the journal proprietor ... but accept that authors may prefer to give Taylor & Francis an exclusive license to publish" (http://www.tandf.co.uk/journals/authorrights.pdf).
2. http://works.bepress.com/chris_boulton/13/.
3. The Code was coordinated and authored by the Media Education Lab at Temple University, the Program on Information Justice and Intellectual Property at American University's Washington College of Law, and the Center for Media & Social Impact at American University. The Code was also endorsed by the Action Coalition for Media Education, the Media Education Foundation, the National Association for Media Literacy Education, the National Council of Teachers of English, and the Visual Communication Studies Division of the International Communication Association.
4. Excerpts of this section first appeared as Boulton (2009) in the Journal of Media Literacy Education, 1(1) licensed under a Creative Commons Attribution-Non Commercial-No Derivs License. In addition to the Code of Best Practices in Fair Use for Media Literacy Education (http://www.cmsimpact.org/fair-use/related-materials/codes/code-best-practices-fair-use-media-literacy-education), the Center for Media and Social Impact has also produced several reports and statements (http://www.cmsimpact.org/fair-use) on fair use for producers of media content that seek to strike a healthy balance between intellectual property and creative freedom.
5. For a charming three minute clarification of the central questions for determining fair use, check out the "User Rights, Section 107" music video: http://media educationlab.com/2-user-rights-section-107-music-video.
6. The video, a mashup of student animation with unlicensed concert footage of a musician who samples other songs without permission is still, for now, up on YouTube with 2 million views and counting: http://www.youtube.com/watch?v=WK3O_qZVqXk.

REFERENCES

Ad Hoc Committee on Fair Use and Academic Freedom, International Communication Association. (2010). *Clipping our own wings: Copyright and creativity in communication research*. Retrieved from http://cmsimpact.org/sites/default/files/documents/pages/ICA_-_Clipping.pdf.

Aufderheide, P., and Peter Jaszi. (2011). *Reclaiming fair use: How to put balance back in copyright*. Chicago: University of Chicago Press.

Best Practices. (2009). *Best practices in fair use in scholarly research*. Retrieved from http://www.natcom.org/fair_use.aspx.

Boulton, C. (2007). *Trophy children don't smile: Fashion advertisements for designer children's clothing in* Cookie Magazine. Retrieved from http:/scholarworks. umass.edu/theses/3/.

Boulton, C. (2009). Review: Code of Best Practices in Fair Use for Media Literacy Education (2008). *Journal of Media Literacy Education, 1*(1). Retrieved from http://digitalcommons.uri.edu/jmle/vol1/iss1/9.

DMCA Info (2010). *Sending a DMCA counter-notification*. Retrieved from http://www.dmca-info.com/sending-a-dmca-counter-notification.html.

Electronic Frontier Foundation. (2014). Lawrence Lessig settles fair use lawsuit over Phoenix Music snippets. Retrieved from https://www.eff.org/press/releases/lawrence-lessig-settles-fair-use-lawsuit-over-phoenix-music-snippets.

Google Support. (2014). *Counter notification basics*. Retrieved from: https://support.google.com/youtube/answer/2807684?hl=en.

International Communication Association. (2010). *Code of best practices in fair use for scholarly research in communication*. Retrieved from http://www.icahdq.org/pubs/reports/fairuse.pdf.

Kreisinger, E. (2014). The impending death of the YouTube mashup. Retrieved from http://www.dailydot.com/opinion/youtube-mashup-remix-copyright-universal/.

Pre-Conference Workshop. (2009). Pre-Conference Workshop presentation, copyright and fair use. Retrieved from http://mediaeducationlab.com/pre-conference-workshop-presentation-copyright-and-fair-use.

SPARC. (2006). Author rights: Using the SPARC author addendum to secure your rights as the author of a journal article. Retrieved from http://www.sparc.arl.org/resources/authors/addendum.

U.S. Copyright Office. (2012). *Fair use*. Retrieved from http://www.copyright.gov/fls/fl102.html.

15 Humoring Youth into Political Engagement through *The Daily Show* and *The Colbert Report*

Satire as Political Critique

Satish Kolluri

TEACHING POLITICAL LITERACY THROUGH POLITICAL HUMOR

In *The Codes of Advertising*, Sut Jhally (1987) uses a Marxist inspired analysis to argue that watching television is a form of work or labor. Similarly today, the more time we spend online, the more we are delivered "algorithmically" to corporate advertisers in this age. Digital technology represents the spirit of capitalist entrepreneurship and creative innovation. Yet in an ironic and troublesome way, our digital age also raises the fundamental issues of human life and dignity and individual privacy—for they have been violated and compromised to a great extent in a physically expanding world of surveillance and a metaphorically shrinking world of sociability in which media ownership gets further consolidated and power becomes privatized. The old definition of the global information society has morphed into a new one that has to be much more expansive, especially if "we live in a multimedia age where the majority of information people receive comes less often from print sources and more typically from highly constructed visual images, complex sound arrangements, and multiple media formats" (Kellner & Share, 2007, p. 3).

Keeping this in mind, the renewal of a call for media and digital literacy across twenty-first century U.S. educational institutions to counter "the influential role that broadcasting and emergent information and computer media play in organizing, shaping, and disseminating information, ideas, and values is creating a powerful *public pedagogy*" that Henry Giroux articulates (ibid., 2007, p. 3). In light of the rapid technological changes that have seen the Internet "absorb" other cultural forms, Kellner and Share (2007, p. 4) argue that

> It is highly irresponsible in the face of saturation by the Internet and media culture to ignore these forms of socialization and education. Consequently, a critical reconstruction of education should produce pedagogies that provide media literacy and enable students, teachers, and citizens to discern the nature and effects of media culture (p. 4).

The question as such is not whether media literacy should be taught, but *how* it should be taught. The need of the hour is to engender more political participation and active citizenship, to become more technologically adept in today's digital culture, to be able to feel empowered, and finally to develop creative and expressive abilities to realize the "transformative potential" of the new media landscape (Frechette & Williams, 2016, p. 2). Today's media literacy must also be global in manifestation, expansive, always in a state of innovative emergence, and able to differentiate itself within and outside the academy. Pedagogical approaches to media literacy should take into account that "today's youth may be engaging in negotiations over developing knowledge and identity, coming of age, and struggling for autonomy" even as "the contexts for communication, friendship, play and self-expression are being reconfigured through their engagement with new media" (Ito et al., 2010, p. 1).

Does that mean the vocabulary of media literacy has to reinvent itself to keep pace with 'newness' in our digital culture? If literacy is a means to an end, what end purpose does it achieve? Is it meant for the self's own use and gratification, *or* is it a means for the self to be in engagement with others? Does that mean all literacy is political and ideological in a fundamental sense? I would argue that they are,

> because literacies are socially constructed in various institutional discourses and practices within educational and cultural sites, cultivating literacies involves attaining competencies in practices in contexts that are governed by rules and conventions. Literacies evolve and shift in response to social and cultural change and the interests of elites who control hegemonic institutions, as well as to the emergence of new technologies.
>
> (Kellner & Share, 2007, p. 5)

For instance, *political literacy* is considered essential to grasp the meaning of citizenship and provides us with abilities to understand the role of government and civil society to fully participate and engage in political and public life, whereas *media literacy* gives us technological competencies and intellectual tools to establish theoretical distance and come up with an immanent critique of the hegemony of that very political and public culture we all inhabit. Both are inextricably linked because we live in a world where our politics are mediated, and media are politicized. In other words, we cannot "do" media literacy without embracing the vocabulary of political literacy, which forms the crux of my chapter.

Following the advice of Kellner and Share, the purpose of this chapter is to "move the discourse beyond the stage of debating whether or not critical media literacy should be taught, and instead focus energy and resources on exploring the best ways for implementing it" (2007). With young people incorporating *The Daily Show* and *The Colbert Report* amidst more established 'news' alternatives as part of their media diet (Pew, 2004; 2008), I employ their 'news sources' as pedagogical material to implement "critical media literacy" in a classroom setting. This takes the form of a course in Political Communication at the intersection of media and politics, and employs the templates of *political literacy* and *political humor* as pedagogical tools to "satirically deconstruct" (Jon Stewart) and "falsely reconstruct" (Stephen Colbert) news and issues of the day. Following this, what are we to make of the state of civic journalism in the United States when the venerated mainstream press itself envies *The Colbert Report* (*TCR*) and *The Daily Show*, (*TDS*) whose only "faux" claim to the institution of journalism is that they are satirists playing journalists? How do we reconcile the trend of youth "tuning out" of news with the increasing initiatives and programs to promote political and civic engagement across campuses in America?

Acknowledging the argument made by Borden and Tew (2007) that "Jon Stewart and Stephen Colbert are better viewed as media critics rather than 'journalists,'" Chris Peters (2012) contends that *TDS* is at the intersection of "journalism, public trust, public pedagogy, and media literacy" (para. 38) and offers a sound rationale for offering such a course:

> What it seems safe to say is that *TDS* is not only an emerging form of journalism, often acting as a substitute or augment of traditional news for its viewers, but a forum where the metanarratives of journalism are frequently discussed, providing young adults with an unexpected avenue for media literacy.
>
> (Peters, 2012, para. 32)

In delineating a subgenre of satire on television from other reality based shows, Gray et al. (2009) contend:

> With the increase in satirical programming, in the socio-cultural status and prominence of such programming ... today's class of Satire TV forms a key part of televised political culture ... and they play a role in nurturing civic culture, as well as their potential place as sources of political information acquisition, deliberation, evaluation, and popular engagement with politics (p. 6).

Concomitantly, there has also been an increase in scholarly research into the effects of political humor (Amarasingam, 2011; Baumgartner and Morris, 2011; Baym, 2009; Gray et al., 2009; Peters, 2012), some of which informed my course as essential to the discussion of political issues that structured it thematically.

In the context of political literacy, several questions arise: At the pedagogical level, how does one negotiate and "operationalize" the practice of political engagement and active citizenship that is situated in the dialectical space between "the subjective component of civic agency at the level of identity" and "the idea of democracy being based on rationality and deliberative engagement at the level of institutions that are committed to produce a civically engaged citizenry?" (Dahlgren, 2004, p. 13). How can we relate to our students' "subjective realities of citizenship, their processes of sense-making in concrete settings" and how these may impact on their political participation and the modes of engagement in making the public sphere more accountable to sociological realities? (Dahlgren, 2009, p. 5). In the context of my approach, what are the important issues that matter to our students, their "subjective realities of citizenship, their processes of sense-making in concrete settings," to quote Dahlgren again, which they can reflect on, and how can they be politically engaged into deliberating them in a civil and reasonable manner after being informed about those very issues through political satire? (Ibid, p. 5).

If being 'politically' informed about news and contemporary issues is a necessary condition for being engaged in worldly matters that determine the quality of their daily lives, then how do students keep themselves suitably informed? And what modes and outlets of civic engagement are available to them, especially in changing media ecology that has become "more commercial, more fragmented, more beholden to technology, and more impacted by temporality over the past few decades?" (Peters, 2012, para. 16). At a time when "corporations are people," corporate lobbyists write public policy, and elected representatives in government are beholden more to the money of the tiny minority on "Wall Street" than the will of the people that constitute the majority on "Main Street," what does "government of, by, and for the people" *really* mean? If the political literacy of elected representatives in our government itself comes into serious question, and the public approval rating for government leaders is at an all-time low, how can we deliberate with our students that political skepticism is better than cynicism, and that civic engagement and political literacy *do* matter?

THE POLITICS OF BEING ENGAGED

Political literacy goes beyond a simple reading of the newspaper or basic knowledge of enrolling as a voter. Ideally, it provides us with higher ordered thinking and engagement on a whole host of issues, including the capacity to critically reflect on political institutions and processes, the role of State, and its exercise of power; an awareness of our news gathering habits to keep pace with events; the ability to interpret and understand the most important issues of the day; and importantly, the fostering of citizenship and civic engagement that ensures that "our rulers are not to be a guardian class set apart from the ruled (and) enabling all to share in and to influence our political debates" (Collins, 1992). Political literacy is of paramount importance because "in the 'marketplace of ideas,' we (as citizen-critics) must learn to protect ourselves against those who may seek to manipulate or deceive us. We must learn how to recognize and resist illogical arguments, misleading or irrelevant evidence, and appeals to our emotions that short-circuit our thinking" (Hogan et al., 2011, p. 9). Simply put, we must stop being a nation of spectators and instead get involved as participants in public life, and realize that we cannot afford to breed cynicism about politics in general and opt out of the system out of a sense of hopelessness. Hogan aptly explains the urgency of political communication:

> For many Americans, "getting involved" means writing a check to a political cause or to some special interest group. In effect, we are paying others to do our politics for *us*! Unfortunately, those paid professionals sometimes degrade the quality of our public discussions. When paid professionals dominate our politics slogans and sound bites replace the voices of ordinary people. Principled leadership gives way to appeals shaped by polling and focus groups, and slick public relations campaigns displace the give-and-take of public debate ... (I)n our legislative assemblies negotiation and compromise has given way to ideological combat and gridlock. Scholars and politicians alike have lamented this loss of civility and substance in our nation's political talk. But the real losers are the citizens, while voices have been drowned out by the voices of more strident activists.
>
> (Hogan, 2011, p.3)

Accordingly, the process of civic engagement and democratic participation is necessary to counter the professionalization and "mediatization" of politics, and privatization of power in a liberal democracy. Fundamentally, civic and political engagement is shaped by political communication that focuses on the "communicative interaction" between political institutions, the media, and citizens, and questions "a transmission view of communication" (Dahlgren, 2009, p. 5).

There are philosophers like Stanley Fish (2004) who contest the idea of educating for civic engagement and citizenship because it impinges on the formation of independent thought among students. For him, the professor's job is to teach, not fashion citizens out of students. He goes on to say:

> There are many in academia who would add to it the larger (or so they would say) tasks of "forming character" and "fashioning citizens." A few years ago, the presidents of nearly 500 universities issued a declaration on the "Civic Responsibility of Higher Education." It called for colleges and universities to take responsibility for helping students "realize the values and skills of our democratic society ... (W)hat practices provide students with the knowledge and commitments to be socially responsible citizens?" That's not a bad question, but the answers to it should not be the content of a college or university course.

But Martha Nussbaum thinks otherwise. In her influential book, *Cultivating Humanity: A Classical Defense of Reform in Liberal Education* (1997), she strongly advocates for the importance of educating "citizens of the world" through the study of non-Western cultures, race, and gender within the liberal education curriculum, and by developing a vital link between liberal education and a deeper, more inclusive kind of citizenship:

> We must ... construct a liberal education that is not only Socratic, emphasizing critical thought and respectful judgment, but also be pluralistic, imparting an understanding of the histories and contributions of groups with whom we interact, both within our nation and in the increasingly international sphere of business and politics. If we cannot teach our students everything they will need to know to be good citizens, we may at least teach them what they do not know and how they may inquire. We can acquaint them with some rudiments about the major non-Western cultures and minority groups within our own. We can show them how to inquire into the history and variety of gender and sexuality. Above all, we can teach them how to argue, rigorously and critically, so that they can call their minds their own.
>
> (Nussbaum, 1997, p. 295)

Nussbaum believes that, to cultivate a sense of humanity in students by evoking the common bond between human populations at large, is of critical importance. She articulates the more recent thought of linking the mission of higher education not only to domestic citizenship, but to the world community through global citizenship. Nussbaum's call for higher education institutions to connect with global issues through the liberal arts curriculum is to be heeded as it will help develop "a global consciousness" among students. As utopian as it sounds, one cannot dismiss the ubiquity of social media and the spread of "hashtag activism" that has made them more virtually connected to global issues than ever before. Whether or not they act on them at the local level remains to be researched. In a similar vein, the call for renewed and increased emphasis on global media literacy is finding favor at different institutional levels, though "it would be probably naively optimistic to overestimate the current degree of news literacy on a global scale ... (but) within certain pockets of young adults, exposure has certainly led to a greater awareness" (Peters, 2012, para. 28). Addressing civic engagement and political literacy through pedagogical efforts in the classroom entails going beyond a superficial 'civics' understanding of engagement and citizenship in order to make it more engaging and participatory. The goal is to generate a more heightened awareness of the 'political' that would in turn lead to more public deliberation and political participation.

TEACHING POLITCAL COMMUNICATION WITH *TDS* AND *TCR*

Like many of their peers, my students consider the realm of politics *incidental* to the terrain of culture. They often display the signs of cynicism and "cool detachment" from the world of politics so characteristic of their age, because the world of (mediated) politics and politicians cannot be trusted. Their basic geographical, historical, and political knowledge of the United States, and general knowledge of the world, leave a lot to be desired, especially in an undergraduate classroom. When asked, "How many members make up the United States House of Representatives and the Senate," only a few students provided correct answers, and even then, they were 'educated' guesses rather than assertive answers. The important question to ask here is what happens to the learning experiences that students collected in school after they make the transition to college? How is it that most students do not know basic facts about the three branches of government despite their relatively heavy use of media? Should we be constructively critical about their lack of political knowledge which is essential to understanding the concept of citizenship and political engagement, or leave them to learn about it on their own?

If the promotion of media awareness is on the rise through media literacy initiatives at the primary and secondary-school levels, and media and journalism studies programs appear across America, then how do we explain our students' sense-making and meaning-making processes of media and politics or lack thereof in the university classroom? As teachers, should we reflect on the problem of 'educating our students for citizenship' to see if it lies in our own pedagogical approaches? Or should we blame the highly commercialized and fragmented media instead for presenting a "dumbed down" version of news in the form of infotainment? In his brilliant delineation of the helpfulness of *media literacy* as a concept to interpret the "the changing audience-journalism relationship" that uses *The Daily Show* as a case study, Chris Peters suggests that the answer is more complex:

> Despite the oft-echoed critique that the news media is turning to tabloid methods, debasing itself as it capitulates to commercial interests, the irony is that, as a workforce, the industry is increasingly demanding that journalists have post-secondary education in order to be admitted into its ranks. So even if we accept contentions of tabloidization and dumbing down at face value, it would seem erroneous to claim that "unintelligent" journalism is resulting from more "uninformed" journalists (2012, para. 17).

It cannot be denied that print journalism in the United States no longer helps us "imagine the nation" as Benedict Anderson had proposed because it is on a serious decline and its traditional readership has almost disappeared:

> A Harvard survey found that only one in 20 teens and one in 12 young adults read a newspaper on close to a daily basis. Online news fares little better. A recent study found that in 2008, roughly 64 percent of 18-to-24-year-olds said they had viewed a newspaper online within

the last year. But by 2009 that had dropped to 54 percent. The figures are even more worrisome when you consider that the study just measured whether a respondent had read online news at all—even once—in the last year.

(Rogers, n.d.)

It is not just print journalism that is struggling to stay afloat financially, as even news channels on network and cable are experiencing similar trends as they attempt to attract younger people by constantly reinventing their programming formats. The latest research shows that television viewers are aging faster than the U.S. population by 5 percent, and that

> The median age of a broadcast or cable television viewer during the 2013–2014 TV season was 44.4 years old, a 6 percent increase in age from four years earlier. Audiences for the major broadcast network shows are much older and aging even faster, with a median age of 53.9 years old, up 7 percent from four years ago.
>
> (Kang, 2014)

If these age trends mean that youths are more or less "tuning out" of mainstream print and broadcast news, then where are they getting their 'serious' news to stay informed? How do they keep themselves informed about issues that matter to them? For important insights into these generational shifts in attitude about news and politics, Kingkade (2012) points to Paula Poindexter's research entitled, "Millennials, News, and Social Media: Is News Engagement a Thing of the Past?":

> Most millennials give the news media average to failing grades when it comes to reporting on their generation. Millennials describe news as garbage, lies, one-sided, propaganda, repetitive and boring. When they consume news, millennials are more likely than their baby boomer parents to access news with smartphones and apps and share news through social media, texting and email. Most millennials do not depend on news to help with their daily lives. The majority of millennials do not feel being informed is important.
>
> (Poindexter, cited in Kingkade, 2012)

Despite these findings, we should not assume that the 'digital generation' does not want serious news. The lore, of course, is that millennials are all selfie-taking egotists who couldn't care less to be informed. But to hear the founder of Ozy.com news, Carlos Watson, explain the news habits of millennials in his pithy way is quite telling: "They just don't want to get it from traditional media for 12 million reasons—whether because they're digital natives, they're not differentiated enough, design matters. Framed differently, the good news is, the space is wide open" (Moses, 2014).

Suffice it to say, those 12 million reasons have been well researched by media scholars over the decades, and this book is an excellent example of why some of those reasons actually constitute the very basis to advance the cause of media literacy. In order to appease millennial tastes and sensibilities for nontraditional sources, more than a few startup "news" websites were founded at the intersections of serious news, entertainment, human interest, and popular culture, offering "sexier" substitutes on digital platforms (Moses, 2014). According to a recent Pew Report (2010), digital platforms played

> a larger role in news consumption … and as a result, the average time Americans spend with the news on a given day is as high as it was in the mid-1990s, when audiences for traditional news sources were much larger. Instead of replacing traditional news platforms, Americans are increasingly integrating new technologies into their news consumption habits. More than a third (36%) of Americans say they got news from both digital and traditional sources yesterday, just shy of the number who relied solely on traditional sources (39%) (Americans Spending More Time Following the News, 2010).

One of the key findings in the report documents that "In terms of age, the 'Colbert Report' (80%), 'Daily Show' (74%) and New York Times (67%) have the biggest percentage of viewers and readers in the coveted 18–49-year-old demographic. Fox News' Bill O'Reilly (35%) and Sean Hannity (33%) have the smallest" (Ibid). Given the immense popularity of Stewart and Colbert, this finding may be more or less consistent across all "generations" on the liberal spectrum.

"IT'S EVEN BETTER THAN BEING INFORMED" AND "THAT'S THE WORD"

The aforementioned findings, in conjunction with the rapidly growing and extremely engaging academic work on the media and political effects of Jon Stewart and Stephen Colbert, and, most importantly, my own interest and investment in politics as an academic-activist, resulted in a course that embraced satire as political critique. It brought together modern political communication theories, academic research on political humor, and *TDS* and *TCR* as pedagogical tools in a course titled "Satire as Political Critique." In the class, students were introduced to political institutions and processes, rhetorical analyses of political speeches and interviews with politicians, ideological analyses of public policies, political protests, and deconstruction of political advertisements and campaigns through the political comedy of Stewart and Colbert. After studying the rich history and development of satire, and its important role in ridiculing and shaming those in power since Greek times, students examined how satire and parody perform the function of critique simultaneously as acts of communication and representation when "comedy becoming political and politics becomes funny" (Gray et al., 2009).

As Compton (2011) explains, earlier academic research on late night television political humor

> focused on viewers' attitudes toward candidates and impacts on voting intentions. With the advent of Jon Stewart's *The Daily Show* (TDS) and Stephen Colbert's *The Colbert Report* (TCR) on Comedy Central, more recent research, however, has approached late night political comedy from a wider perspective, exploring impacts of political humor on viewers' cynicism, civic participation, and perceived efficacy (p. 4).

The use of political humor, specifically satire and parody in *TDS* and *TCR*, to reconstruct and deconstruct the political and mainstream news media establishments, became fairly successful in drawing in otherwise disengaged young people into the political process. But Baumgartner and Morris (2011) caution us about overestimating the seeming potential of these shows because undue reliance on *TDS* does not correlate with increased political knowledge and activity among young adults. However, they are in consonance with the view that many viewers of *TDS* are knowledgeable and engaged, and possibly more cynical due to heavy viewing, and these individuals ensure that they depend on other news sources as well. If satire is laughter with a point attached to it, then what Colbert states here is of significant importance:

When asked whether audiences "get their news" from *The Daily Show,* Colbert expressed doubt and explained:

> I wish people would watch the real news before they watch our show, because we have two games. Our game is we make fun of the newsmakers, but we also make fun of the news style. They're missing half our joke if they don't keep up with up with the day-day changes of mass media news.
>
> (cited in Tally, Jr., 2011, p. 162)

Colbert's observation is useful to students who might otherwise consider Stewart and him as real journalists just because they interview world leaders and newsmakers, or address issues that mainstream mass media is neglecting to cover or analyze. Yet despite Colbert's humble assertions about his lack of established credentials, attempts made to characterize both him and Stewart as real journalists nevertheless reinforce the social and political significance they have had not only in living rooms of America, but also its classrooms.

Sometimes students are unassumingly unaware about socially significant issues that are germane to their demographic until they are specifically introduced to them. Whether their unawareness is from cynicism, a "hip aloofness," or "tuning out," this lack of political knowledge and engagement represents a reality in our classrooms. To have the course centered fundamentally on issues that matter to students' sociological realities despite this "meta-unawareness," and make them read, listen, watch, comprehend, interpret, and produce critiques about them against the larger backdrop of satirical television, makes for an intellectually productive and emotionally satisfying experience in the classroom. Some of the issues that figured in the most recent classes included: public and private education, tuition, and student debt; narcissism and celebrity culture; race, gender and income inequality; congressional gridlock; healthcare and reproductive rights; anti-governmentalism and anti-intellectualism; environment, Ebola and public health; Science and climate change; deregulation; the financial crisis of 2009 and the role of government; Citizens United, The Supreme Court, and corporations; same-sex marriage, religion and politics; journalism, ethics, and media criticism of MSM; ISIS, North Korea, and U.S. foreign policy; and evolution and creationism, to name a few.

In critically analyzing video clips from *TDS* and *TCR* that specifically address the above issues, and engaging in close readings of rigorously researched essays on the effects of their programs, students learned how Stewart and Colbert employ parody and satire in constructing their personae. Moreover, they communicate political humor that not only entertains but informs (Gray et al., 2009).

As Robert Tally explains (2011),

> The hyperreality of these fake news programs is ... that they dramatically enact the underlying critique of the media, by showing that the mainstream news is altogether artificial, constructed according to formulae and processes easily decoded by comedy writers and attentive viewers ... (I)n the hyperreal, the "authentic fake" takes on a reality far more salient than reality itself (p.151).

Hence, it is the "faux journalism" of Stewart and the media criticism of Colbert's "willfully ignorant character" (who modeled himself after right-wing political pundit, Bill O'Reilly) that serves as a meta-critique of journalistic practices.

With the help of examples from *TDS* that feature real news clips, students are able to demonstrate Stewart's ability to import the real into the mimetic frame of his program and to deconstruct or lay bare "the lack of substance behind much political discourse" that naturally encourages audiences to "tune out" (Day, 2009, p. 86). *TDS* and *TCR* have become valuable resources for younger audiences because Stewart and Colbert have established a relationship with the "culture of cool." But does this cachet with young audiences breed a cynical and ironic stance toward "hope and affirmative politics that complements critique ... [which] are key to social transformation?" (Van Heertum, 2011, p. 133). Opinions are divided on this. Peters (2012) recounts that much academic work which focuses specifically on *The Daily Show* investigates the program in this light, discussing its impact on political engagement and attitudes towards the political process. One such case was a forum held during the National Communication Association's annual conference in 2006, which interrogated the claim by Hart and Hartelius that "Stewart's cynical approach to discuss politics was a threat to democracy, resulting in mistrust and antipathy" (para. 36).

Echoing similar sentiments are Baumgartner and Morris, who in their superbly researched essay conclude that "heavy *TDS* viewers do not differ significantly from non-*TDS* viewers with respect to their political knowledge and participation ... and that high levels of exposure to Stewart's sharp and pervasive cynicism may cause that cynicism to rub off" (2011, p. 75). For Hariman though, "Stewart's comedic yet cynical take illustrates the equivalency between the average citizen and politicians, promoting reengagement" (cited in Peters, 2012, para. 36).

Such contestation about the effects of both *TDS* and *TCR* prompt additional inquiry: Do Colbert and Stewart engender a politics of cynicism in their audiences because they do not give them the answers or solutions? Is it proper to ask political humorists on a television channel owned by a giant media corporation to bear the burden of responsibility to bring about "social transformation"?

By watching Colbert's interviews with people who occupy a wide spectrum of name and fame in public life, students watch and learn how, "in breaking down his guests, himself, and the complex issues of our time, he creates a forum through which ... (they) cannot only recognize the paradox of language and politics but also envision alternative possibilities and configure their own beliefs within a larger context" (Wisniewski, 2011, p. 169). His satirical explorations of how ideas as 'memes' are passed along in public discourse make for effective pedagogical tools that expose students to a wide variety of themes and topics that they may or may not have been aware of. For instance, through Colbert's coinage of *Wikiality*, they understand how he decenters "modernity's institutions of knowledge production and its relocation of academic expertise, as Henry Jenkins described, from academic recognized authorities to a form of electronically networked collective intelligence" (Baym, 2009, p.137).

To understand how *TDS* and *TCS* function as valuable political resources and whether they really connect with youth as Van Heertum (2011) suggests, I ask my students to write comedic segments on "the culture of cool" in cultural politics today by establishing an ironic distance between themselves and what they perceive as 'cool.' The exercise is meant to tickle their proverbial funny bone, and also make them think of satire as political critique of public discourse in acerbic and comedic terms. "And it is here is that *TDS* and *TCR* become important in speaking the language of youth—based on irony, or distance from the expected reaction to spectacle society and the absurdity of contemporary politics and essentially cynicism about things ever changing" (ibid., p. 127). In view of the mainstream media largely abrogating its civic responsibility to inform and educate the public, it is not surprising that *TDS* and *TCR* have emerged as 'alternative' sources of news, which ironically perform the function of public pedagogy that still retains its immense entertainment value.

To the critics of Stewart and Colbert who think they breed cultural antipathy, my experience in class has been otherwise because they have actually enabled students to relate to issues relevant to them, and deliberate them in a meaningful and engaging manner. That the course motivated all students to stay connected to issues and the world, and a few of them to seriously consider politics and public service, is a testimony to the profound impact that Colbert and Stewart have had as media avatars of public pedagogy and political engagement in reshaping their understanding of citizenship. The pedagogical challenge to "operationalize" or translate *TDS* and *TCR* as collaborative learning tools is to create an engaged learning community in the classroom to encourage students to critically think about the common good, and engage with each other on issues that matter to their daily lives.

If the goal of political communication is to get students engaged in media genres that are more 'cool' and relevant to the topics and issues affecting them and their generation, then Jon Stewart and Stephen Colbert should be welcomed as guests in today's learning environments. Although further research is necessary to document the long-term impact of watching these programs within and beyond the classroom walls, we can see that *TDS* and *TCR* encourage and prompt sociopolitical engagement among today's youth.

In conclusion, perhaps the best way to articulate a more expansive meaning of political literacy and media education through the use of political humor comes from the late Hannah Arendt, who reminds us that

> Education is the point at which we decide whether we love the world enough to assume responsibility for it and by the same token save it from ruin which, except for renewal, except for the coming of the new and young, would be inevitable. And education, too, is where we decide whether we love our children enough not to expel them from our world and leave them to their own devices, nor to strike from their hands their chance of undertaking something new, something unforeseen by us, but to prepare them in advance for the task of renewing a common world (1968, p. 196).

REFERENCES

Amarasingam, A. (Ed.). (2011). *The Stewart/Colbert effect: Essays on the real impacts of fake news.* Jefferson, N.C.: McFarland & Company.
Americans spending more time following the news (2010). Retrieved from http://www.people-press.org/2010/09/12/americans-spending-more-time-following-the-news/.

Arendt, H. (1968, reprint 1993). *Between past and future.* New York: Penguin Books.

Baumgartner, C., & Morris, J. (2011). Stoned slackers or super citizens? *The Daily Show* viewing and political engagement of adults. In *The Stewart/Colbert effect: Essays on real impacts of fake news* (pp. 63–78). Jefferson, N.C.: McFarland & Company.

Baym, G. (2009). Stephen Colbert's parody of the postmodern. In J. Gray, J. Jones, & E. Thompson (Eds.), *Satire TV: Politics and comedy in the post-network era.* New York and London: NYU Press.

Borden, S., & Tew, C. (2007). The role of journalist and the performance of journalism: Ethical lessons from "fake" news (seriously). *Journal of Mass Media Ethics, 22*(4), 300–314.

Collins, H. (1992). Political literacy: Educating for democracy. Papers on Australian Parliament. Retrieved from http://www.aph.gov.au/About_Parliament/Senate/Research_and_Education/~/~/link.aspx?_id=1322CB719E034CC0AE685C780E53D7FA&_z=z.

Compton, J. (2011). Introduction: Surveying scholarship on *The Daily Show* and *The Colbert Report.* In *The Stewart/Colbert effect: Essays on real impacts of fake news* (pp. 9–23). Jefferson, N.C.: McFarland & Company.

Dahlgren, P. (2004). Theory, boundaries and political communication: The uses of disparity. *European Journal of Communication, 19*(1), 7–18. London: Sage Publications.

Dahlgren, P. (2009). *Media and political engagement: Citizens, communication and democracy.* New York: Cambridge University Press.

Day, A. (2009). And Now … the news? Mimesis and the real in *The Daily Show.* In J. Gray, J. Jones, & E. Thompson (Eds.), *Satire TV: Politics and comedy in the post-network era.* New York and London: NYU Press.

Fish, S. (2004, May 21). Why we built the ivory tower. *The New York Times*, 23.

Frechette, J., & Williams, R. (2015). Introduction. In *Media education for a digital generation* (pp. 1–6). New York: Routledge.

Gray, J., Jones, J., & Thompson, E. (Eds.). 2009. *Satire TV: Politics and comedy in the post-network era.* New York and London: NYU Press.

Hogan, J. (2011). *Public speaking and civic engagement* (2nd ed.). Boston: Allyn & Bacon.

Ito, M. (2010). *Hanging out, messing around, and geeking out: Kids living and learning with new media.* Cambridge, MA: The MIT Press.

Jhally, S. (1987). *The codes of advertising: Fetishism and the political economy of meaning in the consumer society.* New York: St. Martin's Press.

Kang, C. (2014). TV is increasingly for old people. Retrieved from http://www.washingtonpost.com/news/business/wp/2014/09/05/tv-is-increasingly-for-old-people/.

Kellner, D., & Share, J. (2007). *Critical media literacy, democracy, and the reconstruction of education.* Retrieved from file:///C:/Users/skolluri/Downloads/024CritLitDemocracyPP015.pdf.

Kingkade, Tyler (2012). Millennials And News Study: Youth View The News As 'Garbage,' Don't Like Being Talked Down To By It The Huffington Post. Retrieved from http://www.huffingtonpost.com/2012/09/18/millennials-hate-the-news_n_1882080.html.

Moses, L. (2014). Which millennial news sites are really attracting millennials? *Digiday.* Retrieved from http://digiday.com/publishers/millennial-news-sites-really-attracting-millennials/.

Nussbaum, M. (1997). *Cultivating humanity: A classical defense of reform in liberal education*. Cambridge, MA: Harvard University Press.

Peters, C. (2012). 'Even better than being informed': Satirical news and media literacy. Retrieved from https://www.academia.edu/5337727/Even_Better_Than_Being_Informed_Satirical_News_and_Media_Literacy.

Pew Research Center (2004). Cable and Internet Loom Large in Fragmented Political News Universe. Retrieved from http://www.people-press.org/2004/01/11/cable-and-internet-loom-large-in-fragmented-political-news-universe/.

Pew Research Center (2008) What's On—And What's Not On—The Daily Show. Retrieved from http://www.journalism.org/2008/05/08/whats-onand-whats-not-onthe-daily-show/.

Pew Research Center (2010). Americans Spending More Time Following the News: Ideological News Sources: Who Watches and Why. Retrieved from http://www.people-press.org/2010/09/12/americans-spending-more-time-following-the-news/.

Rogers, T. (n.d.). Why don't young people follow the news more closely? Retrieved from http://journalism.about.com/od/trends/a/youngpeople.htm.

Tally, R., Jr. (2011). I am the Mainstream Media (and So Can You!). In *The Stewart/Colbert effect: Essays on real impacts of fake news* (pp. 149–163). Jefferson, N.C.: McFarland & Company.

Van Heertum, R. (2011). Irony and the news: Speaking cool to American youth. In *The Stewart/Colbert effect: Essays on real impacts of fake news* (pp. 63–78). Jefferson, N.C.: McFarland & Company.

Wisniewski, K. A. (2011). It's all about meme: The art of the interview and the insatiable ego of the Colbert bump. In *The Stewart/Colbert effect: Essays on real impacts of fake news* (pp. 164–180). Jefferson, N.C.: McFarland & Company.

16 Back to School

Media Literacy, Graduate Education, and the Digital Age

Lori Bindig

In recent years, there has been much talk about media literacy education as a twenty-first-century skill—something that is vital for life, work, and citizenship in the digital age (Hobbs, 2010; Jenkins, 2013; Thoman & Jolls, 2003). As a result, each state in America has adopted some element of media literacy into its educational curriculum (CIC stats, 2006). Yet, the incorporation and implementation of media literacy curricula not only varies wildly from state to state, but also district to district, and classroom to classroom. The drastically different approaches to media literacy education would not be as problematic if media literacy skills were cultivated in a variety of settings. However, despite the increasing emphasis on media literacy in the digital age, current models typically relegate media literacy education to youth in K-12 classrooms. On occasion, media literacy is also available to young people through nonprofit organizations.[1] While media literacy can be found in the academy, postsecondary education in the United States does not have a standardized media literacy requirement. When colleges and universities do include media literacy in their curricula, often times it is just one (of a number of courses) required for undergraduate college students. In the event that media literacy courses are actually required in higher education, it primarily for those majoring in Communication or Media Studies.

At the same time that media literacy is being emphasized in primary and secondary education, scholars have acknowledged that media literacy itself is changing (Buckingham, 2010; Frechette, 2002; Frechette, 2014; Rushkoff, 2014). In fact, at the 2014 Media Literacy Research Symposium, renowned media scholar Douglas Rushkoff noted that "Media literacy in the digital age is fundamentally different." One obvious reason for this change has been the proliferation of media that is readily accessible to a large number of people through mobile technologies. Digital natives are thought to readily embrace these new platforms because they have grown up using technology (Prensky, 2001). Not only do these digital natives regularly consume media across a myriad of platforms,[2] but they have increasingly becoming media creators (boyd, 2014; Gardner & Davis, 2013). Yet, as Buckingham (2010) notes, "this approach embodies a kind of essentialism, an 'exoticising' of youth, which ignores the diversity and the inequalities in young people's experiences, and the continuities across generations (Facer & Furlong, 2001; Buckingham, 2006; Herring, 2008)" (p. 5).

While digital natives tend to be most closely associated with the changes in digital culture, it is important to remember that people of all ages have the potential to consume and create digital content. For instance, all individuals, not just youth, have the ability to create and maintain relationships as well as collectively and collaboratively build knowledge through social media (Fuchs, 2014). However, as Frechette (2014) reminds us, the very technological advancements that have the potential to bring us together can also keep us apart through cultural niches and targeted marketing. Although digital technologies can and do act as vehicles for facilitating positive social change, the commercialization of media and the rampant consumerism it promotes tends to curtail civic engagement and undermine prosocial endeavors (Frechette, 2014). Furthermore, the "always on" nature of the digital age has created a sense of being tethered to devices with a great deal of time and energy spent living life online rather than in the real world (Chen, 2011; Rushkoff, 2013). As a result we need a media literacy that helps us assess "the social, physical, psychological, and economic costs and benefits of engaging in the digital world" (Frechette, 2014, p. 17).

While technological advancements play a central role in the changes that have occurred within media literacy, there are other factors at play (Buckingham, 2009; Frechette, 2014). For instance, Buckingham (2009) notes, "Current changes in the media environment are not just about technology, but also about how identities are formed and lived out in modern societies" (p. 1). In other words, our understanding of ourselves and the world around us continue to be shaped by media. Therefore, media education in the digital age must provide "the tools through which to examine the political, cultural, historical, economic and social ramifications of all media in a holistic way" (Frechette, 2014, p. 14).

If media literacy has become so central to twenty-first-century citizenship, and if our theory and practice of media literacy have evolved in the digital age, it is necessary to provide comprehensive media education. Yet, the United States overwhelmingly lacks a standardized approach to media literacy education. For instance, although media literacy has the potential to be fostered and utilized in a number of settings (Bergsma, 2004; Bindig, 2012), most media literacy initiatives tend to be implemented in K-12 or undergraduate education. As a result, the majority of media literacy practitioners are either scholars within the academy, or K-12 instructors who may have taken a media literacy course in college or a media literacy workshop as part of their ongoing professional development. In some instances, K-12 instructors of media literacy actually have no formal training; instead, their teaching is based solely on their reflections of their own media use (Risemeyer, 2014). As for the practitioners outside of education, media literacy is typically introduced through a professional association or conference. However, as Buckingham (2001) notes, these practitioners "are often even more inadequately provided with opportunities for training and professional development" (p. 14). Therefore, despite media literacy education becoming an increasingly important skill set, comprehensive training for the very individuals responsible for instilling media literacy skills in youth is limited in the U.S.

This lack of formal education is not a new phenomenon within media literacy. For years, scholarship within the field has continuously recognized the lack of substantive preparation for media literacy practitioners (Buckingham, 2001; Buckingham, 2009; Donnelly, 2011; Silverblatt, 2010). To counter this, Buckingham (2001), in particular, has called for "extensive and sustained" training (p. 14). While he acknowledges "one-off conferences and short courses are obviously of value for those new to the field," Buckingham (2001) has championed the development of more in-depth media literacy training at the Master's level for a range of media literacy practitioners (p. 14). Thus, Buckingham (2001) envisions graduate level media literacy education not just for K-12 educators but also for academics, researchers, activists, community group leaders, parents, religious leaders, and media policy makers and regulators as well as media producers and media company employees (p. 5). Other scholars have expanded upon Buckingham's list and suggested that media literacy is also relevant to those working in psychiatry, nursing, counseling, and coaching (Bindig, 2012; Center for Media Literacy, 2011; Ehrmann et al., 2011; Herzberger, 2008).

Despite this need, U.S. universities and colleges have been slow to develop media literacy graduate programs. In fact, at the time of publication there are only four[3] graduate programs related to media literacy that exist within the United States. Of these four programs, only two are housed in communication. The other two programs are affiliated with education programs and adopt an instructional technology approach, which focus on incorporating computers into a K-12 learning environment. As Tessa Jolls explains in an interview with Henry Jenkins (2014), the technology approach is problematic because it "is often limited to technical proficiency without critical autonomy." Buckingham (2009) suggests that educational media and instructional technology programs take an instrumental approach to media education. In fact, Buckingham (2009) states that in these types of programs "the critical questions we ask as media educators (about who creates media and why they do so, about how media represent the world, and how they work) tend to be marginalized or ignored" (p. 9). Thus, while educational media programs do foster key technological skills for the digital age, they fail to take a holistic approach to media literacy.

While it is easy to critique instructional technology programs for what they lack, it is much more difficult to develop a comprehensive graduate curriculum for media literacy practitioners in the digital age. However, if in-depth media education at the graduate level is ever to occur, it is necessary to consider the components that are essential in this plan of study. If media literacy is conceived as "both critical understanding and active participation," then a critical cultural studies lens may be most useful for developing these types of graduate programs (Buckingham, 2001, p. 2). Critical cultural studies media literacy (CCSML) is often considered the most transformative version of media literacy because it utilizes Freire'ian empowerment theory and focuses on the conscientization of marginalized individuals through media analysis, as well as advocating for social change (Bergsma, 2004; Lewis & Jhally, 1998; Masterman, 2001; Sholle & Denski, 1995). Therefore, CCSML views media literacy as a consciousness-raising tool, which recognizes the interplay[4] between social structures and individual lives.

More specifically, the goal of CCSML is to create well-informed citizens through critical thinking about media messages and an understanding of the political economy of mass media, social engagement, and alternative media production. All this is directed toward the ultimate goal of creating and empowering "effective change agents" (Lewis & Jhally, 1998, p. 110). In other words, through the CCSML lens, media education can be seen as a way to challenge the status quo that is continually reinforced by the mass media. Yet, in this framework, media are not perceived as "all powerful," but rather as "sites of struggle" that allows for participatory engagement and activism.

Although the CCSML conception of media literacy may appear to only reflect the culturalist approach, there are points of convergence with other perspectives within the field (Bindig & Castonguay, 2014). For instance, a CCSML curriculum may appeal to individuals situated within the interventionist framework because it is an intervention in the ubiquitous and toxic—sexist, racist, classist, and homophobic—media culture that surround us today. Likewise, those interested in critical pedagogy, social justice, and health initiatives are also able to embrace a CCSML because of its stress on agency and activism. Therefore, a graduate curriculum grounded in CCSML is able to encompass a number of diverse media literacy paradigms because common goals can be found in thwarting the negative impact of media ideologies and empowering individuals, which ultimately can lead to social change.

The required components of a graduate program in media literacy become clear when the challenges of the digital age are viewed through a CCSML lens. This approach suggests that coursework should encompass five key areas: media studies history and theory, media literacy debates, specialty areas, media literacy research methods, and engaged practice. First and foremost, media literacy practitioners must understand media history, theory, and analysis in order to address the fundamental changes brought forth by the digital age. Courses within this area must also address ethical issues within media industries with regard to how content is created and distributed, underlying ideological values, and the impact of content on both individuals and society as a whole.

With a solid foundation of media studies traditions, practitioners can move on to the second area of coursework where they are exposed to the various approaches within media literacy. These classes provide an overview of the media literacy frameworks that have shaped the field as well as points of convergence and divergence among media literacy scholars. In particular, this set of coursework should explore the seven great debates in media literacy (Hobbs, 1998). These debates coalesce around issues of protectionism and vulnerable populations; media literacy as school-based initiatives and/or specialized subjects; the centrality and value of media production; the incorporation of popular texts as well as ideology and political activism into curricula; and the role of corporate interests in media literacy initiatives.

Once practitioners have a broad understanding of the field they can move on to the third set of courses, which allow for greater exploration of specialty areas. Specialty areas could be conceived as a concentration where a series of courses revolve around a particular topic or theme. Potential concentrations might focus on the relationship between media and health, vulnerable populations, or issues of identity. However, specialty areas could consist of a number of elective courses, which students take based on their own interests and professional goals. In this latter conception of specialty areas, courses may vary thematically. For instance, the subject matter of specialty courses could range from social media and participatory culture to the political economy of media industries to media representations to visual communication. Regardless of whether they are packaged as a concentration or as stand-alone electives, all specialty area courses should further the understanding of media culture in the digital age and develop media literacy skill sets.

While the first three areas of coursework tend to be more theoretical, the last two areas, media literacy research methods and engaged practice, are more applied. Undoubtedly any media literacy research course should provide an overview of the various types of scholarship that has already been conducted within media literacy. Additionally these courses should also outline strategies for designing and implementing original media literacy curricula as well as discuss methodologies for measuring the effectiveness of media literacy initiatives. However, as part of their research coursework, practitioners should be asked to apply their knowledge by designing and revising their own media literacy project in preparation of implementation. Thus, the research component of the curriculum acts as a bridge to the culminating courses in engaged practice.

Engaged practice courses give practitioners the opportunity to develop, execute, and analyze the effectiveness of an original media literacy initiative based on their own career goals and interests.[5] Because a CCSML approach welcomes individuals from a range of professional backgrounds, the process of and product resulting from the engaged practice courses will most likely be unique to each practitioner. Examples of engaged practice may include an elementary school teacher designing a curriculum that introduces the five tenets of media literacy to third graders, a nurse developing a brochure for patients about the relationship between media and obesity, a community organizer creating a public service announcement about the ramifications of new legislation, and a media professional writing a proposal for a diversity workshop. Though these initiatives may differ in topic, goals, target audience, methodology, and effectiveness, the engaged practice courses allow practitioners to gain real world experience and demonstrate their understanding of coursework, as well as act as a vehicle for promoting positive social change. While field experiences may result in logistical challenges[6] for both those taking *and* teaching the engaged practice courses, they are integral to the civic engagement and social awareness that Buckingham views as vital to the future of media literacy (2009; 2010) and considered a best practice for professional development (2001).

In addition to the five key areas of coursework, a graduate program in media literacy must address media production. Rather than approach it from a vocational standpoint, media production can be incorporated into a graduate media literacy curriculum if it is conceived of as a "pedagogical opportunity" (Lewis & Jhally, 1998, p. 115). In other words, media production is not useful if it reinforces consumerism or simply replicates commercial content. In contrast, media production may be of use in graduate media literacy programs if it fosters analytical critique, creates alternative media content, or demonstrates an understanding of curricular concepts. Furthermore, having a working knowledge of basic media production skills, platforms, and techniques is increasingly necessary to be seen as a "credible" media expert among digital natives as well as one who is able to meet them on their own terms.

Beyond the content of the curriculum, when designing a new graduate program (especially in the digital age), it is necessary to specify the mode of delivery. While fully online programs do exist, Buckingham (2001) notes, "Distance learning may be appropriate in many circumstances, but this should be complemented by sustained opportunities for face-to-face tuition" (p. 14). Though Buckingham does not elaborate, the incorporation of engaged practice and media production in graduate coursework may shape his views about best practices. Though online pedagogical strategies can be implemented, face-to-face instruction may be best for skill development, fieldwork supervision, and problem-solving in media production and engaged practice courses. In addition, Buckingham's (2001) call for "self-organization by practitioners" views informal opportunities for consultation and collaboration at the local level as essential for the growth of media literacy (p. 15). As such, it is reasonable to believe that any institution offering a graduate program in media literacy may likely serve as this connecting hub for practitioners. Thus, due to pedagogical and professional development, media literacy graduate programs may best be conceived as "on-ground" or (at the very least) "hybrid" programs.

Although designing the curriculum may seem like the most arduous task in the process of developing a graduate program in media literacy, in today's current economic climate, understanding enrollment is also imperative. This chapter previously discussed a plethora of professionals that may be interested in receiving substantive training in media education. However, determining how to reach out to these individuals may be daunting. Perhaps the easiest way to inform media literacy practitioners of a new media literacy graduate program is through the same channels they currently use to acquire media literacy training. This means contacting colleges and universities that teach undergraduate media literacy courses, as well as school districts and professional organizations that offer media literacy workshops. Beyond those already interested in media education, media literacy graduate programs should recruit students from majors associated with critical analysis, vulnerable populations, and social change such as comparative literature, English, gender studies, global studies, graphic design, health sciences, nursing, political science, psychology, religious studies, sociology, and social work. Likewise, media literacy graduate programs should approach local chapters of professional associations in these related fields, as well as nonprofit organizations associated with prosocial activism and civic engagement. Furthermore, online communities, forums, and listservs related to media literacy and social justice issues provide an inexpensive way for new programs to reach potential students in the digital age.

Even when a proposed new program is pedagogically sound and provides a plan to meet enrollment figures, university administrators may still balk at making an investment of this magnitude. However, several strategies exist for overcoming institutional obstacles. One approach to engaging leery administrators is to highlight how a graduate program in media literacy reflects the mission or strategic plan of the institution. Increasingly, academic institutions tout goals of promoting critical thinking, cultural understanding, technical skills, citizenship, and community involvement. Rather than being simply more empty rhetoric, a media literacy graduate program similar to the one conceptualized in this chapter actually embodies and promotes these crucial values. Sometimes administrators can also be swayed to approve a new program if it will be among the first of its kind. Since so few media literacy graduate programs currently exist in the United States, any new programs that emerge have the potential to create and shape the market or become leaders in the field. Another, more pragmatic, approach to administrators may be to stress the "value-added" aspect of media literacy programs. The required component of engaged practice pushes graduate students outside the university walls and places them in situations where they are creating positive change. If social impact alone is not enough to persuade reluctant administrators, engaged practice is designed to strengthen "town and gown" relations as well as provide positive publicity for the university. Although the emphasis on revenue and public relations may make a CCSML scholar cringe, understanding these aspects of a graduate media literacy program may make the difference in gaining the approval of university administration.

By now, it should be clear that media education at the graduate level is desperately needed in the United States. Current media literacy practitioners require substantive training to adequately address the challenges of the digital age. Because of the ever-expanding reach of media, more and more professions demand a deeper understanding of media and their impact on individuals and culture. This chapter attempts to address these needs by offering a model for a graduate program in media literacy education that simultaneously acknowledges the fundamental changes to media education that have occurred in the digital age and strives for equality and justice both in contemporary media and for our future. In no way should this model be seen as the only option for a graduate program in media literacy. Certainly, there are other theoretical frameworks and rationales that could be utilized in order to produce different, yet still worthwhile, media programs. Instead this chapter should be understood as a call to action to strengthen media education efforts by bringing educators back to school so they can receive the training they need to better foster media literacy education in the digital age.

NOTES

1. One noteworthy example is the Girls Inc. organization, which includes media literacy as part of its educational programming.
2. Croteau and Hoynes (2014) note that youth consumption of television is on the rise while Campbell et al. (2014) note, "Facebook users upload 300 million images each day," "Twitter users send 340 million tweets each day," and "72 hours of video are uploaded to YouTube every minute" while "more than 6 billion text messages are sent each day" (p. 578).
3. These four graduate programs include the online MA in Media Literacy at Webster University (St. Louis, MO), the Sixth Year in Instructional Technologies and Digital Media Literacy program at University of New Haven (New Haven, CT), an online MA in Educational Media with a concentration in Media Literacy at Appalachian State University (Boone, NC) and an on-ground MA in Media Literacy and Digital Culture at Sacred Heart University (Fairfield, CT).
4. As mentioned earlier in this chapter, understanding this interplay is fundamental to media literacy in the digital age.
5. Ideally, practitioners may base their original media literacy initiatives on topics discussed in specialty area courses.
6. Logistical challenges can include a variety of anticipated and unanticipated hardships such as access to participants, time constraints, cost of implementation, technological difficulties, and fieldwork supervision.

REFERENCES

Bergsma, L. J. (2004). Empowerment education: The link between media literacy and health promotion. *The American Behavioral Scientist*, *48*, 152–164.
Bindig, L. (2012). Media literacy in eating disorder treatment (pp. 31–37). In R. A. Lind (Ed.), *Race/gender/class/media* (3rd ed.). New York: Pearson.
Bindig, L., & Castonguay, J. (2014). Should I really kill my television? Negotiating common ground among media literacy scholars, educators, and activists. In B. S. De Abreu & P. Mihailidis (Eds.), *Media literacy education in action*. New York: Routledge.

boyd, d. (2014). *It's complicated*. New Haven, CT: Yale University Press.

Buckingham, D. (2001). *Media education: A global strategy for development*. UNESCO policy paper.

Buckingham, D. (2009). The future of media literacy in the digital age: Some challenges for policy and practice. *Euromeduc: Media literacy in Europe*.

Buckingham, D. (2010). Do we really need media education 2.0? Teaching media in the age of participatory culture. In K. Drotner & K. Schroder (Eds.), *Digital content creation* (pp. 287–304). New York: Peter Lang.

Campbell, R., Martin, C. R., & Fabos, B. (2014). *Media and culture* (9th ed.). Boston: Bedford/St. Martin's.

Center for Media Literacy. (2011). *Voices of media literacy: International pioneers speak*. Retrieved from http://www.medialit.org/voices-media-literacy-international-pioneers-speak.

Chen, B. X. (2011). *Always on: How the iPhone unlocked the anything-anytime-anywhere future—and locked us in*. Cambridge, MA: Da Capo Press.

CIC Stats. (2006). Retrieved from http://meidalit.med.sc.edu/statelit.htm 1/31/2006.

Croteau, D., & Hoynes, W. (2014). *Media and Society* (5th ed.). Thousand Oaks, CA: Sage. Donnelly, K. (2011). 5 great media literacy programs and how to assess their impact. Retrieved from http://www.pbs.org/mediashift/2011/04/5-great-media-literacy-programs-and-how-to-assess-their-impact111/.

Ehrmann, J., Ehrmann, P., & Jordan, G. (2011). *Inside out coaching: How sports can transform lives*. New York: Simon & Schuster.

Frechette, J. D. (2002). *Developing media literacy in cyberspace pedagogy and critical learning for the twenty-first century classroom*. Westport, CT: Praeger.

Frechette, J. (2014). Top ten guiding questions for critical digital literacy. *The Journal of Media Literacy*, 6(1–2): 14–21.

Fuchs, C. (2014). *Social media: a critical introduction*. London: Sage.

Gardner, H., & Davis, K. (2013). *The app generation*. New Haven, CT: Yale University Press.

Herzberger, S. (2008). Nursing media educated patients. *Journal of Nursing Staff Development*, 24(3):101–104.

Hobbs, R. (1998). The seven great debates in the media literacy movement. *Journal of Communication*, 48(1), 16–32.

Hobbs, R. (2010). *Digital and media literacy: A plan of action*. Retrieved from http://www.knightcomm.org/wpcontent/uploads/2010/12/Digital_and_Media_Literacy_A_Plan_of_Action.pdf.

Jenkins, H. (2013). *Confronting the challenges of participatory culture: media education for the 21st century*. MacArthur Foundation. Retrieved from http://www.macfound.org/media/article_pdfs/JENKINS_WHITE_PAPER.PDF.

Jenkins, H. (2014). The value of media literacy education in the 21st century: A conversation with Tessa Jolls (Part One). Retrieved from http://henryjenkins.org/2014/09/the-value-of-media-literacy-education-in-the-21st-century-a-conversation-with-tessa-jolls-part-one.html#sthash.lrxl7d2R.dpuf.

Lewis, J. & Jhally, S. (1998). The struggle over media literacy. *Journal of Communication*, 48(1), 109–120.

Masterman, L. (2001). A rationale for media education. In R. W. Kubey (Ed.), *Media Literacy in the information age: Current perspectives*, (pp.15–68). New Brunswick, NJ: Transaction Publishers.

Prensky, M. (2001). Digital natives, digital immigrants. *On the Horizon*, 9(5), 1–6.

Rushkoff, D. (2013). *Present shock: when everything happens now*. New York: Penguin Press.

Rushkoff, D. (March 2014). Keynote address. Media Literacy Research Symposium, Fairfield, CT.

Sholle, D., & Denski, S. (1995). Critical media literacy: Reading, remapping, rewriting. In P. McLaren, R. Hammer, D. Sholle, & S. Reilly (Eds.), *Rethinking media literacy: A critical pedagogy of representation*. New York: Peter Lang.

Silverblatt, A. (2010). Careers in media literacy. Retrieved from http://www.gmlpstl. org/careers-in-media-literacy-2010/2010/.

Thoman, E., & Jolls, T. (2003). *Literacy for the 21st century: An overview & orientation guide to media literacy education*. Center for Media Literacy. Retrieved from http://www.medialit.org/sites/default/files/mlk/01_MLKorientation.pdf.

Part V
Global

So far, we have explored the evolution of human communication and participation in the Digital Age through our relationships to self, social, local, and national constructs and realms of interconnectivity. In this fifth and final section of *Media Education for a Digital Generation*, we focus on the apex of cultural engagement in our social media ecology—the GLOBAL. Today, digital media afford us a broader networked matrix within which to participate. Our "global village," to borrow Marshall McLuhan's famous phrase, is being transformed in unprecedented ways through the deployment of digital media platforms and networks that provide economic leverage, political participation, and social transformation from the bottom up. Crowdfunding platforms like Kiva.org allow people to lend money to entrepreneurs trying to alleviate poverty in parts of the developing world; social media platforms like Twitter and Facebook allow for instant news aggregation and community formation from almost any spot on the globe; and any citizen with a mobile device is capable of providing on-the-ground reporting on virtually any topic of interest that can be accessed by viewers half a world away. Our first chapter considers how a new mobile generation of digital citizens is reshaping global notions of participation and engagement through cross-cultural connective platforms that unify local-to-global communities. Whether we examine the Arab Spring, Occupy Wall Street, or the Hong Kong Umbrella Revolution, digital media tools are being leveraged by diverse sociopolitical movements, propelling people to engage in collective action through far-reaching networks. Drawing on the power of online networks to serve as collective repositories of cultural knowledge, a new digital platform called FORTEPAN is the subject of our second chapter. By exploring how old photographs can be used by amateurs to crowdsource, catalog, and share archival photos to transform global storytelling, we learn how history can be collectively and inclusively constructed to represent public history beyond the formal structures of official sources. Next, in order to reveal the human costs of our dependence on digital technology, we turn to a provocative chapter that draws attention to the consequences of manufacturing the digital tools we have grown to depend on today. With Apple dominating the global production and sales of digital technology, we'll learn the importance of deconstructing the romanticized mainstream media narratives of this large transnational powerhouse so that we better comprehend the human labor costs of our digital devices, and the ecological impacts of our collective digital footprint. We conclude by unifying our goals for global digital media literacy curricula through the convergence of online and offline social engagements, as well as digital and linear media practices that take place through uni-, bi-, and multidirectional networks across borders. Here, we will consider what one author calls *mediaptation*: the double adaptation of the self and of media, as a pedagogical means to embrace the knowledge production and creativity of youths in the classroom, at home / lifeworld, and 'third spaces.' As all of these chapters make clear, and as our book title suggests, *Media Education for a Digital Generation* requires the development of new literacies of engagement through broader, global contexts that foster civic participation through open and inclusive means for meaningful cultural citizenship in the Digital Age.

17 The Mobile Citizen

How a Media Literate Generation is Reshaping the Global Public Sphere

Paul Mihailidis

THE EMERGING MOBILE CIVIC LANDSCAPE

Across the globe today, the emergence of readily available connective technologies has resulted in the documenting and sharing of daily life in communities of all shapes and sizes. With more mobile phones than humans on the planet, and rapidly rising Internet connectivity throughout the world, mediated platforms have fast become central prerequisites for connecting individuals, communities, and societies. Van Dijck (2013) notes the implications of such a rapid convergence of communication technologies:

> As a result of the interconnection of platforms, a new infrastructure emerged: an ecosystem of connective media with a few large and many small players. The transformation from networked communication to "platformed" sociality, and from a participatory culture to a culture of connectivity, took place in a relatively short time span of ten years (p. 5).

What Van Dijck sees as an emerging "culture of connectivity" has led to the rapid growth of personal expression, sharing, and repurposing of information in peer-to-peer spaces. The active restructuring of forms of engagement and participation in daily life are part of what Castells (2010) understands as the "rise of the networked society" where, "In a world of global flows of wealth, power, and images, the search for identity, collective or individual, ascribed or constructed, becomes the fundamental source of social meaning" (Castells, 2010, p. 3).

The modes of social meaning inherent in these new information landscapes are central to understanding the diversity of motivations driving people to engage in the information sharing process in large-scale connective networks. Sharing information to few and many has become a dominant source of meaning making (Castells, 2012), especially for young people who are growing up in ever-increasing mediated realities (Castells et al., 2006; Mihailidis, 2014). One implication of this public culture of sharing and expression is what Shumow (2014) sees as "formless collective identities" that "often operate without physical dimensions and lack clear connections to both space and place" (Shumow, 2014, p. 6).

Connective networks have often been seen as most vibrant in the context of responsive engagement to large-scale political, economic, and civic oppression—like the Arab Uprisings, the conflict in Ukraine, and Occupy Wall Street (Garrett, 2006; Mercea, 2013; Siegel, 2009; Earl et al., 2013; Thorson et al., 2013; Tufekci & Wilson, 2012). At the same time, such networks have the power to connect communities in the context of addressing everyday problems and challenges that are part of daily life. We have seen such active engagement by recent connective awareness movements for gay rights (HRC), health awareness (ALS Ice Bucket), and civic voices (Carrot Mobs, Citizeninvestor, GoFundMe). Such engagement is facilitated by connective networks, but not motivated because of them. While motivations for engaging are grounded in disputing ideas of personal aggrandizement, egocentrism, and social capital, what we do see clearly is increasing engagement by citizens in connective networks to engage in personal and public issues.

This increase has been largely enabled by the rapid growth of mobile technologies—most specifically mobile "smart" phones—in the daily lives of young people. Recent scholarship has advocated for capitalizing on the potential that mobile technologies play in the formation of digital literacies for an increasingly mobile generation (Ashley et al., 2012; Squire, 2009). This potential has been rooted in avenues of communication, collaboration, and engagement in personal and public communication (McNair, 2009; Papacharissi, 2009), which are embedded in notions of mobility, places, and connective capacities, and in notions of inclusion that "undergird social participation and buttress our sense of belonging to something that transcends the self and the clan" (Lasica, 2008, p. 1). The capacity of mobile technologies, as convergent devices offering an ecosystem of connectivity, sociality, and spreadability, calls into play their role in the facilitation of dynamic collaboration, inclusion in civic life, and the ability to coordinate and engage in new forms of civic practice, design, and participation.

This chapter will focus on the role of digital media education in facilitating the use of mobile technologies as connective platforms for engagement in daily life and more robust information and communication habits across borders and across cultures. The goal of this work will be to help position the critical constructs, competencies, and prototypes that can harness the potential for mobile technologies and connective platforms to engage with global issues to develop a sense of active engagement in daily civic life. These collectively can help position digital media literacy education as a core competency for engagement in ubiquitous twenty-first-century mobile culture.

HOW MEDIA LITERACY APPROACHES MOBILE TECHNOLOGIES

In the Introduction to *Mediated Communities: Civic Voices, Empowerment and Media Literacy in the Digital Era*, Shumow (2014) notes that "if we are going to endow power and agency to the communities and citizens that Shirky (2010) has referred to as the former audience, then we must also think about the tools they will need to survive and thrive in these new environments" (Shumow, 2014, p. 8). Increasingly, the tools that Shumow acknowledges are not simply devices, apps, or platforms, but also the critical skills, dispositions, and constructs that are embedded in the use, design, and practice of digital technologies. As I wrote in Shumow's collection, this becomes an "*active* endeavor that is applied to hands-on experiences with production, creation and expression, and not simply in a responsive context, where viewing and critiquing are central attributes of the process" (Mihailidis, 2014, p. 16).

The evolution of media literacy education as an ecosystem that supports an active and embedded approach to mobility is rooted in a development of the field over the last three or more decades. Foundational work in the media education field largely responded to a growing ubiquity of media in daily life, while at the same time, seeing a need to make distinct the notion of teaching about and with media. Scholarship in media literacy has grown since to incorporate dispositions in media effects, cultural studies, citizenship studies, pedagogies, and technology, all of which are related to how people learn about media's role in daily life and society.

More recently, media education has responded to the convergence of media platforms, the rapid evolution in social and connective technologies, and the ubiquitous presence of mobile devices around the world. At the same time, formal education systems have been hampered by a seemingly impossible mandate to keep up with the pace of technological evolution, something they have not done and will likely never be able to do (Rheingold, 2012). As a result, schools continue to chase technologies and implement systems that quickly become dated. Media education, at the same time, has expanded its reach and breadth to incorporate educational technologies alongside movements in connected learning (Ito et al., 2012), new literacies (Coiro et al., 2008; Lankshear & Knobel, 2006), critical media literacy (Alvermann & Hagood, 2000; Kellner & Share, 2005), and digital citizenship (Hobbs, 2010; Gallagher, 2013). These areas of study have at their core the willingness to understand the situated place of the learner/actor in mediated societies. They discuss a range of modalities and dispositions that are necessary to equip young people with the tools they need to effectively and inclusively engage in digital culture.

The growth of mobile technologies and their now-central place in the daily lives of young people (Bertel, 2013) is increasingly the focus of dialog about how best to prepare future generations for inclusive civic participation. Studies have shown that mobile technologies engage young people in more dynamic consumption, sharing, expression, and participation with information and communication needs (Istvan, 2011; Parry, 2011), and that increased familiarity with mobile technologies can garner a greater sense of agency with mobile technologies for more than personal or social reasons (Squire & Dikkers, 2008).

These works situate mobile technologies in different contexts and with different points of emphasis and skepticism. They embrace the access to technologies that students now see as a default part of their situated identities and experiences in daily life. I want to build from these conceptual works to highlight two specific constructs—connectivity and spreadability—that digital media education must support in the context of ubiquitous mobile adoption in daily life around the world.

CONNECTIVITY

In the context of ubiquitous mobile culture, media literacy's emphasis on *critical thinking* about media texts becomes only one part of a larger system of competencies and constructs. Media education scholars have situated the mode of critical inquiry in cultural (Buckingham, 2003), technological (Rushkoff, 2013), pedagogical (Hobbs, 1998, 2010) and effects (Postman, 1985) traditions, but these have been positioned within the frame of a relationship to and with texts. In a ubiquitous mobile culture, there is an emphasis in understanding the context of connectivity from a textual perspective but also a larger systems perspective. In her recent book, *The Culture of Connectivity*, Van Dijck (2013) highlights the mutually constitutive relationship that users "negotiate" with technological platforms to facilitate information and communication in their daily lives (Van Dijck, 2013, p. 6).

These "platforms of connectivity," Van Dijck argues, are shifting the dialog about users embedded in a "participatory culture" (Jenkins, 2006), to a connective culture where, "sociality coded by technology renders people's activities formal, manageable, and manipulable, enabling platforms to engineer the sociality in people's everyday routines" (Jenkins, 2006, p. 13). In this connective culture, digital media literacy becomes not only about critical inquiry, expression, and dialog, but also about systems, modalities, and designed sociality, where "the choice for a 'like' button betrays an ideological predilection: it favors instant, gut-fired, emotional, positive evaluations. Popularity not only becomes quantifiable but also manipulable: boosting popularity rankings is an important mechanism built into these buttons" (Van Dijck, 2013, p. 13).

Connective culture is further embedded in what Turkle (2008) refers to as a "tethered" generation who use technology as an act of self-establishment, where young people facilitate a sense of self-worth through consistently reaffirming their sense of popularity, place, and belonging online. Nicholas Carr, in *The Shallows* (2009), supports the notion of tethering when he writes, "teens and other young adults have a terrific interest in knowing what's going on in the lives of their peers, couple with a terrific anxiety about being out of the loop ... if they stop sending messages, they risk being invisible" (Carr, 2009, p. 118). Carr asserts that youth trade off their concentration, attention, and focus for a wealth of information that is diverting, short lived, and socially compelling. This shift signifies a need to be consistently visible (Goggin, 2009), which, in turn has been linked to the growing attachment to mobile technologies (Wei & Lo, 2006; Goh et al., 2009).

The emerging connective culture that has been perpetuated by mobile technologies brings great opportunity and challenge to how we prepare young people for lives of inclusive and active engagement in daily life. The work of Jenkins et al. (2009) provides an attempt to situate a new framework for media literacies that are inclusive of digital realities today. Anchored by participation and engagement, the set of skills, from play, performance, and appropriation, to multitasking, judgment, and networking, help facilitate a set of skills for educators to focus on in the context of convergence. Nevertheless, how such literacies are activated in the context of a connected, global culture, will dictate their value to media literacy education as it evolves in a digital context.

SPREADABILITY

Alongside the phenomenon of connective culture is the inherent use of new mobile tools and platforms to "spread" information. Not only do social networks and platforms allow individuals to participate and connect in new and dynamic ways, mobile technologies are also designed to facilitate the spread of information, which is partly the glue that connects communities of interest across the world. As a result, spreadable content has theoretically equalized the potential reach of content from citizens compared to traditional media institutions. In their book *Spreadable Media,* Jenkins, Ford, and Green (2013) understand the concept of spreadability as "the technical resources that make it easier to circulate some kinds of content than others, the economic structures that support or restrict circulation, the attributes of a media text that might appeal to a community's motivation for sharing material, and the social networks that link people through the exchange of meaningful bytes" (Jenkins, Ford, & Green, 2013, p. 4). The landscape that has emerged is one where citizens "count on each other to pass along compelling bits of news, information, and entertainment, often many times over the course of a given day" (Jenkins, Ford, & Green, 2013, p. 13).

What affordances does a spreadable culture allow for digital media literacy? First, it places an emphasis on the role of the public thinker, who creates and shares content with an audience in mind. Clive Thompson, in *Smarter Than You Think* (2013), argues that this mode of thought creates stronger content and a heightened sense of responsibility by authors. Second, the sheer amount of writing and publishing has increased exponentially in a spreadable environment. If we look at large scale global events, like Occupy Wall Street, the Arab Uprisings, or the most recent umbrella protests in Hong Kong, they all began in local contexts, and quickly scaled to national and global levels. This is largely facilitated first by the spread of information from diverse online communities. Third, with the borders of information disintegrating, there is an opportunity, or responsibility, to cultivate what Ethan Zuckerman (2013) understands as a sense of "digital cosmopolitanism" in which he states, "With a fraction of the brainpower that's gone into building the Internet as we know it, we can build a network that helps us discover, understand, and embrace a wider world" (Zuckerman, 2013, p. 9). This sense of cosmopolitanism is a call for a citizenry that is not only skilled in critical engagement with media texts, but also with the capability to extend their online engagement into spaces that transcend cultures and borders.

Media education embraces spreadable media at the point of what Jenkins, Ford, and Green (2013) see as a reengagement with the core human value of storytelling: "Perhaps nothing is more human than sharing stories, whether by fire or by 'cloud' (so to speak). We must all be careful not to suppose that a more participatory means of circulation can be explained solely (or even primarily) by this rise of technological infrastructure" (Jenkins, Ford, & Green, 2013, p. 3). Individuals, and not technologies, are at the heart of this spreadable culture. It is how they perceive their expression and contribution that will dictate the value of these spaces for expression, sharing, collaboration and participation in global culture. The task of preparing individuals for such information and communication infrastructures is at the heart of digital media education in mobile culture.

THE MOBILE CITIZEN: TOWARDS A MEDIA LITERATE ECOSYSTEM FOR ENGAGEMENT IN THE GLOBAL CULTURE

The concepts of connectivity and spreadability are meant to set a constructive context for approaching digital media education as a mechanism to move beyond the primary focus on texts, to a more situated space for practices, modalities, and critical competencies that facilitate the inclusive engagement and participation in global civic life. These constructs are not new, nor are they foreign to the media education field. Rather, to prepare future generations for lives of engagement and civic good, digital media literacy education must extrapolate from a focus on the individual situated in media texts, and towards the actor embedded in a mediated ecosystem of civic life. Only then will the affordances of technologies be understood in more holistic and purposeful ways for daily life, and not reserved for civic dialog in response to oppression, injustice, or marginalization.

Educators, parents, policy makers, and community stakeholders must embrace the connective and spreadable nature of mobile technologies to better harness their potential. This necessarily involves critical media literacy skills of analysis, evaluation, and comprehension and creation, but also those of design, participation, remix, cultural appropriation, engagement in diversity, listening, and cross-cultural exploration. An array of skills and critical constructs that engage at their core with the concepts laid out in this chapter.

This chapter sets some theoretical boundaries for understanding the role of connective and spreadable technologies as they approach media education. Its intention is to provide a baseline for discussion of how media education transcends boundaries, cultures, and divides in both formal and informal education settings. With a more expansive and inclusive global approach to media education, the field may embrace more integrated and viable approaches to participation in digital culture. This will rely on a willingness to engage and embrace the platforms, spaces, and technologies that have increasingly facilitated cross-cultural dialog, engagement, and activity in the global public sphere. As Rheingold notes at the onset of *Net Smart* (2012): "The future of digital culture—yours, mine, ours—depends on how well we learn to use the media that have infiltrated, amplified, distracted, enriched, and complicated our lives" (Rheingold, 2012, p. 1).

REFERENCES

Alvermann, D. E., & Hagood, M. C. (2000). Critical media literacy: Research, theory, and practice in "new times." *The Journal of Educational Research*, 93(3), 193–205.

Ashley, S., Lyden, G., & Fasbinder, D. (2012). Exploring message meaning: A qualitative media literacy study of college freshmen. *The Journal of Media Literacy Education*, 4(3), 229–243.

Bertel, T. F. (2013). "It's like I trust it so much that I don't really check where it is I'm going before I leave": Informational uses of smartphones among Danish youth. *Mobile Media and Communication*, 1(3), 1–15.

Buckingham, D. (2003). *Media education: Literacy, learning and contemporary culture*. Cambridge, UK: Polity Press.

Carr, N. (2009). *The shallows: What the Internet is doing to our brains*. New York: W. W. Norton and Company.

Castells, M. (2010). *End of millennium: The information age: Economy, society, and culture*, Vol. 3. John Wiley & Sons.

Castells, M. (2012). *Networks of outrage and hope: Social movements in the Internet age*. Cambridge, UK: Polity Press.

Castells, M., Qiu, J. L., & Fernandez-Ardevol, M. (2006). *Mobile communication and society: A global perspective*. Cambridge, MA: MIT Press.

Coiro, J., Knobel, M., Lankshear, C., & Leu, D. J. (2008). *The Handbook of research on new literacies*. New York: Routledge.

Earl, J., Hurwitz, H. M., Mesinas, A. M., Tolan, M., & Arlotti, A. (2013). This protest will be tweeted. *Information, Communication, and Society*, 16(4), 459–478.

Gallagher, F. (2013). Media literacy education: A requirement for today's digital citizens. In B. De Abreu & P. Mihailidis (Eds), *Media literacy education in action: Theoretical and pedagogical perspectives* (pp. 173–183). New York: Routledge.

Garrett, R. K. (2006). Protest in an information society: A review of literature on social movements and new ICTs. *Information Communication and Society*, 9(2), 202–224.

Goggin, G. (2009). Adapting the mobile phone: The iPhone and its consumption. *Continuum: Journal of Media and Cultural Studies, 23*(2), 231–244.

Goh, D., Ang, R., Chua, A., & Lee, C. (2009). Why we share: A study of motivations for mobile media sharing. *Lecture Notes in Computer Science, 5820,* 195–206.

Hobbs, R. (1998). The seven great debates in the media literacy movement. *Journal of Communication, 48*(1), 6–32.

Hobbs, R. (2010). *Digital and media literacy: A plan of action.* A white paper on the digital and media literacy recommendations of the Knight Commission on the information needs of communities in a democracy. Washington DC: The Aspen Institute.

Istvan, S. (2011). The media and the literacies: Media literacy, information literacy, digital literacy. *Media Culture & Society, 33*(2), 211–221.

Ito, M., Gutiérrez, K., Livingston, S., Penuel, B., Rhodes, J., Salen, K., Schor, J., Sefton-Green, J., & Watkins, S.C. (2012). *Connected learning: An agenda for research and design.* A research synthesis report of the Connected Learning Research Network http://dmlhub. net/sites/default/files/ConnectedLearning_summary_0.pdf.

Jenkins, H. (2006). *Convergence culture: Where old and new media collide.* New York: NYU Press.

Jenkins, H., Purushotma, R., Weigel, M., Clinton, K., & Robinson, A. J. (2009). Confronting the challenges of participatory culture: Media education for the 21st century. *A Report for the MacArthur Foundation.* Cambridge, MA: MIT Press.

Jenkins, H., Ford, S., & Green, J. (2013). *Spreadable media: Creating value and meaning in a networked culture.* New York: New York University Press.

Kellner, D., & Share, J. (2005). Towards critical media literacy: Core concepts, debates, organizations, and policy. *Discourse: Studies in the Cultural Politics of Education, 26*(3), 369–386.

Lankshear, C., & Knobel, M. (2006). *New literacies: Changing knowledge in the classroom.* London: Open University Press.

Lasica, J. D. (2008). *Civic engagement on the move: How mobile media can serve the public good.* Washington DC: The Aspen Institute.

McNair, B. (2009). The Internet and the changing global media environment. In A. Chadwick & P. Howard (Eds.), *The Routledge handbook of Internet politics* (pp. 217–229). New York, NY: Routledge.

Mercea, D. (2013). Probing the implications of Facebook use for the organizational form of social movement organizations. *Information Communication and Society, 16*(8), 1306–1327.

Mihailidis, P. (2014). *Media literacy and the emerging citizen: Youth, engagement and participation in digital culture.* New York: Peter Lang.

Papacharissi, Z. (2009). The virtual sphere 2.0: The Internet, the public sphere, and beyond. In A. Chadwick & P. Howard (Eds.), *The Routledge handbook of Internet politics* (pp. 230–245). New York: Routledge.

Parry, D. (2011). Mobile perspectives: On teaching mobile literacy. *EDUCAUSE Review, 46*(2), 14–16.

Postman, N. (1985). *Amusing ourselves to death: Public discourse in the age of show business.* New York: Penguin.

Rheingold, H. (2012). *Net smart: How to thrive online.* Cambridge, MA: MIT Press.

Rushkoff, D. (2013). *Present shock: When everything happens now.* New York: Penguin.

Shirky, C. (2010). *Cognitive surplus: How technology makes consumers into collaborators.* New York: Penguin.

Shumow, M. (Ed.). (2014). *Mediated communities: Civic voices, empowerment and media literacy in the digital era.* New York: Peter Lang.

Siegel, D. A. (2009). Social networks and collective action. *American Journal of Political Science, 53*(1), 122–138.

Squire, K. (2009). Mobile media learning: Multiplicities of place. *On the Horizon, 17*(1), 70–80.

Squire, K., & Dikkers, S. (2008). Amplifications of learning: Use of mobile media devices among youth. *Convergence: The International Journal of Research into New Media Technologies, 18*(4), 445–464.

Thompson, C. (2013) *Smarter than you think: How technology is changing our minds for the better.* NY: Penguin.

Thorson, K., Driscoll, K., Ekdale, B., Edgerly, S., Gamber Thompson, L., Schrock, L., … Wells, C. (2013). YouTube, twitter and the occupy movement. *Information, Communication and Society, 16*(3), 421–451.

Tufekci, Z., & Wilson, C. (2012). Social media and the decision to participate in political protest: Observations from Tahrir Square. *Journal of Communication, 62*(2), 363–379.

Turkle, S. (2008). "Always on/always on you: The tethered self." In J. Katz (Ed.),*Handbook of mobile communication and social change* (pp. 1–21). Cambridge, MA: MIT Press.

Van Dijck, J. (2013). *The Culture of connectivity: A critical history of social media.* Oxford, UK: Oxford University Press.

Wei, R., & Lo, V. H. (2006). Staying connected while on the move: Cell phone use and social connectedness. *New Media Society, 8*(1), 53–72.

Zuckerman, E. (2013). *Rewire: Digital cosmpolitans in the age of connection.* New York: W.W. Norton.

18 Digital Literacy, Public History, and FORTEPAN

Bettina Fabos, Leisl Carr Childers, and Sergey Golitsynskiy

As the very title of this book suggests, we are awash with new technology and digital content, and the result is a number of new literacies that are changing the face of education and the way young people learn. Consequently, there is a growing consensus in our educational discourse that our society demands an increase in "digility" (a word we coined within our Interactive Digital Studies program at the University of Northern Iowa), which means an extreme agility with digital technology to innovate, create, plan, and produce digital experiences of all types.

This chapter details our experience in building a vast online collection of curated amateur photographs and the myriad ways we are incorporating the ever-expanding photographic collection into our teaching. First we briefly describe the development of FORTEPAN IOWA. Then we explain how each one of us—a visual communication scholar, a public history scholar, a digital photographer/conceptual artist, and an interactive digital studies web development scholar—are using FORTEPAN IOWA to bring innovative twenty-first century learning practices into our own classrooms. Next, we illustrate numerous best practices for incorporating FORTEPAN IOWA (and any subsequent sister sites) into school curriculums. In conclusion, we illustrate how bringing FORTEPAN IOWA into the teaching of public history can transform the way Iowans (and Iowa's schoolkids) construct our past—collectively, rather than through a top-down dictate of official sources that focus unilaterally on famous people.

BUILDING FORTEPAN IOWA

FORTEPAN started as a single photo archive based in Hungary—the brainchild of two Hungarians committed to public archiving and the beauty and merit of amateur photos. Miklós Tamási and András Szepessy developed an online photo archive of amateur photos of Hungarian life, 1900–1990, that they had been collecting for the past 20 years. Some of the photos came from friends' personal collections, others they found in trash bins or in attics. They arranged the photographs in chronological order, uploaded them at extremely high resolution, and assigned them a Creative Commons license, so anyone doing a noncommercial project could download and use them as they wished.

Figure 18.1 Screenshot of FORTEPAN interface, fortepan.hu.

Today, this photo chronology, called "FORTEPAN," contains more than 40,000 photos and enjoys 180,000 visitors a day. To visit Hungary's FORTEPAN is to glide through twentieth-century Hungarian life and see the character of a nation—in all of its diversity—unfolding across time. The site is brilliant in its ability to convey history so lyrically and so easily: We see an extraordinary country in the 1900s—with all the promise brought by modernization, high literacy rates, and democratic awakenings (such as images of women's suffrage movement). Then we see Hungary getting pummeled by a first, then a second world war—with especially harrowing photographs of a destroyed Budapest in 1945. We see Hungary succumbing to Communist repression and a new landscape of colorless, industrial state farms and rally after official rally. Throughout a century of photographs, we see Hungarians adapting to every new way of life with humor, sometimes dismay, and even sadness—all of this is conveyed through the moments of private everyday snapshots.

Tamási and Szepessy named their archive after a defunct Hungarian company called FORTE, which made and sold the black and white "FORTEPAN" negative film between 1921 and 2001; today the website is an homage to all the amateur photographers who bought FORTEPAN film and with it took pictures of their homes, their lives, and their surroundings. Tamási, who now curates the archive out of his office at the Open Society Archive in Budapest, no longer has to look in attics for images to upload: he has shelves full of glass slides, negatives, and prints donated for him to sort through and digitize. With 180,000 visitors a day (from all over the world), the website has become another one of Hungary's cultural destinations, and, like a public park, it exists for people's various pleasures: to find people or places they may know; to compare streetscapes from an earlier period to the modern streetscapes of today; to download images for personal use (print out and hang on their wall) or for creative digital projects. FORTEPAN simply urges users to "use" the site at their leisure, reflect on the past, and enjoy.

The FORTEPAN website has three significant features for anyone interested in new digital twenty-first century media education. First, the 40,000+ photos are searchable through a sliding interactive timeline. Because they are arranged *chronologically*, the photos are given immediate historical context, and take a visitor, image by image, through the rich and complicated story of Hungarian nationalism, identity, and culture. Second, every photo within the FORTEPAN archive is *generated by amateurs*. Thus, the images tell the story of Hungary from the bottom up, revealing an unofficial and extremely diverse representation of this small country. There are plenty of "official" histories of Hungary. To see the various decades through the eyes of amateur photographers is to gain a valuable perspective that is far more diverse and interesting than any history one might read in a book. Third, every FORTEPAN image can be *instantly downloaded at an extremely high resolution* (in the range of 3000–4000 pixels), and licensed with a Creative Commons Attribution-ShareAlike 4.0 International Public license. This means that anyone, including teachers and their students, can incorporate the archive's high-resolution photographs (as many as they wish) into their creative digital projects without fear of copyright violation.

We have expanded on the FORTEPAN concept by creating FORTEPAN's first sister site: FORTEPAN IOWA. Behind this U.S. initiative are four professors at the University of Northern Iowa: Bettina Fabos (Interactive Digital Studies/Visual Communication); Sergey Golitsynskiy (Interactive Digital Studies/Web Development); Leisl Carr Childers (Public History), and Noah Doely (Digital Photography). All of us come from different disciplines, are impressed by FORTEPAN's mission and simple chronological interface, and see "FORTEPAN" for the state of Iowa is an invaluable public project—for our state, for our university, and for Iowa's schools.

We were able to implement a system with identical look and feel and an interface similar to the original FORTEPAN by late 2014. The system, built using the Python programming language and the Django framework (Django, 2014), introduces a more comprehensive set of searching and browsing features to the front end, making the archive contents more accessible. We have also added functionality that enables our users to personalize their experience by tagging photos, organizing them into their own photo sets, and sharing them through social media. In addition to photos, the content of the archive now includes oral history (audio) components, with plans for a geographical positioning component displaying the location of the photos on a map. The administrative site enables the archive maintainers to easily manage the archive's content. By keeping the logo, as well as the overall visual aspects of the website unchanged, and by linking to the original

FORTEPAN, we moved one step closer towards building an interlinked brand of public photo archives that we hope to turn into larger movement.

As such, we are working with the original FORTEPAN creators to create a sharable toolkit documenting how to identify and work with donors; how to include the source code of the FORTEPAN IOWA web application with documentation of its code, installation, and configuration; how to digitize, curate, and tag archival photos; how to train volunteers and students (who help digitize and enter data); and how to incorporate the archive into University and K-12 curricula, museums, and public life. Our main goal will ultimately be to disseminate the FORTEPAN public archive concept and nonprofit brand across other U.S. states and to other countries around the world. In making FORTEPAN IOWA as successful as the original Hungarian FORTEPAN (which has 180,000 hits daily), we can easily envision the power of multiple FORTEPAN sites, and the impact of a FORTEPAN movement in preserving valuable public memories and bringing them into our public discourse.

INCORPORATING FORTEPAN IOWA IN OUR COLLEGE CLASSES

FORTEPAN IOWA has become an intrinsic part of our college-level classroom instruction at the University of Northern Iowa (UNI). Two of us, Bettina and Leisl, involve our students in *building the archive*, and incorporate FORTEPAN IOWA in units devoted to public archiving in a digital age—one from the angle of copyright and Internet commercialization, the other from the perspective of public history. Bettina and Sergey incorporate FORTEPAN IOWA in a core digital media production class, using images from the archive as a tool for learning Photoshop and working with extremely high-resolution photographs. Sergey also uses FORTEPAN IOWA to teach a variety of web development skills. Below is a discussion of each of our classes in detail.

Digital Culture and Communication: Bettina Fabos

In 2012, UNI's Department of Communication Studies launched a new interdisciplinary program called Interactive Digital Studies (IDS). The program responded to our students' growing need to understand the demands of our digital age, and we developed a customizable curriculum with emphases in digital advertising, visualization, coding, learning, music, imaging, writing, and media and social change, geo-visualization, entrepreneurship, and public history. Each emphasis (we call them "bundles") can be combined to fit a student's interests and needs. Two bundles make a major, one bundle makes a minor, and all IDS students (both majors and minors) are required to take four foundation courses that ground them in the production skills (e.g., Adobe Creative Suite, CSS, and HTML), culture, code, and the historical context of our digital age. Three of these four foundation courses draw heavily on FORTEPAN IOWA as a teaching tool. One of these is the Digital Culture and Communication course, which, like Oral History (described below), involves students building upon the image base of the FORTEPAN IOWA archive.

Our objectives for the Digital Culture and Communication course are to get our IDS students to understand the critical debates that are defining our digital culture. Beyond privacy and surveillance (two important topics), many of these debates involve the battle over who gets to "own" the Internet (commercial vs. public interests), so we teach our students about a wide variety of digital literacy themes: copyright law, the ever-increasing dominance of Google, Microsoft, Apple, Amazon, and Facebook, remix culture, public archives, the Creative Commons, Fair Use, the public domain, and what it means to be a digital citizen. We also ask our students to apply theory to practice by participating in digital culture. For example, students are required to (illegally) download videos from YouTube, edit them into a remixed cultural commentary or critique, and then upload their video creations back to YouTube. The learning moment comes when students receive "take down notices" from Google/YouTube because their pieces—as creative and critically smart as they often are—are in violation of copyright law:

> "Attention: We have received copyright complaint(s) regarding material you posted ... Please note: **Accounts determined to be repeat infringers will be terminated.** Please delete any videos for which you do not own the necessary rights, and refrain from uploading infringing videos."

Today is an era in which regular people, for the first time, have the power to distribute creative work globally via the Internet. It is also an era of digital rights management (DRM), in which copyright holders (usually large corporations) attempt to control the creative work (known as "intellectual property") accessible on the Internet. Take down notices are common occurrences, as we—regular citizens—try to communicate in a world in which public discourse is no longer just spoken or written, but circulates in many forms in a converged online environment. As regular citizens participate in this digital environment, they are testing the boundaries of outdated copyright laws and the limitations of free expression as corporations assert the rights of their intellectual property. For us (who teach about copyright), these takedown notices, however alarming for our students, are a means for discussing the contested terrain of the Internet, dominated as it is by enormous corporations.

We assign the FORTAPAN IOWA PROJECT as a refreshing antidote to the "illegal" remix project because it involves building a digital environment by the public and for the public good. Students in our Digital Culture and Communication class actually locate and digitize many of the photographs uploaded to FORTEPAN IOWA and in doing so, learn why a digital archive such as FORTEPAN IOWA is such a departure from most of the photo offerings (e.g., Google Images) available online. Since the bulk of UNI students come from Iowa, our institution is unique among Iowa's three Regent institutions (i.e., University of Iowa, Iowa State, and UNI) in that we can count on our students to have Iowa family members, and thus Iowa-based photographs that they can (upon family permission) digitize and donate to the archive. For this project, we ask our UNI students to go home, scour through their own family's photo collections, and bring back images for scanning. We give them white cotton gloves and a binder with 30 archival plastic sleeves, and ask them to bring back a minimum of 30 photographs. We also ask them to look out for old negatives or glass slides (these are especially valuable for us because they offer the best digital resolution, and are often first items families throw away), and we ask them to become archive curators as they look through their family photos and tease out those photos that would be best for FORTEPAN IOWA. Here is what we tell them:

> You will be helping us curate the overall collection. Photographs will be chosen to be part of the archive based on their **unique lens into the everyday world of Iowa citizens.** You will likely find a lot of family portraits. Some of these will be interesting for the archive, but too many family portraits will make the archive boring. We are looking for photos with action; that capture a certain public space; that tell a story. We are looking for photos that are perhaps tragic, or funny, or are part of a cultural moment. **We are looking for images with "punctum."**

Punctum, we explain, is a term Roland Barthes used in his famous work, *Camera Lucida*, when referring to a part of a photograph that "pierces the viewer" (Barthes, 1981).

Figure 18.2 A photograph selected for its "punctum" for FORTEPAN IOWA: Carol Mountain, Debbie Robeson, Myrna and Scott Hottle Collection, 1918.

An image with punctum, for example, is this barnyard; notice how one of the horses—the white one, second from the right—seems to be glowing, as if it has special powers.

Figure 18.3 A photograph from FORTEPAN IOWA: Kaye Buch Collection, 1955.

Another example of punctum is found in this photo of a boy and his mother with a little fawn. It takes a minute to realize that the fawn is dead and that the boy is proud because he found it (dead), peeled it off the ground, and posed for this photo.

Besides securing images for digitization, students also have to gain permission from their family members, so they have to explain to their relatives why FORTEPAN IOWA is important, and why their photos are a potentially significant contribution to Iowa identity and culture. Our students know that if their relatives don't want their photographs made public, that is okay; we can help them find other collections to digitize. What is remarkable and heartwarming, however, is that most relatives are thrilled to be a part of this large public project. Moreover, our students often have some of the most memorable conversations they have ever had with their grandparents or even parents as they ask them to tell the stories behind particular photographs. Most significantly, the breadth and depth of the photographs our students are finding—all of which would be lost to the public record—is extraordinary.

Once our students secure their 30+ photos, they learn proper scanning techniques; the proper ways to handle their photographs or negatives; the value of high pixel counts; the differences between TIFF, JPG, GIF, and PNG files; and uniform file-saving and file documentation strategies. Finally, we teach our students documentation skills: once images are digitized, they prepare a table with file names, dates, names, and places carefully documented. All of these data are inputted into the archive and because this is a public project of real consequence, our students are mindful to be as accurate as possible. For additional spins on building the FORTEPAN IOWA Project, Leisl explains in the next section how her students follow similar procedures, but also incorporate an oral history component.

Oral History: Leisl Carr-Childers

FORTEPAN IOWA is at its core a public history project. As a collection of amateur photographs arranged in a visual chronology, it emphasizes change over time, visually capturing and curating how Iowa and the people that lived there once looked. The images, chosen for their piercing, lyrical quality, individually reveal valuable and diverse aspects of family life, place, and community. These details, which provide the context for the images, are captured both visually in the images themselves and through the descriptive information archived with each photograph. The oral history interviews conducted with some of the donors deepen this context by providing the remembrances behind select images. Analyzing and contextualizing sources, such as photographs, and interpreting them for the ways in which cultures, communities, and individuals have changed over time is really the essence of historians' work (Andrews & Burke, 2007). Public historians take this methodology one step further by endeavoring to put those sources and interpretations to work in the world (NCPH, 2014).

Utilizing students in constructing FORTEPAN IOWA involves training them in the standard practices of public history, particularly in archival procedures and oral history. To this end, the Oral History course, a class cross-listed with the Communications Studies and History departments, creates a replicable framework for successive cohorts of students to learn these practices. In the course, students learn how to handle physical photographs and accurately document the dates, places, and people featured in the images. Students are given plastic sleeves to house the photographs and white cotton gloves to prevent the transfer of skin oils to their surfaces while scanning. They are also taught to be conscious of the edges of the photographs and any areas that are already damaged on the images to prevent further degradation. Most importantly, they are taught to catalogue each image according to the protocol established for the project. This includes providing each digital image they generate with a file name, a title, and a detailed description of the people and places featured in each.

This is a highly critical aspect of their training and a fundamental part of engaging in archival work. Historians are trained to locate sources like photographs in space and time—where an image was taken, who is in the image and who took it, and when it was taken must be documented as accurately as possible. Further descriptive details that offer information as to why a photograph was produced and the relationship between the different people in the image is also important. For example, the image below reveals only cursory visual clues as to its actual historical context. A young man dressed in white, skis crossed after what might have been a comical fall, smiles for the camera while one raised gloved hand clutches a ski pole. Who is he? Where is he skiing? What has prompted that boyish smile? Without this information, even with keen visual culture analysis, his location, identity, and purpose remain a mystery.

Figure 18.4 Vernon Nieman skiing in the Bavarian Alps while serving in the military during the Korean Conflict. FORTEPAN IOWA: Carol Eilderts Collection.

Consider then, his name is Vernon Nieman, the year is 1952, he is a soldier during the Korean War, and he is skiing in the Bavarian Alps. Armed with this information, much more can be gleaned from the photograph. He smiles at the camera because he is skiing and because he is not, at the moment, stationed in Korea where the United States military is locked in a deadly stalemate with Chinese and North Korean Communist forces. This was the beginning of the Cold War and a tense time for the nation's military. The Soviet Union, the purported supporter of the northern forces on the Korean peninsula, only a few years before had developed their first atomic weapon, breaking the monopoly on atomic power held by the United States since 1945. The United States saw the conflict in Korea as the first standoff between the two nascent nuclear powers. But Nieman is not in Korea in this image engaged in a firefight with Communist forces, though he likely was or would be, instead he is in Germany skiing.

Beyond the historical context is another layer of information provided by an interview with his daughter, Carol Eilderts, the donor of the photograph. Oral history interviews are tremendously powerful historical sources because they move beyond the data associated with the photograph to the stories behind them. They capture and preserve the voices and memories of ordinary persons, those who are often invisible in the formal historical record (Oral History Assocation, 2012). In the interview, the details of Vernon Nieman's stint in the military are fleshed out (Eilderts, 2014). Nieman never discussed much about his military service from 1952 to 1953 during the Korean War. Drafted in his mid-twenties, the military took him away from his work at his father's farm and stationed him in Germany during the conflict. He never discussed his time in the service with his family after he returned, keeping only a handful of images chronicling his time overseas that his family found after his death. According to his daughter, Nieman never used the word "drafted" to describe his conscription—rather he only mentioned that he was "chosen." He also never traveled after returning to the United States and starting a family. His reluctance to share his experiences during the war and travel to new climes afterward belies the smile that appears on his face in the photograph. Taken in the context of war and before the ramifications of the violence it set in, the image of Vernon Nieman smiling, collapsed onto the snow with skis askew, is that much more poignant.

The oral history interview with Carol Eilderts, in which she discusses her parents, her growing up on a farm in Iowa, and the family traditions she cherishes, narrate the photographs she donated to FORTEPAN IOWA. The interviewer, Carrie Eilderts, was her daughter and a student in the Oral History course. Besides archival work, students in the class learn the best practices of oral history, including proper interviewing techniques, transcription protocols, and editing procedures. They also undergo human subject research training through the university's Institutional Review Board (IRB) and receive their IRB certification. Along with collecting photographs, students in the class interview the donor, using the images as a way into conversations about the stories captured in the snapshots. Through the Oral History course, students build the connections between the visual qualities of the photographs and the historical context in which they were taken. They learn to interpret the images using both visual and material culture.

The course is part of the larger Public History program, an undergraduate and graduate sequence of five classes that provide students intensive training in historical inquiry and in related interdisciplinary skills such as archival work, oral history, material and visual culture. After completing an introductory course in public history, students participate in two internships—one project-based and one individual—and complete their two interdisciplinary classes. These courses fit neatly within the Interactive Digital Studies (IDS) program as a bundle that emphasizes the nascent field of digital history, which uses new media, such as software systems and the Internet, to examine and represent the past (Seefeldt & Thomas, 2009). When digital history is produced for general consumption, it becomes public history. By partnering with Communication Studies in FORTEPAN IOWA, students in the Public History program can expand their training to include digital history. Likewise, students in the IDS program can receive instruction in public history.

Interactive Digital Communication: Bettina Fabos and Sergey Golitsynskiy

Like the Digital Culture and Communication (DCC) class described above, Interactive Digital Communication is one of the four core requirements for our IDS program. It is a skills, production, and theory class where students learn the basic technological requirements behind the Internet/World Wide Web, principles of graphic and web design, intensive Photoshop skills, HTML and CSS coding competencies, and the ins and outs of WordPress customization (which is where they are able to apply their HTML and CSS skills).

When we are teaching our students Photoshop skills, we emphasize working with the highest quality images possible (pixel and file size become a constant conversation). Their first assignment is a multilayered photomontage, where our students practice selecting images from their backgrounds and positioning these selections in a way that is rhetorically meaningful. Working against our students' first impulse to find images via Google search, we require our students to build copyright-free photomontages and teach them about copyright and digital citizenship. We introduce them, accordingly, to the WikiCommons, to the copyright-free collections in the Library of Congress, to the Creative Commons, and of course, to FORTEPAN IOWA.

If our students take this class *after* they take the Digital Culture and Communication class, they are already very familiar with FORTEPAN IOWA and might even choose to work with their own family photos. And if they take this class before DCC, they will understand the value—from the standpoint of creativity and image production—of high-resolution photographs that are in the Creative Commons. The fact that the photographs all come from Iowa—a topic most of my students can relate to deeply, and can be excited by—brings them to a full appreciation of what we are trying to accomplish in terms of public memory and Iowa identity at UNI.

Code and Communication: Sergey Golitsynskiy

The Code and Communication class is one of the four requirements for the IDS program. It is designed to help non–computer science majors learn the computational approach to problem solving in the context of communication systems, processes and tools, and understand the practical uses of code as a critical element of twenty-first century communication. Specifically, its goal is to teach IDS students a set of basic practical skills and concepts that have traditionally been associated with the computer science degree—programming and database design in the context of web development.

The course is centered on a semester-long project through which students learn fundamental web development concepts and obtain skills in client-side coding (i.e., web page markup), basic server-side coding, and simple database design. Selecting an appropriate project can be a challenge: it needs a context that is meaningful to students and is culturally significant; it also must possess a set of characteristics and technical requirements that justify the development of a data-driven website, yet are simple enough to implement by a novice.

FORTEPAN IOWA is the perfect context for such a project—both as a real world system used to study the process of web development, and as a web application to develop in class. On the one hand, its design is simple enough to be understood by students without a technical background. On the other hand, it comes with a rich and large enough data set that justifies the use of a database (one should not write a thousand web pages to display a thousand photos!), yet requires very little code to make it functional—which makes it ideal for a student assignment. Thus, with FORTEPAN IOWA, students get to learn how a real web application functions, as well as practice their new coding skills by designing a database to hold records of historical photos, designing web page templates to display those photos, and write basic server-side code to connect their web page template to the backend database—thus getting to build their very first data-driven website.

INCORPORATING FORTEPAN IOWA IN
IOWA PUBLIC SCHOOLS

So how best to incorporate FORTEPAN IOWA in the public schools? Our FORTEPAN IOWA team at UNI is developing learning modules to help students as young as kindergarten engage with the archive, and in so doing, become adept with digital design and storytelling. It goes without saying that because FORTEPAN IOWA gives our students immediate access to extremely compelling high-resolution images, any of which can be easily downloaded without fear of copyright infringement, the archive liberates any student's digital creativity. For example, students can easily use Photoshop or the free open source equivalent, Gimp, to isolate elements from different photos and animate them across a frame.

FORTEPAN IOWA and its publicly available, high resolution photographs is indeed a gift for any creative Iowa student wanting to simply experiment with new photo manipulation or animation skills. With this in mind, there is tremendous potential to impact various literacy practices by teaching digital media to young people.

First, any work towards narrative construction, no matter what form (words, audio, graphic design, video) helps to promote *traditional* literacy since language construction has much in common with assembling elements on a screen or in a frame (whether the elements are moving or not)

Figure 18.5 A student photomontage drawing upon images from FORTEPAN
     IOWA. Credit: Travis Tjelmeland.

(a)   (b)

(c)

Figure 18.6 a, b, c Inspiring creativity with high quality, downloadable archival
     photographs. This collage is based on FORTEPAN IOWA images.

(Fabos, 2013). By challenging students to understand the language of framing (e.g., high angle vs. low angle, the rule of thirds), the aesthetics of jux-
taposition, the impact of color choices, and the power of movement—is
to teach visual literacy—necessary skills in our increasingly image-driven
culture. Digital media projects also challenge students to think about

representation (media literacy): Why are certain representations stereotypical? Why are minorities represented in such a narrow way? How do power relations play out in the representations? And finally, digital media projects, if taught correctly, can help young people develop critical literacy: the ability to identify alternative, competing narratives that critically evaluate mainstream media representations.

Since the 1970s and 1980s it has been commonly advanced that schooling is a political activity. With these notions came an expanded conception of literacy—critical literacy—that positions all discourse within a political, economic, and social framework (Berlin, 1993; Lankshear & McClaren, 1993). Texts are understood as containing a political perspective and inhabiting a particular place on the political spectrum. Unlike traditional literacy practices, where an apolitical canon is advanced and students are expected to master and imitate these canonical texts, there is no canon in critical literacy. Students are not encouraged, as is common practice, to seek out the various "truths" within a canonical text. Instead, critical literacy students "attain perspective on perspectives" (Lankshear & McClaren, 1993, p. 33). They are taught to understand the relationships between texts, the ideological underpinnings of texts, the struggle behind texts, and all information within a broader cultural context.

We see FORTEPAN IOWA as an unparalleled resource for teaching Iowa history and culture from a critical literacy perspective. We are currently working to assist K-12 teachers in training students in methods commensurate with the best educational practices. Beginning in 2010, Iowa adopted the educational recommendations, called the Common Core, developed by a consortium of states designed to improve students' critical thinking skills and problem solving performance in preparation for introductory careers, further academic training, and workforce training programs. Importantly, these standards include training students to conduct research and make evidence-based arguments (Iowa Department of Education, n.d.).

In the discipline of history, this requires students to learn how to think historically and treat primary sources, the ephemera that provide historians a glimpse of the past. At each grade level, students are exposed to these sources in varying degrees. For example, in fourth grade, when most students receive some Iowa history, they are taught to reconstruct and interpret the past using historical sources, particularly photographs. Students are asked to observe the differences between their world and what they see in the image. They are also exposed to timelines and the concept of change over time. After this initial exposure, Iowa students are asked to increase their capacity to treat primary sources and think historically. In the middle school grades, they learn to evaluate sources and frame them by building historical context so that they may begin to interpret them. By the time they graduate, Iowa students can interpret multiple sources from multiple perspectives and use them to make evidence-based arguments (Iowa Core Social Studies).

FORTEPAN IOWA invites teachers to develop competing and alternative "bottom-up" public histories counter to the hegemonic top-down narratives that so often dominate historical discourse. In fact, the original FORTEPAN (as well as FORTEPAN IOWA) was established with the *very idea* of offering a more nuanced approach to history. As FORTEPAN founders Miklós Tamási and András Szepessy writes in the archives' mission statement:

> When someone wants to research the past century, or to illustrate a story, an article or a paper, he/she always uses press or advertisement or art photos. The heritages of amateur photographers are basically unknown. As if there were not millions of photos made of families, friends—sometimes of the author him/herself from a tripod or in the mirror; sometimes as a silhouette, figure with a hat on his head standing on the bank of a ditch, with the sun behind him. As if only public events took place in the 20th century: inaugurated, signed, sold, cheated, arrested, welcome, buried. In FORTEPAN you won't find photos of this kind.
>
> (Szepessy and Tamási, 2010)

Amateur photos can offer new insights into our past, and help better explain our present. For example, this photograph (below) is not likely to appear in a "traditional" Iowa History textbook.

Figure 18.7 An Iowa Parent Teacher's Association entertaining Iowa schoolchildren in blackface, 1954; FORTEPAN IOWA: Carol Mountain, Debbie Robeson, Myrna and Scott Hottle Collection.

It is an image of Iowans performing a play in 1954. At first glance, it is obvious that the performers on stage are wearing "blackface" makeup and putting on a minstrel show. At second glance it becomes evident that the stage is in a school and that the audience is made up of children. The back story of this image (which appears in FORTEPAN IOWA) is that the performers are all members of the school's Parent Teacher Association; this school is in a suburb outside of Waterloo, Iowa; Waterloo grew in size as a city during the 1950s when large numbers of African Americans from the South relocated to Iowa to work in Waterloo's meat packing industry; the school was filled with children whose white parents "fled" this infiltration; and the PTA was now indoctrinating their children against civil rights. Traditional Iowa history books will talk about the continual progress African Americans made in Iowa, document numerous (prominent) African American Iowans, and explain how they overcame race barriers (Schwieder, Morain, & Nielsen, 2011). The amateur image above was taken by someone who likely endorsed the minstrel show and documents deliberate racism in a public school setting. The story it tells complicates race in Iowa—both then and now—by exposing the institutional barriers to African Americans, not the positive story of progress. This image is all the more powerful juxtaposed with other FORTEPAN IOWA images from 1954.

The relatively new field of public or collective memory studies understands the past as partial and partisan, an "ideologically inflected cultural resource" that is easily contested. "A collective memory perspective," writes Blair, "reminds us to think about how any message alters its context and speaks back to messages that have come before. And because of its focus on what and how we remember, it prompts us to think clearly about what is not said, as well as what is, for forgetfulness is a central operation in the process of constructing coherent and communicatively powerful memories" (Blair, 2006, p. 56, 58). For Blair and other public memory scholars, the idea of a singular, objective, and authoritative "History" became "increasingly (and rightly) untenable," argues Phillips. "Scholars turned to the notion of memory, or perhaps more accurately, 'memories,' as a way of understanding the complex interrelationships among past, present, and future" (Phillips, 2004, p. 2). The above image alone prompts students to think about competing memories, question the stories told in their textbooks, and consider the practices within their own schools, then and now. In short, FORTEPAN IOWA allows us to construct more complicated, multiple histories rather than singular top—down chronicles of influential people and key political events.

To this end, we are working towards curriculum materials that help Iowa students engage with FORTEPAN IOWA photographs and promote an Iowa history that is tangible, visual, complicated, and collective. We are encouraging teachers to let their students examine FORTEPAN IOWA images according to theme, decade, or place; work extremely closely with the images and create digital projects, contribute to the FORTEPAN IOWA archive, and interview their family members to find similar or competing histories.

REFERENCES

Andrews, T., & Burke, F. (2007, January). What does it mean to think historically? *Perspectives on history.* http://www.historians.org/publications-and-directories/perspectives-on-history/january-2007/what-does-it-mean-to-think-historically.

Barthes, R. (1981). *Camera lucida: Reflections on photography* (trans. Richard Howard). New York: Hill and Wang.

Berlin, J. A. (1993). Literacy, pedagogy, and English studies: Postmodern connections. In C. Lankshear & P. McClaren (Eds.), *Critical literacy, politics, praxis, and the postmodern* (pp. 247–270). Albany: State University of New York Press.

Blair, C. (2006). Communication as collective memory. In G. J. Shepherd, J. St. John, & T. Striphas (Eds.), *Communication as ... perspectives on theory* (pp. 51–59). London: Sage.

Django, Version 1.6 [Computer Software] (2014). Retrieved from http://djangoproject.com.

Eilderts, C. (2014, March 20). Interview with Carol Eilderts. FORTEPAN IOWA, University of Northern Iowa.

Fabos, B. (2013). Visual literacy: Aesthetics, semiotics, and the truth behind an image. In J. Jensen, D. Gomery, R. Campbell, B. Fabos, & J. Frechette (Eds.), *Media IN Society.* New York: Bedford/St. Martin's Press.

Iowa Department of Education (n.d.). *Iowa core social studies* [Online]. Retrieved from https://iowacore.gov/iowa-core/subject/social-studies/6/history.

Lankshear, C., & McClaren, P. (1993). *Critical literacy: Politics, praxis, and the postmodern.* Albany: State University of New York Press.

NCPH (National Council on Public History). (2014). What is public history? http://ncph.org/cms/what-is-public-history/.

Oral History Association. (2012). Oral history: Defined. http://www.oralhistory.org/about/do-oral-history/.

Phillips, K. R. (2004). *Framing public memory.* Tuscaloosa, AL: University of Alabama Press.

Schwieder, D., Morain, T., & Nielsen, L. (2011). *Iowa past to present: The people and the prairie.* Iowa City: University Of Iowa Press.

Seefeldt, D., and Thomas, W. G. (2009, May). What is digital history? *Perspectives on history.* http://www.historians.org/publications-and-directories/perspectives-on-history/may-2009/intersections-history-and-new-media/what-is-digital-history.

Szepessy, Á., & Tamási, M. (2010). *About FORTEPAN* [Web page]. Retrieved from http://www.fortepan.hu/?view=fortepan&lang=en&img=445.

19 Tracing the Environmental Impact of Apple

A Case Study of Mobile Technology Production and Consumption

Nicki Lisa Cole

THE TROUBLE WITH CORPORATE NARRATIVES

On October 13, 2012, just three weeks after Apple released iPhone 5, *Saturday Night Live* aired a searing sketch that flipped the script on the company's messaging and the media's reporting on the device. A panel of tech reporters in a talk show setting aired common complaints about the device, like having to use Google Maps in a web browser because Apple had not yet created a map application for its mobile software, and their disdain for the purple hue that discolored photographs of the sun. Others protested that the device scratched easily, and was too light and delicate (King, 2012).

Then, in a satirical twist, the host of the talk show, played by Christina Applegate, introduced "three peasant laborers from the factory in China where the iPhones were manufactured," who offered viciously sarcastic responses to the complainants. One commented, "I guess we just lucky. We don't need map because we sleep where we work." Comparing complaints about "bugs" in iPhone 5 to life in cramped worker dormitories, another said, "Lice are best bug I get. Best!"

Riffing on the "first world problems" meme trending at that moment, the sketch served to trivialize consumer complaints by positioning them next to the realities iPhone workers face, including dangerously long hours, oppressive and unsafe work conditions, and very low pay. With its clever, in-your-face satire, the sketch successfully disrupted the corporate, finance, and consumer-oriented narratives that dominate media coverage of the release of new Apple products.

This "storytelling" disparity—between how our digital technologies are made, and how they are marketed and reported on—was never more severe than in August 2013, when China Labor Watch (CLW) released a damning report on work conditions at several Apple suppliers involved in producing iPhone 5C. The report documented underage workers, required overtime far in excess of Chinese labor law, and university students forced to "intern" for criminally low wages on production lines (China Labor Watch, 2013a). The attention-grabbing story that mainstream media and tech outlets ran in response to this was that Apple would soon release a less expensive, plastic iPhone.

In late September 2014, nearly all press about Apple was focused on the newest features of iPhone 6, 6 Plus, iOS 8, and the newly announced Apple Watch. "Bendgate," or an abundance of stories about how some consumers had been able to bend iPhone 6 Plus, dominated the media conversation, amassing more than 300,000 searchable stories on Google News. Yet, all of this coverage failed to provide substantive discussion about where iPhones are manufactured, by whom, and under what conditions, as well as what the ecological costs of producing these digital tools might be. The absence of this narrative is especially peculiar, given that prominent labor rights organizations, Students and Scholars Against Corporate Misbehavior (SACOM) and CLW, had recently released new reports detailing worker abuse and labor law violations at iPhone 6 suppliers.

Why are reports by the likes of SACOM and CLW ignored by mainstream media and tech outlets? Herman and Chomsky's "propaganda model" provides the answer to this question (Herman and Chomsky, 2011). As they explain in their book, *Manufacturing Consent: The Political Economy of the Mass Media*, the case of Apple illustrates a combination of selective reporting, dependence on advertising revenue, and industry insider sourcing, which yields reporting heavily biased toward corporate interests. They argue that, because corporate media are in the business of selling readers to advertisers, coverage is overwhelmingly skewed in such a way as to please corporate advertisers. Consequently, stories that might conflict with the interests of advertisers are avoided.

Apple happens to have one of the largest advertising budgets among U.S.-based corporations. The company spent $1.2 billion on advertising during its 2014 fiscal year, which came to a close at the end of September (Apple, Inc., 2014a). In 2013, the company spent $351 million just advertising the iPhone, and spent more on TV ads that year than they had spent on all advertising in 2012 (Triggs, 2014). Given this substantial advertising budget— one of the largest among U.S.-based corporations (Taube, 2014)—Apple, as a buyer of readers and viewers from corporate media, is a company that one would do well to keep happy. This undoubtedly has a huge impact on how corporate-owned news media report on Apple.

Sociologists who study consumption also lend valuable insight to understanding which news is reported, why, and how. They would argue that journalists and media outlets, just like us, exist in a consumerist context in which we are socialized to see the world and act in it primarily as consumers (Dunn, 2008). Because of this, they seek to serve us as *consumers* more than they seek to serve us as *citizens*. Rather than providing us with a diverse array of critical perspectives on the important issues of our day, corporate media take for granted that we are consumers interested in knowing about new products and spending money on them, and frame their news coverage and the overall content of media—including advertising—for us in this fashion.

Consequently, we are inundated with advertising and reporting on new products that encourage us to consume ever more, in order to be relevant, on trend, admired, and valued (Bauman, 2007; Schor, 1998), with nary a question about the hidden costs of this economic model and lifestyle. Corporate messaging from companies like Apple, and the frenzied anticipation whipped up by corporate media in advance of and upon the release of new products fuels it too—Think of all the coverage spotlighting masses of eager people waiting outside Apple Stores!—urging us to "upgrade" or switch platforms, regardless of whether we really *need* a new device.

The story we are told about corporations and consumer products is one told by corporations, of corporations, and for corporations. It is a very narrow and uncritical story that obscures many painful realities, like the fact that our planet is pushed already past its ecological limits due to our resource-intensive model of production, consumption, and waste (Klein, 2014); and, that a decades-long and deeply harmful global race-to-the-bottom in wages is well underway (Onaran & Galanis, 2012). Workers around the world, the poor, and the planet are "collateral casualties" of the corporate quest for profit, and of our consumer desires (Bauman, 2007). Following the lead of the *Saturday Night Live* sketch, we need merely compare the corporate media narrative about our digital technology products to reality in order to expose all that it obscures. Teaching students how to do so is an important part of digital media literacy education.

The time has come for a conscientious and informed curriculum to address the impact of living in a digital age. Today's curriculum is increasingly turned toward global issues and context, which helps students understand their social situatedness and connections to others. Examples of this include service learning, civic engagement, and study abroad programs. Similarly, students must also learn to critically analyze the material conditions and consequences of manufacturing the digital tools we depend on today.

Observing with a critical eye how corporate media glorifies corporations while obscuring the human and environmental costs of digital technology production can be an invaluable educational experience. Just as engineering students are taught to disassemble devices like iPhones in order to understand how they work, students who use these tools on a daily basis ought to be able to deconstruct the stories told about them in order to critically analyze the global impact of our growing reliance on digital media. By doing so, we can learn to be more thoughtful, conscientious, and ultimately sociopolitically engaged citizens within a globalized world. Apple—the world's most valuable company (YCharts, 2014), maker of the world's best-selling smartphone (ABIresearch, 2014; Counterpoint, 2014; Kerr, 2014), and owner of the world's most valuable brand (Interbrand, 2014)—which is covered *ad nauseam* by corporate media, makes for a truly compelling and illuminating case.

BEYOND "BENDGATE": THE REAL SCANDALS OF iPHONE 6

In late 2014, the story of Apple would seem to be one of a company mostly in its glory, if one relied only on corporate, mainstream, and tech media sources. Searching for news on Apple, we can read about record-breaking sales of its latest iPhone models, where they will soon be available for purchase around the world, and praise for the "genius" of Jony Ive, who designed both the new Apple Watch and the company's latest mobile operating system, iOS 8. The only bad news for Apple seems to be "bendgate."

The media landscape suggests by omission that Apple has effectively dealt with the ethical and legal labor issues that were previously reported by the *New York Times* and many other media outlets in 2012. Apple now claims that it has taken a lead on improving labor conditions throughout its supply chain. The well-polished pages devoted to supplier responsibility on its website (www.apple.com/supplier-responsibility/), and its annual Supplier Responsibility Progress Report—featuring the faces of smiling young workers—indicate that all is well. Online and in print, Apple asserts, "Each of [the] workers [in our supply chain] has the right to safe and ethical working conditions. So we audit deep into our supply chain and hold our suppliers accountable to some of the industry's strictest standards. In fact, we care as much about how our products are made as we do about how they're designed" (Apple, Inc., 2014b, p. 4). In response to 2013 reports by CLW that detailed labor law violations at several suppliers, Apple continues in the report, "We enforced our Code through 451 audits at multiple levels of our supply chain, and our suppliers trained 1.5 million workers on their rights. We drove our suppliers to achieve an average of 95 percent compliance with our maximum 60-hour work week" (2014b, p. 4).

Yet, recent reports from SACOM and CLW suggest otherwise. From October 2013 through August 2014, members of SACOM conducted undercover research at three Apple suppliers involved in producing iPhone 5C and iPhone 6, and interviewed 103 workers (SACOM, 2014). The suppliers—Maintek Computer, Cotek Electronics, and Casetek Computer— are all in Suzhou, China, and are subsidiaries of Pegatron Corporation, a Taiwanese electronics manufacturing firm that was awarded half of Apple's 2014 iPhone 6 orders (25 million units) (AppleInsider, 2014). Pegatron is also Apple's primary supplier for iPhone 5C (Worstall, 2013). Workers at these factories play a variety of roles in producing components for iPhones and in assembling the devices.

SACOM's report, titled "The Lives of iSlaves," details how workers often labored as much as twelve to fifteen hours per day, sometimes more, and at times worked for *up to ten weeks* without a single day of rest. This unhealthily rigorous work schedule results in as much as 170 to 200 overtime hours per month, which is more than five times China's legal monthly limit (SACOM, 2014). Both the pace and volume of work documented at these suppliers are in violation of Chinese labor laws, as well as Apple's own

Supplier Responsibility code, which states, "a workweek shall be restricted to 60 hours, including overtime, and workers shall take at least one day off every seven days" (Apple, Inc., 2014c, p. 1).

SACOM also found that the factories did not provide workers with necessary safety equipment, that workers suffered medical ailments and injuries including skin allergies, blisters, and fainting due to long hours of standing, and that many reported long-term physical exhaustion. Women who were pregnant while working had no choice but to quit to protect their health and that of their unborn child, because managers were unwilling to reduce their hours to the legal limit. And, workers hired through outside agencies, known as "dispatch workers" in China, were not paid benefits required by law (SACOM, 2014).

What makes these violations reported by SACOM particularly egregious is that many of the same violations were documented at other Pegatron factories during the manufacture of iPhone 5C in 2013, as reported by CLW in July of that year (China Labor Watch, 2013a). Despite this scathing 2013 report, Apple continues to work with Pegatron and grant it lucrative new orders.

Of course, Pegatron is not the only iPhone supplier with which Apple continues to work, despite known ethical and legal violations on-site. In September 2013, CLW released another report that detailed oppressive and unsafe working conditions at Jabil Circuit factory in Wuxi, China—a U.S.-owned corporation—which at the time was making covers for iPhone 5 and iPhone 5C (China Labor Watch, 2013b). A year later, the organization released a second report on the factory that shows that ethical and legal violations continue unabated as workers produce covers for iPhone 6 (China Labor Watch, 2014).

Readers are likely to have heard of labor issues at Foxconn sites throughout China, which made headlines across corporate, mainstream, and independent media outlets in 2012 after a spate of worker suicides drew attention to iPad and iPhone assembly lines. Apple became a member of the Fair Labor Association and promised to conduct audits in response to allegations of labor violations at Foxconn sites following the *New York Times'* in-depth "iEconomy" series. Since then, corporate media have almost universally demonstrated Herman and Chomsky's point about the relationship between sourcing and propaganda, with headlines like "Apple's pressure on Foxconn forces improved working conditions in China,"[1] "Improving Working Conditions at Foxconn,"[2] and "Foxconn's Apple factories start to show signs of improved working conditions"[3] generated by press releases from Apple and Fair Labor Association (an industry group).

Yet, no media coverage has mentioned the contrary research findings of sociologists Jenny Chan, Ngai Pun, and Mark Selden, who have done extensive undercover research at Foxconn facilities and interviewed hundreds of workers. They reported in 2013 that the raising of wages that went through after activist and media scrutiny has been counterbalanced by heightened productivity quotas (Chan, Ngai, & Selden, 2013). So, while workers got a bit more money per hour, they were expected to produce more work for it, effectively nullifying the raise. They also found that while Foxconn management promised to allow workers to unionize, in fact the union leaders were selected by upper management to serve as spies on workers (Chan, Ngai, & Selden, 2013). Instead of moving toward fair labor practices, Foxconn effectively took several steps back. Despite the reality that Foxconn has failed to improve in the ways it has promised to, and that Apple has failed to hold Foxconn accountable in the ways *it* has promised, Foxconn remains the primary producer of iPhones and iPads, and is poised to grow its relationship with Apple with its new contract to produce sapphire glass for screen displays (Chaffin, 2014).

When we pull back the curtain of Apple's carefully constructed and beautifully presented narrative, and we take into account the realities that corporate, mainstream, and tech media choose to ignore, we see that Apple's relationships with its suppliers and hundreds of thousands of young Chinese workers paints a much more disturbing picture. This is why a critical approach to the products that enable digital media and education today *must* be a part of digital media literacy education. There is far too much at stake to simply embrace the power of technology in our classrooms, our homes, and communities without developing an informed awareness about the hidden human costs of production.

THE TRUTH ABOUT CONFLICT MINERALS

> "Greenpeace praises Apple for reducing use of conflict minerals."
> —Neil Hughes, AppleInsider

> "Apple weeds out conflict metals from iPhone and iPad."
> —Shona Ghosh, PCPro

> "Apple cuts conflict minerals and puts its supplier cards on the table."
> —Tom Dowdall, GreenpeaceBlogs

Another arena in which digital media literacy education is deeply necessary has to do with the astonishing lack of mainstream reporting on mining the vast amount of natural resources required to make the tools that enable engagement with digital media. Headlines like those above dominated the media conversation about Apple in early February 2014, after the company released its annual Supplier Responsibility Progress Report, and along with it, a list of smelters in its supply chain. Smelters are factories that turn mined ore into usable metal for electronics components, like gold, tin, and tungsten—to name three out of thirty elements that go into a smartphone (CompoundChem.com, 2014). Apple and its suppliers source from as many as 220 smelters from all over the world at any given time.

Praise for Apple was largely due to its partnership with the Conflict-Free Sourcing Initiative (CFSI), and its participation in the organization's

Conflict-Free Smelter Program (CFSP). Of its stance on conflict minerals—the mining and sale of which funds armed conflict in places like the Democratic Republic of Congo (DRC)—and its relationship with this organization, Apple wrote in the annual report:

> The ethical sourcing of minerals is an important part of our mission to ensure safe and fair working conditions for everyone in our supply chain. We were one of the first companies to survey our suppliers to identify the smelters they use and understand the potential entry points for conflict minerals. We are driving smelters and refiners to be compliant with the Conflict-Free Smelter Program (CFSP) or an equivalent third party audit program. And rather than avoiding minerals from the DRC and neighboring countries entirely, we're supporting verified supply lines and economic development in the region.
>
> (Apple, Inc., 2014b, 15)

At first glance, this progressive mission statement sounds promising. Apple is moving toward transparency by listing its smelters (and many of its other suppliers too, in another document), which is a necessary aspect of being accountable for how it does business. And, it has partnered with an independent organization that will help it to audit and regulate its smelters. Yet, once again, when we dig beneath the surface of the narrative crafted by Apple and the media, we see a much more complicated and troubling picture.

For starters, CFSI, the organization that runs CSFP, is an initiative of the Electronic Industry Citizenship Coalition (EICC) and the Global e-Sustainability Initiative (GeSI) (Conflict-Free Sourcing Initiative, 2014a). The leadership of EICC—including its Board of Directors and its Senior Executive Advisory Council—is composed of executives from major electronics firms like Dell, Qualcomm, Intel, BlackBerry, and Jabil, among others (Electronic Industry Citizenship Coalition, 2014). (You might remember Jabil as the U.S. corporation that owns the Jabil Circuit factory in Wuxi, China, where numerous ethical and legal violations have been recurring for years, as documented by CLW). Meanwhile, GeSI is governed by senior executives from major telecommunications companies based in Europe and the U.S., including several which host contracts for—and sell!—Apple's iPhone (Global e-Sustainability Initiative, 2014).

When we critically examine these entities, what we see is industry regulating itself, which raises serious questions about the validity of the regulation process. To encourage political and economic analysis of today's digital media industries, we need to ask the following questions: Can an organization provide unbiased audits and regulation when it is created, hosted, and run by representatives of the very industry it aims to regulate? Should we trust senior executives of companies that profit from unsustainable and unethical production processes to verify that some aspects of their supply chains are sustainable and just? How thorough will audits be, and how strict enforcement of rules, when the enforcers have a vested interest in the profitability of the targets of enforcement?

The narrative on conflict minerals presented by Apple and corporate news media was further muddied by a report Apple filed with the U.S. Securities and Exchange Commission on May 29, 2014. The Specialized Disclosure Report is required by the Dodd-Frank Wall Street Reform and Consumer Protection Act, passed in 2010 in the wake of the financial crisis. Title XV of the act, "Miscellaneous Provisions," includes a requirement that publicly listed companies disclose the sources of minerals used in their products in order to identify whether the sale of these minerals benefits armed groups in the DRC (Frank, 2009).

In the report, Apple states that most of its supply chain is now conflict-free, per the guidelines of CFSI, and states that its own "conflict minerals policy requires that all of its suppliers map their supply chains through all levels down to the smelters and refiners and report the results to Apple" (Sewell, 2014). The report also states that, between 2010 and 2013, the company surveyed over 400 suppliers. While a cursory look at the report paints a rosy picture, digital media literacy education requires a more investigative and comprehensive analysis, because later in the report, Apple states:

> Based on its due diligence efforts, *Apple does not have sufficient information to conclusively determine the country of origin of the Subject Minerals in its products* or whether the Subject Minerals are from recycled or scrap sources. However, based on the information provided by Apple's suppliers, smelters, and refiners, as well as from other sources, Apple believes that the countries of origin of the Subject Minerals contained in its products include the countries listed in Annex II below, as well as recycled and scrap sources [emphasis added] (Sewell, 2014, p. 3).

Translating this legalese to plain English, Apple states that it cannot confirm, due to insufficient information, the country of origin of the minerals in its supply chain—where the smelters get the minerals. Prior to this paragraph, Apple also admits that it "believes" that the smelters listed are those that its suppliers use. In other words, Apple cannot state with certainty that the smelters it lists are the ones providing the minerals for its products. So, while Apple public relations claims to have a mostly conflict-free supply chain, in reality, Apple really does not know if this is true.

In keeping up with the move to globalize K-12 and higher education curricula, students must learn to analyze the ethical consequences of manufacturing the digital tools they have come to depend on in order to reach their own assessments and evaluative responses. In the case of Apple, its list of suspected mineral supplier countries includes eleven that have extreme to high risk factors for human rights violations, per the U.K.-based Maplecroft's seventh annual Human Rights Risk Atlas. The Maplecroft report specifically implicates four countries from which Apple believes its suppliers source minerals, offering: "The economies of Myanmar, Nigeria, Ethiopia, and Indonesia present a particularly high risk to business. In such economies, a high rate of deforestation, coupled with the unchecked conduct of security forces and a climate of impunity for human rights violations has led to a high risk of 'land grabs' at the expense of indigenous peoples rights, property rights and minority rights" (Maplecroft, 2013). Apple believes that the minerals from its products come from places like this, yet claims that its smelters are conflict-free. At best, such claims are questionable, but no media outlets are asking.

Despite the difficulty of determining whether or not the extraction of minerals for Apple products funds armed conflict, there are still important questions to be raised by Apple's SEC filing. For example, what about the conflicts faced by communities like Bangka, Indonesia, where tin is mined in ways and at a rate that has devastated the local ecology and fishing economy, and injured and killed hundreds of workers (Friends of the Earth, 2012)? Tin from Bangka is hardly free of conflict, though it would meet Apple's and the CFSI's definition of the term. In fact, several Indonesian tin smelters that mine in environmentally destructive ways in and around Bangka, and that buy tin ore from miners often working in dangerous conditions (Matteo, 2014), are on the CFSI's current list of conflict-free smelters (Conflict-Free Sourcing Initiative, 2014b).

With such glaring blind spots in the framework of conflict-free sourcing, and no verifiable information about which mines, regions, or countries Apple's minerals come from, it is hard to swallow Apple's claim that the majority of its supply chain is conflict-free. It also seems fair to criticize mainstream media outlets for failing to critically examine the documents they report on, and instead producing a pro-industry biased fueled by industry advertising and public relations.

USING DIGITAL MEDIA LITERACY EDUCATION TO EMPOWER STUDENTS FOR SOCIAL CHANGE

The goals of digital media literacy education go beyond the ability to see the bias and holes in corporate, mainstream, and tech reporting. The ability to see the kinds of narrative discrepancies described in the previous two sections is a necessary first step to truly understanding one's connection to and impact on other people and the planet. It is also an important step toward being able to identify problems that exist, and to think critically and creatively about solutions. In this way, a curriculum that includes digital media literacy skills can help empower students to become the informed, empathetic, politically engaged global citizens that society needs them to be.

As K-12 and higher education curricula expand to include focus on the social and environmental impacts of our way of life, our relationship with digital technology must be included. While it may be appropriate to blame companies like Apple, Foxconn, and Pegatron for the abuses described in this chapter, we must also recognize our own relationship to these problems, as our collective insatiable demand for the latest devices is a significant driver of them. On average, the U.S. mobile phone user replaces his or her device every 22 months—just shy of every two years (EcoATM, 2014). Companies like Apple fuel this trend with their rapid product cycle. Apple has released ten versions of iPhone since its introduction in 2007. That averages to a new iPhone every 8.4 months! The combination of advertising, incessant news media coverage of the latest products at the expense of more critical reporting, and the centrality of consumer goods in our lives fuels a monstrously unsustainable consumption of natural resources and ecologically disastrous mass disposal of them. We must teach our students to see and respond to these problems, and help them develop careers and lifestyles that fit within a paradigm of solutions. In terms of digital media tools, this means learning about the solutions and careers that lie in ethical production, reduced consumption, repair, reuse, recycling, and responsible management of the waste stream.

On the production side, it's not only important to create ethical supply chains, but also, for companies to design products that are made to last, rather than those that are seemingly impossible to repair, and that are meant to be obsolete within two years' time. Friends of the Earth in the UK has lobbied for laws that would hold companies accountable to standards consistent with these ideals. Their "Make It Better Campaign" encourages companies and lawmakers to build sustainability and long-term durability into product design (Kirby, 2012).

To that end, Fairphone, a company based in the Netherlands, is producing a smartphone with a fully traceable and independently audited supply chain. Not only are they providing a living wage, and safe and stable work environments for those who make their products, but in keeping with the challenge posed by Friends of the Earth, their smartphone was designed with ease of repair and parts replacement as priorities (Fairphone, 2014). While many smartphone users are unable to even open their device to replace a battery or a damaged part, the Fairphone is easy to get into, and the parts inside are labeled to foster ease of replacement and repair.

Across the UK, Europe, and the U.S., citizens are coming together to share and teach the skills necessary to digital products to keep them out of the toxic waste stream. In the UK, The Restart Project, a nonprofit group based in the UK, provides trainings and online tutorials in fixing broken electronics (The Restart Project, 2014). At the Restart Parties hosted by their volunteers, not only do many attendees walk away with working products, but they also leave with an important feeling of community after meeting and working together with neighbors who were otherwise strangers. They also leave with an empowering set of knowledge and skills that serve to redemocratize our relationship with digital technology (J. Gunter and U. Vallauri, in-person interview, December 1, 2014). iFixit, a U.S.-based organization, frames repair of digital technology as a right—a form of freedom. They also point out that a growing repair economy creates jobs and promotes a sustainable future (iFixit.org, 2014).

When they can't be repaired, recycling digital products is an important, meaningful way to reduce our unsustainable demand for fresh raw materials, since they are densely packed with valuable, reusable resources. This aspect of sustainable use and production of digital technology can also provide future jobs for today's current students.

Educational digital media literacy initiatives predicated upon this type of sustainable intervention offer us new avenues to address and remodel our dependence on digital technology. Although the core values of a comprehensive digital media literacy education often conflict with neoliberal values, they present the greatest potential for holistic change to our damaged social, economic, and ecological systems. By combining critical media literacy with an awareness of the political, economic and social impact of digital technology, we can shift the paradigm of learning toward systematic change. This provides us with the best opportunity to make a difference individually and collectively, and to not just survive, but thrive together in the twenty-first century.

NOTES

1. Katie Marsal, AppleInsider (http://appleinsider.com/articles/12/12/27/apples-pressure-on-foxconn-forces-improved-working-conditions-in-china).
2. *New York Times* (http://www.nytimes.com/interactive/2012/12/27/business/Improving-Working-Conditions-at-Foxconn.html?ref=business&_r=0).
3. Juli Clover, MacRumors (http://www.macrumors.com/2013/12/12/foxconn-and-apple-make-strides-towards-improving-work-hours-but-still-violate-chinese-limits/).

REFERENCES

ABI research. (2014, July 7). Samsung and Apple devices dominate Smartphone device model top 20, according to ABI Research. *Business wire.* Retrieved from http://www.businesswire.com/news/home/20140707005601/en/Samsung-Apple-Devices-Dominate-Smartphone-Device-Model#.VCZzgymSzKD.

Apple, Inc. (2014a, September 27). *United States Securities and Exchange Commission form 10-K.* Retrieved from: http://investor.apple.com/secfiling.cfm?filingID=1193125-14-383437&CIK=320193.

Apple, Inc. (2014b, January). *Supplier responsibility 2014 progress report. Apple, Inc.* Retrieved from https://www.apple.com/supplier- responsibility/pdf/Apple_SR_ 2014_ Progress_Report.pdf.

Apple, Inc. (2014c, January). *Supplier responsibility standards, version 4.0.2.* Retrieved from https://www.apple.com/supplier-responsibility/pdf/Apple_Supplier_Responsibility_Standards.pdf.

AppleInsider. (2014, August 14). Rumor: Apple supplier Pegatron nets 50% of 4.7-inch "iPhone 6" production. Retrieved from http://appleinsider.com/articles/14/08/14/rumor-apple-supplier-pegatron-nets-50-of-47-inch-iphone-6-production.

Bauman, Z. (2007). *Consuming life*. Malden, MA: Polity Press.

Chaffin, B. (2014). Apple reportedly building Chinese Sapphire plant with Foxconn. Retrieved from http://www.macobserver.com/tmo/article/apple-reportedly-building-chinese-sapphire-plant-with-foxconn.

Chan, J., Ngai, P., & Selden, M. (2013). The politics of global production: Apple, Foxconn, and China's new working class. *New Technology, Work and Employment, 28*(2), 100–115.

China Labor Watch. (2013a). *Apple's unkept promises: Cheap iPhones come at high cost to Chinese workers*. New York: China Labor Watch. Retrieved from www.chinalaborwath.org/upfile/2013_7_29/apple_s_unkept_promises.pdf.

China Labor Watch. (2013b). *Chinese workers exploited by U.S.-owned iPhone supplier*. New York: China Labor Watch. Retrieved from http://www.chinalaborwatch.org/upfile/Jabil_Green_Point.final.pdf.

China Labor Watch. (2014). *iExploitation: Apple's supplier Jabil Circuit exploits workers to meet iPhone 6 demands*. New York: China Labor Watch. Retrieved from http://www.chinalaborwatch.org/upfile/2014_09_25/2014.09.25%20iExploitation%20at%20Jabil%20Wuxi%20EN.pdf.

CompoundChem.com. (2014). The chemical elements of a smartphone. Retrieved from http://www.compoundchem.com/2014/02/19/the-chemical-elements-of-a-smartphone/.

Conflict-Free Sourcing Initiative. (2014a). About the Conflict-Free Sourcing Initiative. Retrieved October 3, 2014, from http://www.conflictfreesourcing.org/about/.

Conflict-Free Sourcing Initiative. (2014b). Conflict-free tin smelters. Retrieved from http://www.conflictfreesourcing.org/tin-conflict-free-smelters/.

Counterpoint. (2014, July 14). Top 10 smartphones in May 2014—Galaxy S5 fails to displace iPhone 5s. Retrieved from http://www.counterpointresearch.com/top10may2014.

Dunn, R. G. (2008). *Identifying consumption: Subjects and objects in consumer society*. Philadelphia, PA: Temple University Press.

EcoATM. (2014). About us. Retrieved from http://www.ecoatm.com/about-us/.

Electronic Industry Citizenship Coalition. (2014). Boards and advisers. Retrieved from http://www.eiccoalition.org/about/board-advisers/.

Fairphone. (2014). Fairphone story. Retrieved from http://www.fairphone.com/.

Frank, B. (2009, December 2). *H.R.4173—Dodd-Frank Wall Street Reform and Consumer Protection Act* [Legislation]. Retrieved from http://thomas.loc.gov/cgi-bin/bdquery/z?d111:HR04173:@@@L&summ2=m&#major%20actions.

Friends of the Earth. (2012). *Mining for smartphones: The true cost of tin*. London: Friends of the Earth. Retrieved from www.foe.co.uk/sites/default/files/downloads/tin_mining.pdf.

Global e-Sustainability Initiative. (2014). Governance. Retrieved October from http://gesi.org/ICT_sustainability_governance.

Herman, E. S., & Chomsky, N. (2011). *Manufacturing consent: The political economy of mass media* (Google eBook). New York: Knopf Doubleday Publishing Group.

iFixit.org. (2014). Retrieved from http://ifixit.org/.

Interbrand. (2014). 2014 *Best global brands report*. Retrieved from http://bestglobalbrands.com/2014/ranking/.

Kerr, D. (2014, July 16). iPhone 5S is world's bestselling smartphone, report says. Retrieved from http://www.cnet.com/news/iphone-5s-is-the-bestselling-smartphone-worldwide/.

King, D. R. (2012, October 13). Christina Applegate with Passion Pit. *Saturday Night Live*. New York: National Broadcasting Company. Retrieved from http://www.nbc.com/saturday-night-live/episode-guide/season-38/christina-applegate-with-passion-pit/1624.

Kirby, J. (2012, November 23). Make it better: A new campaign for products that don't cost the Earth [Text]. Retrieved from http://www.foe.co.uk/news/better_mine2mobile_38275.

Klein, N. (2014). *This Changes Everything: Capitalism vs. The Climate*. New York, NY: Simon & Schuster.

Maplecroft. (2013, December 4). *Latest products and reports: Human rights risk atlas 2014*. Retrieved from http://maplecroft.com/portfolio/new-analysis/2013/12/04/70-increase-countries-identified-extreme-risk-human-rights-2008-bhuman-rights-risk-atlas-2014b/.

Matteo, F. (2014, March 7). Death metal: The island that's paying the price for your tablet. Retrieved from http://www.wired.co.uk/magazine/archive/2014/03/features/death-metal/page/2.

Onaran, O., & Galanis, G. (2012). *Is aggregate demand wage-led or profit-led? National and global effects*. Geneva, Switzerland: International Labour Office. Retrieved from www.ilo.org/wcmsp5/groups/public/—ed_protect/—protrav/—travail/documents/publication/wcms_192121.pdf.

SACOM. (2014). *The lives of iSlaves: Report on working conditions at Apple's supplier Pegatron*. Hong Kong: SACOM. Retrieved from sacom.hk/wp-content/uploads/2014/09/SACOM-The-Lives-of-iSlaves-Pegatron-20140918.pdf.

Schor, J. B. (1998). *The overspent American: Why we want what we don't need*. New York: Basic Books.

Sewell, D. B. (2014). *Specialized disclosure report* (U.S Securities and Exchange Commission Form SD). Cupertino, CA: Apple, Inc. Retrieved from http://investor.apple.com/secfiling.cfm?filingID=1193125-14-217311&CIK=320193.

Taube, A. (2014). The 12 companies that spend the most on advertising. Retrieved from http://www.businessinsider.com/12-biggest-advertising-spenders-in-2013-2014-6?op=1&IR=T.

The Restart Project. (2014). About. Retrieved from http://therestartproject.org/about/.

Triggs, R. (2014, April 9). Apple closes gap on Samsung's advertising budget. Retrieved from http://www.androidauthority.com/apple-samsung-ad-budget-2013-366238.

Worstall, T. (2013, November 11). Apple's Pegatron, the iPhone 5c assembler, shows how tough it can be to supply the company. Retrieved from http://www.forbes.com/sites/timworstall/2013/11/11/apples-pegatron-the-iphone-5c-assembler-shows-how-tough-it-can-be-to-supply-the-company/.

YCharts. (2014). Apple's Market Cap. Retrieved from http://ycharts.com/companies/AAPL/market_c.

20 'Mediapting' and Curation

Research Informed Pedagogy for (Digital) Media Education Praxis

Julian McDougall

A messy title for this chapter, which would be unwieldy yet convey the thoughts and desires to be expressed in what follows might be something like *Fight the Power? Read (Media), Write (Make or Play), Curate, Argue ... (Double) Mediadapt, then Act (we hope): What counts for (digital) media education, how do we know and what do we do?* Such a crazy description would 'show the working' of media education in the digital age. It signals a desire to break any 'fourth wall' for understanding digital media literacy education as a coherent paradigm. Always at the service of a horizontal discourse, where many flowers continue to bloom, there's little in the way of pedagogic consistency—an ever-incomplete project, for better or worse.

We might reasonably observe that at the *very* moment when global consensus about the pertinence of various new modes of digital practice and engagement might appear to legitimize our work as never before, the media educator finds herself shouting to be heard among all the multiple literacies and (sometimes competing) imperatives. Fortunately, if this is a problem, there is a straightforward solution—we need a research-informed pedagogic shift. To this end, this chapter will consider the research base for understanding the *hybrid* nature of both media learning and digital literacy, and make some recommendations for embracing the complexities of reading, writing, and curating practices and—we all hope, but it's usually optional—social agency. These recommendations will conclude with a pedagogic rationale for an agile, adaptive media education that is based on credible educational research and can at once teach *about* and *with* the digital while seeking to empower students with the capacity for 'digital voice.'

If the 'project' is to be developed, if not ever completed, I propose that every media education encounter should foster incremental change, however small, in media practice and that students' engagements with media—including their own—should adapt to a new, more critical language game. This is what I call double adaptation—of the self and of media, or *mediaptation*. I draw an analogy here with protest camp media from Feigenbaum's research whereby 'dual adaption' arises in the adoption of mainstream media practices while at the same time "protest camps create the power to enforce their own standards on to the media, which has to adapt to protest camps' heterogeneity and refusal to speak with one voice" (Feigenbaum, 2013, p. 224). My proposal is that media education can act in the same way and get closer to the kinds of civic engagement (Mihailidis, 2014) that competence-based approaches find harder to reach. But this cannot be hoped for or planned without a profound shift in how we think about expertise, for which we need—and are building—a credible research base for understanding students' aptitudes for such work and teachers' reflexive identity work.

To start out from the right place, the argument presented here is that 'the (digital) media' are neither objects nor tools—or at least if they are, this is of little educational interest. Rather, the convergence of online and offline, digital and linear media practices by, for, and between people—should constitute our curriculum. Furthermore, the learning spaces in and across which such 'mediadaptive' work is developed and energized must bear witness to the membrane between knowledge production and creative practice in classrooms, homes / lifeworld, and 'third spaces.' This chapter will make recommendations for a more strategic dialogue between literacy research and media education practice, with a particular emphasis on the aspiration for media educators to foster 'critical' thought and 'civic' action in a new (digital) public sphere, arguing that the material (including virtual) conditions for such 'voice' can only be adequately configured with lessons learned from the rich history of 'analog' literacy enquiry.

Firstly, epistemological attention must be paid to 'what counts' as knowledge—and what it means to be an expert—in contemporary literacies. If the international Media Education Summit (2014) conference and it's affiliated *Media Education Research Journal* represent the 'state of the art' for our community of research and practice at the time of writing, then we can group the work disseminated in those outlets into five subfields, with some examples of each here selected from a greater number.

1. **Upskilling:** This research theme describes inquiry into new or emerging digital media practices, articulated as skills, competences, or affinities, covering both the observation of such and the need for educators to respond in kind or in keeping. Frechette and Williams offered a framework for multiliteracies to deal with digital media as 'appendages of self, social, local, national, and global constructs at the core of humanity'—themes which this book seeks to develop. Monteiro and Osorio shared an ethnographic study from Portugal of children's competitiveness, exploring identity and sociability in online peer spaces. Neag assessed the Hungarian media education curriculum against press freedom objectives and human rights criteria, to identify the measurable attributes of a 'media literate child.' Bill Shipman showcased his own practice-based research—*Ruff Ruffman: Humble Media Genius*—an interactive media literacy tool. Readman and Moon grounded digital media production work in processes of critical 'engagement and disengagement,' and Tilleul et al.'s longitudinal study separated technical competences from informational and social—towards what elsewhere I have called a much needed 'untangling' of media literacies (McDougall, 2014). Hiles, Ashton, and

Cownie each reported on research into aspects of practitioner academics and students' commitments and identities in relation to higher education media programs with vocational modalities, while Bosher et al. discussed Internet copyright as positioning education "at the interface of layperson and professional knowledge." In all these cases, research-informed pedagogic strategies for engaging with new dynamics of media literacy and practice were offered.

2. **Discursive terrain enquiry:** Wallis, Kendall, and Murphy; Sanders, Cervi, and my own presentation of our United Kingdom Literacy Association project—where we mapped a composite of international media literacy attributes to a specific qualification, GCSE Media Studies (General Certificate in Secondary Education, examined at 16 years at the end of compulsory schooling in England)—all explored the construction—in teachers' talk and policy rhetoric—of "the discursive terrain that shapes ideas, concepts and practices relating to literacy within the (educational) context and how digital literacies and identities for teachers, students and disciplines are constructed" (Kendall & Murphy, 2015, p. 36). This theme is far more than navel gazing or linguistic fetishism. Rather, as I argue later, developing a critical meta-literacy of how power resides in such terrain is a prerequisite for the kinds of more ethnographic pedagogies that can go beyond competence and key functioning.

3. **Civic action research:** Cortoni et al.; Chu, Monterio and Osorio; Kanizaj et al.; Verdoot, Wilkinson, and Salgado all occupied this well-populated strand with outcomes from research and interventions aiming to transcend the boundaries of educational space to harness action in the public sphere through media work. Aspirations and objectives ranged from "active and responsible citizenship" to "promot[ing] women's empowerment through problematizing media messages and at the same time their gender condition" to "investigating the efficacy of digital media in promoting real-world play between caregivers and young children." The diversity of this theme should be evident here, but the common thread was the availability of findings from action research or similar lines of enquiry.

4. **A new protectionism:** the role of media education as critical safeguard was, as always, a subtheme of the work disseminated. From parental mediation (Stastna) to creating critical distance from everyday media (Chu); media rule-negotiation within families (Hesova et al.) to Sander et al.'s work on parental media-habitus influencing children's gaming choices, these presentations provided methodologically credible explorations of relative levels of media risk and opportunity.

5. **Curation and porous expertise: The 'Third Space':** I am delighted to report that this theme emerged as one of the most abundant. Burn, Carron, and Potter, from the Digital Arts Research in Education collaborative, shared research into signature pedagogies for the 'third space' (networks, across and between school and outside); Mihailidis shared 'the curator's learning curve' with regard to critical analysis, aggregation, and storytelling

competencies; I reported on curational aspects of several pedagogic research projects with shared 'co-creational' objectives; while Parry, Readman, and Moon; Gruhn, Dunford, and Jenkins; and Arnouti and Adamson all shared rich research findings on pedagogic enquiries into the use of media for the reworking of expertise.

Going beyond the Summit, curational pedagogy appears to offer much to media education—both as a way out of the epistemological cul de sacs of 'the media' / 'the digital' and for political renewal. In the twenty-first century, with formal education operating in a 'mixed economy' of home / school / digital learning and the traditional modes of delivery arguably threatened by MOOCS, peer networks, and digital divides, whose knowledge counts? How is the legitimation of expertise negotiated formally and informally across boundaries and between knowledge domains?

Thinking about media engagement as "curated" bears witness to an agentive turn to meta-authorship amongst larger numbers of participants in online media. The way in which digital texts and artifacts combine to make meaning represents, then, a practice of curatorship (Potter, 2011), in and through which a new formulation of knowledge is exchanged between experts who are always 'in progress.' Understood in this way, it is possible that media education as a subject area can now be seen as a rich site for subjectivity and identification and demarginalized—moved towards the center ground of the struggle to locate for education those cultural values that lie outside traditionally prescribed curricula. This cannot be the product of technological determinism, nor from a simple equation of new digital practices with autonomous models, but instead through specific, situated research into the ways in which students move between the worlds of home and school in an actual and metaphorical "third space" between the two. For Guttierez, a third space is mediated by a range of elements including "sociocritical literacy which privileges and is contingent upon students; sociohistorical lives, both proximally and distally" (2008, p. 5). Clear Vygotskyan overtones abound here, and there is an urgent need for media educators to move beyond either an ambitious but overly reductive 'digital turn' or a new protectionism, in order to embrace the rich interactions, embodied practices, and reflexive deep learning that can be fostered in (digital) third spaces. Resisting the either / or tendency of the MOOC and embracing elements instead of the more subtle forms of 'open,'

> a key opportunity is secondary, lying not in the direct provision of education to students but, rather, in how the deliberate restaging of particular pedagogical moments can offer useful insights that are broadly applicable across educational environments [for example, in classroom practice and asynchronous online settings].
>
> (van Mourik Broekman et al., 2014, p. 60)

For media educators, the concept of the 'third space' can be defined as the area between official curriculum and informal knowledge, with skills and dispositions brought in from outside culture. Sometimes this is a literal third space, the actual halfway house of an after-school media education or digital literacy project, a museum, gallery, youth club, or media production / coding space, but in other cases this is co-located in school / college / university as a metaphorical space, negotiated through dialogue and pedagogical strategies designed to mediate expertise and challenge dominant roles and representations of knowledge.

So for Gutierrez (2008), 'Third Space' is where powerful epistemology converges with lifeworld skills and dispositions, and our interest should be where this is made tangible in the digital mediascape. If we accept this premise, then a primary objective of twenty-first century literacy education / entitlement must be the facilitation of informed curational practices in the digital lifeworld. Going further, we can productively draw on creative arts educational practice to draw a parallel between the making of 'the work' and the design of learning (McDougall & Orr, 2013), arguing that digital exchanges provide a 'third studio space' for such collaborative endeavor. We'll return to this later.

Teen 'addiction' to social media is a new extension of typical human engagement. Their use of social media as their primary site of sociality is most often a byproduct of cultural dynamics that have nothing to do with technology, including parental restrictions and highly scheduled lives. Teens turn to, and are obsessed with whichever environment allows them to connect to friends. Most teens aren't addicted to social media; if anything, they're addicted to each other (Boyd, 2014, p. 80).

Another obstacle for media teachers today is the recurring problem of 'the media.' It would appear uncontroversial to say that the hyper-mediation of everyday life, for people in affluent regions of the developed world, at least, makes the study of media something ontologically distinct from everything else redundant. Highmore's (2011) work on the micro-politics of saturation and distraction are helpful here, arguing that our habits of contingent 'mobile attention' present richer research terrain than the 'effects' of something on something else. Yet, the notion of digital literacy as a 'new paradigm' resurrects this impediment. Indeed, the 'big other' of the mass media—to be critically observed, protected against, or to be entered for employment (and usually all of those things at the same time in our tangled discourses)—has been replaced, for some, by new Big Others—the web, new media, digital tools—so debates around liberty and surveillance, creative exchange versus corporate co-option (see Gauntlett, 2015; Merrin, 2014; Morozov, 2013; and Rushkoff, 2014) are sometimes obscured by an unwitting technological determinism that polarizes and simplifies the complexity of cultural practices. We are most guilty of this when we fail to use a research base for our work. One example is the rush for civic engagement, partly driven by funding opportunities and partly because this might offer us political redemption from the 'postmodern turn.' Wanting to facilitate participation in the public sphere, to nurture critical voice, and to aspire for our pedagogies to instill the conviction to take action in the world—these are laudable, even in the perhaps more cynical UK context. I've recently worked with the European Union on ethnographic documentary making for 'digital citizenship,' the *Spirit of 13* project with Ken Loach. My current work on digital literacy and social capability, with Samsung, has more socio-civic objectives for the particular fieldwork community than the funding might suggest. But the research always reveals highly situated practices—even more 'micro' than the family unit or the home, and nowhere near as generalizable as a classroom, a school, 'digital natives,' or 'youth'—to paraphrase Boyd, "it's *complicated*."

It's also *surprising* that so many media educators speak of her work as groundbreaking while retreating to the broad categories of engagement her research so artfully undermines. And, even when we manage 'thick description' of media practices, into this rich (but awkward) mix comes the power dynamics of teacher-student, researcher-participant, which makes genuine, empirically measurable engagement in the lifeworld even harder to reach:

> Young people are actively required to exercise their responsibility as citizens, yet for many the traditional markers of citizenship have been ever more difficult to achieve, and in this context, participation may not be a meaningful practice—and may even prove to be an oppressive imposition.
>
> (Buckingham, Bragg, & Kehily, 2014, p. 280)

Buckingham et al.'s point is clear and, I hope, resonates with my call for a media education 'after the media' (Bennett, Kendall, & McDougall, 2011)—the assumption that digital tools can foster civic action or political appetite is naïve if there is no existing context or driver for such. Furthermore, our recent project for the United Kingdom Literacy Association brought to light absolutely no distinction between the public sphere activity of teenagers in UK schools who had studied media and gained a qualification and those who hadn't:

> Those with a media qualification appear more comfortable in digital spaces and their creativity is more technically coherent and their storytelling more literate. Those who never studied the media are largely more reluctant to participate or to create their own work to disseminate across digital platforms. Successful media students have a more developed, specialist vocabulary to articulate their thoughts on media texts. However, this does not necessarily mean that they are any more instinctively critical. Most significantly, whilst the media students were able to respond to the civic / creative task with more aptitude, they were no more successful in generating an audience and are no more likely to engage in civic activism in the public sphere.
>
> (McDougall et al., 2015, in press)

At the Media Education Association Conference in London (2014), a week after our own Summit, Julian Sefton-Green shared the outcomes of a longitudinal follow-up to his *Cultural Studies Goes to School* project (Buckingham & Sefton-Green, 1994). Sefton-Green caught up with the participants, his ex Media students—including the maker of the parodic text, *Slutmopolitan*, which I and others have taken as some manner of 'benchmark' for situated (political) media education in the Cultural Studies tradition some twenty years on. Back in the role of teacher / researcher, he found that place, identity, and relationships were every bit as meaningful as the arrival of the Internet and digital media in their trajectories—indeed, digital practices were impossible to untangle from life narrative, schooled identity, and, again, the power dynamics of education. Furthermore, perceptions of social class and mobility were as—or even more—powerful now than in the original study:

> These are more macro-sociological issues than normally pertain to studies of the literacy classroom. Questions about their attitude to the media and the current modes of consumption and what it means to consider themselves as media-educated people are inextricably intertwined with these larger social questions.
>
> (Sefton-Green, 2014, p. 58)

I worry that too many of our contemporary 'digital literacy' interventions ignore this 'macro' level, and so doing is far more than an oversight. Rather I see it as complicity in 'zombie politics' as it "feeds off the lawlessness caused by massive inequalities in wealth, income and power" (Giroux, 2014, p. 155).

So far this chapter has established that there is a considerable, powerful and growing research base for the complexities and the politics of media education, the literacies it can develop, and even—if we tread carefully—the voice it can give to students to represent themselves in the digital public sphere and to marginalized groups. We need a big disclaimer here, since the terms on which voice is given and taken, and the material conditions for such are never neutral (Couldry, 2010). That said, the remainder of this contribution will propose a set of 'applications' of the research base in digital media literacy education. These will consist of a set of connections between research into the overlapping research fields of education, curation, and literacy and what we do in the classroom—physical, virtual, or both.

Staying with Giroux for a moment, can we genuinely claim to be using media education in the digital age to attack the long-standing pedagogic violence of the school system, whereby "what is legitimated as privileged experience often represents the endorsement of a particular way of life that signifies its superiority with a "revenge" on those that do not share its attributes" (1988, p. 93)? There is a real danger that our new arrangements of critical literacy, safe use, and civic engagement are merely contemporary reproductions of this hegemonic language game—the validation of particular ways of 'being digital' and the devaluing of others as trivial, self-harming, distracting—either illiterate, or at best marginal.

Education in 2015 is a plethora of empty signifiers, more powerful for their absence of any substance. You can't really be 'against' literacy, competence, or engagement. But the research forces us to at least 'look awry.' More ethnographic educational work around media literacy aligns with Sefton-Green's findings and exposes the cultural politics at work—the inconvenient truth, perhaps. Ethnography has its problems and can be overcelebrated as a panacea, but it offers rich possibilities for media education, if it can be adopted as pedagogy. Just as the ethnographic researcher is explicit about her reflexivity in constructing meaning making from 'data,' the media educator should equally 'lay bare' her authority in generating with students a 'thick description' of their mediated lives—so that media education is not about representing 'the media' and students' media practices, but about re-presenting it, negotiating, or to repeat a new term—*mediapting*. This is messy for any generalizable strategy, or for measurable impact against competencies, of course, because it starts from the premise that every interaction between teacher, students, and media is different, highly specific, and situated in the 'macrosociology' it is so much easier to swerve around. But it is nonetheless relatively easy to map the core principles of ethnography to the pedagogic practices of media education, as follows:

Table 20.1

Research principle (Pole and Morrison, 2003:3)	Pedagogic strategy
Focus on discrete location, setting or event(s)	Every media education encounter is unique.
Concerned with full range of social behavior	Media literacy practices of each students are specific and can be both habitual and idiosyncratic – 'it's complicated'.
Range of research methods	Mixed method teaching / differentiation, resisting theory / practice boundaries.
Thick description to identification of concepts and theories grounded in the data.	Curational approach – co-making 'the work' as both media production and media learning.
Complexities more important than trends.	Student reflexivity – meta-literacy of the self in textual culture / voice privileged over student 'competence'.

From our existing (semi-ethnographic) research findings (McDougall & Potter, 2015), and the work of others, we can propose three recommendations for curating learning in the digital age with adherence to some enduring (but as yet elusive) Vygotskyan (1978) principles:

(1) Literacy practices, resources, and artifactual reflections from lived experience are not easily transmissible across the (only semipermeable) membrane between inside and outside the school (or college or university, or any educational space where power operates). We need, then, to understand

the dispositions evident in the one that can support and develop the other. From the lifeworld, the tactics and strategies of managing multiple presences, anchored and transient affiliations (Merchant, 2005) in a dynamic and seemingly always-visible space; from education, in the other direction, a criticality and distance provided, in the best of these settings, in a moderated place of safety that seeks to work with the habitus and cultural capital of students. Richards (1990) observed the challenges for any education posed by the constraints of broader pedagogic power structures, as inevitably *"Teaching [that] takes place within conditions which are not of its own choosing and its power to intervene in the formation of others, though considerable, is itself historically variable and limited"* (Richards, 1990, pp. 167–168). Two decades on, in the digital age, the profoundly artificial 'in between' (third) space for learning that we try to inhabit should become the explicit focus of our pedagogy as opposed to something we try to ignore. From the research base, this starts to look like a kind of ethnography of mediation across boundaries, rather than the hegemonic intervention in (textual) subjectivity enacted only on the terms of educators exercising power.

(2) Our research shows us that making self-representational texts involves organizing and reordering on and offline, analog, and digital textual practices—acts of assemblage. In this respect, 'knowledge production' moves away from either confirming or challenging the conventions of 'real' academic work and moves towards an auto-ethnographic making of textual meaning and, ultimately, of knowledge (of the self, as opposed to a 'big other' such as 'the media'). The status of educational space as 'in between' habitus (a third space, again) becomes itself the object of study, fostering genuine 'proximal development' of criticality.

(3) Without pedagogic research (in my view most neglected in media education), we start from ignorance in attempting to establish trust in order for students to have voice and exercise more autonomy in digital spaces available to them. Voice (Fielding, 2004) is far from neutral, however, and teacher-researchers need to work hard to understand and apply Couldry's (2010) conception of space for "the conditions under which we can give accounts of our lives and to how these accounts are valued, or perhaps not valued at all" (2010, p. 113). Media education has, ironically, paid insufficient attention to the pedagogic framing of the (textualized) lives of students. Curation has profoundly to do with this kind of textual power-accounting.

In practice, this means genuine knowledge exchange between teacher and student, and students as genuine partners. If the boundaries between technology / user, text / reader, digital platform / audience are to be curated as fluid and unstable, then so too must the boundaries between being a teacher and being a student, being an expert or 'lacking' the capacity to be so. So finally, the design of pedagogy (our 'making' of learning— McDougall & Orr, 2014) must shift to make the 'educational encounter' match the proliferation of deconstructed, fragmented transmedia reading and making practices in the lifeworlds of our students. Put simply, our curation pedagogy embraces the status of the inexpert educator—from Ranciere's 'ignorant schoolmaster' (2009). Going further, we want to mirror transmedia with a pedagogy of blended expertise, so that knowledge and authority—the mantle of the expert—also travel along the membrane between the classroom and, as Stuart Hall used to put it, according to the CCCS50 (Centre for Contemporary Cultural Studies 50 Years On) panel recollections "out there" (see Cannon & McDougall, 2014). A pedagogy framed as curation can help us return to these old questions with a renewal of aspiration, but only with a radical 'reboot' of how we design learning as transdisciplinary and digitally mediated, towards a more porous expertise.

Those 'fault-lines' between literacy, new literacies, time and space based literacies, media literacy, digital literacy, transliteracies, and broader 'safeguarding' objectives have 'always-already' been the subject of dispute and compromised practice. Frau-Meigs argues for transliteracy as a conduit for 'new collective dynamics' (Frau-Meigs, 2012, p. 22), while Comber reflects on decades of her own research with the disclaimer 'the impact of literacy wars and bandwagons has for too long distracted educators from the main game … that people understand how to use texts appropriately to get things done, how to make meaning and how to question the views of the world represented in texts in the interests of particular groups' (Comber, 2014, p. 116). Meanwhile, Burn (2013) calls for a shift in focus to 'media arts' with reciprocal transfer between the 'critical rhetorics' of media education and the creativity and aesthetics of the arts. Policy driven or funded media literacy 'interventions' have generally lacked capacity for exploring the more complex configurations of literacy, such as funds of knowledge (Gonzalez et al., 2005); identify and play repertoires (Marsh, 2009); teacher / student boundary work (Schwartz, 2014); semiotic modes (Parry, 2014); cultural agency (Daniels, 2014) or 'artifactual' literacy ethnographies (Jones, 2014; Pahl & Roswell, 2010).

This complex configuration of media literacy education matters. As the editor of educational research journals and in running a professional doctorate program for media teachers, I have a clear vested interest. But the increasing space, in our hyper-commodity, deprofessionalized education system—Giroux's zombie politics—between research and practice, between serious enquiry into what's going on when young people learn about media, and the proliferation of funded programs and projects assuming problems and solutions—threatens to undermine the credibility of the field and more importantly, leave behind children and young people who do not engage with digital media in the ways their teachers assume. This is why the Media Education Summit, MERJ, the U.K. Media Education Association, our new UKLA research group on media literacies, and all our international counterparts in linking research to media teaching, have to work tremendously hard to have genuine impact on pedagogy 'in the patch.' It was ever thus, but in selecting material to publish in our various outlets, and in the Centre for Excellence in Media Practice, we use the same criteria every time by positing the question, Is this research? Does it generate new knowledge in a field? Are there arising recommendations for practice? What we don't accept as 'of use' are partly formed ideas about what young people are doing with media and what they should be doing instead. In conversation, our friend Paul Mihailidis calls this tendency to assert opinion in the guise of academic knowledge "thoughts I have had, in no particular order." It is an urgent priority for media literacy education to filter these outriders.

To foster such a 'mediapting' mode of media learning and knowledge construction, we must explore the ways that a commitment to process and reflexivity can support the pursuit of pedagogic scholarship and inquiry in the context of media (literacy) education. There are two dimensions to this: firstly, an ethnographic, curational spirit and secondly, thinking about the design of learning and the design of creative media work in parallel.

Understood in this way, and profoundly informed by research, media teachers are creative practitioners in relation to both their activity (helping students design 'the (media) work' *and* their teaching (designing learning). Just as ethnographic research seeks to make the power dynamics of researcher and researched explicit in order to reduce their violence by rendering them 'sayable,' so does drawing out the complementarity between teaching and creative (media) practice. Reflexivity concerns the discovery of how meanings are discursively framed in whatever process generates them—in this case the process of teaching media mirrors both the process of making media and of researching media practices.

Let's return to the legacy of the Birmingham Center, as it remains so influential for our current and future work. At the *CCCS50* conference earlier in 2014 (Cannon & McDougall, 2014), John Clarke, reflecting on the extraordinary 'disproportionate effects' of the Center's impact across disciplines, identified two conditions for this possibility. First, students and teachers co-produced material as the orthodoxy (as the CCCS50 archive itself curates), not an exception to celebrate. Secondly, the Center always worked across and against disciplines, or, in Clarke's words "*they let us mess about*" (2014). In the digital realm today, it is worth asking: Have we, despite ourselves, constructed some unhelpful new disciplines— media education, media literacy, digital literacy, along with maintaining the boundary between media and people and between school and home, or education and lifeworld? Working across and between spaces and classifications, with students as ethnographic partners, across and between formal education and the digital 'out there'—doing teacher-research in messy third spaces where things aren't *either* digital or *not*, media or something else, *this* literacy or *that* literacy, civic action versus reified consumption—this takes effort and patience, but will generate productive frivolity. Such a 'mediaptive' mode of education won't give us any of the 'quick wins' desired for by the new protectionists, civic idealists, and creative fetishists. But I am convinced this kind of research and practice 'fusion' will help the people we work with become more reflexively literate in digital spaces.

REFERENCES

Bennett, P., Kendall, A., & McDougall, J. (2011). *After the media: Culture and identity in the 21st century.* London: Routledge.

boyd, d. (2014). *It's complicated: The social lives of networked teens.* New Haven, CT: Yale University Press.

Buckingham, D & Sefton-Green, J. (Eds), (1994). *Cultural Studies Goes to School.* Abingdon: Taylor and Francis.

Buckingham, D, Bragg, S and Kehily, M. (2014). *Youth Cultures in the Age of Global Media.* London: Palgrave MacMillan.

Burn, A. (2013). Six arguments for the media arts. *Teaching English, 2,* 55–60.

Comber, B. (2014). Literacy, poverty and schooling: What matters in young people's education? *Literacy, 48*(3), 115–123.

Cannon, M., & McDougall, J. (2014). The Centre for Contemporary Cultural Studies: 50 Years On (CCCS50) Conference, Birmingham University, June 2014—a pop-up occupation? *Journal of Media Practice, 15*(2), 147–150.

Clarke, J. (2014). Contribution to roundtable panel on interdisciplinarity: CCCS50 conference, '14. University of Birmingham, UK.

Couldry, N. (2010). *Why voice matters: Culture and politics after neoliberalism.* London: Sage.

Daniels, K. (2014). *Cultural agents creating texts: a collaborative space adventure.* Literacy 48 (2) 103–111.

Feigenbaum, A., Frenzel, F., & McCurdy, P. (2013). *Protest camps.* New York: Zed Books.

Fielding, M. (2004). Transformative approaches to student voice: Theoretical underpinnings, recalcitrant realities. *British Educational Research Journal, 30* (2), 295–311.

Frau-Meigs, D. (2012). Transliteracy as the new research horizon for media and information literacy. *Medijske Studije, 3*(6), 14–27.

Gauntlett, D. (2015). *Making media studies: The creativity turn in media and communications studies.* New York: Peter Lang.

Giroux, H. (1988). *Teachers as intellectuals: Towards a critical pedagogy of learning.* New York: Bergin & Harvey.

Giroux, H. (2014). *Zombie Politics in the Age of Casino Capitalism.* New York: Peter Lang.

Gonzalez, M., Moll, L., & Amanti, C. (2005). *Funds of knowledge: Theorising practices in households, communities and classrooms.* Mahwah, NJ: Erlbaum.

Gutierrez, K. (2008). Developing a sociocritical literacy in the third space. *Reading Research Quarterly, 43*(2), 148–164.

Highmore, B. (2011). *Ordinary lives: Studies in the everyday.* London: Routledge.

Jones, S. (2014). "How people read and write and they don't even notice": everyday lives and literacies on a Midlands council estate. *Literacy, 48*(2), 59–65.

Kendall, A & Murphy, G. (2015), forthcoming. 'Definitions don't matter. Digital literacy and the undoing of Subject Media'. Media Education Research Journal 5(2).

Marsh, J. (2009). Productive pedagogies: play, creativity and digital cultures in the classroom. In R. Willet, M. Robinson, & J. Marsh (Eds), *Play, creativity and digital cultures* (pp. 200–218). New York: Routledge.

McDougall, J. and Livingstone, S. with P. Fraser & J. Sefton-Green (2014). *Media and information education in the UK: Report for cost / ANR.* Retrieved from http://ppemi.ens-cachan.fr/data/media/colloque140528/rapports/UNITED-KINGDOM_2014.pdf.

McDougall, J. (2014). Curating media literacy: A porous expertise. *Journal of Media Literacy, 16*(1/2), 6–9.

McDougall, J., and Orr, S. (2014). Enquiry into learning and teaching in arts and creative practice. In E. Cleaver, M. Lintern, & M. McLinden (Eds.), *Teaching and learning in higher education: Disciplinary approaches to research.* London: Sage.

McDougall, J., Berger, R., Fraser, P., & Zezulkova, M. (2015, in press). Media literacy, education & (civic) capability: A transferable methodology. *Journal of Media Literacy Education* (forthcoming, in press).

McDougall, J., & Potter, J. (2015). Curating media learning. *Journal of E-Learning and Digital Media, 12*(2) (in press).

Media Education Summit. (2014). Goete Institut, Prague 20–21.11.14: Retrieved from http://www.cemp.ac.uk/summit/2014/Summit_Programme_2014.pdf.

Merchant, G. (2005). Electric involvement: Identity performance in informal digital writing. *Discourse: Studies in the Cultural Politics of Education, 26*(3), 301–314.

Merrin, W. (2014). *Media studies 2.0.* London: Routledge.

Mihailidis, P. (2014). *Media literacy and the emerging citizen: Youth, engagement and participation in digital culture.* New York: Peter Lang.

Morozov, E. (2013). *To save everything, click here.* New York: Public Affairs.

Pahl, K. & Roswell, J., R. (2010). *Artifactual literacies: Every object tells a story.* New York: Teachers College Press.

Parry, P. (2014). Popular culture, participation and progression in the literacy classroom. *Literacy, 48*(1), 14–22.

Potter, J. (2011). New literacies, new practices and learner research: Across the semipermeable membrane between home and school. *Lifelong Learning in Europe, XVI,* 174–181. Helsinki, Finland: Kansanvalistusseura.

Ranciere, J. (2009). *The emancipated spectator.* London: Verso.

Richards, C. (1990). 'Intervening in Popular Pleasures: Media Studies and the Politics of Subjectivity' In Buckingham, D (ed), Watching Media Learning: Making Sense of Media Education. London: The Falmer Press.

Rushkoff, D. (2014). *Present shock: When everything happens now.* New York: Penguin.

Schwartz, L. (2014). Challenging the tyranny of the five-paragraph essay: teachers and students as semiotic boundary workers in classroom and digital space. *Literacy, 48*(3), 124–135.

Sefton-Green, J., & Roswell, J. (Eds.). (2014). *Learning and literacy over time: Longitudinal perspectives.* London: Routledge.

van Mourik Broekman, P. , Hall, G. , Byfield, T. , Hides, S., & Worthington, S. (2014). *Open education: A study in disruption.* London: Rowman & Littlefield International.

Vygotsky, L. (1978). *Mind and society: The development of higher psychological processes.* Cambridge, MA: Harvard University Press.

Contributors

Lori Bindig, Ph.D., is an assistant professor of communication in the Department of Communication and Media Studies, director of the Media Literacy and Digital Culture graduate program, and the director of the Performing Arts minor at Sacred Heart University in Fairfield, Connecticut, where she teaches courses on media studies, digital culture, and the persuasion industries. In addition to contributing chapters to the anthologies *September 11 in Popular Culture* (Greenwood Press), *Race/Gender/Media: Considering Diversity across Audiences, Content and Producers* (Pearson), and *Media Literacy Education in Action* (Routledge), she is the coauthor of *The O.C.: A Critical Understanding* and author of *Dawson's Creek: A Critical Understanding*, and *Gossip Girl: A Critical Understanding* (Lexington).

Christopher Boulton, Ph.D., is both a veteran and critic of the creative industries. After working in public and cable television, he earned his doctorate and is now an Assistant Professor at the University of Tampa where he teaches critical media studies and film production. His latest film is a collaboration with the Media Education Foundation entitled *Not Just a Game: Power, Politics, and American Sports*. Boulton's research focuses on the intersection of communication, inequality, and activism and his writing has appeared in the *International Journal of Communication, The Communication Review, Advertising & Society Review, The Routledge Companion to Advertising and Promotional Culture,* and *New Views on Pornography.*

Ben Boyington, M.Ed., is a veteran high school teacher, educational consultant, and former book/magazine editor and film producer. He piloted media studies as a high school course in 2006, founded on the belief that critical thinking and critical consumption are essential dispositions for every citizen. His teaching revolves around the idea that depth of understanding comes from integration, design, and teaching others. Ben has been a member of the Action Coalition for Media Education (ACME) board since 2010 and vice-president since fall 2013. He co-designed the panel discussion "Media Education Programming in Action" for ACME's 2011 National Conference in Boston and presented "Media Studies 7–12: Process to

Attitude," an interactive discussion of media studies in junior high and high school, at ACME's 2013 media education training (in conjunction with the Campaign for a Commercial-Free Childhood's National Summit).

Allison Butler, Ph.D., is a Lecturer-Advisor and Coordinator of the Media Literacy Certificate Program in the Department of Communication at the University of Massachusetts, Amherst where she teaches courses on media, cultural studies, and education, media education, and youth identity development. Butler builds and facilitates workshops on comprehensive media literacy for a variety of schools and organizations across Massachusetts, and is the author of numerous articles and two books on media literacy: *Media Education Goes to School* (Peter Lang, 2010) and *Majoring in Change* (Peter Lang, 2012). Butler co-leads the grassroots organization Mass Media Literacy (www.massmedialiteracy.org), which supports legislation for teacher training in comprehensive media literacy and develops media literacy curriculum for Massachusetts K-12 public schools.

Ryan Cadrette is a doctoral student in the Communications department at the University of Massachusetts, Amherst. His primary research interests concern cultures of narrative production, with a focus on the comparative historical study of digital and print media. He holds an MA in Media Studies from Concordia University, and a BA in Media Studies from Vassar College.

Leisl Carr Childers, Ph.D., is Assistant Professor of History and the Public History Coordinator at the University of Northern Iowa. Her work in public history combines oral history and museum interpretation with traditional research practices. As the assistant director of the award-winning Nevada Test Site Oral History Project, she helped collect, manage, and digitize interviews conducted with those who worked on or were affected by continental nuclear testing in Nevada. She is the author of *The Size of the Risk: Histories of Multiple Use in the Great Basin.*

Nicki Lisa Cole, Ph.D., is a sociologist and Research Fellow at the Institute for Advanced Studies on Science, Technology and Society in Graz, Austria. She has expertise in consumer culture, global production and supply chains, ethical sourcing, and ethical consumption. Nicki has written extensively about fair trade, ethical sourcing, and Apple, Inc. in a variety of academic and popular outlets, including the journals *Race, Gender & Class, Contexts, Sociological Images, CounterPunch,* and *Truth-Out.* Nicki has also contributed chapters to the edited volumes *Censored 2014: Fearless Speech in Fateful Times* (Seven Stories Press, 2013), and *Consumer Culture, Modernity and Identity* (Sage, 2014). She is a member of the American Sociological Association, the Union for Democratic Communications, Editor-in-Chief of *Consumed,* the newsletter for the ASA Section on Consumers and Consumption, founder of the public sociology blog *21 Century Nomad,* and the Sociology Expert for About.com. Her forthcoming book is titled *Blood and Magic: The Hidden Costs of Apple's Rise to the Top.*

Jessica Collins is Program Director of Media Literacy Project (MLP) where she trains youth, educators, and community leaders across the nation on media literacy topics including gender, race, body image, food marketing, reality television, and digital storytelling. She runs MLP's Girl Tech program for young women of color where she teaches media justice, making media, and storytelling for community change. For six years she has taught a media literacy class at Media Arts Collaborative Charter School. She has developed several multimedia educational resources including *Challenging the Debt Industry*, a documentary and media literacy curriculum on predatory lending, and *Media Navigator*, a curriculum and facilitator's guide to teaching media literacy in the United Kingdom. The curriculum was commissioned by How to Thrive. Jessica earned her B.A. in media arts from the University of New Mexico.

Thomas F. Corrigan is an Assistant Professor of Mass Communication in the Department of Communication Studies at California State University—San Bernardino. He teaches undergraduate courses in Digital Media and Communication, Media History, Communication Research Methodologies, and Advertising as Social Communication. He also teaches a graduate course in Digital Culture. His research examines the political economy of communications, particularly the intersections of sports, media, and digital labor. His peer-reviewed work has been published in *The Political Economy of Communication*, *Journalism: Theory, Practice, & Criticism*, *Cultural Studies <=> Critical Methodologies*, *International Journal of Sport Communication*, and *Journal of Sports Media*. He also serves as the book reviews editor for *Democratic Communiqué*—a peer-reviewed journal published by the Union for Democratic Communications.

Kandace Creel Falcon, Ph.D., is Director and Assistant Professor of Women's and Gender Studies at Minnesota State University Moorhead. Her research blurs the boundaries between creative and academic writing with specific attention on the power of storytelling for Chicanas in the Midwest. She utilizes a Chicana feminist praxis to investigate new media practices, specifically making, writing about, and presenting on digital stories and social media activism. The recipient of the Harvard University Schlesinger Library Oral History Grant, her work has been published in women's and gender studies anthologies, *Feminist Cyberspaces: Pedagogies in Transition* (2012), *El Mundo Zurdo 3* (2013), and *Multicultural America* (2013). She is currently working on a book project focusing on Mexican American women in the Midwest and the social, political, and economic impact of the railroad in Kansas.

Bettina Fabos, Ph.D., is Associate Professor of Visual Communication and Interactive Digital Studies at the University of Northern Iowa. Both a scholar and producer of digital culture, her current work revolves around digital culture, digital visualization, digital photo archiving, and public memory. Combining her knowledge of pedagogy and interactive digital studies, Dr. Fabos is currently interested in the pedagogical value of interactive chronologies, the teaching of historical narrative, and collective photographic identity. She is also coauthor of three textbooks: *Media and Culture* (the leading textbook for mass communication survey classes across the U.S.), *Media Essentials*, and *Media in Society.*

Julie Frechette, Ph.D., is Professor and Chair of the Communication Department at Worcester State University, in Massachusetts, where she teaches courses on media studies, critical cultural studies, media education, and gender representations. Her book, *Developing Media Literacy in Cyberspace: Pedagogy and Critical Learning for the Twenty-First-Century Classroom* (Praeger Press, 2002), was among the first to explore the multiple literacies approach for the digital age. She is the coeditor and coauthor of the textbook *Media in Society* (Bedford / St. Martin's Press, 2014), as well as numerous articles and book chapters on media literacy, critical cultural studies, and gender and media. She serves as board co-president of the Action Coalition for Media Education.

Sergey Golitsynskiy, Ph.D., is Assistant Professor in Interactive Digital Studies at the University of Northern Iowa. His interests span the fields of media and communication research, computer science, web development, and digital humanities. His scholarship focuses on the application of computation to a variety of problems in social sciences and the humanities, and has included work in media and communication studies, psychology, and e-discovery. With over 15 years of experience in web application programming and web design, Dr. Golitsynskiy's other passion is digital visual communication, as well as all aspects of building web-based communication tools—from basic websites to digital archives and content management systems.

Paradise Gray, "The Grand Arkitech Traxtitioner Paradise"—Cofounder of the 1Hood Media Academy—is a legendary hip-hop producer, DJ, activist, historian, archivist, writer, photographer, promoter, and manager. In 1987–88 Paradise and Lumumba Carson formed The BlackWatch Movement that spawned several groups including The X-Clan, which was nominated for an NAACP Image Award. BlackWatch Movement was critical to the grassroots consciousness of New York City's youth and was instrumental in changing the face of hip-hop to one of Black Pride in the late 80s to early 90s. In addition to managing entertainment for the legendary hip-hop club "The Latin Quarters," Gray has produced articles and photographs that appeared in *The Source Magazine, XXL, Right On! Magazine, YO!, Wax Poetics, Big Red News,* and *VH1's 30 Years Of*

Hip-hop History TV. From 1999 to 2003 Paradise Gray was the executive director of urban music at the infamous Internet music company MP3.COM, the company that invented the Online Music Revolution and was last big IPO in the Dot.com boom era.

Daniel S. Hunt, Ph.D., is an Assistant Professor of Communication at Worcester State University. He teaches courses in new media and mass communication. His research on social media, interactive technology, and image sharing has been published in scholarly journals such as the *Journal of Broadcasting & Electronic Media, Cyberpsychology, Behavior, and Social Networking, Newspaper Research Journal, The Journal of Social Media in Society, The Journal of Media Literacy*, and *Computers in Human Behavior*. He regularly presents on his research and teaching at national and regional communication conferences.

Morgan Jaffe is the Training, Operations, and Programming Director for KAOS-FM Radio at Evergreen State College. She has worked as a Research Assistant at the Media Education Lab, part of the Harrington School of Communication and Media, University of Rhode Island; taught after-school classes and worked with teachers and administrators for public access TV stations; and worked at college, oldies, Top 40, and alternative radio stations. Morgan graduated from the Warner School of Education in 2013 with her MS in Teaching and Curriculum with a focus in digital media and literacy. As an undergraduate she attended the University of Rochester, where she received her BA in Media and Cultural Studies in American Society and English in 2012.

Satish Kolluri, Ph.D., is Associate Professor of Communication Studies at Pace University and has published in the areas of secularism and nationalism, and participatory development communication. He coedited a special issue of *Cultural Dynamics* on secularism and postcolonial theory. His teaching and research areas center on Indian and Hong Kong cinema, media and politics, intercultural communication, and parenting and education. He also helps curate the New York Indian Film Festival.

Chenjerai Kumanhika, Ph.D., is an artist, activist, and assistant professor in Clemson University's department of Communication Studies. His roots in hip-hop culture have informed his activism, and his scholarship on social movements, popular culture, and digital literacy. His hip-hop band Spook's first commercial album, *S.I.O.S.O.S.* Vol. 1 (2000), produced singles that reached gold-selling status in four countries, and placed highly on top ten charts around the world. During the production of the Spooks second release, *Faster Than You Know* (2003), Chenjerai looked for ways to support a new generation of hip-hop artists and scholars and designed and implemented hip-hop production/media literacy programs in both Philadelphia and Los Angeles. His January 2015 article on "Vocal Color in Public Radio" spawned a nationwide discussion of diversity and voices in public media. It was featured on National Public Radio, the *Washington Post*, and Buzzfeed, and trended nationally on Twitter.

Sun Young Lee, M.A., is currently a corporate copy editor who finished her Master's degree in English Literature, exploring postcolonial topics regarding gender/sexuality, diasporic identity, and translation theory.

Rachael Liberman, Ph.D., teaches media studies courses in the Department of Media, Film and Journalism Studies at University of Denver. Her research tracks the construction, proliferation, and circulation of discourses on gender and sexuality in contemporary media culture; and in particular, the mediation of female sexual subjectivity. Other research interests include negotiations of agency within cultural production, feminist interventions in media studies, the pornography industry, and the politics of media and memory. Her work has been published *Porn Studies*, *Women's Psychology Quarterly*, and *Media/Cultural Studies: Critical Approaches*.

Julian McDougall, Ph.D., is Associate Professor in Media and Education and Head of the Centre of Excellence in Media Practice at Bournemouth University. He is editor of the *Media Education Research Journal* and *Journal of Media Practice*, author of *The Media Teacher's Book, After the Media: Culture and Identity in the 21st Century, Barthes Mythologies Today,* and a range of student textbooks for media / game studies, media literacy / education and cultural studies. He publishes research regularly in academic journals in these fields. At CEMP he runs an educational doctorate program for media educators and convenes the annual Media Education Summit. He is Principal Examiner for Media Studies in the English further education system.

Paul Mihailidis, Ph.D., is an assistant professor in the school of communication at Emerson College in Boston, Massachusetts, where he teaches media literacy and interactive media. He is also the Associate Director of the Engagement Lab at Emerson College, and Director of the Salzburg Academy on Media and Global Change. His research focuses on the nexus of media, education, and civic voices. His new book, *Media Literacy and the Emerging Citizen* (2014, Peter Lang), outline effective practices for participatory citizenship and engagement in digital culture. Under his direction, the Salzburg Academy on Media and Global Change, a global media literacy incubator program, annually gathers 70 students and a dozen faculty to build networks for media innovation, civic voices, and global change. Mihailidis sits on the board of directors for the National Association of Media Literacy Education. He has authored numerous books and papers exploring media education and citizenship, and traveled around the world speaking about media literacy and engagement in digital culture.

Christine J. Olson is a doctoral student in the Department of Communication at the University of Massachusetts Amherst. Her research interests include media production and social participation practices online, social inequality and new media technologies, and digital media literacies. In addition to her work at the university, Christine has facilitated media literacy programs for elementary and middle school students and is currently the coordinator of a local makerspace where she directs an after-school program focused on creative configurations of technology, art, and media. Her work has been presented at International Communication Association conferences.

Andrea Quijada is Executive Director of Media Literacy Project (MLP), where she presents nationally and internationally on the impact of media on culture, politics, and technology. In the past twelve years she has successfully integrated a social justice framework into the programs, curricula, and campaigns of MLP, combining her knowledge of media literacy with her experience as a community organizer. She functioned as an advisor in the creation of Centre for Media Literacy and Community Development in Kampala, Uganda, and is the editor of *Media Navigator*, a curriculum and facilitator's guide to teaching media literacy in the United Kingdom, commissioned by How to Thrive. She also serves on the Consumer Advisory Committee to the Federal Communications Commission. Andrea earned her M.A. in art history from the University of New Mexico.

Andy Lee Roth is the associate director of Project Censored. He has co-edited six volumes of Project Censored's annual book series, including most recently *Censored 2016: Media Freedom on the Line* (Seven Stories Press, 2015). His research, on topics ranging from ritual to broadcast news interviews and communities organizing for parklands, has appeared in journals including the *International Journal of Press/Politics; Social Studies of Science; Media, Culture & Society; City & Community and Sociological Theory*. His book reviews appear in *YES! Magazine*. He earned a PhD in Sociology at the University of California-Los Angeles and a BA in Sociology & Anthropology at Haverford College. He serves on the boards of the Media Freedom Foundation and the Claremont Wildlands Conservancy.

Erica Scharrer, Ph.D., is Professor and Chair in the Department of Communication at the University of Massachusetts Amherst. She studies—and teaches classes that consider—media content, opinions of media, media influence, and media literacy, particularly pertaining to gender and violence. She is editor of the *Media Effects/Media Psychology* volume of the International Encyclopedia of Media Studies (Wiley-Blackwell, 2013) and coauthor of *Media and the American Child* (Elsevier, 2006). Her studies of media literacy education have appeared in *Journal of Children and Media, Journal of Mass Media Ethics*, and *Journal of Media Literacy Education*, among other outlets. She is currently chairing the Children, Adolescents, and Media division of the International Communication Association.

Laras Sekarasih, M.S., is a doctoral candidate in the Department of Communication at the University of Massachusetts Amherst. Her research areas include media, children, and the family, media effects, and media and the consumers. Her work on media literacy has been published in the *Journal of Children and Media*, and is forthcoming in the *Journal of Media Literacy Education*. Her latest work is on parental mediation on young children's use of mobile communication technology that is forthcoming in Lim, S. S. (Ed.), *Mobile Communication and the Family—Asian Experiences in Technology Domestication* (Dordrecht, Germany: Springer, 2015, in press).

Dr. Victor C. Strasburger, M.D., is a pediatrician, adolescent medicine specialist, and Distinguished Professor Emeritus at the University of New Mexico School of Medicine, where he founded the Division of Adolescent Medicine. He has authored 13 books and nearly 200 peer-reviewed journal articles and book chapters on the subjects of adolescent medicine and children, adolescents, and the media. His latest book is *Children, Adolescents, and the Media*, 3rd edition (Sage, 2014), coauthored with Barbara Wilson and Amy Jordan. Dr. Strasburger has also made numerous media appearances, including on *Oprah*, the *Today Show*, National Public Radio, and published in *Time, Newsweek, The New York Times,* and *Washington Post*.

Chyng F. Sun, Ph.D., is a Clinical Professor of Media Studies of McGhee Division, School of Continuing and Professional Studies at New York University. Her teaching and research interests are in media representations of race, class, gender, and sexuality, and their cultural and social impacts. Her recent research focuses on pornography. In addition to directing and producing the documentary film *The Price of Pleasure: Pornography, Sexuality, and Relationships* (2008), Sun has conducted a large-scale content analysis of popular pornography and interviewed male and female pornography users; currently she is leading a multinational research team from nine countries to investigate the connections between pornography and sexual desires, behaviors, and relationships. Sun also has produced and directed three other documentary films: *Mickey Mouse Monopoly: Disney, Childhood and Corporate Power* (2001), *Beyond Good and Evil: Children, Media and Violent Times* (2003), and *Latinos Beyond Reel: Challenging a Media Stereotype* (2012).

Rachel L. Webb currently works as a case manager at Park Avenue Women's Shelter in Manhattan. She graduated summa cum laude from New York University's Gallatin School in 2012 with a concentration in psychology and creativity.

Rob Williams, Ph.D., teaches new/digital and social media, communications, and journalism courses at the University of Vermont and Sacred Heart University. The cofounding president and current board chair of the Action Coalition for Media Education (ACME at www.smartmedia-education.net), he is the author of numerous articles and book chapters about media education, lectures widely on topics and issues related to digital media literacy education, and consults with a number of organizations, including the College for America, PH International, and the U.S. State Department. His latest book is *Most Likely to Secede: What the Vermont Independence Movement Can Teach Us About Reclaiming Community and Creating a Human Scale Vision for the 21st Century* (Vermont Independence Press, 2013).

Elaine Young, Ph.D., is a professor of digital and social media marketing at Champlain College in Burlington, Vermont. She is also the author of *Tuned-In Family: How to Cope, Communicate, and Connect in a Digital World* (Champlain Press, 2014). As a parent and a passionate user of technology, Dr. Young provides teaching, advice, and guidance for individuals and organizations exploring how to best use digital communication technologies for greater benefit. She can be reached on Twitter at @ejyoung67.

Bill Yousman, Ph.D., is the Director of the Media Literacy and Digital Culture Master's Program at Sacred Heart University. Bill served on the board of the Action Coalition for Media Education and is the former Managing Director of the Media Education Foundation. He has published widely on media, race, ideology, and visual culture. His first book, *Prime-Time Prisons on U.S. TV: Representation of Incarceration*, was published in 2009. His most recent book is *The Spike Lee Enigma: Challenge and Incorporation in Media Culture* (Peter Lang Publishing, 2014).

Index